SOCIAL REGULATORY POLICY

Moral Controversies in American Politics

edited by
RAYMOND TATALOVICH
BYRON W. DAYNES
with a Foreword by THEODORE J. LOWI

WESTVIEW PRESS
Boulder and London

Published in 1988 in the United States of America by Westview Press, Inc., 5500 Central Avenue, Boulder, Colorado 80301

Library of Congress Cataloging-in-Publication Data
Social regulatory policy: moral controversies in American politics.
  1. Public policy (Law)—United States—Case
studies. 2. Social problems—United States—Case
studies. 3. United States—Politics and government—
1945–   —Case studies. I. Tatalovich, Raymond.
II. Daynes, Byron W.
JK21.S63 1988   320.973   87-14015
ISBN 0-8133-7386-7
ISBN 0-8133-0612-4 (if published in paperback)

Printed and bound in the United States of America

The paper used in this publication meets the requirements of the American National Standard for Permanence of Paper for Printed Library Materials Z39.48-1984.

10   9   8   7   6   5   4   3   2   1

To our mentor,
THEODORE J. LOWI,
who inspires us
as his teachings continue to guide us

R.T.
B.W.D.

CONTENTS

List of Tables and Figures   viii
Foreword: New Dimensions in Policy and Politics
        Theodore J. Lowi   x
The Contributors   xxii

Introduction: What Is Social Regulatory Policy?
        Raymond Tatalovich and Byron W. Daynes   1

1   School Prayer: Free Exercise of Religion or
     Establishment of Religion?
     John A. Murley   5

2   Pornography: Freedom of Expression or
     Societal Degradation?
     Byron W. Daynes   41

3   Crime: Due Process Liberalism Versus
     Law-and-Order Conservatism
     Brent S. Steel and Mary Ann E. Steger   74

4   Gun Control: Constitutional Mandate or Myth?
     Robert J. Spitzer   111

5   Affirmative Action: Minority Rights or Reverse
     Discrimination?
     Gary C. Bryner   142

6   Abortion: Prochoice Versus Prolife
     Raymond Tatalovich   177

Conclusion: Social Regulatory Policymaking
        Raymond Tatalovich and Byron W. Daynes   210

Notes   227
List of Acronyms   251
Case Index   253
General Index   255

TABLES AND FIGURES

Tables

1.1   Testimony by religious and interest groups before congressional hearings on Bible reading or voluntary prayer in school   8

1.2   *Amicus curiae* briefs to the Supreme Court by interest groups in four school prayer cases   10

1.3   NORC Surveys on school prayer ban, 1974–1986   24

1.4   Legislation on school prayer, introduced in Congress 1962–1986   26

2.1   Legislation on obscenity, introduced in Congress 1956–1985   47

2.2   *Amicus curiae* briefs to the Supreme Court by interest groups in forty-two obscenity cases, 1957–1984   62

2.3   Testimony by interest groups before congressional hearings on obscenity   64

2.4   Public attitudes toward pornography and censorship   71

3.1   Characteristics of offenders in the United States, 1981   76

3.2   Support for the death penalty for murder: Gallup Polls   80

3.3   Reasons for favoring the death penalty among the U.S. public, Gallup Poll   81

3.4   Thirty-nine state actions concerning capital punishment after the *Furman* decisions   90

3.5   Federal prison population and average terms   103

4.1   Top congressional recipients of combined direct and indirect NRA expenditures   116

4.2   Gallup Polls on gun control   123

4.3   NORC Surveys on permits for gun ownership   123

5.1   U.S. budget and administrative activity for civil rights and the EEOC, 1971–1985   166

5.2   *Amicus curiae* briefs to the Supreme Court by interest groups supporting and opposing affirmative action in the *Bakke* case   168

5.3   Percentage of blacks employed in various occupational
            groupings   170
5.4   Smith/Sheatsley index of racial tolerance   171
5.5   Attitudes on whether the federal government should
            help minorities   173
5.6   Attitudes on government responsibility for fair employment
            practices for blacks   174
5.7   Gallup Polls on job hiring: Preferential treatment
            versus ability   175

6.1   States reforming abortion laws, 1966–1972   178
6.2   Gallup Polls on legal conditions for abortion, 1975–1983 187
6.3   NORC Surveys on medical and socioeconomic reasons
            for abortion, 1972–1985   188
6.4   Harris/Gallup Surveys on Supreme Court ruling legalizing
            abortions, 1973–1986   189
6.5   *Amicus curiae* briefs to the Supreme Court by interest
            groups in seventeen abortion cases   192
6.6   Legislation on abortion, introduced in Congress 1973–1986 201

Figures

1   Types of coercion, types of policy, and
            types of politics   xi
2   Public philosophy: Mainstream and radical   xiii
3   How policy problems are defined in mainstream
            and in radical politics   xv
4   Policies and politics in two dimensions   xvii

FOREWORD
New Dimensions in Policy and Politics

Public policy can be defined simply as an officially expressed intention backed by a sanction. Although synonymous with law, rule, statute, edict, and regulation, public policy is the term of preference today probably because it conveys more of an impression of flexibility and compassion than the other terms. But no citizen, especially a student of political science, should ever forget that *policy* and *police* have common origins. Both come from "polis" and "polity," which refer to the political community itself and to the "monopoly of legal coercion" by which government itself has been defined. Consequently, all public policies must be understood as coercive. They may be motivated by the best and most beneficent of intentions, and they may be implemented with utmost care for justice and mercy. But that makes them no less coercive.

There are multitudes of public policies because there are multitudes of social arrangements and conduct that people feel ought to be controlled by coercive means if public order is to be maintained and people are to be able to pursue their private satisfactions in peace. Consequently, some kind of categorization is necessary if meaningful policy analysis is to take place. If the editors and authors of this volume had a particular reason for inviting me to participate in their important project by the writing of this foreword, it was probably because I was young and foolish enough twenty-five years ago to attempt to provide a categorization of public policies and, somewhat later, to describe the logic underlying the categories. If there had been a second reason for involving me it was probably because they found the scheme uncomfortable as well as useful. In brief, I began the categorization with a simple question: If all policies are coercive, is it possible that we can develop a meaningful, small set of policy categories by asking a prior question of jurisprudence: How many kinds of coercion are there? Leaving aside the fine points of definition, I identified four logically distinguishable ways that government can coerce, and I then attempted to demonstrate, with some degree of acceptance in the field, that each of these types of coercion underlies a type of identifiable public policy. The source of each type of policy was, therefore, so close to state power itself that each, I reasoned, should be located in history and that each would, over time, tend

FIGURE 1
Types of Coercion, Types of Policy, and Types of Politics

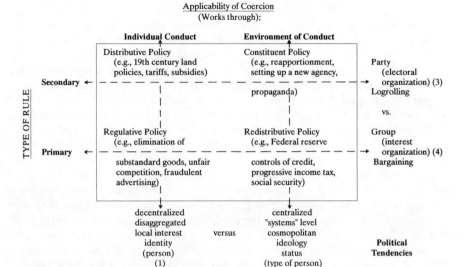

Source: Adapted from Theodore J. Lowi, "Four Systems of Policy, Politics, and Choice," *Public Administration Review* (July-August 1972), p. 300.

to develop its own distinctive political structure. I was attempting to turn political science on its head (or back on its feet) by arguing that "policy causes politics."

The four categories were given the most appropriate names I could contrive at the time: Distributive Policy (or as I have come more recently to call it, Patronage Policy), Regulatory Policy, Redistributive (and Welfare) Policy, and Constituent Policy. (Figure 1 is the four-fold formulation.) Lately I have grown accustomed to a modification of the names of the categories in order to emphasize the intimacy of the historical association between the type of policy and the type of politics that tends to be associated with it: The Distributive (or Patronage) State, the Regulatory State, the Redistributive (or Welfare) State, and the State within the state.

During the very decade (roughly 1964–1974) that these categories were being developed, the national government was going through a virtual second New Deal. There was an explosion of new regulatory and welfare programs. Although most of these new policies fit comfortably enough into the four-fold scheme, there *was* something new about many of them that was not being captured by the scheme. Every scheme of categorization (of anything) sacrifices informational detail and nuance in order to gain analytic power, but is there a point where the sacrifice is too great? Students of these 1960s and 1970s policies referred to them as "new regulation," "social policy," and "social regulation" in order to convey an emerging sense that there is indeed something about these policies that does not fit comfortably into existing categories. Tatalovich, Daynes, and associates do a valiant job of trying to catch the meaning of the "new" and the "social" and why these policies somehow don't fit into any preexisting scheme. In the opinion of these authors, the only way to preserve the four-fold scheme is to add, in effect, a fifth category, which they call "social regulatory policy."

There is no need to take issue directly with the definition of this fifth category. I will try instead to *subsume* it. I recognize at the outset that there is something special about the cases being dealt with in this book. They are cases of regulatory policy in my terms; if they don't seem to fit comfortably it is because the *politics* of the "new" or "social" regulation looks a lot more like what is to be expected with the politics of redistributive policy. The authors discover in their cases that the observed political behavior is more ideological, more moral, more directly derived from fundamental values, more intense, less utilitarian, more polarized, and less prone to compromise.

However, while granting these authors their empirical findings, I hesitate to create a new category to fit the findings until all ways of maintaining the four-fold scheme have been exhausted. This position is one part ego but at least four parts bona fide concern not to destroy the simplicity and, more importantly, the logic of the analysis. For one cannot solve the problem by merely adding a new category. Addition of a category weakens the logic altogether. The fifth category won't work entirely until its logic has been worked out and until a probable sixth is coupled with it to give the new scheme a reasonable symmetry.

In the spirit of trying to preserve the four-fold scheme and at the same time trying to give the new findings their due, I will try an alternative. Some people will agree with me that it is a way to preserve the four-fold scheme. Others will say that I am being too accommodating and will destroy the four-fold scheme by turning it not merely into a six- or eight-fold scheme but in fact (as in Figure 4) into a twelve-fold scheme. Either way, the effort will enhance and dramatize the value of the case materials presented in this volume.

For several years I have shared with these authors a concern for how to make sense of the "new politics" of the public-interest groups on the left and the right in the United States and in Europe. Although these groups seem to be seeking policies that could be categorized as (largely) regulatory or redistributive, they refused to join what most of us would consider mainstream political processes, insisting instead on trying to convert political issues into moral polarities, claims into rights, legislation into litigation, grays into blacks and whites, and campaigns into causes and crusades. If there is confusion among analysts about all this, it is because there is an obvious, age-old fact that we have all been overlooking: that for every type of mainstream politics there is a *radical politics*. Policies can remain the same, insofar as the type of coercion involved is regulatory, or redistributive, or whatever. But just as some mainstream strategies will pay off and some

FIGURE 2
Public Philosophy:
Mainstream and Radical

Direction

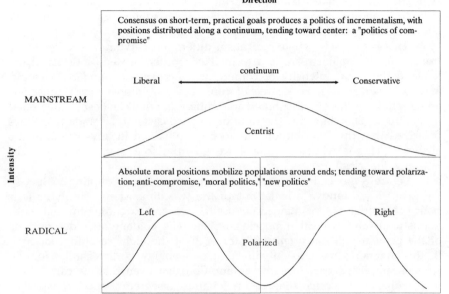

will not (giving each policy type its political distinctiveness) so will radicalization as a strategy sometimes pay off and sometimes will not pay off. When it does pay off, there is likely to be an intensification of all the political elements without necessarily transforming the patterns altogether. And, to repeat, the policy at issue can remain in the same category even as its politics is being radicalized.

Figure 2, a first step toward a new scheme, is an attempt to define radical in relation to mainstream in politics. The *Oxford English Dictionary* defines radical as "of or pertaining to a root or roots." That is also the meaning in mathematics and the origin of the term in politics. It is associated with extremes precisely because people who insist on getting to the root of things are likely to express themselves intensely, rejecting the rules and procedures designed to produce compromise—in other words, rejecting mainstream or ordinary politics. However, as soon as the two dimensions, radical and mainstream, are put side by side it becomes obvious that they are not a simple dichotomy because it is in the nature of radical politics to be so much more ideological that radicalism is at least dichotomous within itself. (I say "at least" because a full-scale analysis of radicalism would require more distinctions than the simple two needed here.) Ideology is not absent in mainstream politics, but lower intensity permits mainstream politicians to practice their skill, which is to obtain practical consensus on goals and to reduce differences to a point where political conflict becomes political competition, strategy becomes tactic, and compromise is possible because the stakes are incremental. To the radical, mainstream means trivialization, and that is absolutely true. Figure 2 attempts to capture this evaluation for the mainstream by placing relevant ideologies on a continuum, with the concentration of positions toward the center, where the frontier between left and right is very fuzzy.

This is precisely where radicalism differs most: What is a rather fuzzy frontier for the mainstream is a formalized border between radicals of the left and the right. Intensity of commitment demands an underlying logic, and logic demands some degree of consistency, reinforced by a conscious affiliation. Positions are distributed accordingly, in what can best be illustrated in Figure 2 as a bimodal distribution. So consistently is radical politics polarized that this distribution has to be maintained in any diagrammatic analysis. (This is why in Figure 4 we go from four mainstream to eight radical categories.)

Figure 3 moves the analysis one step further by attempting to specify the general substantive orientations of the two dimensions. The basic four policy categories are maintained (across the top and extending through both Mainstream and Radical dimensions). The cells contain brief descriptions of the general political orientation for each of the eight resulting patterns. In this diagram, the left-right direction of ideology is disregarded for the sake of simplicity, based on the assumption that even radicals can, in the words of Carl Friedrich, "agree on what to disagree about." A word of explanation is needed mainly for the concepts in boldface. These were the best available words to connote the general orientation; the prose in each box is an effort to spell that out. Note, for example, the distinction between ERROR and SIN; this is an antinomy, which is intended to suggest how differently the two types view the same regulatory issue. The mainstream approach to regulation is as close to instrumental as human beings can get. Mainstream political actors avoid taking a moral posture toward the conduct to be regulated; conduct is to be regulated only because *it is injurious in its consequences*. Though privately the mainstreamer may consider prostitution immoral, the mainstream public position would be that prostitution should be regulated as to its potential for disease or its association with drugs and abduction. The radical would define the conduct moralistically; i.e., for the radical, conduct is to be regulated because *it is good or bad in itself*. From the radical left, prostitution is a sinful product of a sinful economic system; for the radical right it is a sinful expression of bad character. But radicals take a moral posture toward it while mainstreamers can take it as a conduct in need of modification. Regulation is itself a mainstream word, coming from the French, *régle* (rule), so that *réglementation* means "to impose rules upon" or to regularize. From the radical, moralistic standpoint, something like elimination would be a more accurate description.

There is no need to treat the three remaining categories too extensively, since the phenomenon of concern in this book is regulation. Suffice it to

FIGURE 3
How Policy Problems are Defined
in Mainstream and in Radical Politics

	Regulative (Policy toward conduct)	Distributive (Policy toward facilities)	Redistributive (Policy toward status)	Constituent (Policy toward structures)
MAINSTREAM	Control the *consequences* of conduct, consequences defined in purely instrumental terms. Orientation of the discourse is: ERROR	Goals defined instrumentally or denotatively, without a governing rule. Orientation of the discourse is: UTILITY	Class and status relations are specified but redistributive effect minimized by spreading benefits upward and obligations downward. Exclusiveness softened with equities. Orientation of discourse is: ENTITLEMENT	A process definition of the Constitution and rights; a representation definition of government; the good administrator is neutral, obedient to elected officials; decision by competition. Orientation of discourse is: ACCOUNTABILITY
RADICAL	Control of conduct as good or bad *in itself*; consequences defined in moral absolutes; stress particularly on bad conduct. The orientation of discourse is: SIN	Goals defined in terms of consequences but moral consequences, such as improvement of character (right) or defense against capitalism (left). The orientation of discourse is: CIVIC VIRTUE	Class and status relations are exclusive, imbedded in absolutes that transcend policy. Property rights (right) and welfare rights (left); social definitions of rights (left), individualist definitions of rights (right). Orientation of discourse is: RIGHTS	A substantive definition of the Constitution. Good government is commitment to a substantive definition of justice. The good administrator is committed to the program (left) or to good moral character (right). The orientation of discourse is: COMMITMENT

say that the boldface concepts in each of the categories were also selected as antinomies that distinguish most clearly between mainstream and radical discourse, with radicals of both sides agreeing with each other on what to disagree about. Thus, even on something as commonplace as distributive policy (patronage), radicals can be quite moralistic: Railroads should be public corporations because capitalism is bad; museums should be built because art is good. In contrast, for mainstreamers, the whole point of resorting to patronage policies is its UTILITY, its complete amorality; patronage policy is a way to displace conflict, not confront it. For redistributive policy, the near antinomy between ENTITLEMENT and RIGHTS should be close to self-evident. Description in the boxes might help marginally. The constituent policy categories may cause a bit more of a problem, but that need not be a burden for us here. The best way to think about this category is through the history of American approaches to the "good administrator." The mainstream ideal was the "common man"; the modern version of this is the individual trained in the appropriate skills but loyal to majority rule and to the elected representatives of that majority, presumably whatever the "goal." To the radical, majorities and skills are not irrelevant, but they are subordinate to character. Administrators are good if they are committed to virtue (on the right) or "program" (on the left).

We can now turn to Figure 4, the main point and purpose of this enterprise. Figure 4 combines features of Figures 1–3 and joins them to actual policy issues. The antinomies from Figure 3 are repeated in boldface to evoke (without space to be explicit) a sense of the political patterns to be expected.

Figure 4 is a variation on an earlier effort to make sense of environmental policies, which are so rich in "new politics."[1] Only one-quarter of the figure (the Regulatory column, therefore put first) is relevant to the cases in this volume, but the comprehensive (and I hope exhaustive) presentation in the figure makes a productive linkage to the findings in this book and puts these findings in an inherently comparative context.

I like this figure, as revised, not merely because it might preserve my scheme. It confirms my own confidence that policy categorization (not necessarily mine) will in the long run be the route to the new political theory because it arises out of some fundamental political truths: (1) that there are inherent limits to the ways a state can control society, no matter how powerful that state may be; (2) that each of these ways is so fundamental that it has enough of a history and a regularity to become in itself a kind of regime; and (3) that every regime tends to produce a politics consonant with itself. This particular effort has perhaps added a fourth truth: that political leaders can radicalize politics by adding a moral dimension to policy. Radicalizing the policy (i.e., adding the moral dimension) will almost certainly change the political patterns, but even radicalized political patterns will probably vary according to the particular policy category (regime) in question.

Since Tatalovich, Daynes, and associates have concentrated on the regulatory category, I will hold my elaboration of this now two-dimensional

FIGURE 4
Policies and Politics in Two Dimensions

POLICY TYPE

DIMENSION OF POLITICS	1 Regulatory	2 Distributive	3 Redistributive	4 Constituent
MAINSTREAM	**ERROR** Standards of conduct Economic sector regulation Regulation to maintain competition Regulatory taxes Licensing to enforce standards	**UTILITY** Public works Defense installations and stockpiling R & D Sales of public property or access to it Unconditional licensing	**ENTITLEMENT** "Social costs" Income taxation Economic policy through the tax system ("tax expenditure") Social Security Monetary policies	**ACCOUNTABILITY** "Causal theory" Liberal, value-free education Policies restricting state action Administrative reform for neutral, scientific decisionmaking
RADICAL	**SIN** **Left** / **Right** Right to results of regulation (suits to force regulation) / Right to public order & self-defense Cost-oblivious economic regulation / Regulation for moral guidance Affirmative action / Victimless crimes Capitalism as morally suspect / Capitalism as a moral good	**CIVIC VIRTUE** **Left** / **Right** Public ownership of essential service / Public works for private market Displacement of corporate power / Subsidies to industry for the public good Planning for national use of resources Convert distributive to redistributive / Convert distributive to moral regulation	**RIGHTS** **Left** / **Right** Progressive income taxation exclusively / Sales taxes and other regressive taxes exclusively Anti-wealth taxes (estate, luxuries, etc.) / Punitive taxes ("sin" taxes to discourage alcohol, tobacco, etc.) Welfare as a right / Welfare as a moral lesson	**MORAL GOVERNMENT** **Left** "Class theory" / **Right** "Obligation theory" Socialization education / Moral education Bill of Rights (complete nationalization) / State rights Participatory democracy (judicially enforced) / Republicanism ("rightly understood") Programmatic administrator / Good administrator Party executive / Commander-in-chief executive

scheme to the regulatory quadrant alone. But this should not mask the fact that if we had cases here of radicalized policies in, say, the redistributive category, the political pattern, though radicalized, would probably differ from the pattern observed in the radicalized regulatory cases.

Virtually all regulatory policy, as we know it from the familiar economic regulatory programs of the national government, approaches conduct in an almost purely instrumental way. It arises largely out of concern for conduct deemed good or bad *only in its consequences.* (See Figure 4, upper left corner.) The very term *regulation* or *regulatory policy*, as suggested above, became the term of choice by lawyers, economists, and policymakers because the goal of most of these policies is not so much to eliminate the conduct in question but to reduce it, channel it, or otherwise constrain it so that the conduct might persist but with fewer of the injuries (or in some instances, more of the benefits) attributed to it. But there is another whole reality of regulatory policies, and those policies are concerned with conduct *deemed good or bad in itself* (lower left corner in figure). Call the first C_1 and the second C_2. The first type, instrumental regulation, will be abbreviated as C_1. The second, moral regulation, will be referred to as C_2. Most C_2 regulation in the United States has escaped the recent attention of most political scientists (until this volume) because it has been the province of state government. Examples include the criminal law, all the sex and morality laws, most family and divorce laws, the basic compulsory education laws, and the fundamental property laws. The intrinsic moral orientation of this kind of policy accounts also for the fact that state politics in the nineteenth century (when most of these policies were being enacted as a matter of positive, statute law) was far more radical, often violent, than the politics of regulation at the national level. But note well, the descriptions of state politics will reveal that they were dominated not by political parties but by interest groups and movements. Some of those interest groups engaged in mainstream politics—lobbying, bargaining, and compromise like the interest group patterns we associate with the national government. But those groups engaged in "direct-action politics," "single-issue politics," and "social movement politics" to a far greater extent than is found at the national level, except during the epoch of what we now are calling "new politics."

In contrast, the regulatory policies at the national level have not only been quite recent (most of them dating from the New Deal) but have been almost exclusively of the C_1 type. To repeat, the politics is mainstream—dominated by organized interest groups and engaging in lobbying and all the patterns associated with pluralism—and, in a word, regulatory. However, it is an obvious point, though made significant within the context of the cases and my Figure 4, that this standard type of national regulatory policy *can be radicalized by the addition of moral (C_2) considerations.*

An example of radicalization by degree would be elements of the 1964 Civil Rights Act. Most of the titles were by and large of the C_1 type. Following the spirit of *Brown v. Board of Education,* Congress reasoned that separate schools and public facilities and separate criteria of employment

were inherently unequal in their consequences, unconstitutional because
they gave minorities a badge of inferiority and tended to render minority
individuals in actual fact unequal in their ability as well as their opportunity
to enjoy what society had to offer. People who have never read *Brown*
would be surprised at how instrumental and nonmoral (i.e., how mainstream
liberal) the Supreme Court's argument was. Although this same utilitarian,
C_1 rationale was sufficient to win a congressional majority in favor of the
historic 1964 Act, it was far from the full argument the civil rights movement
itself was making. Happy as the movement was to have such a historic
law, the leaders of the movement had good reason to be frustrated by the
public debates and by the modesty of the message and the sanctions in the
regulatory provisions of the Act. The *moral* case against all forms of
discrimination was overwhelming, and there was equally strong moral
justification not only for far stronger and more unilateral sanctions eliminating
all discrimination but also for more direct compensatory policies to overcome
the effects of past discrimination—in other words, affirmative action. This
amounts, as the critics say, to positive and group discrimination that
contradicts the individualist definition of rights as comprehended by the
Constitution and also contradicts the explicit wish of Congress, as expressed,
for example, in the following passage from the employment provisions (Title
VII) prohibiting "preferential treatment to any individual or group . . . on
account of an imbalance which may exist with respect to the total or
percentage of persons of any race, color, religion, sex, or national origin.
. . ." The civil rights movement (note the form: a movement) sought what
amounted to a radicalization of the civil rights laws and, if not the laws,
the implementation of the laws by the agencies and courts. To the extent
that civil rights policy embodied a moral dimension, it both reflected and
contributed to a "new politics"—the politics of morality, of movements, of
polarization, and of what the authors in this book call "social regulatory
policymaking."

Many of the same persons who have decried what I have described
here as the radicalization of civil rights share responsibility not only for
radicalizing the opposition to civil rights but also for radicalizing other
important policies in other subject matter areas. Although the list is longer
than the cases in this volume, all the cases here belong to such a list. And
note well the several following characteristics of these cases:

1. Each C_2 policy had once been the almost exclusive province of state
   government power;
2. Each policy experienced radical politics almost any time the issue got
   on state policy agendas, in the nineteenth or the twentieth centuries;
3. All but gun control were removed altogether or in substantial part from
   state jurisdiction by the Supreme Court;
4. Each in recent years was then nationalized altogether or in substantial
   part.

Thus, none of the politics flowing from these issues was "new." The policies and the politics were relatively new merely to the *national* government. All of the laws and proposals in these cases qualify as "social" in that their focus and preoccupation were not on economic activities as such, even when companies and employers were the main objects of regulation. But now we can get a better sense of what people have been trying to convey by calling policies new or social. If people only meant that these policies were noneconomic, that wouldn't add much to our understanding of policies *or* politics. But if we take *social* to indicate that the policy is aiming at the moral base of conduct, then we have opened an entirely new dimension or have put an old dimension into a new and more useful context. That is at least what I intend to convey by the concept of radicalization. George Will, a self-defined man of the right, provides the distinction between mainstream and radical that I am striving for here: "In a famous opinion in a famous case . . . Justice Felix Frankfurter wrote: 'Law is concerned with external behavior and not with the inner life of man.' I am not sure what Frankfurter meant. I am sure what he said cannot be true. The purpose of this book is to say why that proposition is radically wrong."[2] Taken in moderation, Will's position may be mainstream, simply toward the far right of the mainstream continuum. But embraced to the fullest extent, by our taking Will literally on the desirability of using law to reach "the inner life of man," the continuum becomes a circle, turning downward toward the radical half of Figures 2, 3 or 4. But note well that moral, C_2, considerations can also be introduced from the left, pushing the left side of the continuum in a circular turn downward toward radicalization. In the world of morality and radicalization, the left and the right are a unity of opposites, together as one, logically and empirically apart from the mainstream.

This formulation will, I hope, make a contribution to theory in political science in at least three ways. First, it may make cases like the ones in this volume more interesting and significant by rendering their findings more cumulative, due to their demonstrated membership in a common framework. Second, introduction of the second dimension of policy may contribute to overcoming a long-standing embarrassment in political science: our difficulty in dealing with political radicalism in U.S. history except as something exceptional, sporadic, and temporary. Radical politics is as regular as mainstream, even if less frequent. Some policies are radical from the start, but any area of policy can be radicalized. It depends upon the way the policy or policy proposal is constructed and the severity of the sanctions provided.

Third, success on the first two points would be good for theory in political science. But my hopes expressed in this third point are even more ambitious. Taking away the "new" from the so-called new politics could lead to a richer sense of the historic relation between society and the state in the United States. Radical elements are inevitable in a society as dynamic as ours, and the society would be less healthy and less productive without the radical. The question for the study of political development is how radicalized forces interact with governmental institutions, whether they are channeled into progressive changes, and how they make a place for themselves within the constitutional structure. Was the U.S. system lucky or successful in the great transition through the New Deal to the "Second Republic"?[3] Everyone will agree that the Depression had radicalized an unusually large segment of U.S. society. Yet, it is clear from this analysis that most of the New Deal policies were of the C_1 type. Imagine, if possible, what the outcome would have been if the radicalized groups and movements of the 1930s had succeeded in radicalizing the policies. If there had been in the 1930s a large number of cases at the national level like the cases in this volume, we would not be talking here about the political system as it is today.

Tatalovich, Daynes, and their colleagues have given us not only cases and findings, but more. They have provided an agenda for a new policy analysis appropriate to the new politics.

Theodore J. Lowi

THE CONTRIBUTORS

Gary C. Bryner, Brigham Young University

Byron W. Daynes, DePauw University

Theodore J. Lowi, Cornell University

John A. Murley, Rochester Institute of Technology

Robert J. Spitzer, Cortland State College

Brent S. Steel, Oakland University

Mary Ann E. Steger, Washington State University

Raymond Tatalovich, Loyola University of Chicago

SOCIAL
REGULATORY
POLICY

INTRODUCTION
What Is Social Regulatory Policy?

Raymond Tatalovich and Byron W. Daynes

In a now classic article, Theodore J. Lowi argued that government generates three different categories of policy: distributive, regulatory, and redistributive.[1] In later writings, Lowi added a fourth category: constituent policy. In this volume, we propose an important variant of regulation—social regulatory policy—and outline some of the similarities and differences among the case studies discussed here and the policies encompassed by Lowi's typology.

First, a brief description of Lowi's typology will help to distinguish between and among all the different policy types. *Distributive* policy involves the allocation of federal moneys to subsidize public undertakings; examples are rivers and harbors expenditures, public works projects, and grants for highway construction. *Regulatory* policies impose general rules or laws on various sectors of the economy and include minimum wage and maximum hour laws, strip mining controls, and air pollution standards. Through *redistributive* policies, government seeks to transfer resources from the haves to the have-nots. Included here are welfare programs, social security, medicare, and the income tax from which much of the redistribution flows. *Constituent* policies give substantive content to the political regime and define the relationship of citizens to authority and the structure of government. Examples are the separation of powers principle of government, the civil service norm of "neutral competence," and the concept of legislative supremacy. *Social regulatory policy* as defined here means *the exercise of legal authority to modify or replace community values, moral practices, and norms of interpersonal conduct with new standards of behavior.* The examples included in this volume are those that govern abortion, pornography, gun control, crime, school prayer, and affirmative action. Although these policies share some characteristics with Lowi's regulatory and redistributive policy types, we assert that both the *who* and the *what* of social regulation are different enough to warrant close examination.

First, the *who*. Lowi investigated the policymaking process from the point of view of particular *arenas of power* and of the relationships among the key political actors in these arenas who make policy. These arenas are

1

the president, the Congress, interest groups, and the federal bureaucracy. The importance of each actor, however, depends upon which type of policy is being enacted. The number of political actors involved increases whenever the political resolution of "moral" controversies is attempted—that is, social regulation. In this volume, therefore, each case study is analyzed in terms not only of the four political actors included by Lowi but also in terms of the judiciary, public opinion, and federalism (the role of state and local authorities). To characterize the interrelationships among these seven participants, we formulate fourteen propositions about the process of social regulatory policymaking. These propositions are presented in the conclusion to this volume and serve as an overview of the preceding cases while offering a theoretical framework with which to consider new cases of social regulation.

Now let us return to the *what*. The term *regulation*, especially as Lowi employed it, is generally associated with business and economic activity. Government controls, which are applied to businesses from the auto industry to the stock market, serve to stimulate or restrict competition, change the shape of the market, and ensure economic activity and stability.

With social regulatory policy, *what* is being regulated is not an economic transition but a social relationship. Social relationships historically have been defined by community values, moral codes, and norms of personal conduct. However, there is a change in how those relationships are being governed now that legal authority is being used to regulate the traditional social order and to impose new standards of behavior on citizens.

Social regulations, like economic regulations, deliberately use government authority to change behavior. Rearranging economic relationships, however, is a relatively easy task compared with rearranging long-standing social relationships. Because they impinge on our private lives and define our social positions, social regulations have at their core a moral and normative debate about the place of the individual in the community.

As different as social regulation is from its antecedents, it shares a common regulatory history that logically proceeds to the policies discussed in this volume. A recap of that history will put the cases here in perspective while suggesting some future directions we might want to pursue.

The federal government, beginning with the Interstate Commerce Commission (ICC) of 1887 and until World War II, imposed "controls over the terms of entry and the conditions of operation in particular industries . . . [and] efforts were made to avoid excessive prices in such naturally monopolistic industries as utilities or to prevent destructive competition and ensure market stability."[2] That is, there were federal requirements that the trucking, railroad, and communications industries, for example, had to meet in order to provide services within those markets.

A new breed of government regulation resulted from the enactment of statutes during the 1970s,[3] including the Federal Water Pollution Control Amendments of 1972. These statutes are enforced by federal agencies such as the Environmental Protection Agency, but the objectives of these statutes are more ambitious, and include "the establishment of standards for certain types of activities or the imposition of controls to limit the effects of these activities . . . [and] efforts . . . to prohibit or discourage actions that endanger workers or consumers, pollute the environment, or violate important social goals, such as equal employment."[4]

Randall Ripley and Grace Franklin called ICC-type legislation "competitive regulatory policy" because once the competition among businesses for access to a regulated market is over, those few companies that are victorious enjoy the economic benefits of what essentially is a government-sanctioned oligopoly. In contrast, Ripley and Franklin referred to the 1970s enactments as "protective regulatory policy" because they are intended to "prevent certain types of private activity and require private activities in explicit terms."[5] These federal regulations are more pervasive because they affect the workplace as well as the marketplace and businesses must comply with standards affecting a variety of economic transactions.

Not only are such protective regulations more pervasive; they are more ostensibly concerned with the quality of life, individual welfare, and the common good. The term *social policy* often is used to describe these regulations, but this term is confusing because scholars use various definitions for the term. Charles Murray defined social policy generally as a "transfer of resources from the haves to the have nots" (what Lowi specified as redistribution), and Donald L. Horowitz limited social policies to those affecting "the structure of social norms, social relations, or social decision-making."[6] The Horowitz formulation is closer to what we are presenting here, although it still is too open-ended. Our concept of social regulatory policy builds upon, and fully develops, the previous work by those scholars who began to adapt the Lowi framework to public policies that provoked moral conflict.

The Lowi framework was applied to comparative public policy analysis by T. Alexander Smith,[7] who was influenced by James Christoph's book, *Capital Punishment and British Politics*.[8] Christoph had discovered common attributes shared by such issues as capital punishment, birth control, homosexuality, and prostitution including, most importantly, that they "plumb deep-seated moral codes" whenever these issues arise. Smith drew upon that observation to propose yet another policy category, "emotive symbolism," which "generate[s] emotional support for deeply held values, but unlike the other [policy] types . . . the values sought are essentially noneconomic."[9] He also cited such issues as the death penalty, school prayer, abortion, homosexuality, and racial segregation.

We agree with Christoph and Smith that moral values are the key to understanding certain disputes. Although the social regulatory domain has fewer policies compared to economic regulation, redistribution, or distribution, social regulation provokes intense, persistent controversies. Moreover, these controversies have increased in frequency since the 1950s. Abortion, school prayer, and affirmative action are discussed here. Pornography as well as homosexuality and prostitution involve the sexual mores of a community, just as the Equal Rights Amendment prompted a heated debate about gender roles. Gun control and crime are included in this volume, but patriotism also would illustrate social regulatory policy. Smith studied the political conflict about how to incorporate both French and English symbols within the Canadian flag. In the United States, due to the flood of illegal aliens, conflict regarding bilingualism and the specification of English as the official U.S. language may become our next great debate about social regulatory policy.

∽ Chapter One ∾

SCHOOL PRAYER
Free Exercise of Religion or Establishment of Religion?

John A. Murley

> *In a free government, the security for civil rights must be the same as for religious rights. It consists in the one case in the multiplicity of interests, and in the other, in the multiplicity of sects.*
>
> —*The Federalist, #51*

It has been a quarter of a century since the Supreme Court's ruling in *Engel v. Vitale*, 370 U.S. 421 (1962), declared unconstitutional the Regent's prayer in New York public schools and since the companion cases, *Abington School District v. Schempp* and *Murray v. Curlett*, 374 U.S. 203 (1963), held unconstitutional the reading of passages from the Bible and the saying of the Lord's Prayer in the nation's public schools. Attempts to reverse the school prayer cases have risen, fallen, and risen again during the years, but the Supreme Court has not backed down. In a recent case, *Wallace v. Jaffree*, 105 S.Ct. 2479 (1985), the high court once again rejected an attempt to allow school prayer through "moment of silence" legislation.

The public response to *Engel* and *Schempp* made clear that the Supreme Court had struck a sensitive political nerve. The response was overwhelming, immediate, and generally unfavorable. The range of reactions included abusive denunciation of the Supreme Court as godless, charges that God had been outlawed in schools, and billboards urging citizens to "Keep God in School." Feelings on prayer in public schools ran so deep that for years many school districts simply ignored the Supreme Court decision.

Strict separatists hailed the decision as an additional fortification in "the wall of separation" between church and state, while others applauded the rulings as a contribution to religious freedom. By restricting the states' power to intervene in the sensitive area of prayer, the strict separatists said the Court had advanced and protected the liberty of both believers and nonbelievers in religion.[1]

INTEREST GROUPS

One might assume that the Supreme Court ban on Bible reading and school prayer was viewed by the majority as an assault on Christianity, just as non-Christians and nonbelievers saw the ban as a defense of their civil liberties. But the issue never was joined on these terms. In fact, the rulings were defended by mainstream Protestant denominations, which were joined by mainstream Jewish groups, educators, liberals, civil libertarians, and single-issue coalitions. The primary constituency behind restoring school prayer has included (and still includes) fundamentalists and evangelicals aligned with political conservatives and citizen-based, single-issue groups.

The religious and interest groups that gave testimony on school prayer amendments to the Constitution before congressional committees on six occasions from 1962 through 1985 are categorized in Table 1.1. Compared to other stormy questions before the Congress, this dispute involved relatively few groups. Religious groups and churches were most important on both sides of the question, but especially in *opposition* to school prayer. They represented 63–84 percent of all organizations testifying against school prayer amendments compared to 35–71 percent of those supporting such legislation in these six hearings. A solid phalanx of Jewish groups, opposed to any hint of sectarianism in the public schools, included the Anti-Defamation League of B'nai B'rith, the Synagogue Council of America, and the National Jewish Community Relations Advisory Council. Among the Protestant groups opposed were the Episcopal church, the National Council of the Churches of Christ, the United Methodist church, the Southern Baptist Convention, and the United Presbyterian church.

Roman Catholic, Greek Orthodox, fundamentalist, and evangelical churches favored religious exercises. Most important were the latter—for example, Moral Majority, Christian Voice, and the National Association of Evangelicals, which is composed of thirty-seven evangelical denominations. The Roman Catholic church argued that voluntary prayer, taken alone, was simply a token gesture. In 1983 testimony on S.J. Res. 73, a version of President Reagan's original proposed school prayer amendment, the U.S. Catholic Conference said that although the proposed amendment's intent was a "positive step towards assuring the efficacy of the Religion Clauses . . . [but] in failing to include the right to receive religious instruction, the amendment omits a component which is essential to the integrity of the right to pray."[2] Whereas others tried to find the lowest common denominator, such as a moment of silence, that will allow prayer in the public schools, the Catholic bishops wanted prayer integrated with religious instruction. For this reason, the Roman Catholic church was not the crucial organization behind school prayer.

Single-issue groups were prominent following the *Engel* and *Schempp* cases, and these groups persisted into the 1970s. Representative groups included the Committee for the Preservation of Prayer and Bible Reading in Public Schools, the Constitutional Prayer Foundation, and the Maryland Interfaith Committee for School Prayer. Their political significance was demonstrated by the 1971 crusade that led to the vote in the House of Representatives on the Wylie amendment, which concerned school prayer.

Congressman Chalmers Wylie (R-Ohio) and his allies were able to "discharge" from the Judiciary Committee a constitutional amendment in support of prayer or meditation in publicly funded places thanks in large measure to "Mrs. [Ben] Ruhlin, her Prayer Campaign Committee and related groups . . . [which] mobilized citizen pressure across the country to persuade members to sign the discharge petition."[3] But the intense pressure on Congress may have backfired because the amendment failed by twenty-eight votes.

Beginning in 1970, Mrs. Ruhlin contacted the chairs of the House and Senate Committees on the Judiciary, worked closely with her own congressman, and began a grass-roots organization. She placed $6,000 worth of coupons in newspapers across the country asking supporters to mail them to the House Judiciary Committee, and by the time she visited Wylie on Capitol Hill, one hundred thousand persons supporting a school prayer amendment had signed petitions. Her Prayer Campaign Committee was aided by similar groups, such as the Back to God Movement, Citizens for Public Prayer, Project Prayer, Parents for Prayer, and Citizens for Public Reverence.

There were single-issue groups among the opponents of school prayer as well. The National Coalition for Public Education and Religious Liberty (NCPERL), founded in 1974, represented thirty civil liberties, educational, and religious organizations "dedicated to preserving religious liberty and the principle of separation of church and state and to maintaining the integrity and viability of public education."[4] Its member organizations predominated among those groups that testified against school prayer and included Jewish groups, the American Civil Liberties Union, the National Education Association, and the American Association of School Administrators.

Dating from 1947, there are 55,000 members in Americans United for Separation of Church and State. It monitors legislation and court decisions in the church-state area, does legal work, and educates the public about the importance of the church-state separation principle.[5] People for the American Way (PFAW) was founded by television producer Norman Lear in 1980 "out of a concern that an anti-democratic and divisive climate was being created by groups that sought to use religion and religious symbols for political purposes."[6] The PFAW reportedly has eighty-eight thousand members.

Table 1.2 shows which groups entered friend-of-the-court briefs in four Supreme Court cases on school prayer. Prominent in opposition were Jewish groups (accounting for the majority of *amicus* briefs) and NCPERL as well as some of its member organizations. On the other side were an

TABLE 1.1 Testimony by Religious and Interest Groups Before Congressional Hearings on Bible Reading or Voluntary Prayer in School

	Supporting Bible Reading or Voluntary Prayer						Opposing Bible Reading or Voluntary Prayer					
	Senate 1962	House 1964	Senate 1966	Senate 1982	Senate 1983	Senate 1985	Senate 1962	House 1964	Senate 1966	Senate 1982	Senate 1983	Senate 1985
RELIGIOUS												
Protestant	6	12	5	3		6	2	25	18	5	10	6
Orthodox	1	2	1									
Catholic	4	2	1	1	1							
Jewish				1			14	18	35	2	8	5
INTEREST												
Farmer		1	1		1							
Patriotic/ Political	5	3	4		1			1	1		1	
Business	2								1			
Labor		1	1									
Women			1									
Legal							1				1	
Civil Rights							1			1	3	
Education		2						5	1	1	1	
Civil Liberties			1				1	2	1			

Philosophical	2	3		1	4	3	1
Other	3	2		1	1	1	
Single-Issue	9	3	2	1	2	3	1
	20	35	20	7	23	59	62
	10	1			11	28	16
					3	3	5

Source: Data tabulated from the following hearings: Senate, Committee on the Judiciary, "Prayer in Public Schools and Other Matters," 87th Cong., 2nd sess., 1962; House of Representatives, Committee on the Judiciary, "Proposed Amendments to the Constitution Relating to Prayers and Bible Reading in the Public Schools," 88th Cong., 2nd sess., 1964; Senate, Subcommittee on Constitutional Amendments of the Committee on the Judiciary, "Senate Joint Res. 148 Relating to Prayer in Public Schools," 89th Cong., 2nd sess., 1966; Senate, Committee on the Judiciary, "S.J. Res. 199, A Senate Joint Resolution Proposing an Amendment to the Constitution of the United States," 97th Cong., 2nd sess., 1982; Senate, Committee on the Judiciary, "S.J. Res. 73, A Joint Resolution Proposing an Amendment to the Constitution of the United States Relating to Voluntary School Prayer and S.J. Res. 212, A Joint Resolution Proposing an Amendment to the Constitution of the United States Relating to Voluntary Silent Prayer or Meditation," 98th Cong., 1st sess., 1983; Senate, Subcommittee on the Constitution of the Committee on the Judiciary, "S.J. Res. 2, A Joint Resolution Proposing an Amendment to the Constitution of the United States Relating to Voluntary Silent Prayer or Reflection," 99th Cong., 1st sess., 1985.

TABLE 1.2 *Amicus Curiae* Briefs to the Supreme Court by Interest Groups in Four School Prayer Cases

	Engel v. Vitale (1962)	*Abington Township School District v. Schempp* (1963) and *Murray v. Curlett* (1963)	*Wallace v. Jaffree* (1985)
Support School Prayer/Moment of Silence			
Board of Regents of the University of the State of New York	X		
State attorneys general/state governments	(19)	(1)	(6)
U.S. solicitor general			X
Center for Judicial Studies			X
Christian Legal Society			X
National Association of Evangelicals			X
Freedom Council			X
Legal Foundation of America			X
Moral Majority			X

Oppose School Prayer/Moment of Silence			
American Jewish Committee/American Jewish Congress	X	X	X
Anti-Defamation League of B'nai B'rith		X	X
Synagogue Council of America		X	X
National Community Relations Advisory Council (Jewish)		X	X
American Ethical Union	X	X	X
American Civil Liberties Union	X		
Alabama Civil Liberties Union	X		
National Coalition for Public Education and Religious Liberty			
Senator Lowell P. Weicker (R-Conn.)	X		
American Humanist Association	X		X

array of conservative groups, including the Legal Foundation of America, a conservative public interest law firm, and the Center for Judicial Studies, a policy institute whose goal was to restrict federal judicial powers. Four organizations filing *amicus* briefs in this case reflected the evangelical position, including the Freedom Council, which was affiliated with Pat Robertson's Christian Broadcast Network. State attorneys general or other officials also were involved in *amicus* activity to defend religious practices in their school systems. Nineteen states agreed with New York state in the *Engel* case; Maryland defended Bible readings in a brief accompanying *Schempp* and *Murray;* and six states concurred in arguments to *Wallace* supporting "moment of silence" laws.

The clear division between the interests opposing and those favoring prayer in the classroom reflected differing emphases on how the "establishment" versus "free exercise" clauses of the First Amendment ought to be interpreted. Non-Christians and nonbelievers focused on church-state separation as essential to the protection of freedom of religion in the United States, but some groups in the Christian majority believed that the ban on school prayer violated their religious freedom to engage in prayer, although as taxpayers they, too, supported public schools. This debate was (and is) rich in constitutional and historical argument and looked to the writings of the founding period to determine how the Framers of the Constitution viewed the place of religion in society.

Legal Controversy

Those favoring voluntary prayer point to a long tradition prior to 1963 of religion in schools and other areas of public life. They mention, as examples, "In God We Trust" on the nation's currency, "this nation under God" in the Pledge of Allegiance, the use of public prayer and chaplains at presidential inaugurals, Thanksgiving Day proclamations, the presence of paid chaplains in the Congress and state legislatures, and the invocation "God save the United States and this honorable Court" on behalf of the Supreme Court.

Further, those favoring school prayer claim that the Supreme Court, by denying them the opportunity to engage in publicly recognized prayer, has infringed on their First Amendment free exercise of religion guarantee. They view the result of the Supreme Court decisions not as neutrality among religions or between religion and nonreligion but, at best, as a callous indifference to the religious sentiments of the community and, at worst, as open hostility to those religious sentiments.

Supporters of the Court decisions contend that public school prayer constitutes an establishment of religion and thus contravenes the First Amendment. Even if the original intent of the First Amendment allowed for prayer, the Court's defenders contend that the meaning of "establishment" and "free exercise" must change with the changing social conditions and growing religious diversity of the country. According to this view, public prayers most likely will reflect the view of the dominant religion in any community, thereby violating the rights of nonbelievers or others belonging to minority sects. Even if that were not the case, the opposition to school prayer alleges that any prayer likely to be adopted would be so innocuous and trivial as to not be worthy of the effort. The Court's defenders also insist that voluntary prayer never can be truly voluntary in the public schools. Young students, unlike adults, are captives of a mandatory attendance policy and are unlikely to resist peer pressure to participate in prayer. Finally, Court supporters fear that religion will become a source of irritation, thus fanning religious differences and creating social animosities where none need exist.

It may be that the Supreme Court, given its understanding of the establishment clause, cannot easily resolve this issue. Apart from the First Amendment, religion is mentioned only once in the Constitution: "No religious test shall ever be required as a qualification to any office or public trust under the United States." Until 1947, the meaning of both these provisions was not the subject of constitutional debate. With *Everson v. Board of Education*, 330 U.S. 1 (1947), even though the Court determined that public funding for bus rides to parochial schools was constitutional, the controversy regarding a new interpretation of the establishment clause already was beginning. That new view was reflected in the often quoted, eloquent dictum of Justice Hugo L. Black's majority opinion in *Everson*, where he wrote that the establishment clause "means at least this":

> Neither a state nor the Federal Government can set up a church. Neither can pass laws which aid one religion, aid all religions or prefer one religion over another. Neither can force nor influence a person to go or remain away from church against his will or force him to profess a belief or disbelief in any religion. No person can be punished for entertaining or professing religious beliefs or disbeliefs, for church attendance or nonattendance. No tax in any amount, large or small, can be levied to support any religious activities or institutions, whatever they may be called, or whatever they may adopt to teach or practice religion. Neither a state nor the Federal Government can, openly or secretly, participate in the affairs of a religious organization or groups and vice versa. In the words of Jefferson, the clause against establishment of religion by law was intended to erect "a wall of separation between Church and State."

For forty years, Justice Black's statement has served as the foundation for the Supreme Court's decisions in school prayer cases and in aid to private school cases.

The Supreme Court might have dealt with the school prayer issue in terms of the "free exercise" clause of the First Amendment rather than by relying on church-state separation. This approach was used in the famous flag-salute cases of the 1940s and thus deserves mention here. In the first flag-salute case, *Minersville School District v. Gobitis*, 310 U.S. 586 (1940), the two young Gobitis children were expelled from the Minersville, Pennsylvania, school for refusing to salute the U.S. flag. Saluting the flag was regarded by them as a sin violating their Jehovah's Witness faith, which forbade the worship of graven images. Mr. Gobitis sued to enjoin the school

district from requiring participation in the flag-salute ceremony as a condition
of his children's compulsory attendance in school.

Justice Felix Frankfurter, writing for the Supreme Court, upheld the
expulsion of the Gobitis children. He framed the issue as one of "reconciling
the conflicting claims of liberty and authority" and concluded that "the
mere possession of religious convictions does not relieve the individual from
obedience to a general law not aimed at the promotion or restriction of
religious beliefs."

Justice Harlan Stone, the lone dissenter, argued that "the state seeks
to coerce these children to express a sentiment which, as they interpret it,
they do not entertain, and which violates their deepest religious convictions."
Stone's view eventually prevailed. Three years later, the Court reversed itself
by overturning a West Virginia law requiring students to participate in a
daily flag-salute ceremony. Again, Jehovah's Witnesses sued, but this time,
in *West Virginia State Board of Education v. Barnette*, 319 U.S. 624 (1943),
the Supreme Court said that government had no authority to compel citizens
"to utter what is not in their mind." Justice Robert H. Jackson delivered
the stirring creed: "If there is any fixed star in our Constitutional constellation,
it is that no official, high or petty, can prescribe what shall be orthodox in
politics, nationalism, religion or other matters of opinion or force citizens
to confess by word or act their faith therein."

Can we usefully distinguish between the *Barnette* flag-salute case and
the later *Engel-Schempp-Wallace* line of school prayer cases? In the former,
the Court objected to the use of governmental power to force school children
to participate in patriotic exercises that were against their religious convictions.
At the same time, the Supreme Court did not suggest that West Virginia
had to stop the flag-salute practice in order to remove any embarrassment
or offense to the children.

Nothing in the *Engel-Schempp-Wallace* jurisprudence hinted at any
attempt to coerce children to pray against their will or religious beliefs, and
most Americans undoubtedly agree that people should not be forced to
profess allegiance to any religion. But the Supreme Court has not satisfied
many citizens, particularly advocates of school prayer, with respect to
establishment clause concerns. A foremost concern has been the high court's
view that the First Amendment was designed to erect a "wall" of separation
between church and state. This reference to Thomas Jefferson's metaphor,
in the opinion of some scholars, has had a mischievous effect on the Court's
interpretation of the religion clauses. The critics argue that the Supreme
Court has wrongly interpreted the First Amendment as originally understood
by the Framers. The dispute regarding school prayer thus draws upon a
rigorous scholarly debate about original intent.

Intent of the Framers

School prayer is a political issue that for many citizens goes to the heart
of the nature of their community and to the kind of human beings and
citizens they should be. The Supreme Court has held since 1947 that the

establishment clause requires neutrality among religious sects and also between religion and nonreligion. As such, the school prayer controversy centers around two questions: What is the meaning of the First Amendment? Has the Supreme Court understood that meaning correctly?

The argument that the Founding Fathers intended to have religion play an important public role may prove too much. The religion of the Framers was Protestant Christianity, as George McKenna reminded us: "It was always the King James Bible that was read at public ceremonies and public schools. And it was always assumed America was a Christian nation, in spite of increasing Jewish immigration in the nineteenth century."[7] On the other hand, there is also the tradition expressed in the Northwest Ordinance of 1787, which provided that "religion, morality, and knowledge being necessary to good government and the happiness of mankind, schools and the means of education shall forever be encouraged." Both the First Amendment and the Northwest Ordinance were adopted by the first Congress. Nothing in the legislative history of these provisions suggests that the members of the first Congress understood themselves to be inconsistent or contradictory by adopting both measures. If eighteenth century schools could be encouraged to support religion, education, and morality, cannot twentieth century schools be allowed to do the same, particularly where the community thinks it wise to do so?

The Constitution as written in Philadelphia did not have a Bill of Rights. Many delegates at the Constitutional Convention, moreover, did not think a Bill of Rights was necessary. As James Madison would claim in *The Federalist*, #51, the protection of religious liberty was the same as for civil liberty. This protection resided not in the "paper barriers" of a Bill of Rights but consisted "in the one case in the multiplicity of interests, and in the other, in the multiplicity of sects. The degree of security in both cases will depend on the number of people comprehended under the same government." A large commercial republic with its nearly infinite variety of interests and religious sects would be the assurance against the imposition by government of any one sectarian view.

This argument was not entirely persuasive to many delegates attending the state ratifying conventions who feared that the new government might use its implied powers to enact laws affecting religion and other areas that were the preserve of the states. As a result, there arose a demand that the Constitution be amended. Although the content of the various proposed amendments on religion differed from state to state, both Virginia and North Carolina offered this same version:

> That religion, or the duty which we owe to our Creator, and the manner of discharging it, can be directed only by reason and conviction, not by force and violence; and therefore all men have an equal, natural and inalienable right to the free exercise of religion, according to the dictates of conscience, and that no particular religious sect or society ought to be favored or established by the laws in preference to others.[8]

Support for this view was given by James Madison at the first Congress. When asked how he understood the religion provisions, Madison responded that "Congress should not establish a religion, and enforce the legal observation of it by law, nor compel men to worship God in any manner contrary to their conscience." In Madison's opinion, the First Amendment was intended to meet the objections of anti-Federalists opposed to the Constitution, in part, because they feared the establishment of a national religion. In addressing this concern Madison noted:

> Whether the words [of the religion clauses] are necessary or not, he did not mean to say, but they had been required by some of the State Conventions, who seemed to entertain an opinion that under the clause of the Constitution, which gave power to Congress to make all laws necessary and proper to carry into execution the Constitution, and the laws made under it, enabled them to make laws of such a nature as might infringe the rights of conscience, and establish a national religion; to prevent these effects he presumed the amendment was intended, and he thought it as well expressed as the nature of the language would admit.

Madison further observed that he "thought if the word 'national' was inserted before [the word] religion, it would satisfy the minds of honorable gentlemen. He believed that the people feared one sect might obtain a pre-eminence, or two combine together, and establish a religion to which they would compel others to conform."[9]

In his *Commentaries on the Constitution of the United States*, Justice Joseph Story understood the religion clauses of the First Amendment in essentially the same manner as James Madison had in 1789. "It was impossible that there should not arise perpetual strife and perpetual jealousy on the subject of ecclesiastical ascendancy, if the national government were left free to create a religious establishment."[10] In other words, Justice Story feared that civil and religious strife would result if Congress were allowed to establish a national religion.

However, the Supreme Court in *Everson* adopted Jefferson's "wall of separation between church and state" metaphor as its essential meaning of the establishment clause. Jefferson used this metaphor in a letter to the Danbury Baptists Association (Connecticut) dated January 1, 1802. But recall that Thomas Jefferson was not a member either of the Constitutional Convention of 1787 or of the first Congress of 1789, which wrote and adopted the Bill of Rights. Moreover, Jefferson was widely understood to have views on religion that were not typical of the ordinary colonists, members of the Constitutional Convention, or the first Congress.

Another point of contention from the *Everson* case, although regarded as settled law by the Court, is the Court's application of the religion clauses to the states by the Fourteenth Amendment. Justice Tom Clark writing in *Schempp* made that linkage explicit by stating, "This Court has decisively settled that the First Amendment's mandate that 'Congress shall make no law respecting an establishment of religion, or prohibiting the free exercise thereof' has been made wholly applicable to the States by the Fourteenth Amendment."

But this assertion is not obvious from the history of the Fourteenth Amendment, as George Anastaplo observed, especially with the uses made of the due process clause of the amendment:

> The Fourteenth Amendment *was* peculiarly framed if the intention of its framers was to have made applicable against the States the provisions of the Bill of Rights (such as those of the First Amendment) which had been originally directed only against Congress. Whatever may be supposed about some of the other articles in the Bill of Rights, would not more specific language than that of the Fourteenth Amendment be necessary to incorporate in it the First Amendment with its explicit concern only with Congressional conduct? . . . How *can* the States be limited by the application against them of a provision which was in large part intended to protect them from Congressional interference with whatever religious establishment those States chose to have?[11]

Furthermore, as Edward Dumbauld reminded us, in several New England states an established church was maintained both before and after the First Amendment went into effect.[12] From this perspective, the establishment clause was designed as much to hinder federal interference with states' religious establishments as to forbid the establishment of a national religion by Congress. Speaking to this point, Gerald Gunther contended that

> the "incorporation" in *Everson* of "establishment" took place with considering the textual difficulty of using the "liberty" of the 14th Amendment as the incorporation route. . . . The First Amendment's establishment clause may have been designed primarily as a federalistic limitation: established churches existed in the states when the Bill of Rights was adopted; the main purpose of "establishment" may have been to keep Congress out of that area.[13]

N. Dorsen, P. Bender, and B. Neuborne essentially agreed with that view by arguing that "the purpose of the First Amendment was not to keep government and religion separated" but rather "to forbid the Federal Government from interfering in the manner in which the state governments dealt with religion."[14]

This view makes sense, particularly in light of a later attempt by Congress to pass a constitutional amendment that would have repudiated this understanding. In 1876, Congress attempted to enact the Blaine amendment, which read in part:

> No state shall make any law respecting an establishment of religion or prohibiting the free exercise thereof; and no religion test shall ever be required as a qualification to any office or public trust under any state. . . . This article shall not be construed to prohibit the reading of the Bible in any school or institution; and it shall not have the effect to impair the rights of property already vested.

The amendment obtained the required two-thirds vote in the House of Representatives but failed to do so in the Senate. If the Supreme Court's view in *Everson* of the Fourteenth Amendment vis-à-vis the establishment clause is correct, then one must wonder why Congress thought it necessary to consider the Blaine amendment just eight years *after* the same thing was accomplished through the Fourteenth Amendment.

JUDICIARY

The School Prayer Cases

At the start of each school day, beginning in 1958, in New Hyde Park, New York, a twenty-two word prayer composed by the New York State Board of Regents in 1951 was recited. It read as follows: "Almighty God, we acknowledge our dependence upon Thee, and we beg Thy blessings upon us, our parents, our teachers and our country." This prayer prompted a constitutional challenge, and in 1962 the Supreme Court in *Engel v. Vitale* struck the prayer down as a violation of the First and Fourteenth Amendments' prohibition against establishment of religion. The Supreme Court voted 6–1 with Justices Felix Frankfurter and Byron White abstaining. Justice Hugo L. Black authored the majority opinion in which Chief Justice Earl Warren and Justices William Brennan, Tom Clark, and John Harlan joined, and Justice William O. Douglas wrote a separate concurring opinion. Justice Potter Stewart dissented.

In reaching its decision, the high court did not cite a single case in support of its conclusion that New York state had "adopted a practice wholly inconsistent with the Establishment Clause." After nearly one hundred fifty years, had the practice been wholly inconsistent with the First Amendment, one would have expected some case law on the practice. It seems evident that the Regents Prayer referred to a nondenominational God of the Judeo-Christian tradition, not to the Buddha, Jesus, or Allah of particular religions. The recitation of the prayer at the beginning of each school day also was voluntary; any child who did not wish to participate could remain silent or leave the room. Only one request to be excused from saying the prayer was made, and that was granted. There was no attempt to enter into the record evidence of any effort by school boards or anyone else to impose any particular religious view on students.

However, the absence of coercion was not sufficient protection against the threat of establishment in the view of the Court's majority. Justice Black argued that the establishment clause "must at least mean that in this country it is no part of the business of government to compose official prayers for any group of the American people to recite as part of a religious program carried on by the government." Furthermore, he contended, "neither the fact that the prayer may be denominationally neutral, nor the fact that its observance on the part of the students is voluntary, can serve to free it from the limitations of the Establishment Clause, as it might from the Free

Exercise clause." Black did not explain how a nondenominational prayer equaled an establishment of religion; it was sufficient that the prayer had been composed by the government.

The method of interpretation used in *Engel* has remained constant throughout the succeeding cases. Each time, prayer activities are treated as an immediate and self-evident establishment of religion. There is little or no discussion of what constitutes an establishment of religion or how it applies to the question at hand. In each of the prayer and "minute of silence" cases, questions of nondenominational prayer and of coercion, both physical and psychological, are termed as appropriate only to questions of "free exercise" of religion.

But Justice Stewart, in his dissent, denied that the Regents Prayer had infringed on anyone's free exercise of religion. Moreover, he could not see how "letting those who want to say a prayer say it" established a religion. On the contrary, he thought that prayer allowed children to participate in the religious heritage of the country. What the New York State Board of Regents Prayer had done was what Congress, the president, and the Supreme Court also had done, namely, "to recognize and to follow the deeply entrenched and highly cherished spiritual traditions of our Nation."

At first, the *Engel* decision and Justice Black's opinion gave the impression that what was constitutionally infirm about the Regents Prayer was that the New York State Board of Regents had composed and officially sanctioned the prayer. This view, or hope, was dashed one year later when the Supreme Court decided *Abington Township School District v. Schempp* and *Murray v. Curlett*. The Court held to be unconstitutional a Pennsylvania law requiring at the start of each school day the reading without comment of ten verses from the King James Bible. A Maryland law provided for "the reading without comment of a chapter in the Holy Bible and/or the use of the Lord's Prayer." Any child could be excused from these exercises at his or her parents' request, although in the *Schempp* school the readings were broadcast over the intercom system each day.

This time there was no question about what government agency had written the prayer or Bible verses. The 8–1 decision nullified both practices as being unconstitutional under the establishment clause as applied to the states through the Fourteenth Amendment. Justice Tom Clark wrote the Court's opinion and was joined by Chief Justice Earl Warren and Justices Hugo Black, William Brennan, William Douglas, and Arthur Goldberg. Again only Justice Potter Stewart dissented.

Perhaps as a result of the uproar over *Engel*, Justice Clark retraced the Court's previous rulings on separation of church and state. In doing so he reaffirmed in the strongest manner that the Court "had rejected unequivocally the contention that the establishment clause forbids only governmental preference of one religion over another." The test, said Clark, was, "What are the purpose and primary effect of the enactment? If either is the advancement or inhibition of religion, then the enactment exceeds the scope of the legislative power as circumscribed by the Constitution.

That is to say to withstand the strictures of the Establishment Clause there must be a secular purpose and a primary effect that neither advances nor inhibits religion."

Lower Court Rulings

Following *Engel* and *Schempp*, it became apparent that the Supreme Court would examine very carefully any attempt to get around its interpretation of the establishment clause. During the past twenty-five years, lower federal courts have routinely declared religious activities in public schools to be unconstitutional, and just as routinely the Supreme Court has let those rulings stand. In *DeSpain v. Dekalb County Community School District*, 428, 384 F.2d 836 (7th Cir.), Cert. denied 390 U.S. 906 (1968), an appellate court disallowed kindergarten children from reciting this verse with their morning milk and cookies:

> We thank you for the flowers so sweet;
> We thank you for the food we eat;
> We thank you for the birds that sing;
> We thank you for everything.

In *Karen B. v. Treen*, 653 F.2d 897 (5th Cir. 1981), aff'd, 455 U.S. 913 (1982), the Supreme Court affirmed without an opinion a federal court's striking down a law authorizing "school authorities . . . to allow each classroom teacher to ask if a student wishes to volunteer to offer a prayer and, in the event that no student does volunteer, to allow the teacher to offer a prayer." The high court also let stand the lower federal court ruling in *Collins v. Chandler Unified School District*, 644 F.2d 759 (9th Cir.) Cert. denied, 455 U.S. 863 (1981), which held to be unconstitutional the practice of allowing students to begin school assemblies with a prayer.

In *Stone v. Graham*, 449 U.S. 39 (1980), the Supreme Court declared invalid as a religious activity a Kentucky law that required the Ten Commandments to be posted in public school classrooms. In an attempt to meet the Supreme Court's objections, the bottom of each poster was printed with the following statement: "The secular application of the Ten Commandments is clearly seen in its adoption as the fundamental legal code of Western Civilization and the Common Law of the United States." This avowed secular purpose was not sufficient because, said the Court, "the preeminent purpose for posting the Ten Commandments on schoolroom walls is plainly religious in nature."

Recent attempts to restore religious activity to the public schools have been the "moment of silence" laws. In *Gaines v. Anderson*, 421 F.Supp. 337 (D.Mass. 1976), a federal district court upheld a Massachusetts law requiring at the beginning of the school day a "period of silence not to exceed one minute . . . for meditation or prayer." Although the federal court acknowledged that an earlier version of this law had mentioned only meditation, the present statute, with its reference to both meditation and prayer, nonetheless was sensitive to the "First Amendment's mandate to take a neutral position that neither encourages or discourages prayer." This court believed that providing an opportunity for students to pray did not violate the establishment clause.

An entirely different view was reached by a federal district court in Tennessee. In *Beck v. McElrath*, 548 F.Supp. 1161 (M.D.Tenn. 1982), a nearly identical provision was struck down as violating the establishment clause. In reviewing its legislative history, the court found that when the "terms of the statute are viewed together and accorded reasonable meaning, it is difficult to escape the conclusion that the legislative purpose was advancement of religious exercises in the classroom."

It is readily apparent from these cases that how a judge reads legislative history is all important, be that the legislative history of state laws or of the First and Fourteenth Amendments. This was demonstrated when a district court in *Duffy v. Las Cruces Pub. Schools*, no. 81-876-JB (D.N.M. Feb. 10, 1983), declared null and void a New Mexico law permitting local school boards to allow a minute of silence at the start of each school day, although this law was almost identical to the Massachusetts statute held to be constitutional in *Gaines v. Anderson*. Here the district court saw no secular purpose: "The pre-eminent purpose was to establish a devotional exercise in the classrooms of New Mexico public schools." As evidence, the court pointed out that the sponsor of this legislation had asked the New Mexico State Department of Education "to draft a bill which would allow students to pray in school." Although the law's stated objective was to "enhance discipline and instill in the students the intellectual composure necessary for effective learning," the court said this was "clearly the product of afterthought . . . an elaborate effort to inject a secular purpose into a clearly religious activity."

Wallace v. Jaffree

Since the 1960s, a number of legal scholars have argued that moments of silence might well be an appropriate compromise between proponents and opponents of organized school prayer and one that could pass constitutional muster. Writing in 1963, for example, Jesse Choper suggested that "each school day commence with a quiet moment that would still the tumult of the playground and start a day of study."[15] But now this provision has become yet another constitutional issue dividing the courts and the experts. Faced with conflicting lower court rulings, the Supreme Court took this question under consideration in its 1985 "moment of silence" decision in *Wallace v. Jaffree*. The majority opinion was authored by Justice John Paul Stevens and joined by Justices William Brennan, Thurgood Marshall, Harry Blackmun, and Lewis Powell, with Justice Sandra Day O'Connor filing a separate concurring opinion. Unlike earlier prayer cases, however, *Wallace* called forth a strong, well-reasoned dissenting opinion by Justice William Rehnquist, which questioned the historical and philosophical foundations of the Court's interpretation of the establishment clause.

In 1983, federal district judge William Brevard Hand ruled that the Supreme Court had misinterpreted the establishment clause in previous prayer cases, and he upheld an Alabama law allowing teachers or students to lead voluntary prayers. The Eleventh Court of Appeals was unimpressed, however, and reversed Judge Hand's decision. Alabama's petition for a rehearing was denied, and the state appealed to the high court.

In his opinion for the Supreme Court's majority, Justice Stevens held that Alabama's statute requiring one minute of silence for meditation or voluntary silent prayer was an unconstitutional violation of the establishment clause because the law was "intended to convey a message of State-approval of prayer activities in the public schools." He paid close attention to the idiosyncratic legislative history of Alabama's statute, noting that the only reason put forth for the statute was the express purpose of its primary sponsor to "return voluntary prayer to the public schools." The only change in the revised Alabama statute was to add "or prayer" to the previous meditation law, which was regarded as an obvious violation of the "secular purpose" standard enunciated in *Lemon v. Kurtzman*, 403 U.S. 602 (1971).[16]

Justice Powell wrote a separate concurring opinion in response to the repeated criticisms of *Lemon* that "could encourage other courts to feel free to decide Establishment Clause cases on an *ad hoc* basis." Powell noted that his concurrence was prompted by "Alabama's persistence in enacting three successive statutes." Of importance to Powell was that "the record before us, however, makes clear that Alabama's purpose was solely religious in character." Justice Powell said that he would "vote to uphold the Alabama statute if it also had a clear secular purpose."

Justice O'Connor held the Alabama law unconstitutional but did not join the majority opinion. Although not ready to "abandon all aspects of the *Lemon* test," she concluded that the Court should "frame a principle for constitutional adjudication that is not only grounded in the history and language of the First Amendment, but one that is also capable of consistent application to the relevant problems." She concluded that the "Court holds *only* that Alabama has intentionally crossed the line between creating a quiet moment during which those so inclined may pray, and affirmatively endorsing the particular religious practice of prayer." Justice O'Connor then elaborated:

> By mandating a moment of silence, a State does not necessarily endorse any activity that might occur during the period. Even if a statute specifies that a student may choose to pray silently during a quiet moment, the State has not thereby encouraged prayer over other specified alternatives. . . . The crucial question is whether the State has conveyed or attempted to convey the message children should use the moment of silence for prayer.

In the long run the significance of *Wallace* may well lie in Justice William Rehnquist's dissent. After a lengthy historical survey challenging the Court's reliance on Jefferson's metaphor, he concluded:

> The Establishment Clause did not require government neutrality between religion and irreligion nor did it prohibit the federal government from providing nondiscriminatory aid to religion. There is simply no historical foundation for the propositions that the Framers intended to build the "wall of separation" that was constitutionalized in *Everson*. The "wall of separation between Church and State" is a metaphor based on bad history . . . which has proved useless as a guide. . . . It should be frankly and explicitly abandoned.

Rehnquist argued that the Court's "secular purpose" standard "has no more grounding in the history of the First Amendment than does the wall theory on which it rests." As he explained:

> The Framers intended the Establishment Clause to prohibit the designation of any church as a "national" one. The Clause was also designed to stop the Federal Government from asserting a preference for one religious denomination or sect over others. Given the "incorporation" of the Establishment Clause as against the States via the Fourteenth Amendment in *Everson*, States are prohibited as well from establishing a religion or discriminating between sects.

Justice Rehnquist also called into question the foundation of the Court's interpretation of the First Amendment since the *Everson* case nearly forty years earlier. His dissent marked the first attempt of the Court to challenge the historical support for establishment clause jurisprudence derived from Jefferson's metaphor.

PUBLIC OPINION

In the past twenty-five years, the federal courts have consistently struck down efforts to reintroduce prayer in the public schools, and just as persistently the U.S. population has expressed its support for school prayer. Public opinion polls from 1963 to 1986 indicated that an overwhelming percentage of the population favored some form of voluntary nondenominational prayer, Bible reading, or other pious activity in public schools. The Gallup Poll of June 1963 asked this question: "The United States Supreme Court has ruled that no state or local government may require the reading of the Lord's Prayer or Bible verses in public schools. What are your views on this?" Only 27 percent approved of the decision, whereas 70 percent disapproved.[17] This identical question was asked regularly by the University of Chicago National Opinion Research Center (NORC) since 1974 (see Table 1.3). NORC Surveys showed continued popular support for school prayer.[18]

There is no ready explanation why disapproval of the Supreme Court ruling fell during the early 1980s, just as Ronald Reagan's campaign for school prayer began. Nonetheless, a huge majority consistently has favored prayer in public schools, a fact underscored by other Gallup Polls taken in recent years. Nationwide samples expressed considerable support for a constitutional amendment permitting school prayer when such questions were asked in 1974 (77 percent), 1980 (76 percent), 1982 (73 percent), and 1984 (69 percent).[19]

TABLE 1.3 NORC Surveys on School Prayer Ban, 1974-1986

	1974	1975	1977	1982	1983	1985	1986
Approve	30.7%	35.3%	33.4%	37.4%	39.5%	43.0%	37.0%
Disapprove	65.9%	61.6%	64.1%	60.0%	56.5%	53.7%	60.5%

Source: Based on data from James Allan Davis, General Social Surveys, 1972-1982 (Chicago: National Opinion Research Center, 1982), p. 100; James Allan Davis and Tom W. Smith, General Social Surveys, 1972-1986 (Chicago: National Opinion Research Center, 1986), p. 149.

A cursory look at the Gallup Polls or NORC Surveys on school prayer suggests that the majority viewpoint is shared by virtually every population subgroup regardless of economic, racial, or demographic makeup. But school prayer has more significance for certain voters. One study by William Adams probed the dynamics of public opinion using University of Michigan Survey Research Center (SRC) data of the 1964 and 1968 elections.[20] These election surveys found that nearly three-fourths approved school prayer in 1964 (74.9 percent) and in 1968 (73.4 percent), with only 13 to 15 percent in opposition. In addition to the one-sided quality of mass opinion, tremendous stability in attitudes had obtained during this period.

Agreement existed among Republicans and Democrats, and there was little difference with respect to voters who preferred Lyndon Johnson or Barry Goldwater in 1964 or any of the three presidential candidates in 1968—Richard Nixon, Hubert Humphrey, or George Wallace. In fact, although one question in the Adams study asked which political party "is more likely to allow the schools to start each day with a prayer," 72 percent of the respondents saw no difference between the Republicans and Democrats despite the GOP's endorsement of school prayer in its 1964 platform. Most important was a regional and religious underpinning to public opinion. Support was highest in the South and Northeast and among Baptists, whereas Jews expressed majority opposition. To examine the religious dimension Adams utilized an SRC question asking respondents to assess the Bible. Those people who believed that "the Bible is God's Word and all it says is true" favored school prayer by an 80 percent margin, compared to less than 50 percent of those who viewed the Bible as uninspired and worthless.

The major conclusion drawn by this research was that the differences between public opinion and the positions taken by religious and political leaders "raise once more the paradox of elite liberalism and mass conservatism."[21] This gap between what leaders articulate and what followers believe may explain why the Supreme Court ruling has not been overturned. But majority opinion on school prayer also may lack the intensity needed to inspire political activism. This condition is implied by an SRC open-ended question that allowed respondents to list the six "serious problems" deserving the attention of the national government. Adams noted that only 6 percent cited school prayer as one of their urgent concerns.

A more recent study by Kirk Elifson and C. Kirk Hadaway drew upon NORC data for 1974 and 1982 and the University of Michigan 1980 election survey.[22] Those persons favoring school prayer tended to be older, less educated, and socially, politically, and religiously conservative. These researchers suggested another reason why grass-roots sentiment for school prayer has not yet been translated into public policy: "It may well be that these social characteristics make this majority too silent to be heard by Congress, which itself is comprised of a highly elite group of individuals which our profile would classify as opponents to the issue."[23] Given that often more than two-thirds of survey respondents favor school prayers, the failure of Congress to obtain the two-thirds votes to enact the necessary constitutional amendment implies that the U.S. political leadership is, in fact, more opposed to school prayer than is the mass public.

CONGRESS

Within days of the Court's ruling in *Engel*, 58 proposed amendments to override the school prayer ban were introduced by twenty-five senators and fifty-three representatives (see Table 1.4). The intense congressional reaction swelled to the point where 151 measures were introduced to the House of Representatives during the 88th Congress, which convened in 1963. As Table 1.4 shows, that was the high point of such legislative activity during the past twenty-four years. Compared to the 1960s, legislative activity subsided during the 1970s, although in recent years the advocates of school prayer have had more success in getting their bills voted on by the entire Senate. When Congress was dominated by strong committee chairmen, such as during the Kennedy and Johnson eras, the liberal Democrats who controlled the Judiciary Committees, which had jurisdiction over constitutional amendments, were able to prevent such bills from getting to the floor.

In addition to constitutional amendments to overturn the Supreme Court prayer rulings, other legislation intended to strip federal courts of jurisdiction over these questions or to prevent the enforcement of those judicial decrees by federal agencies such as the Department of Justice has been introduced. The House has been more active than the Senate in terms of measures introduced, in part because senators could co-sponsor bills whereas representatives could not. During the period 1962–1986, there were 66 bills sponsored in the Senate, but in the House there were ten times that number (660). The other significant political finding of Table 1.4 is that school prayer quickly became a partisan issue dividing Republicans from Democrats. In the Senate, Republicans were 48–92 percent of the sponsors

TABLE 1.4 Legislation on School Prayer, Introduced in Congress 1962-1986

	Senate					House of Representatives				
Congress	Number of Sponsors	Republicans	Northern Democrats	Southern Democrats	Number of Proposals	Number of Sponsors	Republicans	Northern Democrats	Southern Democrats	Number of Proposals
87th (1961-1962)	25	48%(12)	16%(4)	36%(9)	5[a]	53	49%(26)	17%(9)	34%(18)	53[a]
88th (1963-1964)	14	64%(9)	7%(1)	29%(4)	9	115	55%(63)	17%(20)	28%(32)	151
89th (1965-1966)	43	62%(27)	19%(8)	19%(8)	3	55	55%(30)	16%(9)	29%(16)	55
90th (1967-1968)	44	61%(27)	12%(5)	27%(12)	2	49	51%(25)	12%(6)	37%(18)	49
91st (1969-1970)	43	68%(29)	16%(7)	16%(7)	5	100	60%(60)	13%(13)	27%(27)	92
92nd (1971-1972)	38[b]	66%(25)	13%(5)	18%(7)	3	169	63%(107)	14%(23)	23%(39)	75
93rd (1973-1974)	19	74%(14)	10%(2)	16%(3)	9	111	61%(68)	15%(17)	24%(26)	37
94th (1975-1976)	12	75%(9)		25%(3)	6	37	62%(23)	22%(8)	16%(6)	36
95th (1977-1978)	10	80%(8)		20%(2)	4	50	74%(37)	14%(7)	12%(6)	25
96th (1979-1980)	6	66%(4)	17%(1)	17%(1)	6	98	64%(63)	15%(15)	21%(20)	29
97th (1981-1982)	9	78%(7)	11%(1)	11%(1)	5	29	62%(18)	7%(2)	31%(9)	26
98th (1983-1984)	15	87%(13)		13%(2)	6	70	71%(50)	13%(9)	16%(11)	19
99th (1985-1986)	13	92%(12)	8%(1)	13%(2)	3	47	74%(35)	11%(5)	15%(7)	13

[a]Proposals include constitutional amendments, bills, amendments to bills, and House and Senate resolutions (simple, joint, and concurrent).
[b]Included among the sponsors was one Independent (Harry Byrd of Virginia) who is not counted in the percentage distributions. Thus, they do not add up to 100 percent.

Sources: Data for this table were derived from Congressional Quarterly Almanacs, Congressional Records, and Commercial Clearing House Congressional Indexes for each Congress.

of pro–school prayer legislation in these thirteen Congresses; in the House, Republicans represented 49–74 percent of the total number. In most cases, southern Democrats sponsored more legislation aimed at promoting school prayer than did northern Democrats, but even southerners were no match for the legislative record established by the GOP on this matter. School prayer is more a partisan issue than a regional issue in the Congress, although among the electorate the reverse probably is true.

When legislation to assist school prayer has reached the full House or Senate, it usually receives a majority vote, but no proposed constitutional amendment ever has obtained the required two-thirds vote in either chamber. On those few occasions when a key vote was taken on a school prayer amendment to the Constitution, the voting mobilized the "conservative coalition" of Republicans and southern Democrats against the northern Democrats, as follows.

- *89th Congress, 1966; S.J.Res. 148,* sponsored by Sen. Everett M. Dirksen (R-Ill.):

  Nothing contained in this Constitution shall prohibit the authority administering any school, school system, educational institution or other public building supported in whole or in part through the expenditure of public funds from providing for or permitting the voluntary participation by students or others in prayer. Nothing contained in this Article shall authorize any such authority to prescribe the form or content of any prayer.

  S.J.Res. 148 did not receive the required two-thirds vote. The vote was 49–37: Reps. 27–3; Dems. 22–34 (N. Dems. 7–29 and S. Dems. 15–5).

- *92nd Congress, 1971; H.J.Res. 191,* sponsored by Rep. Chalmers P. Wylie (R-Ohio):

  Nothing contained in this Constitution shall abridge the right of persons lawfully assembled, in any public building which is supported in whole or in part through the expenditure of public funds, to participate in voluntary prayer or meditation.

  H.J.Res. 191 did not receive the required two-thirds vote. The vote was 240–163: Reps. 138–26; Dems. 102–137 (N. Dems. 48–114 and S. Dems. 54–23).

- *98th Congress, 1984; S.J.Res. 73,* sponsored by Senators Strom Thurmond (R-S.C.), Orrin G. Hatch (R-Utah), Lawton Chiles (D-Fla.), James Abdnor (R-S.D.), Don Nickles (R-Okla.), and Jesse A. Helms (R-N.C.):

  Nothing in this Constitution shall be construed to prohibit individual or group prayer in public schools or other public institutions. No person shall be required by the United States or any state to participate in prayer. Neither the United States nor any state shall compose the words of any prayer to be said in public schools.

S.J.Res. 73 did not receive the required two-thirds vote. The vote was 56–44: Reps. 37–18; Dems. 19–26 (N. Dems. 6–25 and S. Dems 13–1).

As indicated, the reaction to the 1962 *Engel* decision was immediate and quite vociferous. One congressman tried to amend a judiciary appropriations bill to earmark funds to purchase "for the personal use of each [Supreme Court] justice a copy of the Holy Bible," and on September 27 the House voted unanimously to place the motto "In God We Trust" behind the Speaker's desk.[24] In the House, the opposition was led by Congressman Frank J. Becker (R-N.Y.), who proposed a constitutional amendment the day after the decision was rendered that declared, "Prayers may be offered in the course of any program in any public school or other public place in the United States."[25] In the Senate, one month after *Engel*, the Judiciary Committee chaired by Senator James Eastland (D-Miss.) began hearings, although no legislation was enacted by the 87th Congress.

During the 88th Congress, a campaign was led by Congressman Becker, who co-sponsored H.J. Res. 693 the day after the *Schempp* ruling was announced in 1963. The famous Becker amendment stated in part: "Sec. 1. Nothing in this Constitution shall be deemed to prohibit the offering, reading from, or listening to prayers or Biblical scriptures, if participation therein is on a voluntary basis, in any governmental or public school, institution or place."[26]

The House Judiciary Committee was chaired by Emmanuel Celler (D-N.Y.), who was unalterably opposed to any attack on the Court's decisions. Celler planned to ignore the Becker amendment until its supporters began a "discharge" petition to bypass the committee and bring this measure directly to the floor. Celler had little choice but to hold hearings. But the committee hearings, which extended from April 22 to June 3, 1964, and whose testimony filled two thousand eight hundred pages, were designed to dissipate much of the call to overturn the school prayer cases. Although 167 representatives eventually signed Becker's discharge petition, that was short of the 218 needed, and he was unable to bring his measure to the House floor for a vote.

The first vote by either chamber on school prayer came in 1966 when Senator Everett Dirksen (R-Ill.), the minority party leader, sponsored S.J. Res. 148 to amend the Constitution in order to allow school prayer. The amendment eventually had forty-eight co-sponsors. Hearings were scheduled by the Subcommittee on Constitutional Amendments, chaired by liberal Senator Birch Bayh (D-Ind.). Dirksen tried unsuccessfully to persuade the entire Judiciary Committee to report that legislation to the floor without new hearings. But when the hearings were completed, no action was taken by Bayh's subcommittee.

Dirksen then made the motion on the Senate floor to substitute his amendment for a minor bill honoring UNICEF. In reaction, Senator Bayh moved to substitute for Dirksen's amendment a "sense of Congress" resolution that local authorities should be permitted to allow "silent, voluntary prayer or meditation" in public schools and that also provided that a "National Prayer and Meditation Week" be designated each year at Thanksgiving. The Senate rejected Bayh's measure 33–52 and accepted the Dirksen substitute 51–36. On final passage the constitutional amendment fell nine votes short of the required two-thirds. In the Senate debate, Democrats opposing the Dirksen amendment said that the Court would clarify its own rulings and, furthermore, to quote Senator Bayh, that it would be "absolutely ridiculous and a violation of our responsibility as U.S. Senators to amend the Constitution to permit something which the Court has not prohibited."[27]

In 1971, Representative Wylie offered H.J. Res. 191, which was identical to the 1967 amendment by Senator Dirksen. When the House Judiciary Committee refused to report that measure, Wylie and his supporters were able to initiate a discharge petition, which the House passed on a 242–156 vote. After considerable debate, the House accepted a motion replacing "nondenominational prayer" with "voluntary prayer or meditation." This version of the Wylie amendment then passed the House 240–162 but fell short of the required two-thirds.[28]

During the 1970s, there were periodic efforts, mainly by conservative Senator Jesse Helms (R-N.C.), to strip the federal courts and specifically the Supreme Court of jurisdiction over school prayer cases. On April 5, 1979, Helms offered an amendment to legislation designed to create a Department of Education (S. 210).[29] During six hours of stormy debate and wild parliamentary maneuver, the Senate rejected a motion by Senator Abraham Ribicoff (D-Conn.) to table the Helms amendment and then voted 47–37 to accept that motion. The climax was reached four days later when the Senate voted 53–40 to delete that rider from the Department of Education legislation and join it to a minor bill (S. 450) dealing with Supreme Court jurisdiction. President Jimmy Carter made known his opposition to the Helms legislation on school prayer and wanted it detached from his plan to establish a Department of Education. In its amended form, S. 450 was approved 61–30 by the Senate, but languished in the House Judiciary Committee through 1980. School prayer advocates were unable to get the necessary 218 signatures on a discharge petition.

A ploy by Representative Robert S. Walker (R-Pa.) stalled legislative action on a fiscal year 1982 appropriations bill for the Departments of State, Justice, and Commerce, which passed the House in 1981 but not the Senate. The Walker amendment, which the House adopted on a 333–54 vote, barred the Justice Department from using those funds to obstruct programs of voluntary prayer and meditation in public schools. In the Senate, this issue erupted on November 16, 1981, when the floor considered an Appropriations Committee report deleting that amendment. Action turned on a motion by Senator Ernest F. Hollings (D-S.C.) to table the committee language on school prayer. After agreeing to Hollings's motion, the Senate proceeded to vote 93–0 on an amendment by Senator Lowell Weicker (R-Conn.) that nothing herein should be interpreted as "the establishment of religion or prohibiting the free exercise thereof." Senator Jesse Helms then countered with a clarifying amendment that Weicker's proposal would not limit this restriction on Justice Department involvement in school prayer cases. The Helms amendment also was adopted by the Senate on a 58–38 vote.[30]

During 1982, there was considerable debate about school prayer stemming from actions by Senator Helms.[31] On August 18, he offered an amendment to legislation increasing the public debt (H.J. Res. 520) aimed at limiting the appellate jurisdiction of federal courts regarding "voluntary" school prayer cases. Quickly Senators Weicker, a liberal, and Max Baucus (D-Mont.) both offered weakening amendments to the Helms rider. During the course of debate and the parliamentary maneuvers throughout the next month, the Senate seven times rejected attempts to impose cloture to end the liberal filibuster. In the end, a motion to table Helms's motion was accepted 51–48, whereupon the debt ceiling bill was recommitted to committee with instructions that it be reported out free of any amendments.

There were two significant developments in the 98th Congress.[32] One was the passage of the Equal Access Act (P.L. 98-377), which began in the Senate when the Judiciary Committee approved S. 1059, sponsored by Senators Jeremiah Denton (R-Ala.) and Mark Hatfield (R-Ore.). This legislation was added to a House education bill (H.R. 1310) that was accepted by a Senate vote of 88 to 11. When H.R. 1310 was returned to the House, Speaker Thomas P. O'Neill referred the bill to both the Judiciary Committee and the Committee on Education and Labor. Carl D. Perkins (D-Ky.), who chaired the latter committee, allowed the House to vote up or down on the equal access amendment, which was approved by a lopsided 337–77 vote. President Reagan signed this bill into law on August 11, 1984. The Equal Access Act prohibits any public secondary school receiving federal aid from denying equal access to students wishing to conduct a meeting for philosophical, religious, political, or other reasons during nonclass hours.

The second major development was a vote taken on a school prayer amendment backed by President Reagan. In 1983, the Senate Judiciary Committee voted 14–3 to report two proposed amendments but without any recommendation. S.J. Res. 73 was essentially the amendment supported by President Reagan, and S.J. Res. 212 assured "individual or group silent prayer or meditation in public schools" as well as "equal access to the use of public schools facilities" by voluntary student groups. Conservative groups, such as Moral Majority and Christian Voice, lobbied hard for Reagan's amendment and generally viewed S.J. Res. 212, sponsored by Orrin G. Hatch (R-Utah), as being overly narrow. The opposition again was led by Senator Weicker. After much debate and parliamentary maneuver, on March 20, 1984, the Senate voted 56–44, which was 11 votes short of the needed two-thirds.

On January 3, 1985, Senator Hatch introduced S.J. Res. 2 to the 99th Congress; this was an amendment to allow "individual or group silent prayer or reflection in public schools." It was referred to the Judiciary Committee, which in October 1985 voted 12–6 to approve the measure. However, S.J.

Res. 2 never was brought to the Senate floor because Hatch sensed that the necessary votes were not there. Fundamentalists again were opposed to his approach because they favored an amendment permitting organized, recited prayer in the public schools.

On another front, Senator Helms again tried to strip the federal courts of jurisdiction over school prayer cases. The Senate rejected his bill (S. 47) on a 62–36 vote with almost no discussion. The Senate had voted on similar legislation ten times in the past seven years, and this September 10, 1985, vote marked the lowest support given that proposal to date.[33]

As is apparent from this review, Congress has been unable to overturn the Supreme Court rulings on school prayer. Although there seems to be a majority favoring substantive policy to aid school prayer, the support falls short of the two-thirds needed to approve a constitutional amendment. The failure of school prayer advocates to bring about a reversal of public policy would suggest that majority opinion is not intensely committed to that goal.[34] The opposition to school prayer in Congress also has benefited by the lack of presidential leadership on this issue.

PRESIDENCY

Shortly after *Engel*, President John F. Kennedy, a Catholic, in response to a question at a news conference, remarked:

> The Supreme Court has made its judgment. Some will disagree and others will agree. In the efforts we're making to maintain our Constitutional principles, we will have to abide by what the Supreme Court says. We have a very easy remedy here, and that is to pray ourselves. We can pray a good deal more at home and attend our churches with fidelity and emphasize the true meaning of prayer in the lives of our children. I hope, as a result of that decision, all Americans will give prayer a greater emphasis.[35]

At about the same time, former president Herbert Hoover, a Republican, offered a different view: "This interpretation of the Constitution is a disintegration of one of the most sacred of American heritages. The Congress should at once submit an amendment to the Constitution which establishes the right to religious devotion in all government agencies, national, state, or local."[36] These divergent opinions summarize and anticipate the essential nature of the presidential debate on school prayer that would take place during the next quarter century. The presidential candidates or presidents of the Democratic party have ignored the issue or supported the Court's decision, while those of the Republican party have given symbolic support for a constitutional amendment to return prayer to the public schools.

In 1964, the Republican party nominated Senator Barry Goldwater, a well-known conservative, and adopted a platform plank supporting a constitutional amendment that permitted "those individuals and groups who choose to do so, to exercise their religion freely in public places, provided religious exercises are not prepared or prescribed by the state or political subdivision thereof and no person's participation therein is coerced, thus preserving the traditional separation of church and state."[37]

The Democratic party nominated Lyndon B. Johnson by acclamation and adopted a platform that made no mention of school prayer. Goldwater criticized that fact during the campaign and asked "how strongly can you create morality in the minds and hearts of young people when the Supreme Court has said you cannot pray in the schools."[38]

Although President Johnson participated fully in traditional ceremonies, such as the Prayer Breakfast held annually in Washington, D.C., and he issued proclamations for a yearly day of prayer for peace, he did not feel it necessary to address the school prayer question. In 1966, when the Senate was considering Dirksen's constitutional amendment, President Johnson took no position on that legislation. By 1968, the Vietnam War held the national political stage, and neither political party mentioned school prayer in its platform. Richard Nixon won the 1968 election but had nothing to say about school prayer during his first term. The 1972 election was portrayed by both parties as giving the electorate a real choice, and that extended to the school prayer issue as well. The GOP platform "reaffirm[ed] our view that voluntary prayer should be freely permitted in public places—particularly, by school children while attending public schools,"[39] while the Democratic party made no mention of school prayer.

With the 1976 election, President Gerald R. Ford faced Democratic nominee Jimmy Carter, a "born again" Christian and southern Baptist. Carter left no doubt about his religious convictions as this election campaign centered around the ethical issues raised by the Watergate scandals. Once again, the Republican party included a platform plank that "local communities wishing to conduct non-sectarian prayers in their public schools should be able to do so. We favor a Constitutional amendment to achieve this end."[40] It is doubtful that President Ford insisted on that wording given that, in 1975, he had to be reminded by petition to proclaim a national day of prayer, having neglected to do so the previous year.

With President Carter's election, one might have expected to find a sympathetic outlook toward school prayer, but such was not to be the case. When the Senate in 1979 considered S. 450 to deny the Supreme Court jurisdiction over school prayer cases, President Carter expressed his opposition to that bill in a news conference on April 10: "I personally don't think that the Congress ought to pass any legislation requiring or permitting prayer being required or encouraged in school."[41] However, during the 1980 presidential campaign Jimmy Carter was obliged to reconsider his previous position on this question. When asked a question at a town meeting, Carter elaborated:

> The thing that I'm against . . . is the Government telling people they have to worship at a certain time and in a certain way. To me that violates the constitutional separation of church and state. But as long as the Government stays out of it and permits people to worship as we see fit, including in the schools, that's what I want. But I am not in favor of the Government telling

a child "You've got to worship a certain God in a certain way in the classroom."
That's where I draw the line.[42]

It took the candidacy of Ronald Reagan to bring school prayer back
to the political agenda. As part of his strategy to form a new GOP coalition
and to woo southern, working class, and Catholic voters, Reagan promised
to actively support an amendment to the Constitution that would return
prayer to the public schools. At a 1981 press conference for out-of-town
editors, Reagan responded to questions about the Supreme Court's jurisdiction
over sensitive questions such as school prayer, and he cast doubt on the
legitimacy of judge-made law by saying:

> How many people really stop to think that that's no law, that is nothing but
> a case law? That was a decision handed down by a judge, and other judges
> felt bound by the precedent, and so it has become a matter of case law. But
> no legislature and no Congress ever passed that law. For example, I happen
> to believe that the court ruled wrongly with regard to prayer in schools. The
> First Amendment doesn't say anything about that. The First Amendment says
> the Congress shall do nothing to abridge the practice of religion or to create
> a religion.[43]

President Reagan returned to this theme when speaking at the observance of the National Day of Prayer in 1982. After quoting from Abraham
Lincoln, Thomas Jefferson, and Alexis de Tocqueville on the relationship
between prayer and freedom, Reagan announced that he would be submitting
to Congress a proposed amendment "to allow our children to pray in
school." On May 17, 1982, in fulfillment of his campaign pledge, President
Reagan sent Congress what later became known as S.J. Res. 73. It was
accompanied by a message in which President Reagan spelled out many
traditional arguments favoring school prayer. Citing Benjamin Franklin's
request for prayer at the Constitutional Convention, for example, Reagan
expressed his belief that "the founders of our Nation and the Framers of
the First Amendment did not intend to forbid public prayer."[44]

As time passed without any significant movement in Congress, President
Reagan returned again and again to the theme that the Court's decisions
were at odds with the national experience. At Kansas State University he
said,

> One Court has recently ruled that . . . children cannot say grace on their own
> in the school cafeteria before they eat. Now this was done as being in accord
> with the Constitution. But was the First Amendment written to protect American
> people from religion, or was it written to protect religion from government
> tyranny? No one will ever convince me that a moment of voluntary prayer
> can harm a child or threaten a school or a state.[45]

Presidents Kennedy, Johnson, Nixon, Ford, and Carter either shied
away from or ignored altogether the school prayer controversy. Only Ronald
Reagan made school prayer a campaign pledge and supplied presidential

leadership behind a constitutional amendment. In his 1987 State of the Union Address, the president once again called for a restoration of prayer by declaring, "Finally let's stop suppressing the spiritual core of our national being. Our nation could not have been conceived without divine help. Why is it that we can build a nation with our prayers but we can't use a school room for voluntary prayer? The 100th Congress of the United States should be remembered as the one that ended the expulsion of God from America's classrooms."[46] Such action by this Congress was unlikely because the Democrats had regained their Senate majority in the 1986 elections and now held both houses of Congress. But that fact did not deter President Reagan in his challenge to the Congress, just as his administration has not flinched from battle with the Supreme Court over its school prayer decisions.

BUREAUCRACY

The issue of school prayer has not received much attention from the federal bureaucracy because the battle over school prayer has been fought primarily in the courts, in Congress, and in the states. There is also the reality, noted by Chief Justice Warren Burger in *Wallace*, that "no power on earth including this Court and Congress can stop any teacher from opening the school day with a moment of silence for pupils to meditate, to plan their day, or to pray if they voluntarily elect to do so." Because Reagan has advocated school prayer more than has any other president, his support has mobilized federal agencies, particularly the Office of the Solicitor General.

In four recent establishment clause cases, Solicitor General Rex Lee submitted *amicus* briefs supporting religious activity.[47] In *Wallace v. Jaffree*, a short brief supported the Alabama "moment of silence" law. The solicitor general drew upon the accommodation theme put forth by Justice William O. Douglas in *Zorach v. Clauson*, 343 U.S. 306 (1952) (where Justice Douglas noted in dictum "we are a religious people whose institutions presuppose a Supreme Being"). The solicitor general also cited Justice William Brennan's oft-quoted dictum in *Schempp* that "the observance of a moment of reverent silence at the beginning of class" may serve "the solely secular purposes of the devotional activities without jeopardizing either the religious liberties of any members of the community or the proper degree of separation between the spheres of religion and government." Rex Lee supported the moment of silence as a means of bridging the gap between the establishment clause and the free exercise clause of the First Amendment. But his lukewarm defense of the Alabama statute may have been due to his awareness of a more radical critique prepared by the Department of Justice and his desire to place some distance between himself and that statement. Lee's reluctance to push the Reagan administration school prayer policy disturbed conservatives, who favored the appointment of a stronger advocate in that position.[48] When Lee resigned, Reagan appointed Charles Fried as solicitor general, and Fried has taken a more combative approach toward the Court.

In support of S.J. Res. 73, the Justice Department's Office of Legal Policy prepared a lengthy legal analysis, and Deputy Attorney General

Edward C. Schmults drew upon that analysis in his testimony before the Senate Committee on the Judiciary. Both said that the purpose of S.J. Res. 73 was to "restore the status quo with respect to the law governing prayer in public schools that existed before *Engel v. Vitale* and *Abington School District v. Schempp* were decided; i.e., when prayers such as the Regents Prayer and readings from the Bible without comment were not thought to be unconstitutional."[49] Although S.J. Res. 73 expressly protected the right of students not to participate in prayer, it also foreclosed the "implied coercion theory" advanced in both *Engel* and *Schempp*. That is the view that any group prayer by consenting students has a coercive effect upon those students who do not wish to pray and is therefore a violation of their right to the free exercise of religion.

The Justice Department also claimed that the proposed amendment was intended to delegate any decisionmaking to "state or local school authorities and to the individuals themselves." Furthermore, while not requiring school authorities to lead prayer, "the amendment would allow them to do so if desired." But the type of prayer chosen by public schools was *not* understood to be limited to "nondenominational prayer." Choosing an "appropriate prayer" would be left to state and local authorities.

Secretary of Education T. H. Bell devoted much of his testimony supporting the Reagan amendment to the implied coercion theory. Citing public opinion polls showing overwhelming public support for voluntary prayer in schools and for a constitutional amendment, Secretary Bell argued that instead of fearing coercion, "parents would welcome the influence upon their children of other students seeking to develop their character through involvement in religious activities in the public school setting."[50]

The strong implication from this testimony by Reagan administration officials was that S.J. Res. 73 would permit willing teachers and school officials to lead willing students in governmentally composed prayers that easily could have sectarian or denominational content. The Justice Department's legal analysis drew upon the work of constitutional scholars who have been critical of the Supreme Court's establishment clause rulings, and, in general, those scholars relied on the historical record to determine the Framers' original intent. But none had argued, as did the Reagan administration, that the Framers would have supported the use of sectarian prayers composed by public officials to lead students in prayer.

The numerous opinion polls have not cast the question of school prayer in this manner, and public support for sectarian prayers led by school officials may well be problematic. Most critics of the Supreme Court rulings have assumed that any voluntary prayer would be nondenominational and innocuous. The likely possibility of differing religious sects lobbying state and local officials to have their version of school prayer chosen was a concern voiced in the Senate. Just as daunting is the possibility in any community that the majority denomination might have its prayer accepted as the official school policy. These serious concerns explain why there was insufficient support to pass the Reagan amendment.

FEDERALISM

State governments are key actors in the ongoing drama concerning school prayer. The vast majority endorsed school prayer in the years before 1962, and since then state and local officials have tried to circumvent the Supreme Court ban by various methods including the enactment of "moment of silence" statutes.

A count by Donald Boles found that thirty-seven states in 1963 required, permitted, or condoned Bible reading in their school systems.[51] Mississippi upheld Bible reading through a constitutional provision, and eleven states and the District of Columbia had laws requiring Bible reading. They were Alabama, Arkansas, Delaware, Florida, Georgia, Idaho, Kentucky, Maine, Massachusetts, New Jersey, and Tennessee. (Prior to a 1959 District Court ruling that nullified its statute, Pennsylvania also required Bible reading. Later this case was heard by the Supreme Court in its famous *Schempp* decision.) The nature of these laws is illustrated by the wording of the Kentucky statute: "The teacher in charge shall read or cause to be read a portion of the Bible daily in every classroom or session room of the common schools of the state in the presence of the pupils therein assembled, but no child shall be required to read the Bible against the wish of his parents or guardians."[52]

Legislation in Indiana, Iowa, Kansas, North Dakota, Oklahoma, and (as revised) in Pennsylvania permitted Bible reading in school, and nineteen more states condoned the practice without legal authorization.[53] At this time, *no* state constitution forbade Bible reading, although it was deemed a sectarian practice and thus illegal in eleven states. In 1963, according to Dale Doak, thirteen states authorized recitation of the Lord's Prayer in public school, while five prohibited the practice.[54] All thirteen were among the group of thirty-seven that allowed Bible reading, and, with two exceptions, they also are southern or northeastern states.

At Hershey, Pennsylvania, on July 3, 1962, the Governors' Conference unanimously passed (with only New York Governor Nelson Rockefeller abstaining) a resolution that urged "the Congress . . . to propose an amendment to the Constitution of the United States that will make clear and beyond challenge the acknowledgment by our nation and people of their faith in God and permit the free and voluntary participation in prayer in our public schools.[55]

Statements of defiance came from public officials in deep South states where the Bible Belt dominated the political culture. Governor George Wallace of Alabama declared, "I would like for the people of Alabama to be in defiance of such a ruling. . . . I want the Supreme Court to know we are not going to conform to any such decision. I want the State Board of Education to tell the whole world we are not going to abide by it."[56] Governor Ross Barnett announced that he was "going to tell every teacher in Mississippi to conduct prayers and Bible reading despite what the Supreme Court says."[57] In other states, more subtle methods were used, as William Beaney and Edward Beiser explained:

[These methods included] attempting to distinguish the case [as not applying to a state law]; limiting the scope of the case by interpretation (usually by misinterpretation); reading a patriotic song such as "America" or the fourth stanza of the Star Spangled Banner ("In God is our trust"); using hymns, prayers, etc., as part of "music appreciation"; using the Bible as "literature" with no intention of conducting literary study, or . . . making Bible reading part of a "course of study."[58]

What immediate effect did these rhetorical blasts at the Supreme Court have on the state school systems? In Connecticut, less than 20 percent of its 169 towns had implemented the school prayer ban by September 1963, and an April 1964 study in Indiana found that 33 percent of the schools surveyed had Bible reading, nearly 50 percent permitted recitation of the Lord's Prayer, and 60 percent allowed a pupil or teacher to lead the students in prayer, usually at the noon meal.[59] Surveys taken in Texas and Kentucky also found little inclination among these states' populations to abide by the law, whereas a high level of compliance occurred in Minnesota and Ohio schools.[60]

A nationwide study in 1960 by R. G. Dierenfield determined that 42 percent of the responding school districts reported Bible reading.[61] Its incidence was much higher in the South (76 percent) and East (67 percent) but much lower in the Midwest (18 percent) and West (11 percent). In 1966, Dierenfield replicated his analysis but found that only 13 percent of the schools reported Bible reading, although, again, the practice was more common in the South.[62] In 1964–1965, H. Frank Way questioned 2,320 public elementary school teachers from 464 schools across the nation and also discerned a change in routine toward compliance.[63] Before *Schempp*, 60 percent had morning prayers at daily, weekly, or less frequent intervals, but only 28 percent did so afterward. Bible reading also declined; before *Schempp*, 48 percent of the teachers surveyed engaged in that practice, but only 22 percent did so thereafter. Only in the South did the majority of teachers continue Bible reading, prayers, and grace after *Schempp*, and this was attributed to traditional attitudes and school policy.

In 1965, Ellis Katz also compared Bible reading before and after the *Schempp* ruling.[64] Of twenty-nine states reporting Bible reading before *Schempp*, five ended the practice, fourteen more said it almost was stopped, but another six said that Bible reading continued as before. Given the extensive violations he uncovered, Katz concluded that "this study . . . should serve to dispel the notion that society automatically responds to the will of the Supreme Court."[65]

The defiance by southern school districts was illustrated by research on particular states. Tennessee was the focus of research by Robert H. Birkby, who polled school superintendents and members of school boards.[66] Of the 121 who answered his questionnaire, 70 still followed state law, 50 made minor concessions to the Supreme Court ruling, but only 1 school district had completely eliminated devotional practices. By 1971, there was not much compliance in Georgia either, according to Roald Mykkeltvedt.[67]

In response to the Supreme Court, the state legislature enacted a law, which Governor Lester Maddox signed, that permitted "a brief period of silent prayer or meditation with the participation of all the pupils therein assembled." To determine whether schools complied with this law or the Supreme Court, questionnaires were sent to superintendents, principals, and college students who had attended public school in the state. The results were conclusive: "There is massive noncompliance with the *Murray* and *Schempp* decisions in Georgia's public school systems. . . . It exists at every level of the public schools of this state, in every type of community, and in schools of all sizes."[68]

One decade after *Schempp*, Michael La Morte and Fred Dorminy examined compliance from a legal perspective.[69] They asked whether the states had formally accommodated their legal codes to the high court rulings. In 1974, only eight states required or authorized Bible reading or recitation of the Lord's Prayer. Five (western) states had statutory or constitutional provisions outlawing religious observances in public schools; courts had ruled laws null and void in three more states; and state attorneys general issued opinions against existing legislation in seven states. However, by this time, nine states already had enacted laws providing for a "brief period" or "one moment" of silent prayer, reflection, or meditation, and three more states had laws permitting released or dismissed time for students to participate off campus in such exercises.

Because "moment of silence" laws had not been challenged on constitutional grounds, states were turning to that approach as a possible avenue for allowing prayer within the confines of the Court's decisions. By the time *Wallace v. Jaffree* reached the Supreme Court in 1985, twenty-five states had enacted such laws. Eight of these states are located in the South, nine in the Northeast, six in the Midwest, and two in the West. After the Supreme Court in *Wallace* invalidated Alabama's "moment of silence" law, Kenneth Nuger reported on the results of a compliance study focusing on Mobile County, Alabama.[70] He found that 60 percent of the 373 teachers surveyed had admitted to conducting silent meditation or voluntary prayer. Although these activities conformed with Alabama law, they "contravened a long series of Supreme Court decisions denying the permissibility of prayer-related activities in school." But there was community support for the practice insofar as a 1985 University of Alabama poll found that 84 percent of the Alabamians polled favored a constitutional amendment to restore school prayer. After the *Wallace* decision was rendered, Nuger determined that most teachers did stop the practice, but 25 percent of the group that previously conducted voluntary prayer or silent meditation continued to do so.

A key variable affecting compliance is the political culture of the community responding to the ban on school prayer. Resistance has been greatest in the Bible Belt, but the more secularized traditions of California, for example, reinforced the Supreme Court rulings.[71] Three case studies have detailed the crucial role played by local educational and political leaders in gaining compliance with the Supreme Court ban on school prayer. William

K. Muir researched the school system in an Illinois city of 200,000 during 1963–1964, and he found that the force of law had influenced school officials there to accept the ban on Bible reading.[72] Another study by Richard M. Johnson of a downstate Illinois community in 1967 documented the relative ease with which the school system conformed with the ruling.[73]

Kenneth Dolbeare and Phillip Hammond studied five communities in a midwestern state where, five years after *Schempp*, the schools continued to say prayers, read from the Bible, and conduct other religious observances.[74] The reason for these actions was that although "in most cases key members of local power structures only marginally favor schoolhouse religion on its merits, and acknowledge in the abstract a duty to obey the Court, they are unanimous in wanting to avoid public airing of the issue and hence are entirely committed to maintaining the status quo of religious practices."[75] Thus, when Supreme Court rulings strongly clash with prevailing community norms, one cannot assume that citizens will accept those decisions as public policy or that local leaders will readily enforce the law.

SUMMARY

Prior to *Engel*, there was general agreement by the states that voluntary nonsectarian prayer in their public schools was constitutional. Since the *Engel* ruling, the polls continue to show that a majority of the population favors school prayer. But political conflict mainly divides the civil libertarians, mainstream Protestants, and Jewish groups who defend church-state separation from the evangelicals and ideological conservatives.

Since the Supreme Court consistently has denied efforts to introduce religion in the classroom, advocates of school prayer have lobbied Congress to overturn *Engel* by constitutional amendment. Intense opposition also has manifested in noncompliance by school districts with the school prayer ban. Although no president until Ronald Reagan campaigned actively for school prayer, ever since 1962 the federal government has chosen *not* to implement the school prayer ban by executive action. Any enforcement depended upon private lawsuits and the federal courts.

In addition, there have been periodic attempts by various states to circumvent the prayer decisions. Despite the Court's 1985 ruling in the *Wallace* case, its majority and minority opinions implied that other state laws that permitted a "minute of silence" but that lacked Alabama's legislative intent to restore prayer might pass constitutional scrutiny. However, in December 1987, in the case *Alan J. Karcher, Speaker of the New Jersey General Assembly et al. v. Jeffrey May et al.*, 484 U.S. (1987), 98 L. Ed. 2d 327, S.Ct. (1987), the Supreme Court refused to rule on a New Jersey law allowing "a minute of silence before the start of each school day for quiet and private contemplation or introspection." A federal district court and a federal appeals court had found the New Jersey law an unconstitutional violation of the First Amendment requirement for separation of church and state. Although the law did not mention prayer, nor was there any legislative record that suggested prayer was intended, the lower federal courts detected a veiled purpose to allow student prayer.

Writing for a unanimous Supreme Court in *Karcher v. May*, Justice Sandra Day O'Connor dismissed the appeal for want of jurisdiction. The legislators who had sought the appeal in their capacities as legislative officers had been replaced, and their successors had withdrawn the appeal. Thus, the former legislators lacked standing before the Court. However, the Court's decision did not consider the issue of whether the minute of silence law in New Jersey, and by implication similar laws in twenty-five other states, was constitutional.

The Supreme Court may yet accept a "minute of silence" law as the final compromise that removes school prayer as a political issue. If that should occur, there is a certain irony in knowing that this remedy was available twenty-five years ago, at the beginning of the controversy. However, the nature of moral controversies mitigates against so easy a solution. Those opposed to prayer in public schools suspect that supporters of "minute of silence" laws may intend them as a back-door method to restore prayer in the public schools, and fearing this ulterior motive, those who before might have accepted this compromise now have become rigidly opposed.

✃ Chapter Two ✃

PORNOGRAPHY
Freedom of Expression
or Societal Degradation?

Byron W. Daynes

To some people, the obscenity issue (a term used interchangeably with "pornography" to refer to material that is sexually explicit and is designed to cause sexual arousal) is a matter of liberty and privacy, but to others it is an abuse of free expression that is in need of regulation. In the United States, the first judicial ruling on this issue came in 1815, when a Pennsylvania court held it illegal to exhibit any picture of nude bodies for profit. This was followed in 1821 by the enactment in Vermont of the first state antiobscenity law. By 1842, the *U.S. Code* had incorporated a federal statute prohibiting the importation of obscene pictures.

Ever since the eighteenth century, government has tried to cope with the problems associated with obscenity and pornography, but the politicization of this issue had to await Supreme Court decisions of the 1960s and the outcry that followed a 1970 presidential commission report on this subject. There have been laws designed to protect both children and adults from the importation, transportation, sale, and dissemination of obscene materials. Yet despite these laws, which punish distributors of pornography, there have been few major inroads into this lucrative market, a market that is estimated to be an "8-billion-dollar annual business."[1]

One reason for the ineffectiveness of antipornography laws is that demands for their enforcement frequently collide with constitutional guarantees of free expression. Moreover, decisionmakers often act on their own presumptions of what is obscene. In his now famous concurrence in *Jacobellis v. Ohio*, 378 U.S. 184 (1964), the late Supreme Court justice Potter Stewart, after puzzling over its definition, finally said in exasperation: "I shall not today attempt further to define the kinds of material I understand to be embraced within that shorthand description [hardcore pornography], and perhaps I could never succeed in intelligently doing so. But I know it when I see it, and the motion picture involved in this case is not that."

THE JUDICIARY

The judiciary has been actively involved with the pornography issue, but guidelines from court decisions have confused the question and denied to other decisionmakers meaningful standards of judgment. The Warren Court (1953–1969), which was dedicated to free expression, saw the obscenity issue as a barrier to protected expression under the First Amendment and wanted to minimize the issue's impact on free expression. But the Warren Court's approach to obscenity cases, at first, was no different from that of previous courts. Former courts had not defined obscenity before judgment was passed on alleged pornographic materials. It was not until 1957 in *Butler v. Michigan*, 352 U.S. 380 (1957), that the Warren Court first broached the problem of definition. In this case, older standards of judgment were rejected. The "isolated passages" test (which judged the obscenity of a work on the basis of isolated parts of that work without assessing its overall worth or objective) and the "most susceptible persons" test (which considered the concerns of individuals most responsive to the objectionable material, even if those individuals were a socially peripheral or minority group) that the Court had adopted from the 1868 British decision in *Regina v. Hicklin*, L.R. 3Q.B. 360 (1868), were discarded. The Warren Court was unwilling to defer to the judgments of lower federal and state courts and instead insisted on handling these difficult cases firsthand (that is, on acting as a court of original jurisdiction rather than as a court of appeals). The Court insisted on viewing the movies, reading the books, and seeing the artwork. As a result, instead of the value judgments of lower courts, we were left with the tastes and assessments of the Warren Court. This kind of policy response to obscenity caused many legal analysts to question the effectiveness of judicial policymaking in this area.[2]

Although the Warren Court was unable to define what obscenity was, it attempted to determine what obscenity *was not*. The criteria used by the Warren Court to define "the obscene" became so broad and unmanageable that the term *obscene* all but disappeared. This development began in 1957 with *Roth v. U.S.*, 354 U.S. 476 (1957). The Court decided that a work could be considered obscene if it appealed "to the average person, applying contemporary community standards, [and where] the dominant theme of the material taken as a whole appeal[ed] to prurient interests."

The Warren Court continued to broaden its standards in subsequent cases. In *Manual Enterprises v. Day*, 370 U.S. 482 (1962), Justice John Harlan said that for a work to be obscene it should have "prurient interest" as well as being "patently offensive." Furthermore, a work had to fail all the *Roth* tests individually and be "utterly without redeeming social value." This "social value" test, viewed by civil libertarians as the most important criterion, all but eliminated any possibility that a work might be considered obscene because virtually every work, it could be argued, has at least a modicum of social value and importance.

In the last year of its tenure, the Warren Court established no new obscenity standards in the case of *Stanley v. Georgia*, 394 U.S. 557 (1969). Works considered obscene under any standard, regardless of social worth, were protected if they were in an individual's private possession. By 1973, Justice William Brennan, who frequently had been the Warren Court spokesperson in its obscenity decisions, reflected upon the failings of the Warren Court's line of argument in the case of *Paris Adult Theater I v. Slaton*, 413 U.S. 49 (1973).

> No other aspect of the First Amendment has, in recent years, demanded so substantial a commitment of our time, generated such disharmony of views, and remained so resistant to the formulation of stable and manageable standards. I am convinced that the approach initiated 15 years ago in *Roth* . . . and culminating in the Court's decision today, cannot bring stability to this area of the law without jeopardizing fundamental First Amendment values.

Earl Warren was succeeded by Warren Burger as chief justice when Richard Nixon assumed the presidency. In at least two respects the Burger Court's (1969–1986) approach to obscenity was identical to that of the Warren Court. First, the new Court insisted on viewing the movies and reading the books firsthand; second, it was just as reluctant to define obscenity. In the important case of *Miller v. California*, 413 U.S. 15 (1973), the Burger Court decided against the use of expert testimony to aid in defining obscenity because "hard core pornography . . . can and does speak for itself." But the Court moved toward specifying more restrictive standards in making those judgments. In this case, five justices for the first time in many years agreed on what standards ought to prevail. These standards included the following:

1. Whether the average person, applying community standards, would find that the work, taken as a whole, appeals to prurient interest
2. Whether the work depicts or describes, in a patently offensive way, sexual conduct specifically defined by the applicable state law
3. Whether the work, taken as a whole, lacks serious literary, artistic, political, or scientific value

Miller thus substituted a more restrictive "serious value" test for the open-ended "utterly without redeeming social value" test, thereby expanding obscenity as a category of unprotected expression.

The Burger Court also moved close to defining obscenity when in *Miller*, the Court articulated specific acts and words that might be labeled obscene:

1. Patently offensive representations or descriptions of ultimate sexual acts, normal or perverted, actual or simulated

2. Patently offensive representations or descriptions of masturbation, excretory functions, and lewd exhibitions of the genitals

But this list, as the Court later pointed out, was only illustrative and not exhaustive of acts that could be considered obscene. Furthermore, the presence of these specific acts might be compelling enough in some instances to even ignore the *Miller* standards. In the recent case of *New York v. P.J. Video*, 475 U.S. 868 (1986), for example, the Court allowed the state to seize a number of sexually explicit videotapes based solely on an investigator's description of selected scenes of sexual intercourse in the films. This description, the Court felt, gave the judge, who issued the warrant, "probable cause" to believe the films were obscene without the need to consider the films as a whole.

The Burger Court in the *Miller* decision seemed committed to the need for state and local involvement in determining what standards for judging obscenity should prevail in a particular community. Yet at the same time, the Court determined there were certain universal obscene acts that in fact might contradict some community standards. This became a fundamental contradiction of the Burger Court approach. Discretion of juries, legislatures, and judges in determining the nature of community standards was to extend no further than the "universal" list of obscene acts established by the Court. This was further affirmed by the Rehnquist Court's decision in *Pope v. Illinois*, 107 S.Ct. 1918 (1987), in which Justice Byron White, speaking for a 6–3 majority, indicated that community standards could not be used as a guide to determine whether an alleged work had literary, scientific, political, or artistic value. Rather, national standards based on what a "reasonable person" would consider of value were to be the standards of determination.

An unusual problem faced by the courts in dealing with obscenity involved films and live performances. The judiciary first had to decide whether film was even a means of communication. Not until 1952, in the case of *Burstyn v. Wilson*, 343 U.S. 495 (1952), did the Court determine that film was an important means of communicating ideas and therefore deserving of First Amendment protection. Although admittedly there were important distinctions among film, radio, public speech, and the novel in terms of effectiveness, in the case of *Commercial Pictures Corp. v. Regents of the University of the State of New York*, 346 U.S. 587 (1954), Justices Hugo Black and William Douglas hastened to admit that "the First Amendment draws no distinction between the various methods of communicating ideas."

"Live" entertainment also was different in its legal challenges. Although various courts expressed a concern about live entertainment during the 1960s, the stage performance of *Hair* forced the judiciary to reexamine its approach. In 1972, a U.S. district court in Tennessee held that *Hair* violated the public nudity statutes of that state. Eventually, this ruling came before the Supreme Court in the case of *Southeastern Promotions, Ltd. v. Conrad*, 420 U.S. 546 (1975); here the Burger Court retained control of the definition of obscenity. The Court ruled that Tennessee was unnecessarily restrictive of the promoter's access to the auditorium facilities insofar as the restriction was based on what the auditorium director believed was in the community's best interest.

The Burger Court also was concerned with child pornography. Nobody expected the glut of "kiddie porn" that flooded the markets during the 1970s and 1980s. A major problem for the Court in handling child pornography cases was that they fit none of the categories previously established by the Supreme Court. Kiddie porn cases were not considered "child abuse," nor did they fall under the *Miller* standards of obscenity. Consequently, the Supreme Court could not act as it had previously. Instead, Congress and state legislatures took the initiative from the Court by restricting pornographic materials involving children. By 1981, thirty-five states and Congress had prohibited the distribution of child pornography, while twenty of those states restricted such material without reliance on any specific obscenity standard.[3]

Such broad restrictions on free expression collided with the First Amendment and raised questions for the courts. Some legal questions were answered by the Supreme Court in the 1982 case of *New York v. Ferber*, 458 U.S. 747 (1982). Following the lead of Congress and the state legislatures, the Supreme Court determined that stricter standards should govern when children were objects of obscenity. Whether the material was "obscene" or not was of less importance than whether children were being victimized through sexual exploitation. "Childporn" was not to be judged "as a whole" but could be banned based on "isolated passages." Thus, the Burger Court was judging child pornography by the same *Hicklin* standards that the Warren Court had discarded years before.

What of the future actions by the judiciary in handling pornography? Lower federal courts have been no more successful in defining obscenity than has the Supreme Court and, like the high court, have been usually protective of free expression. The most interesting recent case before the federal courts, which involved the city of Indianapolis, was *American Booksellers Association v. Hudnut*; this case eventually was reviewed by the Supreme Court.[4] The city defined pornography as "sexual discrimination" against women, but Judge Sarah Evans Barker, U.S. district court judge for the southern district of Indiana, ruled that the Indianapolis ordinance, which prohibited "all discriminatory practices of sexual subordination or inequality through pornography" (defined as "the graphic depiction of the sexually explicit subordination of women"), was unconstitutionally vague because the definition of pornography also included instances of protected speech. Barker also ruled that the Indianapolis ordinance acted as a prior restraint because there were inadequate procedural safeguards. On February 24, 1986, the Supreme Court held that the Indianapolis ordinance was unconstitutional, but the ruling was issued without an opinion. Justices Warren Burger, William Rehnquist, and Sandra Day O'Connor dissented from the summary affirmance on the ground that the case should have been set down for detailed briefings and oral arguments. Given that the most important legal questions embodying feminist concerns were not confronted in this case, more adjudication on these grounds is likely to be forthcoming.

By virtue of their controversial nature and constitutional sensitivity, interpretations by the Supreme Court on pornography have resulted in split decisions and confusing precedents. Thus far, the one possible exception may be child pornography, where there was a clarity of tone in the *Ferber* case unknown to most of the other obscenity cases.

CONGRESS

Unlike the Supreme Court, congressional response to pornography has spanned many years. Restrictions on obscenity first came in the mid-1800s, with the enactment of the Tariff Act of 1842, which prohibited obscene prints and visual depictions. Since the 1950s, Congress has legislated in several important areas, as Table 2.1 shows, with particular interest in (1) dissemination, exchange, and distribution of obscenity through the U.S. mails and (2) restrictions on child pornography. Unlike the judiciary's approach to antiobscenity policies, the Congress has been guided by an explicit working definition of obscenity.[5] When Congress confronted the problem of child pornography, however, the working definition proved no more useful than had the presumptions maintained by the Court. Like the judiciary's experience in this area, there has been confusion in the Congress as to whether child pornography should be considered "obscenity" or "child abuse." Despite the confusion, in 1984 Congress strengthened previous legislation aimed at protecting minors by significantly raising the penalties against pornographers. First offenders are now liable to a maximum $100,000 fine rather than the previous $10,000, and the fine levied against second offenders has been raised from $15,000 to $200,000. In addition, producers of such materials who are found guilty of sexually exploiting children forfeit all assets used in the production of those materials and any profits accrued from them.

Within the Congress, the principal decisionmakers involved in obscenity policy are members of those standing committees and subcommittees having jurisdiction over areas affected by obscenity. This primarily involves the House and Senate Judiciary Committees, the House Committee on Post Office and Civil Service, and the House District of Columbia Committee. But because obscenity has become so pervasive, other committees also occasionally write legislation; for example, the House Energy and Commerce Committee has written legislation whenever obscenity in cable television is at issue, and the House Government Operations Committee has written legislation when obscenity in the mails is a concern, as it was in 1969. Moreover, when child abuse was examined in 1977, the matter was referred to the House Education and Labor Committee and to the Senate Committee on Human Resources. No one congressional committee in either house of Congress has exclusive jurisdiction over this kind of legislation. Various select committees have been used by Congress to investigate obscenity.

TABLE 2.1 Legislation on Obscenity, Introduced in Congress 1956-1985

	Years						
	1956-1960	1961-1965	1966-1970	1971-1975	1976-1980	1981-1985	Total
Mail/Post Office	7	3	6				16
Protection from obscenity	1						1
State control over obscenity	1						1
Transportation of obscenity	1		2				3
Study of obscenity	3	2	4				9
Sale of obscenity	1						1
Obscenity and subversion		1					1
Criminal Code and obscenity					3	2	5
D.C. bill on obscenity		1	1				2
Obscene communications			1			1	2
Children and obscenity			2	1	9	5	17
Advertising of obscenity			4				4
Definition of obscenity			2	1	2		5
Victims of obscenity						2	2
Importation of obscenity						1	1
Total by year	14	7	22	2	14	11	70

Source: Congressional Records and *Congressional Quarterly Weekly Reports* for the yearly period in question.

Noteworthy among these have been the House Select Committee on Current Pornographic Materials during the 82nd Congress (1951-1952) and the Senate's Special Committee to Investigate Organized Crime in Interstate Commerce, active during both the 81st (1949-1950) and 82nd (1951-1952) Congresses.

Without question, the thrust of legislative activity in this area has been to restrict access to pornography. Few members of Congress could hope to win reelection by campaigning in favor of expanded access to pornography. In fact, for many years, Congress has looked for a far-reaching, structural means of restricting obscenity. Such thinking led the Congress in 1955 to propose a commission to study obscenity. In the 1960 version of that proposal, it was clear that one of the commission's principal tasks would be to study the traffic in obscenity and also to seek ways to inform the public about pornography and to coordinate the work of other agencies examining the same problem. As originally proposed, the study commission was to be a seventeen-member body composed of persons from Congress, the Departments of Health, Education, and Welfare, Justice, and the Post Office and representatives from the clergy, publishing houses, high schools, motion pictures, broadcasting, and state and local law enforcement officers. This proposal was reintroduced in 1963, 1965, and 1966 before finally winning approval in 1967.

Congress may have been anxious to establish this commission, but it was not so eager to receive the commission's final report in 1970. The Senate and President Richard Nixon were upset when the commission report was "leaked" to the press, and on October 13, 1970, the Senate rejected the commission's findings and its recommendations through S. Res. 477, which was passed by a 60–5 vote (with 34 abstentions). In particular, the Senate rejected the following findings and recommendations:

1. That there is "no evidence to date that exposure to explicit sexual materials plays a significant role in the causation of delinquent or criminal behavior among youths or adults"
2. That "a majority of American adults believe that adults should be allowed to read or see any sexual materials they wish"
3. That "there is no reason to suppose that elimination of governmental prohibitions upon the sexual materials which may be made available to adults would adversely affect the availability to the public of other books, magazines, or films"
4. That there is no "evidence that exposure to explicit sexual materials adversely affects character or moral attitudes regarding sex and sexual conduct"
5. That "Federal, State, and Local legislation prohibiting the sale, exhibition, or distribution of sexual materials to consenting adults should be repealed"[6]

The Senate's reasons for rejecting the findings and recommendations were summed up in section 2 of the resolution, which held that (1) generally, the findings and recommendations were not supported by the evidence considered by or available to the commission and (2) the commission had not properly discharged its statutory duties, nor had the commission complied with the mandates of Congress. (The dissenters were five liberal Democrats and Republicans who may have been particularly sympathetic to individual free expression—Walter Mondale [D-Minn.], Clifford Case [R-N.J.], Jacob Javits [R-N.Y.], Steven Young [D-Ohio], and George McGovern [D-S.Dak.].)

There also was a move in the House of Representatives, during the 91st Congress, to reject the majority report of the Presidential Commission on Obscenity and Pornography and to adopt a minority report authored by Father Morton A. Hill, Reverend Winfred C. Link, and Charles H. Keating, Jr. But that resolution was sent to the Commitee on Education and Labor and was never reported out. Another attempt to reject the commission report was made in the 92nd Congress when Representative Chalmers P. Wylie (R-Ohio) introduced H. Res. 485, but again it was referred to the Committee on Education and Labor, where it died. By June 21, 1972, most opposition to the commission report within the House had been expressed. Although the House failed to join the Senate in rejecting the commission report, there were attempts to express such disapproval in other legislation, and there were several attempts to create a select committee on investigation of pornography enterprises.[7]

THE PRESIDENCY

Most contemporary presidents have had little to say about pornography. Democrats John F. Kennedy and Lyndon B. Johnson did give support to existing laws protecting free expression, and Republicans Richard Nixon and Ronald Reagan made obscenity and pornography campaign issues and spoke out forcefully against their spread.

At a news conference on August 29, 1962, John F. Kennedy was asked to comment on a Court decision that prevented the postmaster general from restricting pornographic matter in the mails. He responded that existing laws already governed such distribution and that he believed the Post Office's main responsibility was not to make judgments about the nature of pornography but, rather, to carry out the law. In October of that same year, one of President Kennedy's pocket vetoes returned to Congress a District of Columbia bill to ban obscene publications. The legislation would have required the Post Office to put up public notices to warn citizens of potentially obscene matter in the U.S. mails and to allow citizens to return questionable material to the Post Office. But Kennedy felt that the bill was too broad. As Kennedy stated in his Memorandum of Disapproval: "Such a brief delay in the enactment of this legislation seems a small price to pay in order to obtain an enforceable law which will achieve the worthy objectives which prompted the bill before me."[8]

Barry Goldwater, the Republican candidate for president in 1964, never referred to the problems of pornography, but the 1964 Republican party platform called for the "enactment of legislation, despite Democratic opposition, to curb the flow through the mails of obscene materials which has flourished into a multimillion dollar obscenity racket."[9] Lyndon Johnson's first reaction to obscenity legislation came in the context of the 1966 District of Columbia crime bill, which he vetoed on November 13 of that year. Although it is unclear whether he was generally concerned with the breadth of the legislation or concerned only with the section of the bill that dealt with obscenity, he did believe that the latter posed a threat to First Amendment freedoms. However, two years later, at the request of Congress, President Johnson appointed the well-known, eighteen-member Presidential Commission on Obscenity and Pornography to make a thorough study of obscenity and its effects on society.

Each year from 1969 to 1971, opposition to pornography was a significant issue for Richard Nixon. Much of his concern with pornography grew from his attempt to blame the Democrats in Congress for inaction on his legislative agenda, which included measures opposing obscenity. Even before he took office, in late December 1968, Nixon said legislation was necessary to make it a criminal offense to send pornographic material through the mails to children. The following year in a special message, Nixon announced his intention to propose legislation to Congress that would stop the "peddlers of obscenity."[10] In that May 1969 message, he emphasized the need to halt the traffic in unsolicited sex-oriented material and mentioned how many complaints had been received by the White House and Congress on this matter. He understood that no solution would be easy, given the First Amendment protection of expression, but he proceeded to sponsor various measures.

Nixon proposed making it a federal crime to mail unsolicited pornographic materials to youths (under the age of eighteen); the first offense would carry a penalty of a maximum five years in prison and a $50,000 fine. Violations of proposed antipornographic restrictions on advertising would carry a similar penalty for the first offense but twice that for a second offense. To safeguard personal privacy, Nixon's proposals also extended a 1967 public law against pandering by allowing the recipients of unsolicited pornography to request that their post offices no longer deliver such material to them. Nixon wanted a grass-roots movement against pornography, and he maintained that "when indecent books no longer find a market, when pornographic films can no longer draw an audience, when obscene plays open to empty houses, then the tide will turn. Government can maintain the dikes against obscenity, but only people can turn back the tide."[11]

In a September 1969 speech to the National Governors' Conference, President Nixon again said that antipornography legislation was one of his twenty-four high priority issues for congressional action. Later that month, he complained about congressional inaction on his program and called on the National Federation of Republican Women to urge the legislature to act. These public statements were followed in October 1969 with another special message to Congress in which Nixon reminded the legislators that his proposals had yet to receive action.

President Nixon devoted more energy to the obscenity issue in 1970 than in any other year of his presidency. In his State of the Union Message on January 22, 1970, he echoed the theme that he would carry into the congressional districts as he campaigned for Republicans in the midterm elections: that government has a special responsibility to bring a halt to pornography. But no legislative action was forthcoming in 1970, which prompted Nixon to send Congress another special message on this and other matters in September. During the October 1970 midterm election campaign, Nixon criticized the Congress for doing nothing about his anti-pornography legislation.

The issue was further galvanized by the (1970) report of the President's Commission on Obscenity and Pornography, which President Johnson had staffed two years earlier. Its majority report had been rejected by the Senate one week before being publicly repudiated by President Nixon, who declared, "I have evaluated that report and categorically reject its morally bankrupt conclusions and major recommendations." He indicated further, in one of his most pointed attacks against the commission report, that

> so long as I am in the White House, there will be no relaxation of the national effort to control and eliminate smut from our national life. . . . The warped and brutal portrayal of sex in books, magazines, and movies, if not halted and reversed could poison the wellsprings of American and western culture and civilization. . . . Smut should not be simply contained at its present level; it should be outlawed in every state in the Union. . . . I am well aware of the importance of protecting freedom of expression. But pornography is to freedom of expression what anarchy is to liberty.[12]

President Nixon treated the commission report seriously enough to involve his entire administration in a campaign to discredit the commission's findings. Vice President Spiro Agnew, Nixon's press secretary, the postmaster general, and counselors to the president all made speeches opposing the commission report. These spokespersons blamed the commission report on "radical-liberals" in the Democratic party; as a result, the report itself became a major campaign issue throughout the remainder of the 1970 election campaign.

In 1971, President Nixon made his last, strong appeal to convince Congress to enact antipornography legislation, during which he said, "It would be difficult to overstate the strength of my support for these two pieces of legislation."[13] Although it appears that the president failed to get most of his program enacted, Congress did enact limited prohibitions against obscenity during this period. In 1968, P.L. 90-299 made it a federal crime for anyone to place obscene or abusive telephone calls from the District of Columbia across state lines or in foreign communications. In 1969, three House committees held hearings on obscenity in the mails, but no final action was taken. More hearings were held in 1970 on several portions of the president's program, and while two bills (HR 11031 and HR 11032) were passed by the House and one by the Senate (S 3220), the two chambers failed to act on each other's bills, and they failed to be enacted by adjournment. However, Congress did amend the Postal Reform Act of 1970 (P.L. 91-375) on August 12, 1970, to include a prohibition against mailing sexually oriented commercial advertisements to reluctant adults as well as a prohibition against mailing obscene matter that might appear on envelopes or wrappers. Still another bill (P.L. 91-662) was amended on January 8, 1971, to make it more difficult to import, transport, or send obscene matter through the mails. During the remainder of 1971, the House passed HR 8805, which would have further prohibited mailing of obscene matter, but the Senate took no action on this bill. After 1971, Nixon made no more speeches on the subject, nor did he take any other action against pornography during his second term.

Although there is no evidence that pornography was an issue of concern for either President Gerald Ford or President Jimmy Carter, several political parties did refer to the problems in their 1976 platforms. Lester Maddox's American Independent party stated that it "fully supports laws providing maximum legal penalties for criminal distribution, publication, or exhibition of obscenity."[14] That same year, the Liberation party, in a statement consistent with its philosophy, opposed all "censorship, including anti-pornography laws, whatever the medium involved."[15] Although Gerald Ford paid no attention to the Republican party platform, that year it clearly was concerned with pornography: "The work presently being done to tighten the antiobscenity provisions of the criminal code has our full support. Since the jurisdiction of the federal government in this field is limited to interstate commerce and the mails, we urge state and local governments to assume a major role in limiting the distribution and availability of obscene materials."[16]

Gerald Ford seemed to concentrate on trying to convince a recalcitrant post-Watergate Congress to pass his economic policies on oil and energy independence, and to allow him a freer hand on budget matters and foreign affairs, rather than to adopt social policies. President Carter also focused his attention more on traditional Democratic policy issues, such as welfare, health care, trade, energy, education, and foreign affairs, than on social policy concerns.

The 1980 campaign found none of the major parties interested in the pornography issue. But both the American Independent party and the Libertarian party repeated their concerns of 1976 in their 1980 party platforms. These two minor parties also were joined by the American party, which stated that "neither Congress nor the federal courts should infringe on the rights of states and local governments to enact constitutional laws restricting obscenity, pornography, and illicit sex acts."[17]

In 1984, the Republican party again made clear its opposition to pornography; the party platform stated that "the Republican Party has deep concern about gratuitous sex and violence in the entertainment media, both of which contribute to the problem of crime against children and women. To the victims of such crimes who need protection we gladly offer it."[18]

President Reagan gave full support to this platform statement by focusing considerable attention on the problem, and he escalated his opposition to child pornography. In his 1984 State of the Union Message, President Reagan suggested that parents needed reassurance that their children would not be abducted or become objects of child pornography. Five days later, he repeated those sentiments to the Convention of National Religious Broadcasters and added that he anticipated signing a bill to strengthen the law against child pornography. He reassured the audience that his administration would enforce all antipornography laws.

By May 1984, Congress had enacted the Child Protection Act of 1984 (P.L. 98-292), and at the bill-signing ceremony, President Reagan expressed his disgust for those who abuse children "whether by using them in pornographic material or by encouraging sexual abuse by distributing this material." He added that pornography was "ugly and dangerous" and that despite what the 1967 presidential commission had concluded, there was a link "between child molesting and pornography" as well as one between "pornography and sexual violence."[19] The highlight of his speech was his announcement that the attorney general, at the president's request, would establish a new president's commission to investigate the effects of obscenity on society. In May 1985, Attorney General Edwin Meese named an eleven-member commission to recommend measures, where appropriate, to control the distribution and production of obscene material.

The composition and work of the 1967 and 1985 commissions charged with studying obscenity and pornography show how fundamentally different a liberal Democratic approach can be from a more conservative Republican approach. The 1967 Commission on Obscenity and Pornography was extremely controversial because its recommendations diverged sharply from the general public's beliefs and the politicians' views of those beliefs. In contrast, President Reagan named a commission whose findings, in all probability, will reinforce existing public attitudes about pornography and whose members promised to support the Reagan "social" agenda.

President Johnson's appointees to the 1967 commission included "psychiatrists, sociologists, psychologists, criminologists, jurists, lawyers, and others from organizations and professions who [had] special and practical competence or experience with respect to obscenity laws and their application to juveniles."[20]

The commission's purpose was to investigate whether there was a connection between obscenity and antisocial behavior in adults and in children and to discover ways of monitoring the flow of pornography. The commission also was to formulate a definition of obscenity and pornography. Empirical research, opinion surveys, and extensive interviewing in laboratory settings were thought necessary to obtain because the commission felt there were insufficient data available to answer the inquiries before it.

The 1967 commission findings and recommendations filled ten volumes. The primary recommendations included the following:[21]

1. That a massive sex education effort should be launched

2. That continued open discussion on the issues of pornography and obscenity based on factual information take place
3. That additional factual information be gathered
4. That citizens organize at national, regional, and local levels to implement these recommendations
5. That federal, state, or local legislation should not interfere with the right of adults to obtain, read, or view sexual materials
6. That any federal, state, and local legislation that prohibits the sale, exhibition, or distribution of sexual materials to adults should be repealed
7. That state and local legislation should be enacted to prohibit public displays of sexually explicit pictorial material
8. That federal legislation that prevents unsolicited advertisements of sexually explicit materials through the mails should be continued
9. That prosecutors should have the right to obtain declaratory judgments in order to determine whether material falls within legal prohibition (this will allow civil prosecution rather than criminal)
10. That jurisdiction of the Supreme Court in obscenity cases should not be limited or abolished
11. That commercial distribution and display sale of sexual materials should be prohibited to young people

Because these findings and recommendations did not satisfy everyone, several commissioners filed their own individual statements or reports, and one "minority" report was authored by three members who strongly dissented from the commission's position. Member Irving Lehrman, a rabbi from Florida, criticized the commission for failing to engage in long-range research efforts. Two others who voted with the majority, Joseph T. Klapper, a social researcher and former university professor, and G. William Jones, a faculty member in broadcasting at Southern Methodist University, generally praised the commission's work. The minority statement by Otto Larsen and Marvin E. Wolfgang, both sociologists, however, went well beyond what the commission had recommended and eschewed statutory restrictions on obscenity or pornography in public displays, on unsolicited mail, or on access by juveniles.

Morris Lipton and Edward Greenwood, both psychiatrists, filed a joint statement praising the commission for not endorsing any "simple" solutions to a complex problem and for viewing pornography more as a nuisance than as an "evil." These members did believe, however, that one weakness in the commission's work was its failure to study the effect of erotica on juveniles.

Extremely critical of the majority's opinion were members Morton A. Hill, a Catholic priest and president of Morality in Media; Winfrey C. Link, a Methodist minister; and Charles H. Keating, Jr., founder of Citizens for Decent Literature, who filed a joint statement calling the majority report a "Magna Carta for the pornographer" and insisting that it was "slanted and biased in favor of protecting the business of obscenity and pornography, which the Commission was mandated by the Congress to regulate." These members charged the commission with exceeding its mandate and assuming the role of "counsel for the filth merchants." The minority report charged the commission with ignoring important studies that contradicted the majority's viewpoint. The research that was used, the minority further contended, was misquoted, misrepresented, and distorted. With this harsh criticism from dissenters on the commission, it is not surprising that public release of its report was greeted with controversy. Before the report was formally released, in fact, versions of the final report were "leaked" to columnist Jack Anderson and to Congressman Robert Nix (D-Pa.), who immediately called the House Post Office and Civil Service Subcommittee of the Postal Operations Committee into special session to hold hearings on the report. The leaked report also was given to Stein and Day, a publishing house, which printed it as an "unofficial" *Obscenity Report* before the *Final Report* was made public.[22]

The Nixon administration quickly placed some distance between itself, the commission, and its Democratic sponsors. As Vice President Spiro Agnew stated in a speech on September 30, 1970, in Salt Lake City, "Just today, the lame duck Commission on Obscenity and Pornography weighed in with its final report. Its views do not represent the thinking of the Nixon Administration. This Commission was not named by President Nixon. No Sir, your honor, it's not our baby."[23]

Lingering doubts about the wisdom of its recommendations coupled with a political backlash encouraged the Reagan administration, sixteen years after the first commission report, to establish a second eleven-member commission to study obscenity and to recommend ways to control its spread.

The 1985 Attorney General's Commission on Pornography (the Meese Commission) was strikingly different from the 1967 commission. The recent commission was established under President Reagan, who proclaimed an early interest in the potential threats posed by pornography as well as a dissatisfaction with the findings of the 1967 commission. Differences between the two commissions could be seen in their memberships. The 1985 commission was more heavily staffed by law-enforcement persons; there were few social scientists among the commission membership.[24] Unlike the 1967 commission, the 1985 panel not only accepted research from the social sciences but drew on data from a number of fields outside of the social sciences on which to base its conclusions.

The 1985 commission, in contrast to the earlier commission, worked from an agreed-upon definition of pornography as material that is "predominantly sexually explicit and intended primarily for the purpose of sexual arousal."[25] Budgetary and time constraints were also a factor and concern of the 1985 commission. This commission was limited to a one-year time period and to budgetary constraints of $500,000, which, in the opinion of some panelists, "prevented us from commissioning independent research."[26]

One of the 1985 commission's most controversial methods was a letter sent to some 8,000 retail chain stores warning them that they were guilty of displaying popular soft-pornography if they sold magazines such as *Playboy* and *Penthouse* and therefore would be identified as distributors of pornography. Playboy Enterprises and the American Booksellers Association immediately brought suit against the commission, charging it with attempting to suppress adult books and magazines and accusing it of harassment and blacklisting. Federal district judge John Garret Penn issued a preliminary injunction to the commission that prevented it from publishing the list of retailers. The court also required the commission to send a follow-up letter to each of the retailers notifying them that the first letter was to be withdrawn and that retailers' names would not be used in the final 1986 commission report.[27]

Findings of the 1985 commission focused on two main areas—child pornography and the pornography of sexual violence—areas that some commissioners on the 1967 commission thought had been ignored. In the area of sex and violence, the commission drew one of the sharpest distinctions from its 1967 counterpart when concluding that "the available evidence strongly supports the hypothesis that substantial exposure to sexually violent materials . . . bears a causal relationship to antisocial acts of sexual violence and, for some subgroups, possibly to unlawful acts of sexual violence."[28] In all, there were ninety-two commission recommendations for dealing with pornography. A number of the recommendations encouraged stern enforcement of obscenity laws already a part of state and federal legal codes. At the federal level, Congress, the cabinet, and regulatory agencies were asked to develop new laws and regulations to comply with the commission's objectives and goals. At the state level, state legislatures and prosecutorial staffs were to enforce antiobscenity restrictions. Judges were asked to sentence convicted child pornographers to lifetime probations with appropriate imprisonment in order to monitor their actions. The Department of Justice was urged to develop an informational data base on pornography as well as to more actively use present laws to prosecute the main producers and distributors of pornography.

The 1985 commission saw a need for state legislatures to update their obscenity statutes and to make them consistent with standards in the landmark 1973 obscenity case of *Miller v. California*, 413 U.S. 15 (1973). State legislatures were asked to increase penalties for second violators of antipornography statutes and to enact racketeering statutes that would weaken organized crime's hold on the pornography trade. State and local public health agencies also were requested to investigate adult establishments and arcades in order to enforce relevant health standards. Each level of government was asked to become more vigorous in halting the use and spread of pornography. Citizen groups opposed to the spread of pornography that were using such methods as boycotting, picketing, and other lawful means of protest were given encouragement by the commission report.

Reactions to these recommendations, even among the commission members, were not unanimous. Two of the eleven members, Ellen Levine and Judith Becker, while indicating that much of the report could be considered intelligent and reasonable, asserted in a twenty-page written statement that the evidence examined by the commission had been "skewed to the very violent and extremely degrading"[29] and that the limited budget and examination period had proved impossible barriers to properly assess commission findings. Outside reactions to the report thus far have varied across liberal/conservative lines. Liberal groups such as the American Civil Liberties Union (ACLU), in the person of Barry Lynn, its legal counsel, attended most of the commission hearings and monitored them. The commission's final report raised, for Lynn, "enough constitutional questions to litigate for the next 20 years."[30]

Christie Hefner's response to the report was equally critical. As president of Playboy Enterprises, she was particularly concerned with the encouragement given by the report to grass-roots opposition to adult magazines and other pornography. Hefner indicated that "the notion of citizen vigilantism against magazines, books, films or video cassettes is something I think conjures up visions of Nazi Germany, not of the United States."[31]

Supporters of the commission report included Christian Voice, the Liberty Federation, and, to a limited extent, the National Organization for Women (NOW). Bruce Hallam of Christian Voice asserted that this report would make "headway in eliminating the plague of pornographic pollution which has ravaged our society." Jerry Falwell, for the Liberty Foundation, extolled the report and indicated that it was a "good and healthy report that places the United States Government clearly in concert with grass roots America."[32]

Spokespersons for NOW supported the commission's recommendation that "legislatures should consider legislation recognizing civil remedies for harm directly attributable to pornography," but NOW could not support the commission's focus on law enforcement. NOW was particularly concerned with such groups as those affiliated with the religious Right that might gain strength from the report's conclusions.[33]

These commission recommendations, despite their controversial nature, may well have greater impact on society than did the 1967 commission findings. Chances of implementation are much greater for the findings of the later commission, given the president's and attorney general's support of this commission and the importance of pornography as an agenda item on the president's schedule. The further strength of these recommendations comes from the fact that many of them only require additional enforcement of laws already in the state codes.

BUREAUCRACY

On occasion, leading White House officials have received assignments directly from the president to speak out against pornography, as was the case during the Nixon administration. More often, however, entire agencies and bureaus have become involved in restricting pornographic traffic; these actions have derived from the primary functions of the agencies or from decisions made by senior bureaucratic officers in these agencies. Agencies that have been involved during the years have included the Federal Communications Commission (FCC), the Federal Bureau of Investigation (FBI), the Post Office (as both a cabinet department as well as an independent agency), and the U.S. Customs Bureau.

The FCC

When pornography and the media are the focus of attention, the FCC becomes an agency of great importance. Although the Federal Communications Act forbids the FCC from censoring questionable material, the *U.S. Code* (18 USC K 1464) prohibits obscene and profane language in broadcasting. The FCC thus is encouraged to act as a watchdog over broadcasting in order to screen questionable material. Although reluctant to use its most effective sanction, in extreme circumstances the FCC will use its control over licensing to pressure an outlet. "Intent" has been an important consideration in some of the FCC policy judgments. The FCC declared in the *Jack Straw Memorial Foundation* case that, although a Seattle FM radio station had broadcast some questionable programs in the past, the FCC decided to renew the station's three-year license because "they did not do so with any intent to give offense, to pander, to sensationalize, to shock, or to break community standards."[34]

In most cases, the FCC supports station management's control over content. In the July 9, 1981, memorandum opinion on commission rules and regulations for cable television channel capacity the FCC ruled that a cable system operation should not be allowed to censor programming "on a channel set aside as a public forum, to which the programmer has a right of access by virtue of local, state or federal law" because this would "impose a system of prior restraint."[35] Likewise, in June 1983, the FCC affirmed the decision of Mass Media Bureau in Indiana over the objections of Decency in Broadcasting, Inc. that "certain obscene, indecent and profane material had been broadcast over station WFBQ (FM)." The FCC indicated that it had no prerogative to intervene where the language spoken "was not profane within the meaning of that word as described in court opinions and, based upon current case law, it was unlikely that any sanction imposed by the Commission for the broadcast of profane language in this situation would be judicially upheld."[36] Similarly, in August 1984, the FCC, in a license renewal case of KISW (FM) in Seattle, Washington, denied complaints by Vincent Hoffart of Hoffart Broadcasting that offensive material had been heard on a live interview program. The FCC was not impressed by the complaint because the station had taken measures to correct the situation by halting the interview when the person being interviewed would not change his language and by repeatedly broadcasting a later apology by that person.[37] Over time, the FCC has given much of its support to the stations.

The FBI

The FBI also has been involved on occasion in antiobscenity campaigns. This is particularly true when interstate transportation of obscene materials has been in question. Prior to 1955, the FBI could arrest only individuals carrying obscene materials if they were transported on common carriers. In 1955, Congress passed a law that made any interstate transportation of pornography illegal whether it came by common carrier or private automobile. This legislation has increased FBI effectiveness, although the Bureau is usually called upon only when hard-core pornography or other unusual cases are at issue. One unusual case occurred in 1983 when, in cooperation with the Postal Inspection Service, the Bureau succeeded in indicting Catherine S. Wilson of Los Angeles on fifteen counts of major violations of the child pornography laws.[38] The FBI also becomes involved in pornography investigations when the Mann Act (18 USC Sec. 2423) is used to indict violators of pornography. At one time, this act was concerned only with the transportation of females across state lines for illicit purposes; in recent years, the act has been broadened to include the transportation of males as well as females across state lines for purposes of prostitution and the transportation of minors for the purpose of engaging in sexual conduct for commercial reasons.[39]

U.S. Customs

None of these agencies has had quite the impact on the pornographic trade that U.S. Customs and the Postal Service have. These two agencies are the institutions that primarily monitor the flow of pornography within the country. Although U.S. Customs has no official authority to make judgments about obscenity, the nature of the agency's work puts it in a position to determine what books, magazines, devices, and films enter the country. Most foreign films, in fact, have been given Customs's review before entering the United States. Customs also spot-checks suspicious packages and, in conjunction with the Postal Service, on occasion withholds first-class mail. Customs also has authority to prohibit the mailing of sexually oriented advertisements; to prohibit any "office of the United States" from aiding in the importation of obscene or "treasonous" books or articles;[40] and to prohibit the actual "importation or transportation into the United States" of any obscene material.[41]

Critics of the U.S. Customs have suggested that although Customs does not have the authority to determine what is and is not obscene, agents in effect can censor because the importer or producer of the material must spend precious time and money in courts to reacquire the material that is seized by Customs. Furthermore, the limited route of appeal that can be taken by those accused of producing and distributing pornography may work in Customs's favor. As James Paul and Murray Schwartz contended, "The absence of administrative formality makes it easier for the government official to decide against the contesting citizen in a borderline case. Precisely because there is not the check of a formal adversary hearing nor easy review in the courts, Customs procedure delegates considerable power to the few who decide what publications shall be suppressed."[42]

Much of the focus of U.S. Customs from 1983 to 1985 was on child pornography under investigation in conjunction with U.S. Postal Service inspectors and local police. In November 1984, Customs agents, along with Postal Service inspectors and Montgomery, Alabama, police, had Wallace Miller indicted for violating the Child Protection Act of 1984. He had received materials through the mails showing minors engaged in sexually explicit acts.[43]

Although Customs appears to have been fairly active in combating the traffic in pornography, seizures have dropped off significantly during the 1980s. The General Accounting Office (GAO) Report for April 20, 1982, for example, indicated that pornography seizures in New York decreased from 15,020 in 1975 to 1,580 in 1980. The report attributed this difference to an increase in federal statutes against pornography as well as to a reduction in the number of Customs agents serving this area. In addition, the report indicated that the reduction also may have been because pornographers were using other techniques, such as domestic reproduction of pornographic foreign films, thereby making it unnecessary to import so many of them through Customs.[44]

The Postal Service

The Postal Service has long been of greater concern to civil libertarians than has the Customs Bureau. The Postal Service has been quite restrictive of the flow of obscenity throughout the country. Congress has provided the Post Office with sufficient leverage through statutory authority to detain and restrain the mail.

Civil libertarians have been concerned with the techniques the Post Office has used to restrict the flow of questionable materials. This agency has resorted to seizure, exclusion, branding certain publications as unmailable, blocking the mail sent to certain persons through the use of mail covers, and revoking mailing privileges, which thus allows the Post Office to be a stern overseer of the mails.

Since 1984, postal officers and inspectors have been very active in working for the indictments of persons violating the strict child pornography laws. This activity is the result of recently passed federal statutes against child pornography. Prior to 1977, few such laws were on the books, but since then most states as well as the federal government have such laws.

At times, postal inspectors have operated independently in their prosecutions as they did in 1982 when they arrested a Cleveland couple who were charged with sexual battery and corruption of a minor. Sexually explicit pictures also were found in the house.[45] The next year, in Waukegan, Illinois, an undercover postal service inspector was instrumental in the sentencing of David Petrovic to twenty-six years in prison for violating the Illinois state laws against taking indecent liberties with children.[46] Information provided by postal inspectors was responsible for indictments against individuals in nine separate child pornography cases in 1984 and four more child pornography cases in 1985. The most successful indictment came against Cathy Wilson, a Los Angeles "kiddie porn queen," who, once a purveyor of adult pornography, became one of the major distributors of child pornography in the country. She is currently serving ten years in prison as a result of an eight-year Postal Service investigation.[47]

The Postal Service also has worked in conjunction with state and local police, the FBI, U.S. Customs, and in cooperation with U.S. attorneys to combat the spread of pornography. Because sex crimes and distribution of pornography so frequently overlap jurisdictions, so often involve more than one city, town, and county, even involve international contacts, this cooperative effort is probably the most common pattern for the Postal Service. In January 1984, for example, postal inspectors, Las Vegas metropolitan police, and the U.S. Attorneys Office, after an eight-year investigation, indicted Sheldon Heiman, who founded and operated the Church of the Children of the Desert, after it was found the church was a front to support Heiman's possession of pornography and bondage devices.[48]

Although such activity seems fairly constant on the part of the Postal Service, the 1982 General Accounting Office Report on "Sexual Exploitation of Children—A Problem of Unknown Magnitude" stated that pornography inspection was not considered a very high priority by police and Postal Service employees. The Postal Service, for example, had only one inspector for the entire New York City area during that year.[49] This was not peculiar to New York City. In fact, a significant decline in complaints about child pornography has occurred since 1970; the Post Office received nearly three hundred thousand complaints that year compared to less than fifteen thousand in 1982.[50] This decrease may be due to the increased number of strict state and federal laws and the willingness of juries to prosecute those creating child pornography. The GAO Report also suggested that the 1979 bans in Denmark and Sweden on child pornography severely restricted the worldwide market for child pornography.[51]

INTEREST GROUPS

Interest group activity against pornography has existed since the mid-nineteenth century in the United States. From the beginning, the two political institutions that have attracted the most interest group attention have been the Supreme Court and the Congress. *Amicus curiae* (friend-of-the-court) briefs filed before the Supreme Court and public testimony before Congress can suggest which groups have been most active in influencing obscenity policy at the national level. Table 2.2 indicates the types of interest groups that filed *amicus* briefs in major Supreme Court obscenity cases from 1957 to 1984. As is evident, interest groups seeking to expand public access to obscenity, pornography, and freedom of expression were far more likely to seek judicial resolution of the controversy than were those "single-issue" groups wanting to restrict access. The most important nationwide single-issue group seeking to influence judicial action in this area was founded in 1957 as the Citizens for Decent Literature (now known as Citizens for

TABLE 2.2 *Amicus Curiae* Briefs to the Supreme Court by Interest Groups in Forty-two Obscenity Cases, 1957-1984

| | Classification of Interest Groups Filing Briefs | |
| | To Restrict Access | To Expand Access |
Interest Group	Number of Briefs Filed	Number of Briefs Filed
Parent/child	2	
Single-issue	2	
Law-related		2
Religious	1	2
Museums/libraries		2
Multi-issue		9
Arts		5
Authors/press		23
Total	5	43

Most Active Interest Groups Filing Briefs

Citizens for Decency Through Law (formerly Citizens for Decent Literature)	8[a]	American Civil Liberties Union and affiliates	22
Morality in Media	2	Council for Periodical Distributors Assoc.	6
American Parents Committee	1	Assoc. of American Publishers	6
Covenant House	1	Authors League of America	5
N.Y. State Catholic Welfare Committee	1	American Library Assoc. and affiliates	4
		International Periodical Distributors Assoc.	5
		American Book Publishers Council	4
		American Booksellers Assoc.	4
		Motion Picture Assoc. of America	3
		National Assoc. of College Stores	3

[a]In addition to the group *amicus* briefs, C. Keating, the organization's founder, filed 8 additional briefs.

Decency Through Law). This group filed eight *amicus* briefs, while its founder, Charles H. Keating, Jr., filed eight additional briefs for a total of sixteen in the forty-two cases analyzed.

The other single-issue group desiring to restrict access rights was the New York–based antipornography organization, Morality in Media, founded in 1962, which filed *amicus* briefs in two cases. Three more groups supporting restricted access were two family- and child-oriented organizations—American Parents Committee and Covenant House—and the New York State Catholic Welfare Committee. Each of these groups filed one *amicus* brief.

A narrow range of interest groups have petitioned the Supreme Court to expand public access to information with no limitations. These included the American Civil Liberties Union and its state affiliates and groups representing authors, publishing houses, and the arts. The American Library Association, the American Jewish Congress, the Metropolitan Committee for Religious Liberty, the Committee on Constitutional Liberties, and the National Lawyers Guild also filed such briefs. Among these groups, the ACLU traditionally has been most active in lobbying both the Supreme Court and Congress on free speech and press issues. During this period, the ACLU or its state affiliates filed twenty-two *amicus* briefs in twelve different cases.

The largest number of organizations petitioning the Supreme Court are motivated by self-interest and principle. These include organizations of authors, publishing houses, presses, and distributors such as the Council for Periodical Distributors Association and the Association of American Publishers, both filing *amicus* briefs in six cases each. The Authors League of America, which submitted five briefs, has been active before the Supreme Court, the Congress, and administrative agencies. Civil libertarians, libraries, museums, artists, and presses all have favored free access to pornography except where minors and nonconsenting adults were involved. Among those groups representing the press, the more established groups filed *amicus* briefs in support of media access to obscenity. Because the Supreme Court was supportive of the free press during the period in question, the antipornography watchdog groups focused their energies on the legislative branch.

Table 2.3 indicates which groups either testified before the Congress or submitted written statements on the question of pornography during the years 1953–1982. A very different pattern of group access emerges than in the case of the judiciary. More than three times as many groups favoring restrictions on obscenity testified before Congress as did organizations in favor of expanded public access. Among the 107 groups that testified against obscenity, religious organizations predominated. The major exceptions to this pattern were the American Lutheran church and the Methodist TV, Radio, and Film, Committee, both of which favored greater public access. However, despite their increased numbers, the Catholic and Protestant groups that testified against pornography generally did not express the same sort of stridency as did single-issue groups such as Citizens for Decency Through

TABLE 2.3 Testimony by Interest Groups Before Congressional Hearings on Obscenity[a]

	Classification of Interest Groups Giving Testimony	
	To Restrict Access	To Expand Access
Government	8	4
Parent/child	1	
Single-issue	14	
Law-related	1	4
Religious	38	2
Health-related	11	1
Education	3	1
Multi-issue	10	2
Arts	3	2
Authors/press	7	13
Fraternal/ethnic	3	
Labor/business	4	1
Women's groups	4	
Museums/libraries	—	1
Total	107	31

Most Active Interest Groups Giving Testimony

	Number of Statements		Number of Statements
Citizens for Decency Through Law	18	American Civil Liberties Union and affiliates	13
U.S. Postal Service	16	American Book Publishers Council	6
American Legion	6	Authors League of America	4
National Assoc. of Evangelicals	3	U. S. Postal Service	4
Methodist Church--Bd. of Temperance	3	Assoc. of American Publishers	3
National Council of Catholic Men	3	Direct Mail Advertising Assoc.	2
National Assoc. of Letter Carriers	3	American Library Assoc.	2
Morality in Media	2	American Lutheran Church	2
Philadelphia Citizens Committee Against Pornography	2		
Catholic War Veterans of U.S.A.	2		
St. Barnabas Medical Center (N.J.)	2		
National Womens' Christian Temperance Union	2		

[a]Includes testimony or written statements before thirty-seven congressional hearings during the period 1957-1984.

Law. This group, a legally oriented antiobscenity organization, has been involved for years in filing *amicus* briefs and in staging grass-roots campaigns against pornography. Most of the single-issue groups to petition the Congress, in fact, were affiliates of the Citizens for Decency Through Law, except for testimony from Eradication of Smut and Morality in Media. The U.S. Postal Service appeared before every committee of Congress when the mailing of pornography was at issue. As expected, Postal Service representatives tended to be sympathetic to restrictions on pornography, although the Postal Service did testify on behalf of expanded access in a few of the hearings. Groups of physicians, hospitals, and psychiatrists also were supportive of restricting access.

The American Library Association, arts groups, and associations of authors and press associations testified in favor of public access, just as they had done before the Supreme Court. But there were exceptions. Those author and press groups affiliated with religious organizations, such as the *Christian Science Monitor, Christian Herald,* and the children's publication *Jack and Jill,* argued for restrictions. Veterans organizations, school groups, and local chambers of commerce generally favored restricting access to obscenity. The American Legion, in fact, most frequently advocated restrictions. One curious omission from these data are feminist groups, which, by and large, have been extremely critical of pornography. Yet the only women's groups to offer testimony before Congress were the more traditional organizations, such as the Federation of Women's Clubs, the National Women's Christian Temperance Union, and the Women's Democratic Club of Philadelphia. Newer feminist groups such as Women Against Pornography, Take Back the Night, Women Against Violence in Pornography, the Feminist Anti-Censorship Task Force, and Women Against Violence Against Women, although concerned about pornography and violence against women, chose not to express their views before Congress.

Apart from the lobbying activities of antiobscenity groups at the national level, how effective are such organizations at the grass-roots level? Their effectiveness seems to be uneven at best. Local affiliates of national organizations often have engaged in censorship campaigns. Morality in Media, a single-issue antipornography group active in various cities, focused its efforts in 1984 on Buffalo, New York. The group wanted to remove nudity and sex from the Playboy TV channel there, but Morality in Media's protests were not persuasive with the Buffalo City Council because cable TV still was considered a personal option paid for by the subscriber. In other instances where similar campaigns have been mounted, success has been limited. A study by Harrell R. Rodgers of censorship campaigns in eighteen communities found that most ended in failure in terms of any long-run suppression. In the short run, such efforts kept some publications off the newsstands temporarily. But only rarely was anyone prosecuted. Any agreements between the wholesalers and the retailers to suppress obscene publications never lasted long. In five communities where the censorship campaigns were very active, nevertheless, they had no real impact on newsdealers and minimal effect on community leaders. Censorship failed because the booksellers successfully appealed to the courts and local officials failed to back the censorship campaigns. Rodgers concluded that because antipornography groups were unable to rally public opinion, "those who attempted to censor basically had to do so alone," and they had to settle for limited, short-term, or symbolic successes.[52]

FEDERALISM

Because Supreme Court rulings on pornography often have been vague and imprecise, the Court's guidelines frequently have been misunderstood or simply ignored by states and localities. As a result, compliance with the Supreme Court decisions on obscenity and pornography was uncertain in many states.

Localities have allowed and, in some instances, encouraged restrictive antiobscenity campaigns in their communities, but most have not been too successful, even in conservative areas. One such campaign in Atlanta was directed by Hinson McAuliffe, the Fulton County solicitor general. In 1977, he made an all-out attempt not only to arrest the actors and actresses involved in the production of *Oh, Calcutta,* but he also attempted to take such soft-core publications as *Playboy, Penthouse,* and *Hustler* from city bookstores. Larry Flynt, the publisher of *Hustler,* traveled to Atlanta in order to operate a newsstand for one day and thereby dare the prosecutor to arrest him. McAuliffe quickly obliged. But McAuliffe's efforts were not supported by most city officials; the Atlanta police refused to assist him, and he was forced to use county deputies to make arrests. His actions also aroused the opposition of civil libertarians, newspaper editorialists, and media elites. With such opposition, public apathy, and indifference by law enforcement officials, long-term reform became impossible in Atlanta, and McAuliffe's zealous activities were brought to an end.

The situation in Des Moines, Iowa, illustrates the frustrations of many cities trying to control pornography without going to the lengths Atlanta did. Here the city council passed an ordinance in 1975 requiring masseuses to obtain permits from the city and forbidding masseuses from offering "sexual services." That law zoned massage parlors to the outer limits of the city and banned "outcalls" of sexual services to residents of motels and homes. Yet Des Moines was unable to bar nude photography sessions or nude encounters, where an undressed woman discussed sex problems with her customer. Nor did the city have a law against pornographic movie houses or bookstores so long as these establishments did not allow minors on their premises; nor could the city ordinance restrict massage parlors, nude dancing, or outcall sexual services located in the county. Prosecution rarely occurred because open soliciting did not take place.[53]

That same year, the city of Chicago, under the leadership of Mayor Richard J. Daley, devised a unique system to counteract pornography. Chicago political leaders in cooperation with the Cook County Chancery Court padlocked twenty-four massage parlors under authority of the common law courts of equity. The city ordinance allowed the city to "abate a nuisance by locking it up."[54]

Cities and counties also have written some unusual ordinances that raise important constitutional questions. On November 23, 1983, an ordinance introduced in the Minneapolis City Council held that pornography discriminated against women. The ordinance defined pornography as "the sexually explicit subordination of women; graphically depicted, whether in pictures or words" and categorized it as one type of discrimination based on gender.[55] By defining pornography in this way, individuals could bring lawsuits based on the city's civil rights ordinance. The antipornography ordinance was supported by the Minneapolis City Council, but Mayor Donald Fraser vetoed it on the grounds that it was ambiguous and vague.

Although this approach failed in Minneapolis, its effect was felt in other communities throughout the United States. One direct consequence of the Minneapolis experiment was the enactment of a similar antipornography ordinance in Indianapolis, which was adopted by the Indianapolis City and County Council in May 1984. The ordinance would have allowed city residents who believed their rights were violated by obscene material to file complaints with the city Office of Equal Opportunity, which could issue, subject to court review, a cease-and-desist order against the distributor.

Civil libertarians viewed the Minneapolis and Indianapolis ordinances as legal censorship. That logic swayed federal district court judge Sarah Evans Barker who, although a Reagan appointee, declared the Indianapolis ordinance unconstitutional because it encroached on the right of free expression. That view was upheld by the Supreme Court on February 24, 1986, when it deemed the Indianapolis law to be unconstitutional. In light of the high court's action, a similar antipornography ordinance ready for enactment in Suffolk County, New York, was withdrawn from consideration.

In addition to these innovative but unsuccessful local approaches to pornography, voters in several states also have had opportunities to express their views on limiting pornography through referenda. The results show no obvious consistency. In 1977, a Washington state referendum that prohibited the additional establishment of adult bookstores and movie theaters in the state was passed by 54.4 percent of the voting electorate. But a 1984 referendum in conservative, Mormon-dominated Utah to prevent "indecent material" on cable television was rejected by a two-to-one margin. Likewise, in the small town of Vista, California, a proposition demanding that "indecent material" not be shown on the Playboy cable TV narrowly lost, with 7,323 opposing it and 6,394 in favor.[56]

One of the few policies on which state, local, and federal government can agree is opposition to child pornography. Since 1977, almost every state has enacted strong regulations against child pornography. Except for Minnesota and California, the states generally require felony penalties for violating child antipornography laws. Less than half of these states restricting "kiddieporn" require that legal obscenity be proved before a work can be banned.

For example, twenty states prohibit child pornography whether or not it is obscene, while fifteen others require that material must be proven obscene before action is taken.[57]

There remains a fundamental problem regarding a state's right to determine obscenity standards: It is not obvious that the Supreme Court is willing to grant much authority to the states and localities in order to control obscenity. Nor is it obvious what "local community standards" means or which agency of local government would determine its meaning. Looking back to the 1964 case of *Jacobellis v. Ohio,* 378 U.S. 184 (1964), for example, Justice William Brennan said that "an allegedly obscene work must be determined on the basis of a national Constitution," but Justices Earl Warren and Tom Clark, although they concurred, argued to the contrary: "I believe that there is no provable 'national standard' and perhaps there should be none. At all events, this court has not been able to enunciate one, and it would be unreasonable to expect local courts to divine one." As a result of this decision, states themselves felt free to disagree as to what standard of obscenity ought to prevail. Nine states argued for a national standard, four states opted for a state standard, and four more looked to "local standards" as the preferred measure of pornography.

Nor has a resolution of this policy confusion come from the Burger Court, because it retains the final say on what is considered obscene. In the case of *Jenkins v. Georgia,* 413 U.S. 160 (1974), the Burger Court refused to accept the judgment of the Georgia Supreme Court that, in Albany, Georgia, at least, the movie *Carnal Knowledge* was considered obscene. The Court asserted that *Carnal Knowledge* could not be considered obscene by any standard and argued further that "it would be a serious misreading of *Miller [Miller v. California]* to conclude that juries have unbridled discretion in determining what is 'patently offensive.'" The "local community standard" was further weakened in *Pope v. Illinois,* no. 85-1973 (1987), where the Court said that it had to give way to a "reasonable person" standard for assessing the literary, artistic, political, or scientific value of explicit material.

Even had the high court supported local standards in such cases, it is doubtful whether there would be sufficient consensus among local decision-makers to agree on what community standard would prevail. In a study of Detroit, for example, Douglas H. Wallace found that "there was no uniform standard or criterion being used by these subjects [those being tested] as they evaluated the stimulus items. The variability of their responses . . . in their mean ratings of the pictures, and the differences between the 'sexual liberals' and 'sexual conservatives' do not support the *single contemporary community standard* hypothesis."[58] Even in an Idaho town of forty-three thousand, whose views one might expect to be more homogeneous, a 1978 study found that "pornography was dichotomized differently by different individuals."[59] Thus, not even in this medium-sized city did an obvious community standard emerge.

A new device for combatting pornography—the use of zoning laws to segregate purveyors of obscenity—was upheld by the Supreme Court in

1986. In the case of *City of Renton v. Playtime Theatres*, no. 84-1360 (1986), the Supreme Court permitted local zoning boards broad authority to control the location of adult movie theaters. In Renton, Washington, a zoning ordinance isolated adult theaters to an industrial area. Justice William Rehnquist argued that although adult movie theaters needed "a reasonable opportunity to open and operate," there was no requirement that they "be able to obtain sites at bargain prices." The zoning ordinance did not suppress a protected right, Rehnquist argued, because the ordinance was not directed at the contents of the film. Instead, he saw the law as designed to protect the "quality of urban life" as well as to show concern for the potential harm to children and for "neighborhood blight." But Justices William Brennan and Thurgood Marshall dissented on the grounds that the ordinance could "selectively impose limitations on the location of a movie theater based exclusively on the content of the films showing there." The law, they felt, was designed to "suppress the content of adult movies" because some local people were offended. Brennan also countered that the argument that zoning helped prevent neighborhood blight was a "purely speculative conclusion" based upon no evidence.[60]

PUBLIC OPINION

Is pornography a salient issue for most citizens? There is enough opinion research on this topic to draw some conclusions about how the public assesses this problem. At the outset, one thing is certain: Pornography is pervasive in almost all communities. A 1977 Gallup Poll found that x-rated movies, adult bookstores, and even massage parlors existed in communities of all sizes, ranging from those with more than 1 million people to towns with populations of 2,500. Only in rural areas where there were less than 2,500 inhabitants were movie theaters not showing x-rated films.[61] Moreover, this situation was troubling to the public. A 1985 *Time*–Yankelovich Clancy Shulman poll indicated that 63 percent of the public was "somewhat concerned" with the proliferation of pornography.[62] Despite the 1967 president's commission, which suggested that there was no evidence linking pornography to social deviancy, most citizens saw such a relationship. A large majority in a 1985 *Newsweek* poll believed that explicit pornography can encourge some people to commit rape or sexual violence (73 percent) and 76 percent felt that people exposed to pornography lost respect for women. Moreover, 67 percent said that pornographic materials could lead to a breakdown of public morals.[63] Research by Herbert McClosky and Alida Brill in 1978–1979 found that 58 percent of their respondents believed that selling pornographic films, books, and magazines lowered a community's moral standards. This view was held by a majority (52 percent) of community leaders but only 33 percent of the legal elites, which suggested a division between the legal system and the political community.[64]

While most people in the country (92 percent in 1986), much like the late Supreme Court justice Potter Stewart, had confidence in their innate ability to determine for themselves what pornography was,[65] agreement on what to do about it was less obvious, although in most cases a majority favored restrictions. Most commonly branded pornographic by the public were depictions of sexual intercourse in magazines (84 percent), x-rated movies (77 percent), and depictions of homosexual sex acts (86 percent).[66] The 1985 *Newsweek* survey also revealed that most people would ban violence in pornography. The respondents favored a ban on sexual violence in magazines (73 percent), in movies (68 percent), and in video cassettes (63 percent). Where there was no violence portrayed in sexual materials, the public's tolerance increased. However, there remained considerable support among a plurality of the respondents in two instances (magazines showing sex acts and x-rated movies) for a complete ban on obscene materials (see Table 2.4).[67]

Opinion surveys also have validated arguments that the public wanted to adopt more protective standards for minors under eighteen years of age, who were exposed most frequently to pornography.[68] Some 53 percent of the public supported laws restricting the distribution of pornography to youth, while fewer than 50 percent would support such a ban for all persons.[69]

The 1977 Gallup Poll revealed that opposition to pornography hardened to the extent that 45 percent wanted stricter standards compared to the 6 percent who favored a relaxation.[70] Demographic breakdowns in this survey found that greater support for stricter standards came from people living in the South (53 percent) and Midwest (48 percent), while those in the East (41 percent) and the West (36 percent) were less supportive. Persons with less education, who were older, married, and female also tended to favor stricter pornography standards. A 1986 poll confirmed these findings: 49 percent of respondents with less than a high school education, 67 percent of those greater than sixty years of age, 45 percent of those married, and 52 percent of the women favored laws against the distribution of pornography. When questioned about whether only persons under eighteen should be protected, the percentage in these categories jumped to 96–97 percent support for laws restricting distribution to youth.[71]

An early study based on 1970 data by Marc Glassman determined that tolerance for pornography varied according to residence. Persons in metropolitan areas were more willing to accept "visual and textual depictions of nudity and intercourse as well as some textual depictions of presumably deviant sexual behavior" than were those in nonmetropolitan areas.[72] But very different findings were revealed in the 1977 Gallup Poll noted previously, with greatest support (52 percent) for stricter standards being expressed by residents of cities with 1 million or more population, which suggested that big city residents might be tiring of the spread of obscenity. The research also showed a gender gap in attitudes about pornography. A 1986 *Washington Post*–ABC News poll found that, compared to 41 percent of the men who held this opinion, 72 percent of the women felt that current laws were not strict enough.[73]

TABLE 2.4 Public Attitudes Toward Pornography and Censorship

	1973	1986
"There should be laws against the distribution of pornography to persons under 18"	48%	53%
"There should be laws against the distribution of pornography whatever the age"	43%	43%
"There should be no laws forbidding the distribution of pornography"	9%	4%

"Do you think laws should totally ban any of the following activities in your community, allow them as long as there is no public display--or impose no restrictions at all for adult audiences?"

	Total ban	No public display	No restrictions on adults
Magazines that show nudity	21%	52%	26%
Magazines that show adults having sexual relations	47%	40%	12%
Magazines that show sexual violence	73%	20%	6%
Theaters showing X-rated movies	40%	37%	20%
Theaters showing movies that depict sexual violence	68%	21%	9%
Sale or rental of X-rated video cassettes for home viewing	32%	39%	27%
Sale or rental of video cassettes featuring sexual violence	63%	23%	13%

Source: Reported in "Opinion Roundup: A Pornography Report," *Public Opinion* (September/October, 1986), pp. 31, 33. The top three questions were asked in the NORC General Social Survey of 1986; the bottom seven questions were asked in a Gallup Poll done for *Newsweek* in 1985.

But should there be a national or local standard on pornography? The 1977 Gallup Poll found that people in localities with adult bookstores and massage parlors divided about evenly in favoring a national (41 percent) or a community (42 percent) standard, but 51 percent of the residents of communities without such establishments wanted a national standard.[74] McClosky and Brill reported that 43 percent of the public, 40 percent of the community leaders, and 29 percent of the legal elites favored community standards for judging pornographic films.[75] By 1985, according to the *Newsweek* poll, 47 percent wanted a national standard, but 43 percent favored community standards. Only 5 percent of the sample wanted no standards for judging obscenity.[76]

SUMMARY

Obscenity is a classic example of the fundamental conflict between the constitutional guarantees of free expression and the collective goal that society represent some kind of moral order. Beginning in the nineteenth century, the existence of antiobscenity laws represented the majority will of the body politic, as reflected in the actions of state legislatures and the Congress, and the judiciary did not upset this normative structure until the 1960s. Then an activist Warren Court refused to ban publications on the grounds that Congress and the states had used. This gave the Supreme Court an exclusive authority to define obscenity on a case-by-case basis.

Given the constitutional obstacles to limiting the spread of obscenity to adults, the states and Congress turned to child pornography as their overriding concern. Various enactments since the late 1970s regulated child "porn" without bothering, in many cases, to prove the materials "obscene" before action could be taken to restrict public access. This approach by Congress has since been upheld by the Burger Court in its *Ferber* ruling.

More recently, pornography has been exploited by Republican presidents as a campaign issue. Richard Nixon focused public attention on his anti-pornography legislation as a means of dramatizing congressional inaction on his domestic program. For Ronald Reagan, antipornography was one objective in his broad-based conservative "social" agenda. That Democrats Kennedy, Johnson, and Carter did not exploit this issue politically shows the more liberal constituency base of the Democratic party and its traditional concern with civil liberties.

Although the nation's citizens generally oppose rigid censorship of books and films, there exists a consensus against absolute free expression. The polls show that most people want some type of obscenity standard regarding the materials available for public distribution, and recent legislation to curb child pornography finds a sympathetic public opinion. Even groups representing authors, presses, and distributors reluctantly testify before Congress in favor of limiting obscene materials to adults only. Opponents of government censorship, notably the ACLU, focus their energies on the judiciary, which is receptive to arguments upholding freedom of expression.

Against this background, the 1985 Meese Commission reopened the debate about obscenity by embracing a conservative, law-and-order approach to the problem. The commission's report comes at a time of political reaction against the social permissiveness of the 1960s and 1970s and of heightened concern about child pornography. There are signs, therefore, that the 1985 commission report may have more impact on sympathetic policymakers than the 1967 commission study had on the political leadership.

Chapter Three

CRIME

Due Process Liberalism Versus Law-and-Order Conservatism

Brent S. Steel and Mary Ann E. Steger

During the course of the last several decades, debate about appropriate public policy on crime has been particularly intense in the United States. The debate reflects an underlying conflict between two schools of thought about how those accused and convicted should be treated by government. The *civil libertarian* approach emphasizes the rights of such individuals; the opposing *law-and-order* approach is primarily concerned with protecting the public order.

Since the Warren Court (1953–1969) began to demonstrate its concern with the expansion of due process and legal counsel rights of defendants, one very contentious point in this debate has been illegal search and seizure, in particular the use of evidence gained by police in unauthorized searches and seizures. Civil libertarians support the prevailing Court view that such evidence must be excluded and argue that without this "exclusionary" rule, the police would have little incentive to respect citizens' privacy rights. Law-and-order advocates would use such evidence at trial because they believe that legal technicalities allow defendants who are indisputably guilty to escape conviction and punishment.

Most criminal laws are regulatory because their intent is to define what behavior is prohibited and punishable in U.S. society. But criminal regulations are different from economic regulations, where one side usually wants government controls while the other is opposed, because conflict instead focuses on the *types* of solution to crime. Crime policy also involves conflict about moral questions because it regulates the "moral temper" of society.

The Debate on the Causes of Crime

The debate about crime policy is fueled by a profound disagreement about the causes of crime. On this issue criminologists disagree, although most identify three major types of causal explanation of crime. The "sociogenic" school focuses on the environment and places primary responsibility for crime on society.[1] Poverty, lack of education, and high unemployment often are cited as significant causes of crime. This explanation also considers the impact on the individual of unstable homes, the absence of affection, lack of discipline, and improper socialization into social norms. The sociogenic approach reflects a liberal political ideology. Proponents argue that if sufficient social welfare programs were available, the disadvantaged would not turn to criminal behavior. Given that the disadvantaged are overrepresented among convicted felons, there is prima facie evidence to this line of argument.

The "psychogenic" school is a psychological approach that considers the individual's *propensity* and *inducement* to commit crime.[2] That propensity is determined by the individual's ability to conceptualize right and wrong, to manage impulses, and to anticipate future consequences. Acceptance of risk and willingness to inflict injury also are predispositions to crime. Inducement refers to situational factors, such as access and opportunity, that act as incentives to crime. According to this view, the individual is responsible for his/her behavior because a *choice* is made whether to commit a crime. This view underlies conservative thought and explains why the view's advocates favor severe penalties (such as capital punishment) thought to *deter* individuals from making the *wrong* choices. Considerable prima facie evidence also exists for this position. Given that human behavior is generally rational, it stands to reason that the manipulation of penalties would affect choices to commit or to avoid unlawful acts.

The third approach is referred to as the "biogenic" or "sociobiological" explanation. This view is less common among criminologists but has been popularized by James Q. Wilson. This school relates criminal behavior to such biological phenomena as brain tumors, endocrine abnormalities, neurological dysfunctions from prenatal and postnatal experiences, and chromosomal abnormalities.[3] Preventive crime policies favored by the proponents of this theoretical perspective entail the development of appropriate screening and other diagnostic tests for persons suspected of such physical or mental disorders. As in the case of the first two types of explanations of crime, there again is considerable prima facie support for this approach to the etiology of crime. Sensationalized stories and news coverage of mass murderers, serial killers, arsonists, and sex offenders often describe perpetrators of such gruesome crimes as sociopathic personalities.

Characteristics of Offenders

Given these differing explanations for criminal behavior, it is instructive to observe just who are the criminal offenders in the United States. The statistics displayed in Table 3.1 provide information on the gender, race, ethnic origin, and age of persons arrested and convicted of crimes in 1981. These statistics

TABLE 3.1 Characteristics of Offenders in the United States, 1981

| | U.S. Population, 1980 (226,545,805) | Index Crime Arrestees | | Convicted Jail Inmates (91,411) | State Prison Inmates (340,639) | Federal Prison Inmates (28,133) |
		Violent (464,826)	Property (1,828,928)			
Gender						
Male	49%	90%	79%	94%	96%	94%
Female	51	10	21	6	4	6
Race						
White	86	53	67	58	52	63
Black	12	46	31	40	47	35
Other	2	1	2	2	1	2
Ethnic Origin						
Hispanic	6	12	10	10	9	16
Non-Hispanic	94	88	90	90	91	84
Age						
-15	23	5	14	0	0	0
15-19	9	25	36	14	7	0
20-29	18	42	31	53	56	34
30-39	14	17	11	19	25	40
40-49	10	7	4	9	8	17
50-59	16	3	2	4	3	7
60+	16	1	2	1	1	2

Source: U.S. Department of Justice, *Report to the Nation on Crime and Justice* (Washington, D.C.: U.S. Government Printing Office, (October 1983), p. 31.

indicate that the majority of offenders arrested and convicted for all offenses were white, male, and young. This pattern held true for persons arrested for both violent and property crimes, and it applied equally for inmates of county jails, state prisons, and federal prisons. It should be noted, of course, that blacks were greatly overrepresented vis-à-vis their percentage of the U.S. population. While blacks constituted only 12 percent of the U.S. population, they constituted between 31 and 47 percent of the persons convicted of crimes in the several categories of violent and property crimes. This disproportionate representation was directly equivalent to socioeconomic inequalities obtaining among whites and blacks, a fact that led many scholars of the sociogenic school to final proof of their argument concerning the societal origins of criminal behavior.

Although this pattern of background characteristics was similar for persons arrested and convicted for crimes considered in the aggregate, arrest rates for specific crimes exhibited somewhat diverse patterns. For example, homicide was most prevalent among those older than twenty-five, car theft was most prevalent among those younger than eighteen, and white collar crime was most likely committed by older, more affluent persons. Crimes of violence were committed most frequently by persons of low socioeconomic status. Burglary rates were highest among those younger than eighteen, and robbery was most prevalent among those between eighteen and twenty-four years old. Most other offenses—such as fraud, gambling, vagrancy, drunken behavior, and crimes against the family—most likely were committed by those older than twenty-five years of age.[4] Males, rather than females, were much more likely to be arrested for a criminal offense, although there has been some decline in this difference. In sheer numbers, many more whites were arrested each year than blacks, but the rate of arrest—as a percentage of black and nonblack populations—was much higher for blacks. In recent years, however, these racial differences in arrest rates have declined.

PUBLIC OPINION

There are many forms of criminal behavior in the United States; the most commonly referred-to categories of crime include violent crimes against persons (street crime), property crime, white collar crime, victimless crime, and organized crime. The general public seems to pay little attention to most types of crime except for violent street crime and property crime— crimes that tend to be accorded considerable attention by the media. White collar crime, which involves millions and millions of dollars each year in tax evasion, embezzlement, price fixing, and stock fraud, generally goes unreported in the media and is seldom thought of among the public. Former attorney general Ramsey Clark has observed that bank embezzlements annually cost ten times more than bank robberies do. In this connection, Clark has noted that "one corporate price-fixing conspiracy criminally converted more money each year it continued than all of the hundreds of thousands of burglaries, larcenies, or thefts in the entire nation during those same years."[5] Despite this fact, there seems to be far less public concern for this type of crime than for violent street or property crime; it should be noted, moreover, that penalties for white collar crimes usually are light.

In 1977, a national survey of crime severity was conducted in the United States; the survey asked the U.S. public to rank the seriousness of several specific kinds of offenses. The results of this survey indicated, in part, that citizens made distinctions about the seriousness of crimes depending on the circumstances involved. For example, "an assault [was] viewed as more serious if a parent assault[ed] a child than if a man assault[ed] his wife, even though both victims require[d] hospitalization. These differences [were] greater for assaults that result in death."[6] In general, crimes involving the use of violence were most likely to be perceived as very serious by the public. High on the public's list of severe crimes were planting a bomb that killed people in a public building, robbing at gunpoint a victim who then was killed after a struggle, stabbing someone to death, running a narcotics ring, and forcible rape. Much less severe were petty crimes—such as picking a victim's pocket of $100—or so-called victimless crimes—prostitution, smoking marijuana, public drunkenness, vagrancy, and the like.

In regard to frequency of crime occurrence, it is true that the United States has a distinctly high rate of both violent and property crime when compared to other advanced democratic nations.[7] In comparison to West Germany, England and Wales, France, Australia, and Japan for the year 1978, the United States had the highest overall crime rate, which included all reported crimes. The pattern was similar for the criminal ratio (the number of criminals per 100,000 population) and the homicide and larceny rates. In fact, the homicide rate in the United States was more than double that of any other country in this group. Given these unfavorable comparisons with nations the United States likes to compare itself against, it seems clear that concern for and dialogue about crime in the United States are well justified.

The public is very concerned about violent crime and property crime, and a major reason for this concern is that during 1981 nearly 33 percent of all households in the United States (around 25 million) were victimized by violence or theft. Approximately 21 percent of the nation's households were victimized by at least one theft, 2 percent were victimized by theft of a motor vehicle, and 6 percent had members of the household who were victims of at least one violent crime of rape, robbery, or aggravated/simple assault. Businesses, during this same time period, were robbed at a rate ten times higher than was the rate for private persons. Overall, property crimes outnumbered violent crimes by a ratio of nine to one.[8]

The public is most concerned with specific violent and property crimes, and these include murder, rape, aggravated assault, robbery, and burglary. A presidential commission in the 1960s concluded that the "prevalence of the two crimes of burglary and robbery is a significant, if not a major, reason for America's alarm about crime."[9] National surveys conducted at this time by the President's Commission on Law Enforcement and the Administration of Justice found that more than half the respondents were concerned about robbery and burglary. One third of the public also indicated that they felt unsafe about walking alone at night in their own neighborhoods.[10]

As the public became more concerned about crime during the 1960s, "law and order" became a rallying point for politicians on the conservative end of the political spectrum. It should be noted that public desire for greater police authority and more forceful anticrime action was not limited to consideration of violent and property crime alone. A survey conducted among homeowners in the Boston metropolitan area found that the public also was concerned about public immorality, disorderly youth, juvenile delinquency, and unruly behavior in public places.[11] The elderly and poor in particular were extremely concerned about crime, and concern about crime as a social problem was greater than that for other more traditional urban concerns such as job opportunities, affordable housing, environmental pollution, and mass transportation. These findings are not surprising, of course, because the poor and elderly are most likely to live in older city neighborhoods where the occurrence of violent and property crimes is the most frequent.

Although the public's focus is primarily on violent and property crime, crime in general typically has been considered an important national problem by the U.S. public. Although crime never has ranked as the "most important issue" nationally, it has appeared consistently in polls asking people to enumerate the nation's problems. These findings attest to the fact that crime concerns remain among the most salient for U.S. citizens. In a December 1985 Gallup Poll, for example, crime was considered the nation's "most important problem" by 3 percent of the population. Although seven other national problems were considered more important by the public in this survey, among the "top ten" problems listed *only crime* remains among the "top ten" throughout the length of time that Gallup has been asking this survey question.

The belief among the population that crime is a national problem leads to a fear of being victimized by crime, and this fear is likely to be stronger in metropolitan centers than in the United States as a whole. In addition, some groups in society tend to express more fearfulness than others. In general, blacks are more fearful than are other racial or ethnic groups, people who are widowed, separated or divorced are more fearful than are the never or currently married, and older people are more fearful than are younger people. When comparing men and women, it is interesting to note that the fear of crime falls disproportionately on women, even though men are twice as likely to suffer from crime as are women.[12]

Generally speaking, the more a person is concerned about crime and disorder, the more likely it is that that person will support more stringent "punishment" as a "deterrent" against crime. For example, as drug addiction becomes of increasingly greater concern, some demands for governmental actions are translated into legislation. Efforts to "toughen the law" include more serious penalties for the manufacture, sale, and use of banned substances. Support for the death penalty for persons convicted of murder is another example of where this logic applies. There has been substantial support in the United States during the past forty years for the death penalty, and the percentage in favor of capital punishment is currently at its nadir. Statistics on the percentage of the population favoring and opposing the death penalty since 1936 are reported in Table 3.2; these figures indicate that 72 percent of those surveyed in 1985 expressed support for the death penalty. Of course, for law-and-order proponents the death penalty has been among the most favored public policies because it is a means to curb the incidence of violent crimes *and* a just punishment (an eye for an eye, a tooth for a tooth) for a grievous offense against society.

TABLE 3.2 Support for the Death Penalty for Murder: Gallup Polls

	1936	1937	1953	1960	1965	1966	1969	1971	1972	1976	1978	1981	1985
percent favor	61	65	68	51	45	42	51	49	57	65	62	66	72

Source: Based on data from *The Gallup Report* (January/February 1985), Nos. 232-233, p. 4.

This increase in support for the death penalty coincides with a rising fear of crime among the U.S. public. The Gallup Poll's 1985 report on crime showed that nearly half of the public was fearful of venturing out after dark. This poll also found that one person in four nationally said that he or she had been physically assaulted or had his or her home broken into during a twelve-month period.[13] The question on the death penalty, given Gallup Poll experience, is a good barometer of hard-line or soft-line moods in the nation toward crime. Among those who support capital punishment, the survey showed that "support would decline dramatically (from 72 percent to 56 percent) if life imprisonment, without any possibility of parole, were a certainty for murderers."[14] Support also would decline (from 72 percent to 51 percent) if studies could show conclusively that the death penalty does not act as a deterrent to murder. However, revenge ("an eye for an eye") was given as the favorite reason among supporters to justify the death penalty (Table 3.3). This certainly corresponds to more conservative law-and-order views on crime policy.

This idea of revenge was given some legitimacy in the Supreme Court's decisions on capital punishment. Justice Potter Stewart, writing on *Gregg v. Georgia*, 428 U.S. 153 (1976), stated that "capital punishment is an expression of society's moral outrage at particularly offensive conduct." Stewart went on to say, "Retribution is no longer the dominant objective of the criminal law . . . but neither is it a forbidden objective nor one inconsistent with our respect for the dignity of men." In this case, Justice Stewart wrote the majority opinion, and this majority opinion condoned the use of capital punishment as retribution when grievous crimes were involved.

Nevertheless, most of the populace believe that the death penalty is unfairly applied. "Two-thirds (64 percent) think poor persons are more likely than average or above-average income people to receive the death penalty for the same crime. And four in ten (39 percent) believe blacks are more likely than whites to be sentenced to death for the same crime."[15] There is quite strong support for the death penalty as a policy option among the public, even though the public is aware that capital punishment may not be "fairly" applied across social classes and races.

An indicator of extremist public sentiment on the issue of crime, which reflects a self-sufficiency orientation toward the law-and-order approach to

TABLE 3.3 Reasons for Favoring the Death Penalty Among the U.S. Public, Gallup Poll

Revenge: an "eye for an eye"	30%
Acts as a deterrent	22
Murderers deserve punishment	18
Costly to keep murderers in prison	11
Keeps murderers from killing again	9
Removes potential risk to the community	7
All others	13
No opinion	2
	112[a]

[a]Total adds to more than 100 percent due to multiple responses.

Source: The Gallup Report, nos. 232-233 (January/February 1985): p. 3. Reprinted by permission.

crime prevention, is support for vigilantism. Bernard Goetz, the "subway vigilante" who shot four youths in a New York City subway, has become the subject of much public attention on this topic. National surveys of the public indicate that a large majority hold the view that occurrences such as the New York incident are "sometimes justified" by the circumstances. "A total of 72 percent of Americans hold this view, while an additional 8 percent of hard-liners volunteer that taking the law into one's hands . . . is always justified. Only 17 percent in the survey maintain that such action is never justified."[16] The fear people have of potential victimization is most likely related to this acceptance of methods outside the normal legal process.

JUDICIARY

Although public opinion on the use of the death penalty is likely to be a good measure of the public's mood concerning hard-line policies that fit into the law-and-order tradition, the U.S. Supreme Court nevertheless most directly sets these policies. The Court is sensitive to public sentiments to be sure, but the justices of the federal appellate bench do not necessarily reflect public opinion in their individual and collective decisions. In the area of crime policy in particular, the U.S. Supreme Court often has been a major source of frustration for those subscribing to the law-and-order perspective because of the Court's decisions concerning the constitutional rights of the accused. Since the Warren Court decisions of the 1960s, law-and-order advocates have been most unhappy with the evidentiary rules governing search and seizure, police interrogations, and the taking of confessions. The prevailing sentiment was that "most persons arrested for the more common serious crimes, such as burglary and robbery, have been arrested under circumstances such that no confession is required, no searches need be conducted, and scarcely any police interrogation occurs."[17]

The U.S. Supreme Court under Chief Justice Earl Warren made the protection of the constitutional right to due process the basis of many of its decisions on the rights of the accused. However, not all violations of procedural justice were protected by the Supreme Court. In *Harrington v. California*, 395 U.S. 250 (1969), the Warren Court held that some violations of procedural justice may be regarded as only "harmless error." If there is overwhelming evidence pointing to the guilt of a defendant, a technical violation of due process may not necessarily bring about a reversal of a conviction. Even so, the Warren Court is remembered for those important decisions that extended the rights of citizens in their relationship with the federal government to defendants in their relation to general legal criminal practice; this extension was accomplished by means of the due process clause of the Fourteenth Amendment.

A key concern of procedural justice is the application of the protections found in the Bill of Rights to state courts. After all, most criminal cases are tried in the state courts. During the 1930s and 1940s, some criminal procedural safeguards were "incorporated" into the Fourteenth Amendment in a few cases. These protections included the right to a fair trial and the right to counsel in capital cases (*Powell v. Alabama*, 287 U.S. 45 [1932]); the right to a public trial (in re *Oliver*, 333 U.S. 257 [1948]); and protection against unreasonable searches and seizures (*Wolf v. Colorado*, 338 U.S. 25 [1949]). Notwithstanding these earlier developments, however, the great thrust of incorporation came under the Warren Court. Beginning with *Mapp v. Ohio*, 367 U.S. 643 (1961), the Warren Court incorporated into the Fourteenth Amendment various provisions of the Fourth, Fifth, Sixth, and Eighth Amendments. By the end of the 1960s, protections existed in both federal and state law against unlawful searches and seizures, the right to protection against self-incrimination, and the right to legal counsel for indigent persons accused of serious crimes.

The protections established by the Warren Court were viewed by law-and-order advocates as unnecessary protections for wrongdoers that imposed unwise restraints on the activities of law enforcement personnel; critics of these developments accused the Court of "coddling criminals" and "tying the hands of law enforcement." Subsequent Supreme Court decisions modified many of these protections, and this is especially evident in the interpretation of Fourth Amendment rights against unlawful searches and seizures. In the courtroom, the exclusionary rule—as first defined in *Mapp v. Ohio*—makes illegally obtained evidence inadmissible in federal and state courts. In *U.S. v. Leon*, et al., 52 LW 5155 (1984), the Burger Court (1969–1986) established a good-faith exception to the exclusionary rule in cases where police officers reasonably relied on search warrants issued by a judge or magistrate. The

Court under Chief Justice Warren Burger changed the degree of Fourth Amendment protection provided to citizens in this case by expanding significantly the power of law enforcement agencies to make searches and introduce evidence of questionable origin into court proceedings.

Even though some degree of loosening in Fourth Amendment rights occurred under the auspices of the Burger Court, significant Fourth Amendment protections remain in effect. For example, in *Brown v. Texas*, 443 U.S. 47 (1979), the Court ruled that the police may "stop and frisk" a person only when circumstances justify a reasonable suspicion that the person was involved in a criminal activity. Some protections also exist in cases where the evidence is obtained by electronic surveillance because wiretapping is not allowed without permission from a court (for example, *Silverman v. United States*, 365 U.S. 505 [1961]). Justice Lewis Powell, who has been one of the Court's consistent law-and-order advocates, suggested in 1986 that the Court had gone far enough in trimming Fourth Amendment protections when he led dissenters in two 5–4 decisions involving aerial searches without a warrant. Powell was quoted as saying that authorizing such searches would allow a "gradual decay in Fourth Amendment rights as technology advances."

The Court's decision in *Miranda v. Arizona*, 384 U.S. 436 (1966), also dealt with the rights of suspects. Here the Warren Court laid out a specific code of police conduct. Prior to interrogating suspects, officers must inform suspects of their rights, including the right to be silent and to see an attorney. As was the case with the original decision on illegal searches and seizures, this particular decision angered those advocating a law-and-order perspective. This feeling toward the *Miranda* decision continued into the Reagan administration and was expressed in the following statement by Attorney General Edwin Meese: "The *Miranda* decision was wrong. We managed very well in this country for 175 years without it. Its practical effect is to prevent the police from talking to the person who knows the most about the crime—namely, the perpetrator."[18] The Burger Court modified the *Miranda* rule in *Harris v. New York*, 401 U.S. 222 (1971), when the Court allowed defendants who took the stand to be questioned even if they had never received a *Miranda* warning.

Even though the Burger Court modified the *Miranda* warning requirement in the direction of greater flexibility, which benefited prosecutors, the Court acted to uphold the *Miranda* right in general. In two Michigan murder cases, in which the police continued to question suspects after they had requested attorneys but without the attorneys being present, the Burger Court upheld the *Miranda* ruling. By a 6–3 vote, the convictions in these cases were overturned, and the cases will have to be retried without the benefit of the evidence gained from illegal interrogation. Justice John Paul Stevens wrote for the majority that "the reasons for prohibiting the interrogation of an uncounseled prisoner who has asked for the help of a lawyer are even stronger after he has been formally charged with an offense than before." In addition to *Miranda*, the Court ruled that confessions must be voluntary (*Rogers v. Richmond*, 365 U.S. 534 [1961]), and must result from a free and rational choice (*Spano v. New York*, 360 U.S. 315 [1959]).

The exclusionary rule and the *Miranda* warning are not the only Supreme Court policies that have fueled the civil libertarian–law-and-order debate. This debate has extended to Fifth Amendment protections against double jeopardy, which were applied to the states in *Benton v. Maryland,* 395 U.S. 784 (1969). Defendants also are allowed freedom from excessive bail (*Stack v. Boyle,* 342 U.S. 1 [1951]), and right to trial by jury is required in criminal cases. Most importantly, in 1963 the Supreme Court held that an attorney is constitutionally required for indigent defendants in felony cases (*Gideon v. Wainwright,* 372 U.S. 335 [1963]). This right to counsel regardless of ability to pay was expanded nine years later in *Argersinger v. Hamlin,* 407 U.S. 25 (1972), to misdemeanor cases that might lead to punishment by imprisonment.

Those convicted of crimes are protected by constitutional safeguards imposed upon governmental corrections agencies by the Supreme Court. The Eighth Amendment forbids "cruel and unusual punishments." The Supreme Court has interpreted this language of the Eighth Amendment to greatly limit the use of the death penalty today. For example, capital punishment has been prohibited for some crimes, such as rape (*Coker v. Georgia,* 433 U.S. 584 [1977]). Although in several cases the Court has imposed limits on the use of capital punishment, in principle the Supreme Court has upheld the death penalty and has not considered it in violation of the "cruel and unusual punishment" standard. For crimes such as premeditated murder wherein suitable appeal rights have been observed, the Court permits states to administer the death penalty in pursuit of justice (*Gregg v. Georgia*). Further, the Court has ruled that when applying the death penalty to juveniles, their emotional and mental development must be taken into consideration (*Eddings v. Oklahoma,* 455 U.S. 584 [1977]). The Court has further ruled that persons who participate in robberies where a killing occurs may not be put to death if they themselves did not kill or intend to kill the victim of the crime (*Edmund v. Florida,* 458 U.S. 782 [1982]).

The law-and-order critique of these procedural protections of individuals is based upon the assumption that "it is the defendant, not the state, that has the upper hand. Part of the problem stems from the expansion of the due process rights by the Warren Court." This, then, enhances the possibility that a defendant can be let go because of "a plethora of legal rights as well as attorneys who know how to use these rights to maximize the defendants' chances of acquittal on some legal technicality or other."[19] The result, as Chief Justice Warren Burger has remarked, is that "we have eager and extraordinarily bright young men going into criminal law. They make every motion in the book. It is good to have them, and there has been a lot of good effects from them. But there is also the tendency of defense lawyers today to make a federal case out of every trial. . . . Defense counsel generally are clogging the system by an excess of zeal."[20]

This overload upon the system increases the chances that plea bargaining will take place—a process of negotiation of pleas and charges whereby prosecutors gain convictions to crimes significantly less severe than the actual crimes committed. According to the law-and-order school of thought, defendants are in the position to manipulate the system to their own advantage and avoid responsibility for their choices to commit crimes. Such advocates also argue that plea bargaining practices serve to demoralize the police in their pursuit of criminals; evildoers are apprehended and evidence is amassed for the prosecution of felons, only to have them set free after brief incarceration for a lesser crime.

Civil libertarians and liberals have a vastly different view of the Warren Court rulings on the rights of the accused, as might well be imagined. According to this approach, which has been referred to as the "coercive critique" of the criminal justice system, procedural regulations protecting the accused are necessary because "once arrested, those accused of crime are presumed to be guilty and then subjected to virtually irresistible pressures to plead guilty."[21] Consequently, to the civil libertarians, the *Miranda* warning regarding the individual's right to protection from self-incrimination and right to legal counsel represents some of the best protections imaginable. In this regard, Stuart Scheingold quoted Abraham Blumberg's observation that

> the accused is confronted by definitions of himself which reflect the various worlds of [those who mediate between the accused and the criminal courts]— yet are consistent for the most part in their negative evaluations of him. [They] seize upon a wholly unflattering aspect of his biography to reinterpret his entire personality and justify their present attitude and conduct toward him. Even an individual with considerable personal and economic resources has great difficulty resisting pressures to redefine himself under these circumstances. For the ordinary accused of modest personal, economic, and social resources, the group pressures and definitions of himself are simply too much to bear.[22]

The 1986–1987 term of the U.S. Supreme Court represented the inauguration of the Rehnquist era of the high court, with several cases pending for review. They raised such questions as whether the exclusionary rule should be further modified, whether confessions by mentally ill criminal defendants are acceptable as evidence, and whether defendants' rights are violated in cases where oral testimony is given voluntarily but without a lawyer present after the *Miranda* warning is read. One major ruling issued by the Rehnquist Court in 1987 involved a challenge to Georgia's death penalty law on the grounds that statistical evidence showed that killers of white victims received death sentences more frequently than did killers of black victims. In *McCleskey v. Kemp*, 107 S.Ct. 1756 (1987), the Supreme Court turned back that legal challenge in a close 5–4 vote and argued that statistics showing race-related disparities in the imposition of the death penalty were not enough to sustain constitutional challenges to existing capital punishment laws. This decision was a major blow to the opponents of capital punishment and paved the way for the execution of hundreds of black inmates whose victims were white. Thus, the conflict between civil libertarians and law-and-order proponents is already evident in the early decisions of the Rehnquist Court, as it was in the Warren and Burger years.

FEDERALISM

It is a mistake to assume that constitutional law is created only by a federal judiciary unaffected by state influence. For example, although the exclusionary rule is commonly thought to derive from the Supreme Court decision *Weeks v. U.S.*, 232 U.S. 383 (1914), in actuality, a ruling to the same effect was rendered a decade or so earlier by the Iowa Supreme Court in *State v. Sheridan*, 96 N.W. 730 (1903). Although many people are familiar with *Gideon v. Wainwright* through the writing of Anthony Lewis and the popularization of his historical novel as a major film, hardly anyone knows that the Wisconsin Supreme Court ruled that the state's bill of rights mandated the publicly supported appointment of counsel for indigent defendants, and that this state decision occurred more than a century before *Gideon*.[23] One scholar concluded that since 1970 alone, state high courts have handed down more than two hundred fifty published opinions that held that the constitutional minimums announced by the U.S. Supreme Court were insufficient to satisfy the more stringent requirements of state law.[24]

These recent state court activities are designated the "new federalism" in constitutional law by scholars in the field.[25] Reliance on independent state grounds for court decisions has allowed state appellate courts to avoid potentially adverse reviews by the U.S. Supreme Court. Consequently, this new federalism is generally well received by state court officials. During the era of the Warren Court's activism, many state judges acquiesced to the high court's lead in setting constitutional policy. The Burger Court largely abandoned the leadership role established by the previous court in the area of civil liberties, and during the 1970s many state courts once again actively participated in making policy involving rights for the accused. This newly emboldened state-level court activity is especially evident in social regulatory policymaking; state court opinions reflecting this new activism have been handed down on subjects of direct concern to the law-and-order–civil liberties debate—namely, freedom of expression, equality of treatment, economic due process, criminal procedure.[26]

Between 1974 and 1984, several state courts rendered decisions in favor of criminal defendants that were broader than or co-extensive with the analogous federal rights.[27] In a state of Washington search and seizure case (*State v. Ringer*, 100 Wn. 2nd 686 [1983]), a majority of the court concluded that the protections of Article 1, Section 7 of Washington's Declaration of Rights exceeded the federal Constitution's Fourth Amendment requirements. This conclusion led the Washington high bench to overrule previous decisions and interpret the citizens' right to protection from un-reasonable searches and seizures more broadly than had the Burger Court. The dissenters on the Washington court argued the law-and-order position in stating that the "majority was handcuffing the police." In a second case involving a search and seizure issue, the Washington Supreme Court issued a majority opinion stating that the "federal Constitution only provides minimum protection of individual rights" and does not limit the authority of states "to accord . . . greater rights."[28]

The Case of Capital Punishment

Federal rulings to expand the rights of criminal defendants in the area of the death penalty have followed a clearly liberal, due process line of argument. In contrast, much state action dealing with the issues of the *morality* and *utility* of the death penalty has been in a rather conservative, law-and-order direction. This divergence of perspectives is especially apparent since the *Furman v. Georgia*, 408 U.S. 238 (1972), decision, a case in which five Supreme Court justices declared "capital punishment, as currently administered in the U.S. . . . constitute(s) 'cruel and unusual punishment' as prohibited by the Constitution in the Eighth Amendment . . . and the Fourteenth Amendment" (which prohibits a state from depriving any person of life, liberty, or property without due process of law). This decision spared some 645 death row persons throughout the United States from execution and also overruled the death penalty provisions of forty states, the District of Columbia, and the federal government.[29]

Only two of the five justices constituting the majority in the *Furman* case wrote that capital punishment in and of itself constituted a cruel and unusual punishment. The majority's disapproval centered on the "relatively rare and arbitrary manner in which capital punishment was imposed," but constitutional experts generally assumed that the Supreme Court had not declared capital punishment "unconstitutional per se, but only its unpredictable and fortuitous use."[30] As a result, thirty-five states tightened the laws under which the death penalty was to be inflicted. These state actions after *Furman* characteristically took two directions: (1) the "mandatory" death sentence, which was designed to eliminate sentencing discretion by removing all flexibility from the sentencing process; and (2) "guided discretion" statutes, which were designed to require sentencing judges and juries to consider certain specified "aggravating or mitigating circumstances of the crime and the offender."[31] Ten states, including North Carolina, Louisiana, and Oklahoma, met the *Furman* objections by requiring mandatory death sentences for specified offenses, while other states, such as Georgia, Florida, and Texas, wrote guided discretion statutes that allowed the courts to decide whether the death penalty was fair in light of sentences for similar offenses. In both sets of cases, the states were writing laws that reduced the arbitrariness denounced in *Furman*.

In *Gregg v. Georgia* and the companion cases that were decided on July 2, 1976, the Supreme Court of the United States rejected the mandatory death penalty statutes of Louisiana and North Carolina and upheld the guided discretion statutes of Florida, Georgia, and Texas. The Court also ruled that the death penalty was not inherently cruel and unusual punishment, and the justices in the majority agreed that the Georgia law (and the Texas and Florida laws) did not "wantonly and freakishly impose the death sentence; it is always circumscribed by the legislative guidelines."[32] The actions of the thirty-five state legislatures in response to the *Furman* decision were of evident concern to the justices; in recording his views on the matter, Justice Stewart referred to "society's endorsement of the death penalty for murder," and he noted further that "a heavy burden rests on those who would attack the judgment of the representatives of the people."

In the *Furman* decision, Stewart's concurring opinion stated,

> The instinct for retribution is part of the nature of man, and channeling that instinct in the administration of criminal justice serves an important purpose in promoting the stability of a society governed by law. When people begin to believe that organized society is unwilling or unable to impose upon criminal offenders the punishment they "deserve," then there are sown the seeds of anarchy—of self-help, vigilante justice, and lynch law.

In the *Gregg* decision, Stewart quoted the foregoing opinion and went on to argue,

> Retribution is no longer the dominant objective of the criminal law . . . but neither is it a forbidden objective nor one inconsistent with our respect for the dignity of men. Indeed, the decision that capital punishment may be the appropriate sanction in extreme cases is an expression of the community's belief that certain crimes are themselves so grievous an affront to humanity that the only adequate response may be the penalty of death.

Given that the *Gregg* decision was "announced" by Justice Potter Stewart on behalf of himself and Justices Lewis Powell and John Paul Stevens, with the concurrence of Chief Justice Warren Burger and Justices Byron White, Harry Blackmun, and William Rehnquist, it is evident that even members of the high court have viewed the death penalty as a just punishment for grievous offenses against society in certain circumstances.

In 1967, a nationwide moratorium on executions was imposed in anticipation of the 1972 Supreme Court decision, and this moratorium was not broken until 1977. Actually, few persons were executed after 1977, but a substantial number of prisoners were living under the sentence of death. By 1983, 1,050 persons were on death row, mostly in Florida, Texas, and Georgia, and more than 40 percent of these felons were black.[33] State action to reestablish capital punishment after the *Furman* decision took a variety of forms and occurred during a number of years. The actions taken by state legislatures from 1972 to 1982 are summarized in Table 3.4. Thirty-nine states enacted legislation establishing (or reestablishing) the death penalty.

In the case of twenty-two of these states, newly enacted capital punishment laws were invalidated as unconstitutional either by state benches or federal appellate courts. The states of Alabama, Arizona, Mississippi, and North Carolina went on to revise their statutes through the judicial action of state supreme courts. This revision occurred when courts acted to reinterpret existing death penalty statutes so as to keep them in force as law or to modify them to the same effect. Twenty-six of the states reenacted their post-*Furman* capital punishment laws after state legislatures reworked those statutes to comply with U.S. Supreme Court directives. Nine of the states that went through a process of reenactment also amended the statutes in question through minor additions to or alterations of statutory aggravating circumstances, and six additional states amended their original post-*Furman* statutes without a thorough reworking or reenactment of these pieces of legislation. Information for eleven states does not appear in Table 3.4. Five of these states—Michigan, Minnesota, Wisconsin, Hawaii, and Alaska—have never authorized capital punishment at the state level. The remaining six states—Iowa, Kansas, Maine, Vermont, West Virginia, and North Dakota—have not replaced the statutes under which pre-*Furman* executions were ordered.

State Law Enforcement

In addition to setting crime policy, states along with local governments have the principal responsibility for law enforcement. In recent decades, the role of the federal government in law enforcement has grown, but state and local governments nevertheless continue to carry the major burdens of providing police protection, operating judicial systems, offering probation and parole programs, and maintaining correctional facilities. This primary state/local responsibility is emphasized by the fact that more than one-half million people are employed as state and local government law enforcement personnel, while the federal government employs fewer than fifty thousand persons in all its law enforcement activities. Similarly, state prisons have approximately three hundred thousand inmates compared with about twenty-five thousand in federal prisons.

Generally speaking, the states tend to pursue a law-and-order–high efficiency, deinstitutionalization direction in their decisions on the punishment of state offenders. On the one hand, mandatory minimum sentencing laws requiring prison sentences for certain serious offenses are quite common, and a number of states are using determinate sentencing and elimination of parole in order to "toughen up punishments." Such actions proceed from the law-and-order belief that punishments should fit their crimes and that persons convicted of serious crimes must not "get off easy" through release on parole. On the efficiency side, however, most states are seeking ways of dealing with offenders other than *imprisonment*, which is an expensive proposition given federal standards for human incarceration. Mississippi, Kansas, and Minnesota are experimenting with programs such as "community-based" corrections and expanded work-release opportunities. The Kansas program focuses on lesser property offenders and allows for work release, community services counseling, and restitution to victims. Although the initiation of such programs is motivated largely by the states' desire to reduce spending, these programs receive the support of liberal civil libertarians and from time to time are attacked by law-and-order advocates who view

TABLE 3.4 Thirty-nine State Actions Concerning Capital Punishment After the *Furman* Decisions

State	Enactment[a]	Invalidation	Revision	Reenactment	Amendment
Ala.	3/7/76	6/20/80	12/19/80	7/1/81	
Ariz.	8/8/73	4/21/78	7/20/78	5/1/79	
Ark.	7/24/73			1/1/76	3/17/77
Calif.	1/1/74	12/7/76		8/11/77	11/7/78
Colo.	1/1/75	10/23/78		7/1/79	
Conn.	10/1/73			7/1/81	
Del.	3/29/74	10/22/76		4/14/77	
Fla.	12/8/72				7/3/79
Ga.	3/28/73				
Idaho	3/27/73			3/28/77	
Ill.	7/1/74	9/29/75		6/21/77	
Ind.	4/24/73	4/6/77		10/1/77	
Ky.	1/1/75			12/22/76	
La.	7/2/73	7/2/76		10/2/76	
Md.	7/1/75	11/9/76		7/1/78	7/1/79
Mass.	11/13/79	10/28/80		12/22/82	
Miss.	4/23/74		10/5/76 ·	4/13/77	
Mo.	9/28/75	3/15/77		5/26/77	5/20/80
Mont.	1/1/74			4/8/77	
Nebr.	4/20/73				4/19/78
Nev.	7/1/73				7/1/77
N.H.	4/15/74				9/3/77
N.J.	8/6/82				
N. Mex.	3/23/73	8/20/76		7/1/79	3/17/81
N.Y.	9/1/74	11/15/77			
N.C.	4/8/74	7/2/76	1/18/73	6/1/77	5/14/79
Ohio	1/1/74	7/3/78		10/19/81	

the programs as seriously compromising the value of just retribution and effective incapacitation of wrongdoers.

An old stereotype of state-level politicians presents them as "unenlightened about justice policy and as advocating a narrow law-and-order posture," but that is untrue according to a study of Illinois legislators that concluded that they were

> quite diverse in their criminal justice ideology. . . . They manifested a pronounced conservative strain in their thinking, trumpeting the importance of crime control and advocating stiff prison terms aimed at effecting deterrence, incapacitation, and retribution. Yet they also evidenced an affinity for elements of the traditional liberal agenda. . . . They tended to agree that crime has causes rooted in social inequality . . . that rehabilitation is an important goal . . . that prisons

TABLE 3.4 (continued)

State	Enactment[a]	Invalidation	Revision	Reenactment	Amendment
Okla.	5/17/73			7/24/76	5/8/81
Ore.	12/7/78	1/20/81			
Pa.	3/26/74	11/30/77		9/13/78	
R.I.	6/26/73	2/19/79			
S.C.	7/2/74	7/21/76		6/8/77	6/30/78
S.D.	2/27/79				
Tenn.	2/27/74	1/24/77		4/11/77	3/19/81
Tex.	6/14/73				
Utah	7/1/73				5/10/77
Va.	10/1/75				7/1/77
Wash.	11/4/75	4/16/81		5/14/81	
Wyo.	2/24/73	1/27/77		2/28/77	

[a]*Enactment* of the original legislation establishing the death penalty after *Furman*. *Invalidation* by the judicial action of a state or federal appellate court ruling against the constitutionality of the particular death penalty statute. *Revision* by the judicial action of a state supreme court interpreting a statute so as to keep it in force as law or altering the statute to the same effect. *Reenactment* by a state legislature typically reworking the statute so as to comply with Supreme Court directives. *Amendment* by legislative action, which is considerably less far-reaching than is reenactment (minor additions to or alterations of statutory aggravating circumstances).

Source: Based on data from William J. Bowers with Glen L. Pierce and John F. McDevitt, *Legal Homicide: Death as Punishment in America, 1864-1982* (Boston: Northeastern University Press, 1984), Appendix B.

should be reasonably humane, and that community corrections is an idea worth exploring.[34]

Crime Policy at the City Level

The rising crime rates for both violent crime and property crime have primarily affected cities with populations of more than fifty thousand; crime rates for these cities very nearly quintupled between 1948 and 1978.[35] As a consequence of this increase, crime is one of the core issues of city-level politics. City governments generally seek to stem the rising tide of crime by authorizing more anticrime or crime prevention spending and adding personnel to the police force. Unfortunately, a comparative longitudinal study of crime policies in ten U.S. cities during this thirty-year period strongly suggested that police departments were unable to translate increased resources into effective crime containment outcomes; in five cities where investments in crime fighting and crime prevention were particularly great (Philadelphia, Newark, San Jose, Phoenix, and Minneapolis), municipal crime rates rose at the same rate as those in similar cities lacking such investments.[36]

In a number of cities, vocal and well-organized segments of rank-and-file law enforcement personnel have made use of direct political action to undermine the policies of moderate police managers and elected officials. For example, groups of police officers in Boston, Cleveland, and Detroit organized and coordinated opposition to incumbent mayors perceived as too liberal (pro–citizen rights) in their efforts to improve police-community relations; in Philadelphia and Minneapolis ex-police chiefs exploited law-and-order themes to challenge incumbent mayors they viewed as being overly lax on crime and won these mayoral elections.[37] Some students of city crime policy believe that "the political arena will be receptive to rank and file demands for a more punitive policy posture as long as the politics of law and order continue to predominate," particularly in cities where leaders have been "traditionally receptive to reform, good government, and less harsh forms of law enforcement."[38]

INTEREST GROUPS

Interest groups are active participants in the ongoing struggle concerning the rights of defendants and those convicted of crimes. Many such organized groups wish to influence public policy in this area—some because of their professional concerns, some for their economic gain (manufacturers and purveyors of anticrime equipment, technology, training programs), and some for their moral commitment to justice (for example, the American Civil Liberties Union and Mothers Against Drunk Drivers). Legislation and administrative decisions that enhance the resources of law enforcement agencies are promoted for the most part by management and rank-and-file law enforcement groups and their closely associated allies. These groups have relatively little clout in the national political arena, which led one scholar to conclude that "the fight against crime was mounted by pygmies rather than giants in the world of interest groups."[39]

Those interest groups that are most prominent in trying to influence the major outlines and legal parameters of crime policy, especially as such crime policy emanates from Supreme Court decisions, can be thought of in two basic categories: (1) *consumer groups,* whose members are directly affected by the policy; and (2) *secondary groups,* whose members are interested in the policy but are not directly affected by it.[40] Consumer groups include such associations as the International Association of Chiefs of Police, the Fraternal Order of Police, the Patrolmen's Benevolent Association, the State Patrol and Probation Officers' Association, the National Sheriffs' Association, the National Union of Police Officers, the National Association of Attorneys General, the American Bar Association, the National Legal Aid and Defender

Association, and similar professional associations representing key actors in the criminal justice process. Such groups manifest a persistent presence in the crime policymaking process.

The specific groups found in the second category change depending on the policy under discussion, but a number of groups are active in most issues involving criminal procedures and treatment accorded those convicted of committing crimes. These groups include the American Civil Liberties Union (ACLU), the National Association for the Advancement of Colored People (NAACP), the League of Women Voters, the Washington Legal Foundation, Americans for Effective Law Enforcement, the American Jewish Congress, and the American Judicature Society. Courts depend on intermediaries such as these to assist in the enforcement of their interpretations of precedent, judgments on administrative regulations, and declarations on statutory or constitutional law. For their part, most of these interest groups see a favorable court decision as an important resource serving to advance their goals; these groups tend to make litigation the primary expression of their pressure group activities.

Consumer Groups

When Supreme Court decisions involve the rights of defendants and those convicted of crimes, state and local criminal authorities are under legal obligation to uphold these decisions. The implementation of these policies falls upon the shoulders of the key actors who maintain the criminal justice system—defense attorneys, prosecutors, police, judges, and corrections officials. These professional actors are organized into professional associations of long-standing and considerable political experience, and these groups are wont to advocate their views on all important legal issues that affect their fellow professional members.

The U.S. system of adversary justice gives rise to a tripartite division of labor—prosecutors, defense counsel, and judges—within the criminal law system, and this specialization of tasks and responsibilities affects the personnel in each of the divisions.[41] All three types of courtroom actor have distinct responsibilities, which lead to disagreements as to how the values of law and order and the values of civil liberties ought to be balanced in any particular situation. Judges bear responsibility for managing conflict and maintaining the flow of cases. If they are to be effective, judges must be impartial, fair, and detached from the issues dividing the defense and the prosecution. In contrast, the professional success and career interests of defense attorneys are tied directly to the interests of the accused. Finally, prosecutors tend to identify closely with law enforcement because their success depends mightily upon the ability of police to secure damning evidence of the commission of a crime.

Of course, these natural antagonisms do not necessarily place their respective interest groups on different sides of all crime policy issues. Each actor in the criminal justice process has a stake in the maintenance of a legal culture that emphasizes professionalism and practicable procedures for processing cases. Stuart Scheingold argued that professionals in the criminal justice system divide ideologically along the same lines as do other citizens, but the former's legal training and organizational responsibilities tend to complicate their values.[42] Criminal professionals who think in liberal legal terms (primarily defense attorneys and some judges) will attempt to maximize the rights of defendants in order to protect them from all forms of coercion, and due process liberals tend to choose the least onerous and most humane sentences.

Moderate conservatives, whom Scheingold expected to find represented among judges and prosecutors, are likely to be comfortable with policies that emphasize either deterrence or retribution. Both are consistent with predetermined sentences based on the seriousness of the crime and the offenders' records. Punitive conservatives who favor heavy sentences that strike fear in the hearts of would-be offenders tend to be found in police departments, with some found in the ranks of judges and prosecutors.

One comparative study of criminal courts in U.S. urban cities concluded that the ideological positions taken by court personnel tended to be influenced by the political styles predominating in cities.[43] Metropolitan areas with a reform style of politics tended to recruit judges from the ranks of middle-class lawyers engaged in private legal practice who came to the bench with strong preferences for legal consistency and business values. These preferences among jurists tended to give rise to uniformity and severity in sentencing practices. Cities with "machine-style" politics, in contrast, tended to recruit judges primarily through the party system. Consequently, judges from minority, ethnic, and lower income backgrounds were more frequently in evidence. Such judges tended to be more lenient in the assignment of penalties and more comfortable with a discretionary form of sentencing.

All of these professional actors are expected to comply with Supreme Court decisions involving the rights of defendants and those convicted of crimes. State and local criminal justice authorities for the most part have done so, primarily because these authorities are to a considerable degree vulnerable to judicial sanctions if they fail to comply. However, certain consumer groups are as intent on blocking or minimizing the implementation of judicial decisions as others may be on implementing them. Interest groups that oppose particular policies often work to minimize the impact of unliked policies by disseminating information about how the decision might be narrowly applied or interpreted in the course of official criminal law business.

Consumer groups, and especially national law enforcement associations, are frequently a good source of this kind of information and advice for local police departments. For example, a number of researchers investigating the behavior of local police departments have noted that law enforcement associations commonly pass along information to local agencies on how the *Miranda* decision on notification of rights can be minimized in practice.[44] Lectures and workshops by such associations have manifested a "definite unwillingness to accept what lawyers would call the 'spirit' of the decision." Local police personnel were instructed to recognize situations where the

Miranda warnings were not required and were advised to make every effort to keep interrogation sessions "noncustodial" so warnings concerning suspects' rights would not have to be read.[45] Such research also illustrated that police departments and associations representing law enforcement personnel were most likely to be associated with a law-and-order perspective; however, this did not hold for all law enforcement officials.

Interest groups other than those representing law enforcement professionals also can be expected to advocate public positions on crime policy. For example, the National Association of Attorneys General opposed moves by the Carter administration to initiate court action when state or federal prisons were judged to be engaging in institutional abuses that fell into a broad, repeated pattern of "cruel and unusual punishment." Legislation to this effect was criticized on the grounds that enactment would lend congressional endorsement to a growing intrusion of federal courts into state affairs. Even though the Carter administration wanted to ensure minimum federal standards for all prisons—standards that would affect the way prisoners were housed and treated in these institutions—the proposal was fought principally because federally mandated institutional changes would require additional state spending in an area that was a *state* as opposed to a *federal* function.[46]

The American Bar Association

The American Bar Association (ABA) is the foremost nationwide organization representing attorneys, and it is considered an interest group that has high status, effective organization, and skilled leadership. The ABA is very active concerning issues of crime policy and criminal procedures, and the association often takes public stands on these issues. It is a professional organization that controls entry to the legal profession and carries considerable weight in the criminal law policymaking process. ABA representatives constitute the key bearers of testimony at congressional hearings on legislative proposals to reform the *U.S. Criminal Code*. The ABA also is highly influential in the nomination processes that surround the selection of federal judges and is one of the chief proponents of legal reform in states. While the ABA exercises its influence in all these arenas on the national level, state and local bar associations perform similar roles on the state and local levels.

The American Bar Association is in some respects a conservative organization whose leadership traditionally has held laissez-faire attitudes on economic questions and has advocated positions supportive of states' rights. During the 1950s, the ABA was openly hostile toward the liberal direction of the Warren Court's decisions, but this hostility was tempered by the association's traditional defense of the judicial branch. Such professional cross-pressures were in evidence in a 1958 debate in the ABA's House of Delegates concerning a congressional bill that would have restricted the appellate jurisdiction of the Supreme Court. One description of the debate remarked that "many members felt obliged to rally to the defense of the Court as an institution. . . . On the other hand, a great number of lawyers, especially those from the South, were totally out of sympathy with the Warren court's jurisprudence."[47]

In more recent times, the association has defended the civil libertarian perspective rather more often than the law-and-order viewpoint. For example, along with the ACLU, the ABA opposed the easing of restrictions on the use of illegally seized evidence in criminal cases; this position was taken in response to antidrug legislation enacted by the U.S. House of Representatives in September 1986. This particular antidrug legislation proposed a broadening of the good-faith exception to the exclusionary rule (which would be an extension of *U.S. v. Leon*) to cover the large number of situations in which police officers act without a warrant in the investigation of drug-related crimes. The ABA and ACLU considered this proposal unconstitutional and argued that the only reason the police, Drug Enforcement Administration officials, and the FBI take the citizen's Fourth Amendment rights seriously is because law enforcement officials realize that evidence seized in violation of these rights will be suppressed.[48]

The ABA considers itself somewhat above the political fray; hence, the association is not easily placed in either a law-and-order or civil libertarian position. ABA representatives consider themselves to be impartial experts aiding elected decisionmakers in obtaining worthy goals, and ABA recommendations generally are regarded as nonpartisan and objective. The ABA's underlying logical foundation is legalism, and such reasoning places the ABA on the high plane of "a government of laws rather than of men" in the eyes of many governmental officials and much of the U.S. public.

Considerable attention and respect were given to the recommendations made by the ABA during the troubled 1970s when Congress was discussing reforms in the *U.S. Criminal Code*. During an eight-year period, representatives of the various sections of the association (including the sections on criminal law, criminal justice, business law, taxation, and antitrust) offered testimony on most parts of the code, including criminal sentencing, probation, insanity defenses, the death penalty, and bail jumping.[49] Rather than argue for a particular ideological position, the ABA commonly fought to remedy the inconsistencies, ambiguities, confusions, and out-of-date aspects of the nation's criminal code that cause the most concern to the country's practicing attorneys.

Secondary Groups

The secondary groups active in the area of crime policy most clearly represent the two sides of the law-and-order versus civil liberties debate. In this debate, interest groups on both sides of the issue assist and are assisted by consumer groups. For example, the ACLU (a secondary group) and the American Bar Association (a consumer group) both oppose the easing of restrictions on the use of illegally seized evidence in criminal cases.

Many secondary groups that get involved in issues of crime policy are not single-issue groups. Organizations such as the NAACP, the ACLU, the American Jewish Congress, the League of Women Voters, the Washington Legal Foundation, and Americans for Effective Law Enforcement are actively working to influence many types of policy. However, some national single-issue organizations have formed around the death penalty and drunk driving issues, and in local jurisdictions single-issue campaigns for a host of purposes are in evidence. These campaigns range from demands for more women and minority representation in the criminal justice system and stricter enforcement of antipornography laws to greater local press and electronic media access to courtroom proceedings. The National Coalition Against the Death Penalty, one such organization, acts as a clearinghouse for approximately forty state-level groups organized to fight the death penalty. In addition, multi-issue interest groups occasionally form sections within their organization that deal with single issues. For example, the ACLU has a Capital Punishment Project, whose director is now active in a 1988 case involving a teenage girl from Gary, Indiana, under a death sentence for stabbing an elderly lady repeatedly. The girl was fifteen at the time, and she has become a cause célèbre for death penalty opponents. Even the pope has asked for mercy in this instance. What troubles many people, and constitutes the legal challenge to the Indiana capital punishment statute, is that Indiana has the lowest age threshold for the imposition of the death penalty of any state in the union.

Not all secondary groups have a civil libertarian viewpoint on the death penalty or other crime issues. For example, single-issue groups representing crime victims and missing persons support the death penalty as a necessary punishment for some grievous crimes of murder. The nationwide organizations devoted to stiffer penalties for driving while under the influence (DWI) of alcohol—Mothers Against Drunk Driving and the Citizens Against Alcohol Related Traffic Accidents—constitute a significant influence on DWI dispensations and enforcement in many areas. In addition, there are organizations that consistently argue the law-and-order viewpoint in the nation's courts. The Washington Legal Foundation advocates a conservative, law-and-order viewpoint; the foundation argues that the enlargement of the investigative powers of government permitted by the Burger Court should be applauded as essential for the important task of prosecuting criminals. Conservative groups generally argue that the Burger Court merely engaged in the process of correcting the liberal excesses of the Warren Court rulings of the 1950s and 1960s. According to this view, the Burger Court was not acting to curb civil liberties in any substantial way, but was only adding to the likelihood that obviously guilty criminals were rightfully convicted rather than being released on legal technicalities.[50]

One important way that interest groups attempt to influence the making of crime policy is by means of *amicus curiae* (friends-of-the-court) briefs, which the groups use to add new points of law, provide expertise, or add important jurisprudential arguments to specific Supreme Court cases. For example, twenty-one of the fifty-two cases involving the rights of the accused and convicted accepted by the Supreme Court in its important 1967–1968 term were brought by the NAACP, the ACLU, and the American Jewish Congress. Such *amicus* activity by groups interested in promoting civil

liberties and due process led to the formation of an opposing organization—
Americans for Effective Enforcement—whose purpose is to provide expert
amicus support in favor of capital punishment and strong law enforcement
and to provide conservative support for policy issues other than crime.[51]

PRESIDENCY

Presidents on occasion have initiated crime policies and created programs
that reflect their beliefs about the causes of criminal behavior and the proper
anticrime and crime prevention policies to be pursued. James Calder suggested
that "each of these Presidents [since Hoover] injected into their respective
anti-crime programs obvious ideological precommitments that anticipated
significant reductions in crime."[52] These ideological precommitments by and
large fit into the two perspectives on crime policy being discussed here.
Herbert Packer described the conflict in this manner: "Two models of the
criminal process will let us perceive the normative antimony at the heart
of the criminal law. . . . I call these two models the Due Process Model
and the Crime Control Model."[53] Stuart Scheingold also has commented
on the linkage evident between public opinion toward crime and the positions
taken by many politicians.

> Because the American public is responsive to the myth of crime and punishment
> (deterrence), politicians are tempted to campaign on the issue. Not only is the
> public united in its opposition to crime, especially street crime, but it is also
> an issue that arouses strong feelings. . . . The politician who embraces the
> cause of law and order need not, for example, confront nor communicate
> obtruse economic ideas.[54]

Kennedy's Crime Policies

Beginning in the 1960s, crime became a central issue on the political agenda
for presidential candidates. President John Kennedy, who subscribed to the
sociogenic school of thought, promoted crime policies based upon the notion
that the lack of opportunity for youths in urban ghettos was the primary
cause of much personal and property crime. Kennedy sought to engage
youth in physical fitness programs and job opportunities in order to create
a "nation of participants" instead of a "nation of spectators," and he
concluded that "we cannot effectively attack the problem of teenage crime
and delinquency as long as so many of our young people are out of work."[55]
Implicit here is the view that socioeconomic conditions and a person's
environment are important in creating criminals. Thus, stiffer penalties to
deter crime by youth were not an essential part of Kennedy's crime policies.

The Kennedy administration also wanted to abolish what Attorney
General Robert Kennedy identified as "two systems of justice" in the United
States—one for the rich and one for the poor. The administration was
concerned that poor defendants could not afford the proper means of legal
defense that were readily available to the more affluent. An Office of Criminal
Justice was established to provide free counsel for poor defendants and to

fight for reasonable bail guidelines. Legislative funding to implement this program came with the Supreme Court 1963 ruling on indigent rights to counsel in *Gideon v. Wainwright*. In March 1963, President Kennedy proposed the Criminal Justice Act to Congress, which explicitly linked poverty, opportunity, and criminal behavior. Although this bill failed to pass the Congress in the period following Kennedy's assassination, it did influence the content of President Lyndon Johnson's crime policy agenda.

Kennedy's response to organized crime was much different; he wanted a "chance to get tough with the 'enemy within'—the allegedly evil, suppressive, monopolistic and manipulative characters of the underworld."[56] Kennedy's approach reflected more fully the ideas of the law-and-order school of thought, which held that leaders of organized crime were not "victims" of environmental or socioeconomic factors. Accordingly, the power of government would be used to pursue, apprehend, and incarcerate persons involved in interstate travel to commit bribery or extortion, interstate transmission of betting information, interstate transportation of wagering paraphernalia, interstate flight to avoid prosecution, and interstate shipment of firearms to known felons.

Johnson's Crime Policies

It was during the Johnson administration that crime emerged as a highly visible political issue. Both the Kennedy administration and urban riots of the late 1960s brought the problem of violence and crime to the attention of the public, and President Johnson was well aware of public sentiment. President Johnson used very strong language to describe his "war" or "battle" against the "menace" of crime, which he characterized as a "malignant enemy," but his approach was similar to Kennedy's and involved a mixture of law-and-order policies based on psychogenic explanations and social programs based on sociogenic explanations of criminal behavior.

In 1965, the president directed his Commission on Law Enforcement and the Administration of Justice to study the crime problem and issue recommendations to alleviate it. Poverty was viewed by the commission as the major cause of crime, and Johnson was quoted as saying: "Strike poverty down tonight and much of the crime will fall down with it." He further stated that "there are very few affluent and educated Americans that are attracted to crime, and very few of them have criminal records."[57] Thus, Johnson's main policy for dealing with the causes of criminal behavior was his Great Society program, which included massive expenditures for social welfare, education, and training programs intended to alleviate the problem of crime.

Nixon's Crime Policies

The sociogenic view of criminal behavior espoused by Lyndon Johnson took a back seat to the psychogenic/deterrence approach of Richard M. Nixon. The major reason for this policy shift may have been the civil disorder brought on by the Vietnam War. Massive and sometimes violent public demonstrations resulting from President Johnson's escalation of the Southeast Asian war led to much public clamor for law and order in the streets. Upheaval in urban areas and on college campuses caused the Nixon administration to attack the so-called fallacies of the sociogenic approach to crime. President Nixon focused his blame upon the decline of traditional family values and the rise of "permissiveness" in child rearing, sexual mores, and discipline generally.

President Nixon also attacked the liberal "permissiveness" of the Warren Court, which he said favored the criminal element over justice for the "silent majority" of law-abiding Americans. Crime, according to Nixon, was primarily the product of calculated choices by ill-intentioned individuals who were not in the least representative of the average citizen. In his view, the socioeconomic focus of the sociogenic school was used as a self-serving excuse for not obeying the fair laws of U.S. society.

President Nixon's attempt to reestablish traditional values concentrated on the home. This approach was evident in his establishment of the Office of Child Development: "When there is little stimulus for the mind and especially when there is little interaction between parent and child, the child suffers lasting disabilities, particularly of a sense of control of his environment. None of this follows from the simple fact of being poor."[58] Whether or not the family was economically deprived was irrelevant to Nixon; he stressed the teaching of moral values that encouraged individual initiative and self-help.

President Nixon's view of crime policy was, in many respects, a complete repudiation of the sociogenic school of thought. According to his view, drug addicts, thieves, and other lawbreakers were rational persons who chose to violate the rules of society, and as such they should be sternly dealt with by law enforcement agencies. Thus, criminals should be deterred by strict enforcement of the law, and where deterrence fails, they should be incarcerated. Nixon understood the role of government to be law enforcer rather than socioeconomic engineer. His administration also saw crime as an obstacle to individual freedom because the threat of crime or its actual occurrence violated the victim's or potential victim's individual rights. As President Nixon stated, "The issue of crime is freedom. When individual citizens are the direct victims of violence, or the indirect victims when they are forced to restrict their own movements out of fear of violence, fundamental liberty is not worthy of the name."[59] Following this line of thought, President Nixon pushed for stringent punishments: "The death penalty is not a sanction to be employed loosely or considered lightly, but neither is it to be ignored as a fitting penalty, in exceptional circumstances, for the purpose of preventing or deterring."[60]

Ford's Crime Policies

Gerald Ford was concerned about the fear individuals have of everyday street crime, and in a 1975 message to Congress he said, "America has been far from successful in dealing with the sort of crime that obsesses

America day and night—I mean street crime, crime that invades our neighborhoods and our homes . . . the kind of brutal violence that makes us fearful of strangers and afraid to go out at night."[61] Ford believed that much of the rising crime rate resulted from a disregard for the law. Like his predecessor, Ford criticized the Supreme Court for its permissiveness; indeed, the Court's decisions on rules of evidence and criminal rights led Ford to declare, "Because of their complexity, the laws invite technical arguments that waste court time without ever going to the heart of the question of the accused's guilt or innocence."[62]

The Ford administration also was concerned about the deterrence impact of existing laws. The erratic and inconsistent application of law "is profoundly unfair and breeds disrespect for the law."[63] President Ford believed likewise that criminal fines were inadequate to deter the offenders "whose business is crime." Thus, he favored mandatory incarceration for anyone using a dangerous weapon when committing an offense; for serious crimes such as hijacking, kidnapping, or trafficking in hard drugs; and for repeat offenders.

But two aspects of Ford's crime philosophy were not indicative of a law-and-order approach. These were his preference for rehabilitation of some first-time offenders and the building of humanitarian prisons that minimized the violence prisoners may experience. As Ford stated in a special message to Congress, "While the problem of criminal rehabilitation is difficult, we must not give up our efforts to achieve it, especially in dealing with youthful offenders."[64] Much of his concern with rehabilitation was based on his concern for the young, and he directed the secretary of health, education, and welfare and the attorney general to ensure that the federal government helped young ex-convicts receive jobs after prison.

President Ford maintained the funding of the Law Enforcement Assistance Administration by supporting a $6.8 billion allocation that kept the Law Enforcement Assistance Administration (LEAA) operating until 1981. This decision reflected his belief that the federal government ought to assist state and local governments in crime prevention. All in all, therefore, President Ford's attitudes toward crime prevention policy were more moderate than those of President Nixon.

Carter's Crime Policies

With Jimmy Carter, a new emphasis in crime policy became evident. President Carter was very interested in persons of all economic classes having "equal access" to justice. He sought to create an image of U.S. justice as fully representative of the nation's diverse peoples, and Carter stressed "special efforts to identify qualified minority and female candidates for judgeships."[65] A more representative judiciary, he believed, would give disadvantaged groups more reason to respect the legal process and would increase the likelihood that their grievances would be treated more fairly. As Carter said in 1978, "Too often, the amount of justice that a person gets depends on the amount of money that he or she can pay. Access to justice must not depend on economic status, and it must not be thwarted by arbitrary procedural rules."[66]

President Carter's concern for the rights of the accused, who often were economically disadvantaged, extended to his doubling the budget of the Legal Services Corporation in 1979. Although he did not emphasize crime issues as much as did Nixon or Ford, Carter nonetheless was deeply committed to making the criminal justice system more fair in its dealings with the less fortunate.

Reagan's Crime Policies

Having interpreted his landslide victory in the 1980 election as direct evidence of a "conservative realignment" in U.S. politics, President Reagan was reported to have said that "the public wants criminals clobbered, and that is what we are going to do."[67] In his first public speech on crime (before the International Association of Chiefs of Police in 1981), Reagan unveiled his ideological attack on the "social thinkers of the 1950s and 1960s who discussed crime only in the context of disadvantaged childhoods and poverty-striken neighborhoods" and who "thought that massive government spending could wipe away our social ills." He concluded that speech with the call that only appropriate morals "can hold back the jungle and restrain the darker impulses of human nature."[68]

With comments like these, it is clear that President Reagan endorsed not only a psychogenic view of crime but also a biogenic view. His tough law-and-order agenda, with the exception of Nixon's, was unprecedented in recent times. Reagan and his (second) attorney general, Edwin Meese, wanted to do more than convict and imprison criminals. Reagan's goal was to make basic changes in the criminal justice system that would "tip the balance" from the accused to the victims. The Reagan administration also believed that the judicial branch was too lenient and thereby brought on a surge in crime. President Reagan sought to appoint federal judges who were inclined to favor the prosecution in criminal cases. Because of the greater use of fixed sentences, tougher penalties, and more flexibility in the hands of prosecutors, during Reagan's tenure there were more persons incarcerated in federal prisons with longer sentences (see Table 3.5).[69]

The Reagan approach to crime policy is summarized by the Comprehensive Crime Control Act of 1983, which Reagan proposed to Congress.[70] This bill would make it more difficult for a defendant to be released on *bail* pending trial. *Sentencing* requirements would be consistent throughout the federal system, with no parole possible, and the *exclusionary rule* would be weakened by allowing evidence seized in "good faith" to be used as evidence in criminal cases. The use of *criminal forfeitures*, where federal prosecutors could confiscate the assets and profits of criminal enterprises, would be strengthened. The *insanity defense* would be limited to only those persons unable to understand the nature and wrongfulness of their criminal acts, and *narcotics enforcement* would produce increased penalties for traf-

TABLE 3.5 Federal Prison Population and Average Terms

	1980	1983	1985
Federal prison population	24,153	30,474	35,593
Average prison sentence	52 months	57 months	60 months

Source: Data supplied to the authors by the U.S.
Bureau of Prisons, Administrative Office of the United
States Courts, Washington, D.C., 1985.

ficking in drugs while more regulatory authority would be given to the Drug Enforcement Administration.

Acting on the last provision, the President's Commission on Organized Crime recommended on March 4, 1986, that a widespread national program to test most working Americans for drug use should be implemented. The program was intended to dry up the market for illegal drugs and thus put organized crime out of business. Many civil libertarians opposed such methods, but the Reagan administration countered that "those who say it is too intrusive" should consider that federal drug-enforcement officers are "putting their lives on the line" because of drug users' "weekend activities."[71]

CONGRESS

While most crime policy is under state jurisdiction, Congress plays a key role in setting crime policy in response to crime control problems that become national issues. Some problems that do reach the national policy-making agenda are gun control, organized crime and drugs, highjacking, terrorism, and bank robbery. Organized crime has been a source of concern for the U.S. Justice Department during all of the post–World War I administrations. Government efforts to prosecute syndicate leaders have been hampered greatly throughout this long period by the refusal of major crime figures to testify before grand juries and by their invocation of Fifth Amendment rights in doing so. In 1970, the Justice Department pressed hard in Congress to gain passage of the Organized Crime Control Act (P.L. 91-452), a statute containing provisions that "severely restricted the use of the Fifth Amendment by grand jury witnesses."[72]

In addition to legislation dealing with the rights of persons accused or convicted of crimes, Congress also has established crime programs that provide for the distribution of funds to state and local governments. The most prominent example of such legislation is the Omnibus Crime Control and Safe Streets Act of 1968. This enactment represents one of the first large-scale attempts to establish a block grant mechanism within the U.S. federalist governmental structure. Block grants endowed state and local governments with the direct funds and decisional authority required to accomplish the ends for which the grant program was established.

The Safe Streets Act provided funding for a variety of criminal justice activities, and through this act Congress earmarked fixed percentages of expenditures at local levels for correctional institutions, juvenile delinquency programs, and neighborhood crime prevention.[73] Congress also required the annual submission by states of comprehensive plans for the use of their funds to the LEAA—which was created to implement the act—for review and approval. These dimensions of federal oversight of LEAA program decisions led some to call the Safe Streets program a "closely related set of categorical grants masquerading under a block grant guise."[74]

In some respects, the Safe Streets Act is a direct reflection of *both* sides of the law-and-order versus civil liberties political struggle. On the one hand, the major portion of the funds expended by the LEAA in the early years of the program was used by police departments to enhance their crime fighting abilities; the purchase of communications equipment, high technology surveillance and analysis devices, and weaponry was commonplace. In addition, the Safe Streets Act extended the use of wiretapping by law enforcement officials.[75] On the other hand, the LEAA supported a variety of rather liberal programs, which often were innovative undertakings that emphasized experimentation in the areas of police–minority community relations and the "diversion of juveniles from the criminal justice system, neighborhood justice to resolve minor criminal disputes by informal mediation, and reforms aimed at more effective policing."[76] Nevertheless, the funding for these experimental programs was a very small part of the total amount expended by the LEAA.

The Omnibus Crime Control and Safe Streets Act was the realization of ideas that had been under discussion in the legislative and executive branches of the federal government for a number of years. Law and order first became a major public issue in the presidential campaign of Barry Goldwater in 1964. In 1968, both Richard Nixon and George Wallace played on the law-and-order theme in their respective presidential campaigns, and this focus on the crime problem raised public expectations about the possibilities for a clear governmental response to the problem of crime containment.

President Johnson considered the antipoverty programs of his administration as the primary answer to the crime problems facing the nation. On the heels of his overwhelming electoral victory in the 1964 presidential election, President Johnson created the Commission on Law Enforcement and the Administration of Justice in 1965 to recommend policy solutions to the nation's crime problems. In its report, the commission articulated a definite liberal perspective on crime. The commission's first recommendation was to eliminate the social conditions associated with crime, and although the commission saw the need to suppress riots in impoverished urban areas, the members argued that what was really needed was a "far more determined effort . . . to eradicate conditions that invite riots."[77] President Johnson sought to meet the criticisms of the report made by law-and-order advocates by introducing comprehensive proposals for a large-scale grant program to assist state and local units of government in crime reduction and law enforcement efforts in a message to Congress in February 1967.[78] These proposals become the basis for the congressional discussions that in time led to the Safe Streets Act.

Congressional deliberation on the Johnson administration proposals and the report of the advisory commission began against a backdrop of a "national wave of violence." Forty-three people had died in the Detroit rioting of July 22, 1967, and elsewhere many others had been killed or injured in the worst series of violent civil disturbances in the country's history.[79] In addition, the country was faced with the rise of the Black Power movement, the militant anti–Vietnam War movement, and the assassinations of President John F. Kennedy, Malcolm X, Martin Luther King, Jr., and Robert F. Kennedy. Consequently, many members of Congress were interested in taking a strong stand against the perceived lack of law and order and the growing violence evident in U.S. society.

At this point, when the subject of crime began to reach its nadir in the Gallup Polls, interest groups representing both sides of the law-and-order versus civil liberties debate made serious efforts to influence congressional discussion on crime legislation. These groups included the ACLU, Americans for Democratic Action, the International Association of Chiefs of Police, the National Association of Attorneys General, the National Council on Crime and Delinquency, the National Sheriffs' Association, and interest groups representing the government officials likely to benefit from the program (the National Association of Counties, the National Governors' Conference, the National League of Cities, and the U.S. Conference of Mayors). Although these groups did not agree on specific policy approaches, all agreed that some comprehensive national response to crime was needed.

Despite President Johnson's past legislative successes, the administration's liberally oriented proposals were not well received in Congress. Many members of Congress were disenchanted with the Great Society programs and were not anxious to fund another set of costly categorical grants. President Johnson's bill called for direct grants to local governments, required state matching contributions to these grants, placed the authority for running the proposed program in the Justice Department, and gave the attorney general broad discretionary powers in developing the program and in directing funding decisions.[80]

The democratic chair of the House Judiciary Committee, Emmanuel Celler (D-N.Y.), was able to report out a bill that provided for direct grants to local law enforcement agencies and was in accord with most of the other provisions of the administration's bill. However, twelve of the fifteen Republicans on this committee strongly disagreed with the committee bill and took their case to the full House. This group of Republicans was under the leadership of William Cahill (R-N.J.), Thomas Railsback (R-Ill.), and Edward Beister (R-Pa.) and had the blessing of House Minority Leader Gerald R. Ford.[81] These Republicans mobilized the rest of their party colleagues and also mobilized many southern Democrats against the administration's bill.

This coalition opposed the president's proposals for several reasons, primary among them being that the proposals were a continuation of the administration's erosion of state's rights through direct grants to local governments. Another widely shared objection concerned the authority granted to the attorney general to dictate policies to local law enforcement officials. The administration's attorney general, Ramsey Clark, was considered very "soft on crime" by many law enforcement officials inasmuch as he was a major spokesperson for the civil libertarian perspective. The administration's bill was soundly defeated in the House in favor of the version proposed by the coalition of Republicans and southern Democrats. It was clear that these members of Congress wanted to create a national-level response to the problem of crime, but it also was clear that the Republicans did not want to create a program similar to the War on Poverty, which produced disproportionate political benefits for the Democrats.

The Senate followed suit as well, making short shrift of the Johnson administration's legislative initiative. In addition to defeating the president's bill, the Senate's version of the bill contained two provisions that demonstrated that body's determination to produce a piece of legislation that took a strong law-and-order approach. The first provision eventually became Title II of the Act and represented an attempt to overrule the Supreme Court's *Miranda* decision by granting the admissibility of confessions at trial. The second provision (Title III of the enacted legislation) expanded the use of electronic wiretapping.[82] The conference committee retained the Senate's additions, and the final legislation was sent to President Johnson for his signature on June 19, 1968.

BUREAUCRACY

To orchestrate this full-scale attack on crime, the Safe Streets Act sets out five major titles: Title I—Law Enforcement; Title II—Admissibility of Confession; Title III—Wiretap and Electronic Surveillance; Title IV—State Firearms Control Assistance; and Title V—General Provisions. Under Title I, the LEAA was created within the Department of Justice and became the principal federal agency dealing with crime problems at state and local levels of government. According to the provisions of the Act, LEAA would perform this role in five ways:

> (1) by supporting statewide planning in the field of criminal justice through the creation of state planning agencies; (2) by supplying the states and localities with block grants of federal funds to improve their criminal justice systems;

(3) by making discretionary grants to special programs in the field of criminal justice; (4) by developing new devices, techniques, and approaches in law enforcement through the National Institute of Law Enforcement and Criminal Justice, LEAA's research arm; and (5) by supplying money for the training and education of criminal justice personnel.[83]

The Administrative Complexity of the LEAA

At the outset, the LEAA was directed by three coequal administrators (the "troika") who were bipartisan, appointed by the president, and confirmed by the Senate. This troika was created by Congress to provide national-level administration, but the difficulty the three administrators had in achieving unanimity on policy and personnel decisions severely hampered the operation of LEAA programs.[84] The troika later was replaced by a single administrator assisted by two deputies. During its existence, the LEAA consisted of five main operating parts: (1) the block grant program, which received most of the funding ($452.4 million in 1976, which was one of the last years of substantial LEAA appropriations); (2) the discretionary fund grants ($118.5 million in 1976); (3) the National Institute of Law Enforcement and Criminal Justice ($32 million in 1976); (4) education and training programs ($43 million in 1976); and (5) the Juvenile Justice Office, which began operating in 1975.[85]

Under the block grant, LEAA distributed the greatest share of its funds to state planning agencies (SPAs), which were created in each state and were under the direct control of state governors. These SPAs received both planning grants and action grants, but in order to receive money for programs (under the action grants), "comprehensive" plans had to be prepared that accounted for a coordinated, systematic use of funds available under the planning grants. LEAA officials reviewed such plans, although they did not have the authority to veto specific projects included in the plans. The act required that 50 percent of the membership of state planning boards be local elected officials so that officials from fields other than law enforcement would be represented. However, the reality in most states was that law enforcement personnel were very much overrepresented on LEAA's state and regional planning boards.[86]

Critics of these LEAA arrangements charged that the state planning units were "created only in order to obtain federal funds and were not serious planning agencies or strategically situated to assume leadership."[87] Some support for this criticism exists in the fact that since the termination of the LEAA program during the Reagan administration's first term, most states remain very involved in fighting the problem of crime. Even if a harsh review of LEAA is not fully warranted, the SPAs indeed were faced with a nearly impossible task of coordination. The staffs of these agencies had to create comprehensive plans for extremely fragmented criminal justice systems within the context of state planning boards that were dominated by the very groups the SPAs were supposed to constrain.

In addition to planning and action grants, the LEAA also distributed discretionary grants, which could be used to fund innovative programs.

Because these discretionary grants could be used to fund projects outside a given state's planned funding priorities, projects funded by discretionary grants often conflicted with the comprehensive planning process of the state planning agencies. This same lack of coordination among parts of the program was evident in the activities of the National Institute of Law Enforcement and Criminal Justice. The institute supported research, but the findings of this research "had little effect on the distribution of LEAA's discretionary grants and virtually no impact on the states' use of block grants."[88]

To carry out the LEAA's education and training mandate, four other programs were created: (1) the Law Enforcement Education Program; (2) the National Criminal Justice Education Consortium; (3) the Graduate Research Fellowship Program; and (4) the Internship Program. Funding was available to provide college educations for criminal justice personnel, to improve criminal justice curricula in universities, to support criminal justice doctoral candidates writing their dissertations, and to supplement salaries of undergraduate, graduate, and professional interns in criminal justice agencies. This particular aspect of the LEAA structure was not funded to the same degree as was the block grant and discretionary grant sections of the LEAA anticrime program.

The administration of LEAA programs indeed was complex; many new agencies had to be created, including the LEAA itself. The authorizing legislation did not simply provide additional funds to an ongoing program; entirely new bureaucratic structures and procedures were created and put into operation. In addition, the block grant structure of a major portion of the program required that the implementation process involve federal, state, and local authorities, thereby creating a "multiplicity of bureaucratic structures with overlapping responsibilities."[89] Although the LEAA was funded from 1969 to 1981, many knowledgeable observers believe that the full range of LEAA programs was not operational during the early years because of the substantial start-up costs associated with the establishment of such complex bureaucratic structures.

Impact of the LEAA's Programs

The implementation of the Safe Streets Act by the LEAA had both its critics and its supporters. Critics tended to charge that in spite of LEAA programs, national crime rates escalated, conditions in jails and prisons did not noticeably improve, and the abuse of justice continued in courts that remained overloaded with cases. Although planning in the area of criminal justice improved under the LEAA's programs, this planning did not have the dramatic impact so broadly anticipated. In addition, there was no separation in the implementation process of planning and granting responsibilities, and this led administrators to use planning only to "service the distribution of funds, with the result being a minimal satisfaction of the planning requirements."[90] In 1976, the Office of Management and Budget concluded:

LEAA funds have been used for projects which have little or no relationship to improving criminal justice programming. Funds are so widely dispersed that their potential impact is reduced, and the absence of program evaluation severely limits the agency's ability to identify useful projects and provide for their transfer, and too frequently LEAA funds have been used to subsidize the procurement of interesting but unnecessary equipment.[91]

Supporters of the program responded to these criticisms by saying that too much was expected of the LEAA. According to the Twentieth Century Fund Task Force on the LEAA, funds from this agency made up only 5 percent of the average state's criminal justice budget and represented approximately 10 percent of the total amount that the federal government was disbursing under the General Revenue Sharing program.[92] Supporters also argued that LEAA programs had some important but generally unappreciated intangible impacts. Even though the block grant structure made the administration of the program difficult, for example, the structure in fact did force various components of the nation's criminal justice community to work together cooperatively. The criminal justice system has remained fragmented for the most part, and the persistence of this system of "checks and balances" quieted fears expressed by some that the federal program would produce a national police state.

SUMMARY

It is clear that a moral dimension underlies the debate about crime in the United States. We predict that the current controversy about drug testing—in the workplace, in school, in athletics—will be the next great policy conflict to develop in the context of the debate about crime. During the 1960s, drug abuse was considered by some people to be a "victimless" crime, and thus reformers wanted to lift criminal penalties from offenses such as marijuana use. With the changed social and political milieu of the 1980s, there is new concern about the ill-effects of drug use, and opponents now advocate more intrusive methods of detecting drug abuse by middle class citizens as well as by addicts. This political debate will again be taken up by interest groups in the defense of civil liberties versus the protection of social mores.

A moral dimension also affects the activities of the major decisionmakers in the policy drama about crime. Presidents, members of Congress, federal and state judges, interest groups, and state and local criminal justice authorities are wont to explain their involvement in terms of fundamental assumptions about human nature—about individual responsibility versus social disadvantage, about fear of an oppressive government versus fear of disorder, about the justice of taking human life as a fit punishment for heinous crimes versus the sacredness of human life. But this moral dimension is everpresent and represents the basic conflict between liberal and conservative ideologies in U.S. politics.

Liberals consistently have favored the civil libertarian side of the debate, while conservatives are usually in the law-and-order camp. Much of this dispute was generated by Supreme Court decisions, and these liberal-conservative labels have been attached to the high court at various times. The liberal Warren Court was succeeded by the conservative Burger Court, and we are now in the era of the most conservative chief justice in modern times. We are also at the end of a presidential administration that strongly favored a law-and-order approach. Attorney General Edwin Meese even wanted a Supreme Court review of the *Miranda* decision, and his desire stemmed from a Justice Department report that maintained this decision hindered criminal investigations by preventing the police from obtaining confessions and other information from suspects. As that report concluded, "The interesting question is not whether *Miranda* should go, but how we should facilitate its demise, and what we should replace it with."[93] The answer to that question is not apparent, given the moral dilemma involved. For this reason, public policymaking of social regulations such as the criminal code does indeed warrant the serious attention of political scientists and other social scientists.

ACKNOWLEDGMENTS

We thank Professor Nicholas P. Lovrich of Washington State University, our colleague and teacher, whose invaluable advice and editorial comment guided the preparation of this chapter.

GUN CONTROL
Constitutional Mandate or Myth?

Robert J. Spitzer

A well regulated Militia, being necessary to the security of a free state, the right of the people to keep and bear Arms, shall not be infringed.
——Second Amendment, U.S. Constitution

The NRA, the foremost guardian of the traditional right to "keep and bear arms," believes that every law-abiding citizen is entitled to the ownership and legal use of firearms, and that every reputable gun owner should be an NRA member.
——Motto, *The American Rifleman*

A powerful lobby dins into the ears of our citizenry that . . . gun purchases are constitutional rights protected by the Second Amendment. . . . There is under our decisions no reason why stiff state laws governing the purchase and possession of pistols may not be enacted. There is no reason why pistols may not be barred from anyone with a police record. There is no reason why a State may not require a purchaser of a pistol to pass a psychiatric test. There is no reason why all pistols should not be barred to everyone except the police.
——Associate Justice William O. Douglas,
Adams v. Williams (1972)

Since 1964, abundant research has employed Theodore Lowi's arenas of power scheme, including the work of this author,[1] to analyze the policymaking process. The purpose of this chapter is twofold. One is to test hypotheses about social regulatory policy as they apply to the gun control issue. The second is to explore this issue by washing away as much polemical froth as possible. Surprisingly few works on this controversial topic involve a dispassionate examination of gun control policies and politics. My primary concern is whether the state has *authority* to regulate guns under the Second Amendment and, if so, how to explain the existing pattern of weak gun controls. I begin with historical antecedents.

Any people who can argue successfully that their contemporary view of the Second Amendment stems from the intent of the Framers can claim a certain moral high ground that lends weight and legitimacy to their cause. Firearms possession was, without a doubt, a common and necessary part of colonial and frontier life. Settlers had to rely on their own wits and skills to protect themselves against Indians and foreign armies and to keep food on the table. Thus, the idea of settlers banding together to provide mutual protection was integral to colonial life. At the same time, the colonists' experiences with regular standing armies generated considerable cause for suspicion. This suspicion partly had its roots in the English Bill of Rights of 1689, which resulted after Catholic James II attempted to promote the cause of "papism" by filling the leading ranks of the army with Catholics, to the exclusion of Protestants. King James's oppressive practices eventually led to his overthrow and replacement by William of Orange. This history led to a reference to a right to bear arms in the English Bill of Rights and to subsequent mistrust of standing armies.

Mistrust of standing armies was a pervasive sentiment during the revolutionary period in America and was related directly to the bearing of arms by citizens. Samuel Adams wrote in 1776, for example, that a "standing army, however necessary it be at some times, is always dangerous to the liberties of the people."[2] In 1771, James Lovell wrote that "the true strength and safety of every commonwealth or limited monarchy, is the bravery of its freeholders, its militia. By brave militias they rise to grandeur; and they come to ruin by a mercenary army."[3] Samuel Seabury characterized the standing army as "the MONSTER,"[4] and George Washington observed that "mercenary armies . . . have at one time or another subverted the liberties of almost all the Countries they have been raised to defend."[5] Thus, a reliance on the citizen-soldier became synonymous with the revolutionary spirit, and these sentiments also were reflected in the political thought of such philosophers as François-Marie Voltaire, Anne-Robert-Jacques Turgot, François Quesnay, and Jean-Jacques Rousseau.

Concerns about the adverse effects of standing armies found specific expression in the Declaration of Independence where, in reaction to the presence of the British military, Thomas Jefferson complained that "he [the King] has kept among us, in Times of Peace, Standing Armies, without the consent of our Legislatures. He has affected to render the Military independent of and superior to the Civil Power." The Declaration of Independence also complained that the British were "quartering large Bodies of Armed Troops among us" and "protecting them, by a mock Trial, from Punishment for any Murders which they should commit on the Inhabitants of these States." The British only compounded these grievances by hiring Hessian mercenaries to fight against colonial troops during the revolution. The colonists relied on state-based militias to fight the war, rather than risk vesting a national government with a national army that might later pose a threat to the people's liberties. Indeed, even by 1788, the Army of the Confederation consisted of only 697 men and officers.[6]

Yet despite these concerns, the Framers recognized that a standing army was a necessity. Article I, Section 8 of the Constitution grants Congress the power "to raise and support armies" (although the fear of standing armies caused the Framers to limit appropriations for the military to two years), to "provide for calling forth the militia," and to "provide for organizing, arming, and disciplining, the militia."[7] The modern militia is no longer a citizen army as it was during the eighteenth century but now is recognized as the National Guard since passage of the National Defense Act of 1916.

Fears of a standing army also influenced the writing of the U.S. Bill of Rights. During the first session of Congress, when Elbridge Gerry was asked about the connection between a militia and a secure, free state, he replied, "What, sir, is the use of a militia? It is to prevent the establishment of a standing army, the bane of liberty."[8] The congressional committee reviewing proposed amendments reported out this text for what eventually became the Second Amendment: "A well regulated militia, composed of the body of the people, being the best security of a free state, the right of the people to keep and bear arms shall not be infringed; but no person religiously scrupulous shall be compelled to bear arms."[9] The primary change in the final text was the omission of the last phrase; Gerry and others felt that the religious exemption could result in numerous citizens exempting themselves from military service, which might necessitate the baneful standing army.[10]

Knowing that political power stemmed from military power and that history was replete with examples of this pattern, the Founders sought in the Second Amendment insurance that states could maintain their militias against a mischievous federal army. Absent from these debates was anything resembling an a priori individual "right" to bear arms. The concept of individualism had relevance only insofar as individuals had to supply their own arms while serving in the militia. For example, Congress created uniform state militias through the Militia Law of 1792, which allowed the calling up of "every free, able-bodied, white male citizen of the respective States [between the ages of 18 and 45] in the militia. Each man was to provide his own weapons, two flints, 24 rounds of ammunition for a musket or 20 rounds for a rifle."[11] This kind of armed force was mobilized by President Washington in 1794 to suppress the Whiskey Rebellion.

The debate today about whether the Second Amendment refers to an "individual" or "collective" right to bear arms is directly relevant to the gun control issue. The individual interpretation, which confers greater rights to firearm possession, is championed by the National Rifle Association (NRA). The weight of scholarly opinion argues against the NRA position,[12] but others interpret the Second Amendment as securing an individual right to bear arms.[13]

INTEREST GROUPS

The NRA

The National Rifle Association was formed in 1871 by Colonel William C. Church, editor of the *Army and Navy Journal*, and by George W. Wingate, an officer in the New York National Guard. The NRA beginnings paralleled a rising interest in rifle shooting competitions, which resulted partly from the Union Army's relatively poor marksmanship skills during the Civil War. In 1900, Albert Jones, an officer in the New Jersey National Guard, with the aid of New York governor Theodore Roosevelt, solicited interest in forming a group to support U.S. marksmen. The then-forgotten NRA became the vehicle for implementing Jones's plan, and in 1905 the NRA became the primary channel for the sale of government surplus weapons and ammunition to rifle clubs under P.L. 149. In 1921, C. B. Lister, a promotions manager, assumed leadership of the NRA, and due to his efforts, the NRA became affiliated with two thousand local sportsmen's clubs and its membership grew tenfold by 1934. The NRA swiftly became the largest and best organized association of firearms users in the nation.

The NRA is now headquartered in Washington, D.C., in a building whose front entrance is flanked by two marble plaques. One says, "Firearms Safety Education. Marksmanship Training. Shooting for Recreation." The other reads, "The Right of the People to Keep and Bear Arms Shall Not Be Infringed." Inside rows of sophisticated computers keep information on the NRA's 3 million members and on legislators. In a few hours, thousands of letters and mailgrams can be routed to Congress by mobilizing this huge membership. The NRA operates on a reported annual budget of $53.5 million, and the current president, Harlon B. Carter, commands an $85,000 per year salary.[14] Fifty percent of the NRA's revenues come from membership fees and another 15 percent from advertising, mainly by gun manufacturers, in its monthly magazines: *The American Rifleman, The American Hunter,* and *The American Marksman.*[15] In 1979, the NRA reported assets of $46.7 million.[16]

With a paid staff of nearly three hundred, the NRA coordinates a network of fifty-four state groups and about ten thousand local gun clubs. The heart of the NRA organization lies in its mass membership. As the *Congressional Quarterly* observed, the unique success of the NRA rests with "a body of gun lovers linked by a common activity that continues even when the legislative front is quiet."[17] The NRA fosters this devotion by emphasizing the gun as a cultural phenomenon, not simply a political issue. As a former Treasury Department official noted, "Gun owners operate with such high emotion, that to have them as an enemy is unpleasant."[18] Beyond this, the NRA has benefited from a kind of quasi-governmental status. Federal law stipulated that surplus military arms could be sold only to civilians who belonged to the NRA. This led to an ironic occurrence in 1967 when 400 members of the Detroit Police Department had to join the NRA in order to obtain surplus army carbines for riot control.[19] A court order ended this special privilege in 1979, the result of a legal challenge by the National Coalition to Ban Handguns (NCBH).

Institute for Legislative Action (ILA). This special branch of the NRA coordinates legislative efforts. Its specialists are scattered throughout the nation at the state and local levels and in Washington, D.C. One of ILA's primary responsibilities is to provide the membership with up-to-date information and alerts on impending firearms legislation and court rulings. The ILA operates through news bulletins and a biweekly newspaper called *Monitor*.

In 1982, the National Rifle Association reported spending $450,737 on lobbying, a relatively modest sum for an organization of its size.[20] However, this figure did not include expenses for communications with the NRA's 3 million members. Because these communications do not involve direct contact with Congress, the NRA does not consider them to be lobbying. Although these communications may not be "lobbying" in the strict sense, they do produce grass-roots lobbying, and most other groups include this sum in their lobbying disclosures.

During the 1983–1984 period, the NRA ranked second only to the AFL-CIO in spending on internal communications.[21] These costs include phone banks urging members to support candidates, distribution of literature promoting or attacking candidates, and related get-out-the-vote drives. But this period represents something of an exception because the NRA has ranked first in this kind of spending at least since 1979. Expenditures of this kind by the AFL-CIO for Walter Mondale amounted to more than $1.2 of its $1.4 million total. The NRA spread its money across more races; intraorganizational communications money was allocated to more than three times as many elections as compared to the next most active organization. (During 1981–1982, the NRA led all other organizations in such spending with $803,656; in 1980 the NRA also ranked first with $803,839.) One measure of the potency of this effort is the NRA's claim that it defeated proposed gun curbs in twenty-eight cities in 1981.[22]

NRA-PAC. The Institute for Legislative Action also manages the NRA's Political Action Committee (PAC), which is called the Political Victory Fund. In 1980, the Political Victory Fund spent $1.5 million in congressional campaign contributions,[23] not including $171,000 to help Ronald Reagan, a long-time NRA member, become president.[24] In all, the NRA-PAC gave contributions to more than three hundred congressional contenders. Although many of these contributions were small, 80 successful aspirants to the House had received more than $1,000 each, as did 18 senators.[25] In 1982, the Political Victory Fund spent almost $2.3 million on 226 congressional races; of these, 177 NRA supporters won.[26] During the 1981–1982 period, the NRA was one of the top five raisers and spenders of PAC funds among trade/membership/health PACs.[27]

In the congressional elections of 1983–1984 and in senatorial elections during the 1979–1984 period, the NRA-PAC spent a total $1,469,865 on direct contributions to and independent expenditures on behalf of congress-persons. Like other PACs, the NRA is careful to target its money. For example, 97 percent of the money spent on senators was allocated to those who supported the NRA on a key vote during the 1985 consideration of the McClure-Volkmer Bill. During the 1983–1984 period, the NRA was the tenth largest money raiser and the fifth largest spender.[28] The NRA also makes expenditures to defeat specific candidates. It spent about $230,000

TABLE 4.1 Top Congressional Recipients of Combined Direct and Indirect NRA Expenditures[a]

Senate	Total NRA contributions/ expenditures, 1979-1984	House of Representatives	Total NRA contributions/ expenditures, 1983-1984
Gramm (R-Tex.)	$332,797	Lightfoot (R-Ia.)	$21,061
Helms (R-N.C.)	96,827	Schaefer (R-Colo.)	20,988
Grassley (R-Ia.)	29,281	Smith (R-N.H.)	19,122
Eagleton (D-Mo.)	26,574	Volkmer (D-Mo.)	15,805
Abdnor (R-S.D.)	25,911	Vucanovich (R-Nev.)	11,977
Trible (R-Va.)	21,229	Dickinson (R-Ala.)	10,917
Byrd (D-W.Va.)	19,328	Bilirakis (R-Fla.)	10,523
D'Amato (R-N.Y.)	16,278	Carney (R-N.Y.)	9,981
Weicker (R-Conn.)	14,515	Jones (D-Okla.)	9,920
Durenberger (R-Minn.)	14,427	Chappell (D-Fla.)	9,252
Deconcini (D-Ariz.)	14,299	Marlenee (R-Mont.)	8,853
Thurmond (R-S.C.)	13,169	Mollohan (D-W.V.)	8,653
		Kasich (R-Ohio)	8,444
		Cobey (R-N.C.)	8,176
		Fields (R-Tex.)	7,604
		Stump (R-Ariz.)	7,527
		Franklin (R-Miss.)	6,742
		Foley (D-Wash.)	6,337
		Snyder (R-Ky.)	6,048

[a]Direct expenditures are those given by a PAC to a candidate's campaign committee. Indirect expenditures are purchases of goods and services (media ads) that advocate election or defeat of a particular candidate.

Source: Data taken from *Common Cause News*, August 30, 1985.

in the 1980 presidential primaries to stop Edward Kennedy from winning the Democratic nomination.[29]

Although the NRA gives to both political parties, the lion's share goes to Republicans (see Table 4.1). During the 1981–1982 period, the NRA gave $540,000 to Republicans and $176,000 to Democrats.[30] One recipient was Senator Orrin Hatch (R-Utah), a long-time NRA defender who, during the period when the Republicans were the majority, chaired a Judiciary Committee subcommittee with jurisdiction over gun legislation.[31]

Heavy campaign involvement is a primary tactic used by the gun lobby. By helping those candidates who support its position, the NRA has secured a strong and reliable voice in both state legislatures and Congress. But the NRA does not confine its activities to the legislative branch. Through its Firearms Civil Rights Legal Defense Fund, the NRA helps to finance legal battles in the courts. This organization is a tax exempt fund supported by individual and corporate donations and under the guidance of the Institute for Legislative Action.

Other Progun Groups

Single-issue progun groups have sprung up mainly because they believe that the NRA is not strident enough in its opposition to gun control legislation.[32] One such group, the second largest progun organization, is the Citizens Committee for the Right to Keep and Bear Arms, headquartered in Washington, D.C. With a reputed membership of 300,000 in 1981, the Citizens Committee operated on a $1.7 million budget. Led by full-time lobbyist John Snyder, a former Jesuit seminarian disgruntled with the activities of the NRA, the Citizens Committee publishes a monthly newsletter called *Point Blank*.[33] Of the $2 million raised by the committee in the early 1980s, only $15,000 was spent on political races. The rest was channeled into a television documentary and a wide range of propaganda materials. The research arm of the Citizens Committee, the Second Amendment Foundation, publishes progun literature.[34]

The Gun Owners of America (GOA) was founded in 1974 by H. L. Richardson, a California state senator and former director of the NRA. The goals of the GOA, which boasts more than three hundred fifty thousand members, are more narrow than the NRA's insofar as GOA is concerned only with contributing money to elections, for or against candidates. In the 1980 campaign, the GOA spent about $1.3 million, some 80 percent of its total budget, on campaign activities. Since its inception, the GOA has helped to raise $5 million for candidates around the country. Based in Sacramento, California, the GOA's lobbying effort on Capitol Hill is practically nonexistent.

Progun Arguments

Among all the groups on both sides of the gun controversy, the NRA is by far the most prolific in terms of distributing literature. The NRA's publications include general descriptive literature on the organization, information on firearms laws and regulations, booklets and flyers on gun ownership, use and safety information, reprints of sympathetic articles from law journals and elsewhere, and political advocacy literature. The symbolic importance of the Constitution is evidenced in much NRA literature. Listed on the reverse side of its membership application ("What is NRA?") are the purposes and objectives, of which the first is "to protect and defend the Constitution of the United States, especially with reference to the inalienable right of the individual American citizen guaranteed by such Constitution to acquire, possess, transport, carry, transfer ownership of, and enjoy the right to use arms." The second purpose—"to promote public safety, law and order, and the national defense"—uses inflated rhetoric tied to broad national concerns.

One recurring theme in the literature is the argument that the Second Amendment does protect absolutely any individual's right to own guns. The NRA also argues against waiting periods for gun ownership and for the elimination of gun regulations, stiffer laws, and any restrictions on handguns, including "Saturday night specials." One especially interesting use of these arguments has to do with the subject of public opinion. NRA literature boldly asserts popular support for its position. In one flyer entitled "Ten Myths About Gun Control," the NRA labels as myth the assertion that "the majority of Americans favor strict new additional Federal gun laws." In actuality, Gallup, Harris, and NORC Polls show that most people do favor stricter gun control laws.

An analysis of the NRA's rhetorical style was done by Raymond S. Rodgers,[35] who identified five logical and rhetorical fallacies in the NRA's publications. The first was the failure to define terms, for example the options that are included under the term *gun control*. The second was the use of the "big lie"—that the Second Amendment guarantees an inalienable right to bear arms. The third, the "slippery slope" fallacy, argued that any gun regulation invariably will lead to a total ban on guns and even to authoritarianism.[36] The fourth was the use of "bully tactics" such as name calling, as when gun control advocates were called "gun-grabbers." The fifth was improper appeals to authority, such as using endorsements by John Wayne, Roy Rogers, and Wally Schirra rather than relying on evidence or reasoning. Although such tactics are utilized by most interest groups, these tactics are a mainstay of the NRA's political efforts.

One singular example of how effectively the antigun control lobby has legitimized its viewpoint is evident in a 1982 report of the Senate's Subcommittee on the Constitution.[37] Although admittedly the NRA had an ally in the chairman, Orrin Hatch, this report went far beyond even the conventional anti–gun control arguments. The Subcommittee report ignored three Supreme Court cases (*U.S. v. Cruikshank* [1876]; *Presser v. Illinois* [1886]; *Miller v. Texas* [1894]) whose relevance as precedent was acknowledged by both proponents and opponents of gun control. The report erroneously stated, "The United States Supreme Court has only three times commented upon the meaning of the second amendment," and the cases mentioned were *Dred Scott v. Sandford* (1857), *U.S. v. Miller* (1939), and *Lewis v. United States* (1980).

The *Dred Scott* opinion was cited because it "indicated strongly that the right to keep and bear arms was an individual right; the Court noted that, were it to hold free blacks to be entitled to equality of citizenship, they would be entitled to keep and carry arms wherever they want." In fact, *Dred Scott* is not considered in the usual Second Amendment legal literature; indeed, the Court ruled that blacks were not citizens and any argument based on this ruling shows a priori why the concern about blacks carrying guns arose in the first place. The *Lewis* reference is even more obscure, as the report commented: "A footnote in *Lewis v. United States* indicated only that 'these legislative restrictions on the use of firearms'—a ban on possession by felons—were permissible. But since felons may constitutionally be deprived of many of the rights of citizens, including that of voting, this dicta reveals little." In fact, to the contrary, *Lewis* reveals a great deal about the Supreme Court's thinking as reflected earlier in the *Miller* case. The full text of that footnote, in what was Justice Harry Blackmun's majority opinion, is as follows: "These legislative restrictions on the use of firearms are neither based upon constitutionally suspect criteria, nor do they trench upon any constitutionally protected liberties. See *United States v. Miller* . . . (the Second Amendment guarantees no right to keep and bear a firearm that does not have 'some reasonable relationship to the preservation or efficiency of a well regulated militia')." The remainder of the footnote to *Lewis* cites recent lower federal court rulings that support the legality of firearms regulation.

Thus, this Senate subcommittee boldly misinterpreted the obvious point made in *Lewis* just as it erroneously elevated the significance of *Dred Scott* to the gun issue. The subcommittee's references to the important *U.S. v. Miller* case attempted to blunt its primary gun control thrust. But beyond the apparent willful manipulation of historical facts in this subcommittee report, the episode speaks powerfully to the ability of anti–gun control groups to legitimize and popularize their extreme views on the meaning of the Second Amendment.

Antigun Groups

The ideological antithesis of the NRA is Handgun Control. Although certainly not equal in membership or financial resources to the NRA, Handgun Control nonetheless tries to battle the NRA on its own terms by using the same style and methods. Based in Washington, D.C., Handgun Control is the largest of the antigun groups. Although formed in 1974, the organization had few resources and capabilities until the early 1980s, especially following the murder of ex-Beatle John Lennon. The organization now claims more than 1 million members, and many of those new recruits are people in their twenties and thirties who felt an emotional attachment to Lennon and were outraged at his death. Handgun Control lobbies heavily and in 1980 contributed money to congressional candidates for the first time, giving $75,000.[38] In contrast, that year the NRA spent $1.5 million for campaigns. In 1982, Handgun Control contributed to 120 congressional candidates; during the period 1983–1984, it gave $88,000 to various congressional races. The organization's political funding remains modest given the scope of campaign spending by the opposition.

Handgun Control wants to restrict, but not ban, the ownership of pistols and revolvers (in particular Saturday night specials), and to accomplish this objective, the organization has adopted some NRA tactics. Handgun Control is beginning to build its own portfolio of members who are willing to write legislators urging stricter gun control measures. Under the chairmanship of Pete Shields and Charles Orasin, Handgun Control targeted substantial funds for newspaper advertisements designed to generate mail to Congress on regulating handguns. Aside from generating 450,000 letters to Congress, these advertisements also gained for Handgun Control a list of 450,000 recruits for its membership rolls.

Drawing on this expanded membership, Handgun Control in 1986 spearheaded a political effort to block any weakening of the 1968 Gun Control Act (see later discussion of the McClure-Volkmer Bill). The nationwide campaign focused, in particular, on Sarah Brady, wife of presidential press secretary James Brady who was seriously wounded during the assassination attempt on President Reagan in 1981. As a board member of Handgun Control, Sarah Brady was a leader of its nationwide publicity campaign as well as its lobbying efforts on Capitol Hill. (She is also the daughter of an FBI agent and a marksperson trained on an FBI range.) But despite these heightened efforts by Handgun Control, combined as they were with those of many police organizations that opposed any relaxation of gun regulations, the NRA again prevailed in this legislative battle.

Another antigun group, the National Coalition to Ban Handguns, was founded in 1974 with a grant from the United Methodist church. The NCBH is composed of thirty national religious, educational, and social organizations and has about eighty-five thousand members. The NCBH tends to be more militant and aggressive in its lobbying efforts, and it wants handguns to be used only by the police, the military, properly secured gun clubs, and, to some extent, gun collectors. The NCBH favors a ban on Saturday night specials as well as stricter controls on other types of handguns. In contrast to Handgun Control, the NCBH concentrates its lobbying efforts on the state and local levels. Both NCBH and Handgun Control operated on annual budgets of approximately $1 million in 1981.[39] During the period 1983–1984, NCBH contributed only $11,595 to congressional candidates.

Still other single-issue groups have entered the gun control fray, although their impact has been relatively minor. In 1980, *Rolling Stone* publisher Jann Wenner formed the Foundation on Violence in America. Wenner had been a friend of John Lennon, and Lennon's death spurred the creation of this organization. In addition, some groups focus their efforts on educating the public about guns and gun safety from a gun control perspective. Such groups include the National Alliance for Handgun Control Education, the Committee for the Study of Handgun Misuse, the Foundation for Handgun Education, the National Alliance Against Violence, the Gun Safety Institute, and the Medical Council on Handgun Violence.

Unlike the anti–gun control groups, the proponents of stricter regulations have rallied the support of other organizations not exclusively concerned about the gun issue. As mentioned, the NCBH is a coalition of diverse religious and other organizations. The U.S. Conference of Mayors also is involved in this campaign. In 1972, the conference adopted a strongly worded resolution stating that the organization "takes a position of leadership and urges national legislation against the manufacture, importation, sale and private possession of handguns" and that it "urges its members to extend every effort to educate the American public to the dangerous and appalling realities resulting from the private possession of handguns." The NAACP also has endorsed stricter gun laws.

Gun Control Advocacy Literature

The publications of antigun groups cannot match the NRA in volume or intensity. The two principal sources of this literature are the NCBH and Handgun Control. General uniformity of content is to be found to the degree that such literature emphasizes crime statistics and the "collective" meaning of the Second Amendment as well as supplying anecdotes to buttress arguments for more gun regulations.

Each year in the United States, 30,000 people die as a result of the suicidal, criminal, or accidental use of guns. Since 1968, the number of firearms in private ownership has dramatically increased from approximately 60 million to the 150 million guns in circulation in 1982.[40] Americans own 55 million handguns and are purchasing 2.5 million more every year—one pistol for every four Americans. Indeed, a handgun is sold in the United States every thirteen seconds.[41] Nearly 5.5 million firearms are manufactured in this country each year, and 750,000 more weapons are imported into the country each year. All told, of the estimated 150 million guns in the United States today, nearly 40 million are handguns. Antigun literature emphasizes that handguns are the weapon used in more than one-half of the nation's 22,000 murders each year. Annually in the United States 1 million gun incidents occur, including 15,000 suicides, 1,800 accidental deaths, 157,000 assaults, 221,000 robberies, and 200,000 injuries.[42]

Historian Richard Hofstadter observed that the United States is the only modern Western nation that clings to the "gun culture."[43] This fact is dramatized by cross-cultural statistics. In 1979, for example, Sweden reported 21 deaths from handguns, Japan had 48, and Canada had 52; deaths from all guns equalled 55 in Britain and 800 in France. But in the United States, 9,848 persons died from handguns alone.[44] In 1980, Switzerland reported 24 handgun deaths as compared to 4 in Australia and 23 in Israel; in the United States, the toll was 11,522.[45] Thus, despite population size differences, it is obvious that U.S. gun-related deaths are far greater in absolute numbers and proportionately than in other industrial nations. The advocates of stricter gun control legislation claim that other nations' much lower death rates from guns are a consequence of stronger laws.[46] In their defense, opponents of gun controls argue that those statistics reflect deep-seated cultural differences that cannot be erased through legislation.

If one underlying theme predominates throughout the antigun literature, it is a rebuttal of the NRA's arguments about the legal and political justifications for firearms and the alleged adverse consequences from gun control. This "truth squad" approach is illustrated in various gun control newsletters. In the Fall 1983 issue of the NCBH's "News and Views," for example, the back page was devoted mostly to a story about a sixty-seven-year-old Alabama woman who, with an empty .32 caliber handgun, ostensibly held off a street gang of young males that she claimed tried to rob her while she was visiting New York City. The *New York Post* and the *Daily News* gave big coverage to the story and particularly to the fact that the woman was arrested, in addition to her alleged assailants, for not having a city pistol permit. Her story was widely trumpeted in several anti–gun control publications.

According to the NCBH's account, however, subsequent investigation determined that the "gang" included a forty-seven-year-old woman and two fifteen-year-old girls. The woman later admitted that she never was actually robbed or accosted, contrary to the first reports, but that she merely had suspected that her purse might be snatched. This incident was used by NCBH to argue for stricter gun laws because the woman's willingness to pull a gun evidently was not warranted by the circumstances. Nonetheless, a New York state rifle and pistol club awarded the woman $500 for her "brave actions" and also replaced her confiscated pistol.

Gun control groups struggle to wage this rhetorical war against progun groups on their home turf, and the proponents of gun controls say that the weight of law and fact rests with them. The outcome of the gun control struggle will not depend on factual information alone, although both sides seek to establish a kind of symbolic high ground in the dispute. In one important way this has been achieved by the gun control lobby because most citizens do favor stricter gun laws. The problem is that antigun groups lack the level of political resources of the NRA; in addition, the zealotry of the NRA's membership may be more than any match for public opinion.

PUBLIC OPINION

As early as 1938, pollsters began measuring public opinion on gun control. The Gallup Poll in that year found that 79 percent of the respondents favored "gun control."[47] Since 1959, Gallup has asked, "Would you favor or oppose a law which would require a person to obtain a police permit before he or she could buy a gun?" The affirmative response rate to that question has fluctuated between 68 and 78 percent.[48]

Gallup also asked whether laws concerning handgun sales should be strengthened, weakened, or kept as they are now. Table 4.2 gives those responses.[49] A breakdown of the 1983 responses shows that women were more likely to favor stricter laws than were men, as were young adults (18–29), the college educated, and people living in the East and in urban areas. Almost half (47 percent) of all gun owners favored stricter handgun laws, although this percentage did drop to 39 percent among handgun owners specifically. In addition, the National Opinion Research Center surveyed the public on whether police permits should be required for gun ownership. The responses in Table 4.3 show much public support for that requirement.[50]

A variation of that question was used by researchers Howard Schuman and Stanley Presser to measure intensity of feelings on both sides of the

TABLE 4.2 Gallup Polls on Gun Control

	1975	1980	1981	1983	1986
More strict	69%	59%	65%	59%	60%
Less strict	3	6	3	4	8
Kept as is	24	29	30	31	30

Source: Data taken from *The Gallup Report*, No. 248
(May 1986), p. 17.

TABLE 4.3 NORC Surveys on Permits for Gun Ownership

	1972	1973	1974	1975	1976	1977	1980	1982
Favor	70%	73%	75%	74%	72%	72%	69%	72%
Oppose	27	25	23	24	27	26	29	26

Source: Data derived from the National Opinion Research Center, *General Social Surveys* (July 1982): p. 87. The question was, "Would you favor or oppose a law which would require a person to obtain a police permit before he or she could buy a gun?"

gun controversy.[51] What these researchers found was that at the purely subjective level, supporters of the permit law responded with slightly more intensity than did the opponents; however, when the respondents were asked whether they ever wrote letters or contributed money to support their position on this issue, the opponents were much more likely to have done so than were the supporters. One reason for this differential, the authors suggested, was the superior organizational effectiveness of anti–gun control forces. Schuman and Presser concluded that single-issue politics was more complex than was previously believed, but their findings did affirm what case studies have suggested—namely, that the progun lobby has a more determined constituency as compared to the majority who favor gun controls.

Even the most extreme handgun proposals find substantial support from the public. The 1983 Gallup Poll also asked respondents if they would support a ban on the sale and possession of handguns in their community. Forty-four percent said they would (although a plurality of 48 percent was opposed), and the pattern of approval for this proposal among subgroups in the population was roughly the same as that reported in favor of stricter gun laws. The same question was asked in 1985, this time with 40 percent favoring but 56 percent opposing the proposal.[52]

Despite the wealth of public opinion findings favoring gun control, the opposition can point to survey results indicating support for the use of guns in hypothetical situations of danger or criminal assault. A 1968 Harris Survey found that 51 percent would "use your gun to shoot other people in case of a riot."[53] That question probably was triggered by the urban disturbances and rioting that occurred in several U.S. cities during 1968. More recently, a Gallup Poll found overwhelming support (72 percent) for using a gun against a likely assailant.[54] This question was prompted by a well-publicized incident in New York City where a white man shot four minority youths he alleged were going to rob him. The fear of violent crime that rationalizes the use of force in self-defense is one sentiment progun groups exploit in their arguments.

The statistics on the availability of guns in the United States are staggering, and this fact is underscored by 1983 and 1985 Gallup Polls that asked, "Do you have any guns in the house?" Four in ten respondents in both surveys claimed to own one or more guns.[55] There were more gun owners among men rather than women, whites rather than blacks, as well as among the less educated, older persons, and people with higher incomes. Also, Republicans were more likely to own guns than were Democrats, Protestants more than Catholics, and manual workers more than other occupational groupings. But a majority of only two subgroups owned guns: residents of the South (53 percent in 1983/54 percent in 1984) and persons living in towns with populations of less than 2,500 and in rural areas (where 65 percent owned guns). If there is a gun culture in the United States, these data suggest that it is a rural and southern phenomenon. In contrast, fewest guns were owned by easterners and by people living in cities of 1 million or more population.

FEDERALISM

Much of the emotional commitment that feeds the gun culture stems from a long tradition linking guns to the nation's frontier development. Few would deny the vital role of the Pennsylvania rifle in helping yeoman colonists defeat European professional soldiers and protect property. But to claim that "the American experiment was made possible by the gun"[56] is to ignore the political economy of colonial America. Similarly, axioms such as "the guns that won the West" and "arm[s] that opened the West and tamed the wild land"[57] underestimate the central role played by homesteaders, ranchers, businesspeople, and the general movement of civilization. Even after the frontier disappeared, mythic attachments to the gun remained; otherwise, how else can one explain the argument that a boy should be allowed to own a gun because a .22 caliber rifle was a "character builder"?[58]

It is difficult to overemphasize the grass-roots nature of the gun culture. Obvious regional differences do exist, for example, between Morton Grove,

Illinois, where handgun ownership in the home was banned, and Kenesaw County, Georgia, where local leaders passed an admittedly frivolous law making it a crime *not* to own a handgun. This action was taken in direct response to Morton Grove. Thirty-nine states make some mention of a right to bear arms in their constitutions; those that do not are California, Delaware, Iowa, Maryland, Minnesota, Nebraska, New Jersey, New York, North Dakota, West Virginia, and Wisconsin. Except for California, none of these eleven states is located in the South or West where the gun culture is presumably strongest.

One study devised a measure of the strictness of state handgun laws using seven possible types of regulation. Most states fell in the middle of the distribution, having neither very strict nor very weak gun laws. Generally, the states with stricter handgun control laws tended to have larger populations, were eastern, and committed more resources to criminal justice.[59]

Lacking an ostensibly strong progun tradition, New York state makes no mention of any right to bear arms in its constitution and has one of the strictest handgun control laws. Yet a recent battle about "cop-killer" bullets shows how grass-roots activism by progun advocates can affect local decisionmaking on gun control even in a state as liberal as New York.

During the summer of 1982, the otherwise placid Long Island community of Brookhaven erupted in political controversy. The issue that rocked this New York township was an attempt by the Brookhaven Town Board to outlaw the possession of handgun bullets capable of piercing a police officer's bulletproof vest. The armor-piercing bullet, the most commonly mentioned being the teflon-coated KTW bullet, is capable of blasting through auto engine blocks. This penetration capacity has caused police departments uniformly to discontinue using the bullet and to advocate its ban. The president of the International Association of Chiefs of Police stated flatly that KTW bullets have "no legitimate use . . . either in or out of law enforcement."[60]

Armor-piercing bullets are capable of passing through up to seventy-two layers of Kevlar, the material from which body armor is made. Typical vests are composed of eighteen layers. Insofar as body armor has been credited with saving the lives of more than four hundred police officers from 1974 to 1982,[61] police officials argue that public safety is served by banning these bullets, especially because the bullet has no hunting or recreational value. In its literature, the NRA claims that no police officer has ever been killed by the KTW bullet and that recent publicity about the bullet serves simply to inform criminals of its availability and capability.[62] But the National Coalition to Ban Handguns alleges to have documented at least two cases where police have been shot by these bullets.[63] Recently, New York police uncovered thirty-two armor-piercing handgun bullets in the home of a suspected bank robber on Long Island.[64] The NRA blames media publicity for spreading information on this deadly bullet, but an "NBC Magazine" segment aired on January 8, 1987, showed that various gun magazines featured stories about the bullets in 1981.

Despite the many questions raised about this ammunition, the Brookhaven Town Board's effort to ban the "super bullets" (a ban supported by the Suffolk Police Patrolmen's Benevolent Association and other police departments, including New York City's) was defeated when hundreds of local residents turned out at a town meeting to denounce the proposal. The outpouring was prompted by the NRA, which sent "alert" telegrams to its members in the area. Speaking against the ordinance, NRA lobbyist James Baker commented, "You can't moderate behavior by controlling objects," and a local spokesperson observed that mere possession of the bullets would constitute "presumptive intent. . . . dangerous words when it comes to the liberties of an American citizen."[65] The opponents of the town ordinance raised moral and constitutional objections that any restrictions eventually would lead to the banning of all guns. Eventually an ordinance was passed, but it was weakened further by a provision that made possession a criminal offense only if criminal intent could be demonstrated.

The Brookhaven case illustrates several points: the zealotry of the NRA's grass-roots operations; the NRA's refusal to compromise on its absolutist approach to gun ownership; the NRA's readiness to tie specific cases to moral and constitutional issues; and the NRA's ability to displace the burden of proof onto the media and gun control proponents. As a final note to this story, Congress enacted a ban on the importation, manufacture, and sale of KTW bullets (P.L. 99-408) that was signed into law August 20, 1986. Attempts to pass this legislation, which went back four years, had been opposed by the NRA. This time, however, it did not actively oppose the law,[66] a move motivated partly by the alienating effect the NRA's opposition had on police organizations as well as the NRA's preoccupation with defeating the McClure-Volkmer Bill under consideration at the same time. A similar ban was enacted by New York state in August 1986, and at least fourteen other states passed such prohibitions by the end of 1985. The federal and New York state laws prohibit bullets made from tungsten alloys, steel, iron, brass, bronze, beryllium copper, or uranium.

THE PRESIDENCY

Involvement of the presidency with the issue of gun control has occurred primarily on a symbolic level; that is, presidents periodically have expressed their views on the subject but rarely have played an active role in gun-related policymaking (see subsequent discussion of Congress). The first president to associate himself aggressively with organized gun interests was soldier-hunter-sportsman Theodore Roosevelt. While governor of New York, Roosevelt took an active hand in helping to form an organization to support marksmanship. As president, Roosevelt took an active interest in the revival of the National Rifle Association and was himself a member. He also helped to encourage the establishment of firing ranges in public schools.

During the term of President Calvin Coolidge, Congress dealt with several modest but controversial gun control measures. Yet Coolidge offered no leadership on the issue, in part because it raised the specter of federal involvement in policing activities that otherwise had been reserved to the states. Franklin D. Roosevelt was the first president to actively promote gun-restricting legislation as part of a larger federal assault on crime and gangsterism. The modest gun control legislation that was enacted into law in 1934 and 1938 was the result of this effort.

Gun issues surfaced little during the next thirty years, and for most subsequent presidents the gun issue was primarily one more symbolic ribbon to be acquired. Notably, Presidents Dwight Eisenhower, John Kennedy, Richard Nixon, and Ronald Reagan (as well as Vice President George Bush) were/are all life members of the NRA. Ironically, it was the Kennedy assassination that prompted renewed interest in stronger gun regulations. President Lyndon B. Johnson stood behind the gun control efforts of the 1960s, but he was not especially successful in exerting a decisive political influence as compared to his enormous impact on major social welfare legislation during his term in office.[67]

President Reagan has taken a consistent and prominent stand against gun control. Even after the nearly successful attempt on his life in 1981, he made it clear that his position had not changed. In a subsequent interview, Reagan said that "if anything, I'm a little disturbed that focusing on gun control as an answer to the crime problem today could very well be diverting us from really paying attention to what needs to be done if we're to solve the crime problem." He also said that existing gun control laws had proven ineffective in regulating guns.[68]

Like other social issues, such as abortion and women's rights, the national political parties consistently have disagreed with each other on gun control, although the degree of rhetorical stridency in each party's platform has varied. The Republicans have articulated a long-standing support for gun ownership, and the Democrats exhibit a similar consistency in favor of stronger gun regulations. The issue first appeared in party platforms in 1968,[69] and both political parties have treated the issue in their platforms under the category of crime and criminal justice.

The 1968 Republican party platform urged "control [of] indiscriminate availability of firearms" but also "safeguarding the right of responsible citizens to collect, own and use firearms . . . retaining primary responsibility at the state level." The 1972 Republican platform again endorsed citizen rights to "collect, own and use firearms," but also included "self-defense" as a purpose and emphasized efforts "to prevent criminal access to all weapons," especially cheap handguns, while relying mainly on state en-forcement. The 1976 GOP platform was more terse; it simply stated, "We support the right of citizens to keep and bear arms." The Republican party also stated its opposition to federal registration of firearms and advocated harsher sentences for crimes committed with guns. If the previous GOP platforms had contained at least a nod to gun regulation, the 1976 document conformed fully to NRA policy.

In 1980, the Republican platform wording was the same as in 1976, with an added phrase urging removal of "those provisions of the Gun

Control Act of 1968 that do not significantly impact on crime but serve rather to restrain the law-abiding citizen in his legitimate use of firearms." The 1984 platform dropped any reference to the Gun Control Act or to gun registration and said instead that citizens ought not to be blamed for "exercising their constitutional rights" (which presumably meant an "individual" right to bear arms).

The 1968 Democratic party platform, in its mention of gun control, urged "the passage and enforcement of effective federal, state and local gun control legislation." A specific proposal appeared for the first time in 1972 when, after calling for "laws to control the improper use of hand guns," the Democratic party asked for a ban on Saturday night specials. The 1976 platform again called for strengthening existing handgun controls as well as banning Saturday night specials. But the platform also urged tougher sentencing for crimes committed with guns and—in a partial reversal— affirmed "the right of sportsmen to possess guns for purely hunting and target-shooting purposes." The 1980 platform advocated the same position and reaffirmed that the Democratic party supported the rights of sportsmen to possess guns for sporting purposes.

This softening of the Democratic party's stand on gun control probably reflected the caution of its presidential candidate, Jimmy Carter. Carter certainly was preferable to the progun lobby than was his arch rival, Senator Edward Kennedy (D-Mass.). During his 1980 primary campaign to unseat President Carter, Kennedy found his trail dogged by progun activists. He persistently faced union members who had been told by the NRA that Kennedy favored the confiscation of firearms. As the senator observed, "It was not true, but it was believed, because the gun lobby had repeated it over and over."[70] The 1984 Democratic party platform, reflecting the liberal views of nominee Walter Mondale, made a modest turn to the left by dropping any reference to the sporting use of guns. The platform again called for tough restraints on snub-nosed handguns.

This overview indicates scant presidential involvement with the gun control issue. Modest gun control laws were enacted during the terms of Democratic presidents FDR and LBJ, whereas President Reagan was adamantly opposed to more regulations on guns, even handguns. The increasingly pro-NRA wording of GOP platforms since the early 1970s seems to parallel the rising influence of the NRA. In contrast, the Democratic party platforms generally have adhered to a gun control philosophy.

CONGRESS

Only five gun control enactments merit any consideration. The first is the National Firearms Act of 1934. It came as a response to gang violence and the attempted assassination of President Roosevelt the year before. The act's main purpose was to end possession of machine guns, sawed-off shotguns, silencers, and other gangster weapons. Congress went a step further in 1938 by passing the Federal Firearms Act, which tried to regulate the interstate shipment of firearms and ammunition by establishing federal licensing of manufacturers, importers, and dealers of guns and ammunition. The act also prohibited the shipment of firearms to people under indictment, fugitives, and some convicted felons.

Two laws were passed in 1968. One was incorporated in Title IV of the Omnibus Crime Control and Safe Streets Act, which banned the transportation of pistols and revolvers across state lines and forbade the purchase of handguns in stores in a state where the buyer did not reside. The Omnibus Crime Control and Safe Street Act was passed the day after the assassination of Robert Kennedy and two months after the murder of Martin Luther King.

Gun Control Act of 1968

The key provisions of the Omnibus Act were incorporated into the Gun Control Act of 1968, the second enactment of the year. This statute provides an ideal case study to highlight the political processes affecting a direct effort to regulate firearms. The main arena of conflict was Congress, where numerous efforts were made on the floor to amend this legislation. Lobbying by interest groups was heavy, but the president's influence over the final bill was minimal.[71] The enactment of P.L. 90-618 was spurred by recent assassinations and a wave of public sentiment favoring tougher gun laws. President Johnson had been outspoken in his support for stronger gun laws ever since taking office in 1963, but congressional action was not forthcoming, even during LBJ's period of maximum influence during 1964–1965. On June 6, 1968, President Johnson urged Congress "in the name of sanity . . . in the name of safety and in the name of an aroused nation to give America the gun-control law it needs."[72]

The Johnson proposal was introduced into the House on June 10, 1968, as HR 17735 by Judiciary Committee chairman Emanuel Celler (D-N.Y.), a gun control advocate, and by Senator Thomas Dodd (D-Conn.), also a champion of gun control, who chaired the Judiciary's Subcommittee on Juvenile Delinquency. The House Judiciary Committee initially voted 16–16 on the bill, thus keeping it in the committee. An agreement was made to reconsider the legislation, however, and it was finally reported out on June 21, after the addition of some qualifying amendments. The House Rules Committee approved a rule for the bill on July 9, after holding the legislation for nearly three weeks. Rules Committee chairman William Colmer (D-Miss.), a gun control opponent, released the bill only after extracting a promise from Celler that he would oppose any efforts to add registration and licensing provisions to the bill on the floor of the House.

The House of Representatives passed HR 17735 on July 24 after four days of vigorous floor consideration characterized by numerous attempts to amend the bill. Efforts were made to strengthen registration and licensing provisions, increase penalties, deregulate ammunition sales, provide exceptions for collectors, and curtail importation of foreign military weapons. Overall, forty-five attempts were made to amend this legislation on the floor of the House, including four roll call votes plus one more on final passage. In the more liberal Senate, the gun control bill met with greater support, and more debate centered on whether to strengthen the law or not. Subcommittee hearings began on June 26, and testimony was received from a wide variety of persons including NRA president Harold W. Glassen, who said that the legislation was part of an effort to "foist upon an unsuspecting and aroused public a law that would, through its operation, sound the death knell for the shooting sport and eventually disarm the American public."[73]

The Senate subcommittee approved the measure unanimously and forwarded it to the full committee where the bill encountered stiff opposition. The bill was delayed and weakened by gun control opponents, including Judiciary Committee chair James Eastland (D-Miss.). Efforts to push the bill through were hampered by the absence at various times of gun control supporters, including Senator Edward Kennedy (D-Mass.), who was still mourning the loss of his brother. Finally, the bill was sent by committee to the Senate floor, where it was debated for five days. The opening salvo came from Senator Dodd, who accused the NRA of "blackmail, intimidation and unscrupulous propaganda."[74] Debate centered on attempts to nationalize gun registration, strengthen criminal penalties, and create special exemptions for gun collectors and sportsmen. In all, seventeen formal motions were made to amend this bill in the Senate. After the bill's passage on September 18, a conference committee ironed out differences with the House, and President Johnson signed the bill on October 22.

As enacted, P.L. 90-618 restricted interstate shipment of firearms and ammunition and prohibited the sale of guns to minors, drug addicts, mental incompetents, and convicted felons. The act strengthened licensing and record-keeping requirements for gun dealers and collectors, extended the tax provisions of the National Firearms Act of 1934 to include destructive devices not originally covered, and banned the importation of foreign-made surplus firearms. But the law did not ban the importation of handgun parts, which effectively allowed for the circumvention of the import ban.

Opposition to this modest gun law did not end in 1968, however. One year later a key provision of the act requiring sellers of shotgun and rifle ammunition to register purchasers was repealed in an amendment tacked onto a tax bill. This rider was authored by Senator Wallace F. Bennett (R-Utah) along with forty-six Senate co-sponsors.[75]

The Firearms Owners Protection Act of 1986

Repeated efforts were made throughout the years to weaken the 1968 gun law. The most important, and successful, attempt came in 1986, with enactment of the Firearms Owners Protection Act, also known as the McClure-Volkmer Bill (S. 49, H.R. 4332, P.L. 99-308). This act amended the 1968 Gun Control Act by allowing for the legal interstate sale of rifles and shotguns as long as the sale is legal in the states of the buyer and seller. The act also eliminated record-keeping requirements for ammunition dealers, made it easier for individuals selling guns to do so without a license unless they did so "regularly," allowed gun dealers to do business at gun shows, and prohibited the Bureau of Alcohol, Tobacco, and Firearms (BATF) from issuing regulations requiring centralized records of gun dealers. In addition, the act limited to one per year the number of unannounced inspections of gun dealers by the BATF and prohibited the establishment of any system of comprehensive firearms registration. Finally, the act barred future possession or transfer of machine guns and retained existing restrictions (except for transport) on handguns. The passage of this legislation spanned two years and was the culmination of a protracted lobbying effort by the NRA, joined by the Gun Owners of America and the Citizens Committee for the Right to Keep and Bear Arms.

Consideration of S. 49 began first in the Senate, where attempts to weaken the 1968 gun law had been approved by the Judiciary Committee in 1982 and 1984. Floor consideration was not obtained, however, until 1985, the first time the full Senate had considered any gun legislation since 1972. Once on the floor, the bill was subjected to a barrage of amendments designed to strengthen gun controls; none of these amendments, however, was accepted. Senator Edward Kennedy proposed that the ban on the interstate sale of handguns be retained because this prohibition was lifted in the original Senate Bill. Senator Charles McC. Mathias (R-Md.) moved to eliminate a provision requiring that gun dealers be given prior notice before routine inspections by federal investigators are made. Senator Daniel K. Inouye (D-Hawaii) proposed a fourteen-day waiting period between purchase and delivery of handguns, a provision that was recommended by law enforcement groups.

But the bill's chief Senate sponsors, James A. McClure (R-Idaho) and Orrin Hatch (R-Utah), argued that the proposed restrictions would have no effect on crime-fighting but instead represented unjustified limitations on sportsmen, hunters, and dealers. The one significant restriction imposed by the Senate was a ban on the importation of Saturday night special gun parts. The final vote on S. 49 was 79–15, with the strongest support coming from western supporters. The relatively speedy passage of this bill was attributed to the pressure of the NRA and its allies and to the fact that the Republican-controlled Senate had a sympathetic Judiciary Committee chairman (Strom Thurmond, R-S.C.) and majority leader (Robert Dole, R-Kans.).[76]

In many respects, gun control forces were caught unawares by the speedy Senate action in committee and on the floor. This set the stage for a full-scale fight in the House of Representatives in 1986. Although the progun lobby achieved an important victory, in the process the lobby alienated some key, long-time allies—police groups and organizations. Police dissatisfaction with NRA positions had been growing for some time, and even during Senate consideration of S. 49, Handgun Control had enlisted the support of five national police organizations. In 1986, national law enforcement groups lined up almost unanimously with gun control proponents. Such organizations as the National Sheriffs' Association, the International Association of Chiefs of Police, the National Organization of

Black Law Enforcement Executives, the National Troopers Association, the Police Executive Research Forum, the Police Foundation, and the Fraternal Order of Police have become increasingly alarmed about the criminal and safety consequences of weak gun regulations. In particular, law enforcement officials were alienated by the NRA's stand against controlling armor-piercing bullets and in favor of legal possession of submachine guns and automatic weapons. The NRA responded that those national police organizations were out of touch with their memberships and that most rank-and-file police continued to support the NRA.[77]

Deliberations on the McClure-Volkmer Bill in the Democratic-controlled House posed a far greater problem for the progun lobby. Judiciary Committee chairman Peter Rodino (D-N.J.), a staunch proponent of gun control, had announced that the bill came "D.O.A.—Dead on Arrival." Many proponents of gun control felt reassured, despite the Senate action, because they had confidence that Rodino would not allow a gun decontrol bill out of his committee. Rodino's comments infuriated the gun lobby, however, and a discharge petition was begun, spearheaded by bill sponsor Representative Harold L. Volkmer (D-Mo.). If signed by a majority of the House membership, a discharge petition would force the bill from the committee to the House floor. The opponents of gun control argued that this bill was necessary to eliminate burdensome and unnecessary restrictions on gun dealers and legitimate owners as well as to provide a means for curtailing what these opponents perceived to be harassment by federal bureaucrats. The BATF countered that, in fact, most of its prosecutions under the gun law involved individuals with prior criminal or felony records.[78]

Despite its well-known support for the NRA, the Reagan administration played a minimal role in these proceedings. Officially, the administration supported S. 49, but the Justice Department offered no testimony at committee hearings, and internal BATF memos released to the press revealed doubts about some of the decontrol provisions. Public comments by Attorney General Edwin Meese were similarly equivocal.[79]

Despite the firm opposition of Congressmen Peter Rodino and William J. Hughes (D-N.J., chairman of the Subcommittee on Crime), the full Judiciary Committee held a markup session on the bill and reported it to the floor by a unanimous vote. This remarkable turn of events occurred in March as the result of a successful discharge petition—the first successful petition since 1983. By reporting to the floor first (March 11) before completion and filing of the discharge petition (March 13), gun control forces hoped to salvage some parliamentary flexibility that would allow prior consideration of this legislation, which retained more gun restrictions. This maneuver failed, however, because Representative Volkmer was able to offer his version of the bill as a substitute for that of the Judiciary Committee.

On April 9, Congressman Hughes offered a package of law enforcement amendments, including a ban on interstate sale and transport of handguns and stricter record-keeping regulations. The package was rejected by a wide margin (176–248). During the vote, police officers stood in full uniform at "parade rest" at the entrance to the House floor. After several other votes on motions to strengthen certain gun control provisions (none was successful), the House adjourned and then reconvened the next day. This time, on the third try, the House approved (233–184) a ban on interstate handgun sales after proponents stressed the difference between sale and transport. A final amendment to bar all future possession and sale of machine guns by private citizens also passed. The bill was approved by a lopsided 292–130 vote on April 10.

Analysis of the voting behavior on the key package of amendments offered by Congressman Hughes revealed that anti–gun control support was strongest in the South and Border states (83 percent voting against), followed by the West/Rocky Mountain region (59 percent against), the Midwest (50 percent against), and then the East (38 percent against). Those regions with more rural populations and greater gun ownership (and presumably greater NRA influence) provided the strongest support for the progun lobby. Among the representatives from Alabama, Alaska, Arizona, Idaho, Louisiana, Maine, Mississippi, Montana, Nebraska, Nevada, New Hampshire, New Mexico, North Carolina, North Dakota, Oregon, South Carolina, South Dakota, Utah, West Virginia, and Wyoming (twenty states), *none* registered an anti-NRA vote. In four other states—Arkansas, Georgia, Kentucky, and Tennessee—the NRA lost only one vote among their congresspersons. The NRA even did well in some larger states such as Pennsylvania and Texas. In terms of partisanship, House Republicans heavily favored the NRA, with only 40 voting for the Hughes package versus 138 against. The Democrats were less cohesive on this question; they split almost evenly, with 138 for the amendments and 110 against. Thus, the key variables influencing this vote were region, constituency, and attendant ideological disposition toward the gun issue.

NRA applied dual pressure from below (grass roots) and above (lobbying) on the Congress. In all, the NRA devoted $1.6 million to its efforts compared to the paltry sum of about $15,000 spent by police organizations.[80] The relative inexperience of police lobbying also hurt their cause. As one congressman observed, "The police misunderstood the force of lobbying. Lobbying is not standing in long lines at the door. Lobbying is good information early; it is a presence when minds are being made up."[81] Moreover, relatively little attention was devoted to the efforts of Handgun Control, despite its high-visibility national campaign spearheaded by Sarah Brady.

The House-passed bill, H.R. 4332, differed from the Senate version in a few specifics. They were resolved by the unusual action of enacting a separate bill (S. 2414). Its purpose was to clarify certain sections and to appease police interests, which finally succeeded in persuading Senator Thurmond to take up their appeal. The added provision made clear that guns transported across state lines must be unloaded and locked in an area of the motor vehicle other than the passenger compartment. The clarifying bill also provided for easier government traces of guns and restored certain recordkeeping provisions. In this form the bill was signed into law by President Reagan on May 19, 1986.

This legislative case study parallels the experience of the 1968 Gun Control Act in important ways. First, President Reagan's impact was minimal, despite his clear opinions on this subject. Second, the level of political intensity was high, especially in the House. The successful and rare application of a discharge petition coupled with the unusual clarifying bill at final passage illustrate how both conflict and political instability caused these disruptions in legislative routine. The large number of floor amendments revealed the inability of the proponents and opponents of decontrol to resolve their differences within the committees of either house. Third, interest group activity again was abundant and of critical importance to the final outcome. Because of the NRA's political skill, pressure on Congress from constituents and lobbyists, and substantial financial commitment, the underfunded and poorly organized coalition of police groups was no match for the National Rifle Association.

BUREAUCRACY

The Bureau of Alcohol, Tobacco, and Firearms (BATF) was established in 1972 when legal authority related to alcohol, tobacco, firearms, and explosives was transferred from the Internal Revenue Service. Although the bureau's headquarters are located in Washington, D.C. (under the Treasury Department), its operations are relatively decentralized, as most BATF personnel operate from regional offices around the country. The bureau is organized according to two sections: regulatory enforcement and criminal enforcement. Matters dealing with gun regulations, including licensing, gun tracing, illegal firearms transport and possession, and explosives are handled by the Section on Criminal Enforcement.[82] Much of the reputed laxity of the BATF can be traced to its stated objective of relying on voluntary compliance with the laws the BATF is supposed to enforce, but the problem of promoting strict gun control enforcement existed long before the creation of the BATF.

During congressional hearings in 1965, for example, Treasury Department officials acknowledged that only five BATF employees were assigned full-time to enforce the 1934 and 1938 gun laws. *Congressional Quarterly* reported that in the previous thirty years the Treasury Department had obtained only one conviction involving the improper mailing of firearms to individuals in states that required purchase permits.[83] More recently, government officials from the BATF and elsewhere have admitted that gun smuggling and other illegal gun trafficking have not been high enforcement priorities.[84] An examination of BATF activities reveals that despite NRA criticism, the BATF and its predecessor have not posed a major regulatory threat to gun owners. The pattern of sporadic enforcement by the BATF extends to the present day.

A spokesperson for the BATF told the *Washington Star* that during 1980 the bureau conducted only 103 investigations of firearms dealers and that 10 dealer licenses out of the 180,000 nationwide were revoked.[85] In 1985, BATF fielded only 400 inspectors to monitor more than two hundred thousand gun merchants.[86] To cite another example, the BATF has been criticized for its handling of the Ingram MAC-10 pistol. In 1979, the BATF's firearms-technology branch examined the weapon and recommended that it be classified as a machine gun. This classification would have placed strict controls on the weapon, but this recommendation was overturned by the agency's firearms-classification panel (meaning that the weapon would get a classification of semiautomatic and therefore be free of significant regulations). At this time, fewer than one thousand of these weapons had been produced. But in the next three years, production increased and the weapon was used in a variety of crimes, including the murder of a Missouri state trooper. In 1982, the BATF reassessed the status of the weapon, but this time classified it as a machine gun (the weapon is easily converted to either semi- or fully automatic use). But in this reclassification process, BATF exempted those MAC-10s produced or sold before 1982. Finally, the NCBH succeeded in prodding the Congress to consider legislation in 1985 to resolve the status of the MAC-10.[87]

Much of BATF's reticence to implement more aggressive gun control enforcement stems from continued NRA harassment. When the bureau proposed regulations to centralize gun records in 1978, NRA members flooded the agency with 350,000 letters in opposition. NRA allies in Congress also regularly call BATF representatives before congressional committees to respond to charges of harassment of innocent gun dealers and collectors. According to the Carter administration's assistant treasury secretary who oversaw the BATF, "The NRA set them [BATF] up as a bogeyman to raise funds and rally support."[88]

Despite this record of administrative weakness in relation to gun control, the Reagan administration moved early in 1981 to abolish the BATF by proposing to shift its responsibilities back to the Internal Revenue Service (IRS). The proposal was appealing because the BATF had few friends and many enemies and because the proposal conformed to President Reagan's antiregulation, budget-cutting themes. In September 1981, the administration moved ahead by recommending to Congress that as a cost cutting venture, the agency be eliminated by surrendering its functions to the IRS and, with regard to its law enforcement duties, to the Secret Service or the Department of Justice. At this time, the BATF employed 3,900 people and had an operating budget of $160 million.

That recommendation prompted numerous comments of dismay from BATF officials and gun control proponents. One BATF employee said, "The N.R.A. has finally won," and Director G. R. Dickerson commented that his agency was being "destroyed by cuts that are in large measure due to the N.R.A. campaign against us." NCBH Director Michael Beard added, "I fear it may be a major step backward and another victory for the N.R.A."[89] The anti-BATF campaign by the NRA, highlighted by an NRA-produced film depicting BATF agents as "Nazi gestapos" and "jackbooted fascists," left little doubt about the NRA's views of the agency.[90]

Although the Reagan proposal generated much outcry from gun control advocates, it died in Congress with the ironic assistance of the NRA. (The BATF did suffer some budgetary and personnel cuts.) The final Reagan administration proposal advocated a division of BATF responsibilities between the U.S. Customs Service and the Secret Service. The NRA turned thumbs down on this recommendation because of the organization's concern that the Secret Service, by reputation a highly efficient agency, would prove to be even more effective at enforcing gun regulations than the BATF had. In fact, gun control proponents had long sought to transfer BATF enforcement authority to an agency like the Department of Justice in the hopes of improving supervision over gun laws. According to *Congressional Quarterly*, the Reagan proposal died because it met with "fierce opposition from gun owners."[91]

JUDICIARY

Courts initiate change in social regulatory policy and shift legal jurisdiction from the states to the federal government. Gun control does not immediately conjure up this image of judicial activism because the Second Amendment has not been centrally involved in fundamental rights adjudication. This amendment is accorded low status by most legal experts. Irving Brant argued that the Second Amendment "comes to life chiefly on the parade floats of rifle associations and in the propaganda of mail-order houses selling pistols to teenage gangsters."[92] Robert Rutland considered the Second as he did the Third Amendment: "Gradually, the need to insure citizens the right to bear arms or the prohibition on quartering troops have become obsolete."[93] J. W. Peltason wrote that the Second Amendment "was designed to prevent Congress from disarming the state militias, not to prevent it from regulating private ownership of firearms."[94]

Despite the widely held view among constitutional scholars that the Second Amendment is largely obsolete as the basis of any legal doctrine (including the "right to bear arms"), the amendment nonetheless continues to be the focus of the political debate between pro- and antigun groups. Each side seeks the mantle of constitutional legitimacy not so much for any possible legal remedy (although both welcome favorable court rulings) but rather for the symbolic gains associated with anything labeled as a constitutional right. The legal battles fought in court have been won usually by pro–gun control factions. In state courts, various rulings generally have upheld the power of states to regulate firearms and have associated the right to bear arms with service in a militia.[95]

Supreme Court Cases

There is little constitutional law on gun control, but four Supreme Court cases serve as precedent for interpreting the Second Amendment. These cases are acknowledged by both pro- and antigun groups to be central to the question.

The first was *U.S. v. Cruikshank*, 92 U.S. 553 (1876). Cruikshank was charged with thirty-two counts of depriving blacks of their constitutional rights, including two alleging that he had deprived blacks of firearms possession. The Court ruled that the right "of bearing arms for a lawful purpose is not a right granted by the Constitution, nor is it in any manner dependent upon that instrument for its existence." Speaking for the Court, Chief Justice Morrison Waite said that "the Second Amendment declares that it shall not be infringed; but this, as has been seen, means no more than that it shall not be infringed by Congress." At this juncture, the Supreme Court established two principles that it (and most other courts) consistently have upheld. First, the Second Amendment does not simply afford any individual the right to bear arms, lawfully or otherwise; second, the Second Amendment is not "incorporated" or applied to the states through the due process and equal protection clauses of the Fourteenth Amendment. The Court would not begin to incorporate parts of the Bill of Rights until 1925, but it never accepted the notion of total incorporation and to date has made no effort to incorporate anything in the Second Amendment.

Ten years later, the Supreme Court ruled in *Presser v. Illinois*, 116 U.S. 252 (1886), that an Illinois law that barred paramilitary organizations from drilling or parading in cities or towns without a license from the governor was constitutional. Herman Presser challenged the law after he was arrested for marching his fringe group, Lehr und Wehr Verein, through Chicago streets. In upholding the Illinois statute, the Supreme Court reaffirmed that the Second Amendment did not apply to the states. In his majority opinion Justice William B. Woods discussed the relationship between the citizen, the militia, and the government.

> It is undoubtedly true that all citizens capable of bearing arms constitute the reserved military force or reserve militia of the United States as well as the States; and, in view of this prerogative of the General Government, as well as of its general powers, the States cannot, even laying the constitutional provisions in question out of view, prohibit the people from keeping and bearing arms, so as to deprive the United States of their rightful resource for maintaining the public security, and disable the people from performing their duty to the General Government. But, as already stated, we think it clear that sections [of Illinois State law] under consideration do not have this effect.

Thus, the states may not prevent the federal government from creating a militia, as it is a "prerogative of the General Government," but, short of this, the states are free to regulate the circumstances under which citizens bear arms, subject to the parameters of state constitutions. The *Presser* case also demonstrated the inextricable link between the right to bear arms and the formation and conduct of a militia. This link between bearing arms and the militia requirement was reaffirmed in subsequent rulings.

In 1894, the Supreme Court ruled in *Miller v. Texas*, 153 U.S. 535 (1894), that a Texas law prohibiting the carrying of dangerous weapons did not violate the Second Amendment. Here again the Court said that the right to bear arms did not apply to the states. This reasoning was reaffirmed three years later in the case of *Robertson v. Baldwin*, 165 U.S. 275 (1897).[96]

The final, critical case in this sequence was *U.S. v. Miller*, 307 U.S. 174 (1939). The *Miller* case was founded on a challenge to the National Firearms Act of 1934, which regulated the interstate transport of certain weapons. Jack Miller and Frank Layton, both of whom were convicted of transporting an unregistered 12-gauge sawed-off shotgun (having a barrel less than 18″ long) across state lines under the 1934 act, challenged its constitutionality by claiming that the law violated the Second Amendment and also represented an improper use of the commerce power. The Court turned aside those arguments and ruled that the federal taxing power could be used to regulate firearms and that firearms registration was legal. Beyond this, the Supreme Court was unequivocal in saying that the Second Amendment must be interpreted by its "obvious purpose" of assuring the effectiveness of the militia. Speaking for the Court, Justice James C. McReynolds wrote:

> In the absence of any evidence tending to show that possession or use of a "shotgun having a barrel of less than eighteen inches in length" at this time has some reasonable relationship to the preservation or efficiency of a well regulated militia, we cannot say that the Second Amendment guarantees the right to keep and bear such an instrument. Certainly, it is not within judicial notice that this weapon is any part of the ordinary equipment or that its use could contribute to the common defense.

The Court thus stated that citizens only possess a constitutional right to bear arms in connection with service in a militia, which would naturally exclude the vast majority of gun owners in the United States. In upholding the National Firearms Act, the Court affirmed the constitutional power of the Congress in addition to that of the states to regulate firearms use. This did not imply that citizens may not own guns per se; rather it meant that gun ownership may be regulated as the states and the federal government see fit, except during instances when average citizens are called on to serve or protect their nation or both.

Much of the *Miller* ruling was devoted to an extended discussion of the historical antecedents of the Second Amendment. Justice McReynolds' citations included *Blackstone's Commentaries*, Adam Smith's *Wealth of Nations*, colonial practices, and early state laws and constitutions. The thrust of this entire discussion was that the country's military defense was predicated on a citizen-army, which derived from the prevailing fear that large standing armies posed a threat to liberty and democracy. With modern mass armies and the National Guard, the need for militia of the sort envisioned by the Framers disappeared.

The *Miller* case continues to be cited in subsequent gun cases. In the case of *Adams v. Williams*, 407 U.S. 143 (1972), the Supreme Court upheld the conviction of a man (overruling a lower court) based partly on his illegal possession of a weapon, which was uncovered by a policeman as the result of an informant tip (the suspect was carrying the weapon on his person at the time). In a dissenting opinion authored by Justice William O. Douglas (quoted at the beginning of this chapter), with Justice Thurgood Marshall concurring, Douglas acknowledged the state's power to regulate if not prohibit the possession of firearms. He then cited the *Miller* case and related the militia concept to the right to bear arms. Because this opinion did not pertain directly to the issues being raised in *Adams* and appeared in a dissenting opinion, it is not accorded great weight; but the fact that two justices added this perspective so clearly in a case involving gun possession shows the persistence of that interpretation of the Second Amendment. Another example is found in a footnote that accompanied Justice Blackmun's majority opinion in *Lewis v. United States,* 445 U.S. 95 (1980). This case involved a man convicted for unlawfully possessing a weapon under the Omnibus Crime Control and Safe Streets Act of 1968 (he was previously convicted of a felony and therefore was not allowed to own firearms under that law). He challenged his conviction on the grounds it was based on a prior criminal record resulting from a trial for which he had no lawyer (that is, was pre–*Gideon v. Wainwright,* which established the right of all suspects accused of felonies to a lawyer during trial). He thus contended that the prior conviction should not have been used against him. The Court ruled against Lewis. The footnote by Blackmun (reprinted in a previous section of this chapter) acknowledged the propriety of the gun law and reaffirmed the *Miller* precedent.

The Morton Grove Case

One recent case to reach the federal courts merits specific attention. On June 8, 1981, the village of Morton Grove, Illinois, passed a local ordinance banning, with exceptions, the possession of handguns. The ordinance banned the ownership of working handguns except for possession by peace officers and security guards so long as such possession was in accordance with their official duties. The ordinance also exempted licensed gun collectors and dealers in antique firearms. Residents were not denied their handguns, however; rather they could keep their handguns in licensed gun clubs. Nor did the ordinance bar the possession of long guns. Offenders convicted under this law were subject to fines of up to $500 and up to six months imprisonment.

Gun control opponents filed suit against the ordinance, claiming that it violated the Second, Fifth, Ninth, and Fourteenth Amendments as well as Article I, Section 22 of the Illinois Constitution. In particular, these opponents argued that the Second Amendment provided an individual right to bear arms, rather than a collective right as part of a well-regulated militia. They also contended that the Second Amendment should be applicable to the states by incorporation through the Fourteenth Amendment, that the Morton Grove law deprived citizens of property without due process, and that the Ninth Amendment provided an inherent right of self-defense through its "enumeration . . . of certain rights."

In *Quilici v. Village of Morton Grove*, 532 F. Supp. 1169 (1981), a federal court for the northern district of Illinois ruled in favor of the village by arguing that the Second Amendment did not apply to the states, nor did it provide an individual right to bear arms. The court also declared that the Morton Grove ordinance was a reasonable exercise of police power and, in any case, did not result in the elimination of individuals' use of firearms. With regard to the Ninth Amendment, the court pointed out that the Supreme Court had never recognized any particular right stemming from it nor any constitutional right of self-defense. Article I, Section 22 of the Illinois Constitution refers to "the right of the individual citizen to keep and bear arms," but here, too, the court rejected the claims of gun control opponents. The court ruled that this constitutional provision did not prohibit the government from validly exercising its police power. The town ordinance was not found by the district court to be unreasonable, arbitrary, or simplistic.[97]

An appellate court in *Quilici v. Village of Morton Grove*, 695 F. 2d 261 (1982), upheld the district court ruling by observing that possession of handguns by individuals is not part of the right to keep and bear arms. This court also said that the Supreme Court had consistently held that the Second Amendment did not apply to the states, "even if opponents to gun control find it illogical." The court further ruled that the right to bear arms extended only to those arms that were necessary to maintain a well-regulated militia. The motion for *certiorari* to the Supreme Court was denied, thereby letting the district court opinion stand. As a footnote to this case, as of 1985, at least three other cities—Evanston, Illinois; Oak Park, Illinois; and Washington, D.C.—had adopted similar ordinances.

Legal Remedies Through Product Liability Law

Since the end of the 1970s, victims of crimes committed with handguns have sought compensation by relying on a citizen's right of legal redress. These victims have filed suit against handgun manufacturers, alleging that handguns violate product liability laws because they are dangerous and unsafely distributed. These litigants argued that these guns were manufactured and sold with the purpose of killing people and that the harm caused by such weapons was so great that the manufacturers who profited should be held financially accountable. In particular, these tort law proceedings were aimed at inexpensive (less than $50), small-caliber (less than .38), short-barreled (3" or less), lightweight, and easily concealable handguns. This novel approach was popularized by a New York tort lawyer, Stuart Speiser, in a book called *Lawsuit*.[98] Not surprisingly, this unusual approach has been criticized by other lawyers as well as by gun control opponents.[99]

By the end of 1982, about sixty such lawsuits had been filed, and this increased to an estimated two hundred cases by the end of 1983. The most celebrated lawsuit involved President Reagan's former press secretary, James Brady. He filed a $100 million suit against a German gun manufacturer and its U.S. importing outlet for manufacturing and distributing the gun John Hinckley used in his assassination attempt against the president (in which Brady was wounded).[100] An important court ruling in this area was handed down in October 1985, when Maryland's highest court, the court of appeals, ruled unanimously that anyone shot during a criminal act with a Saturday night special could sue the manufacturer, distributors, and seller of the weapon. The suit was brought by a man shot during a 1981 supermarket robbery and is expected to serve as a legal precedent for similar cases in other states.[101] This attempt to employ economic sanctions in order to impel greater gun control does represent a creative, although controversial, use of the judiciary in the ongoing political struggle about gun control.

SUMMARY

Since President Johnson's advocacy of gun controls, no other president has taken a leadership role in opposing the NRA, and President Reagan's hostility to gun control was reflected in his attempt to abolish the BATF. Congress has enacted only four gun control laws, which barely addressed the monumental problem of gun ownership, and the Bureau of Alcohol, Tobacco, and Firearms has been a timid enforcer of existing gun control statutes.

The Supreme Court (unlike other policies analyzed in this volume) has not been involved in much litigation, but the Court's rulings consistently have paved the way for gun controls by government. The high court's support for gun control has caused the NRA to sustain political pressure on Congress, the executive, and state and local officials in order to stave off greater gun regulation. As the Morton Grove case and recent use of tort law illustrate, if the debate about gun control is as old as the Republic (and it is), we can only look forward to the debate's continuation.

Debate already is starting to simmer about a product of technological innovation, the plastic gun. Law enforcement officials are concerned that terrorists and criminals can evade the standard metal detectors used at airports and elsewhere, according to a 1986 report by the Office of Technology Assessment. Plastic weapons may have uses for the police and the military, but no sporting or recreational purpose is foreseen. Nevertheless, NRA spokespeople already have expressed misgivings about possible attempts to regulate these new weapons.[102]

The NRA continues to be the pivotal political force in this controversy. The organization's success has come from keeping gun control reforms off the political agenda both at the state and national levels. By its very effective use of propaganda and the mythology of the Second Amendment, the NRA has imposed significant political barriers against constitutional arguments favoring gun control. The NRA has kept the political offensive in its ongoing war of words with gun control advocates, and, so far, the NRA has held the decisive advantage.

ACKNOWLEDGMENTS

My special and most sincere thanks to Grant Podelco, David Solar, and Mark Eichin for their important and valuable assistance. My thanks also to Loretta Padavona and Marcia Carlson and to the Cornell Law Library for its accessibility and receptivity to an outsider.

❧ Chapter Five ❧

AFFIRMATIVE ACTION
Minority Rights or
Reverse Discrimination?

Gary C. Bryner

The politics of fair employment policy revolves around the shift from equal employment opportunity to affirmative action. Federal judges, presidents and bureaucrats, members of Congress, political parties, coalitions of interest groups, and political activists have functioned within a political environment that has evolved from great controversy and divisiveness to general consensus and agreement to renewed conflict and tension. Although there is general acceptance of the goal of assuring equal employment opportunity for women and minorities, there are large rifts concerning the appropriate means of achieving this objective. Equal employment opportunity and affirmative action raise fundamental questions about the nature of justice, the meaning of equality and of merit, the relationship between government regulation and voluntary efforts, and the practical difficulties of implementing an effective program to accomplish this purpose.

Equal employment opportunity generally has been understood to mean that decisions concerning the selection, promotion, termination, and treatment of individuals in employment must be free of considerations of race, color, national origin, religion, and sex. Equal employment opportunity rests upon the idea of nondiscrimination—that these kinds of considerations are unconstitutional and morally unacceptable.

Affirmative action is defined here, following the U.S. Civil Rights Commission, as having three components. First, it is remedial: Affirmative action denotes efforts that take race, sex, and national origin into account for the purpose of remedying discrimination and its effects. Second, affirmative action seeks ultimately to bring about equal opportunity: Affirmative action assumes that "race, sex or national origin [must be considered] in order to eliminate considerations of race, sex and national origin," that "because of the duration, intensity, scope and intransigence of the discrimination women and minority groups experience, affirmative action plans are needed to assure equal employment opportunity."[1] Third, affirmative action specifies what racial groups are to be considered part of the "protected class" covered by its policies.

The discussion that follows is primarily concerned with racial preference, not gender. Although affirmative action affects women as well as minorities, the primary focus of civil rights laws and their administration has been on the discrimination suffered by minorities, particularly blacks.

However, there is no universally accepted definition of affirmative action. For some, it is an attempt to establish an equality of results rather than of opportunity or a means of assuring that the distribution of employment opportunities mirrors the distribution of groups in society. Others call affirmative action "reverse discrimination" or racial discrimination in reverse (against whites). Still others emphasize the concept of "preferential treatment" and view it either as an imperative to overcome the effects of past discrimination or as an evil that perpetuates race consciousness and injustice.[2]

Nor is there clear agreement about which groups are to benefit from affirmative action, although blacks are of central concern to those who make affirmative action policy. Under Title IV of the 1964 Civil Rights Act, the primary equal employment opportunity statute, minority groups include blacks, Hispanics, Asian or Pacific islanders, and Native Americans or Alaskan natives. Under public works legislation that sets aside 10 percent of funds for minority-run enterprises, groups included are blacks, Spanish-speaking persons, Orientals, Native Americans, Eskimos, and Aleuts. Federal agencies with policy responsibility in this area define protected groups as blacks (all racial groups of Africa except North Africa), Hispanics (Mexicans, Puerto Ricans, Cubans, Central or South Americans, and members of other Spanish cultures), Asian/Pacific islanders (from the Far East, Southeast Asia, the Indian subcontinent, and Pacific islands), and Native Americans (original people of North America who maintain their tribal identity). But none of these definitions indicates what percentage of an individual's ancestors must fall within one of these groups in order to trigger the requirements of the law or how far ancestry can or should be traced back.

FEDERALISM

Following the Civil War, Amendments thirteen, fourteen, and fifteen were passed in order to assure the rights of blacks, and legislation to guarantee their political and personal liberties, notably the Civil Rights Act of 1866, was enacted. Congress established affirmative action programs such as the Freedman's Bureau, whose purpose was to develop employment and educational opportunities for blacks. By 1876, however, the federal government largely abandoned these efforts, and blacks became subject to discriminatory actions by private interests as well as by state governments. Supreme Court rulings, notably *Plessy v. Ferguson*, 163 U.S. 537 (1896), reinforced those practices. For almost a century, blacks had to depend on state governments to protect their civil rights, although many states adopted policies that kept blacks in a subservient legal and social position. Despite *Plessy*, state programs for blacks were separate and unequal to those for whites.

After World War II, some states began to enact laws and programs to protect the civil rights of blacks. One of the first states to take such action was New York, which passed a fair employment practices law in 1945. New York also was the first state to use the term *affirmative action* in providing for remedies to victims of employment discrimination. A 1964 study by the U.S. Department of Labor (done in response to the passage of Title VII of the Civil Rights Act) found that twenty-five states had fair employment laws that prohibited private employers from discriminating on the basis of race, color, creed, and national origin in decisions relating to hiring or discharging employees and in wages and other conditions of employment.[3] None of these twenty-five states was in the South, however. Louisiana and Texas did have fair employment laws that prohibited discrimination on the basis of age, as did ten other northern, midwestern, and western states. Two states—Nevada and West Virginia—made compliance with nondiscrimination statutes voluntary, and Oklahoma's law applied only to state employees. The Labor Department study concluded that twenty-two of the twenty-five state laws were essentially compatible with the provisions of the Civil Rights Act of 1964. Thus, by the time Congress passed the Civil Rights Act—although many states had passed laws prohibiting employment discrimination based upon race, color, creed, and national origin—such coverage did not extend to the majority of states, and to none in the South.

Title VII of the 1964 Civil Rights Act encouraged states to enact and implement their own fair employment laws and assumed that much of the enforcement of Title VII would take place in state agencies. In 1965, the Equal Employment Opportunity Commission (EEOC) agreed to permit agencies in some twenty-two states to begin enforcing the federal law, including the Civil Rights Act of 1964. Title VII clearly was aimed at the southern states that had no laws protecting blacks from discrimination. Much of the impetus for this and later civil rights laws was the hostile actions of many southern state legislatures and governors against blacks.

CONGRESS

Congress was slow to respond to demands for civil rights legislation; no such action was taken between Reconstruction and 1957. In that year, and again in 1960, Congress passed legislation to ensure voting rights for blacks, and Congress, for a relatively short period of time, became the focal point of interest in equal employment opportunity.

As the peaceful, nonviolent civil rights protests and demonstrations by ad hoc groups of students and community activists in the late 1950s were transformed into violent confrontations in the early 1960s, civil rights groups and political activists, trade unions, civil liberty associations, and religious leaders joined together in a broad-based social movement to lobby the Congress and the Kennedy administration for decisive action. The AFL-CIO and most major trade unions—including the autoworkers, steelworkers, textile and clothing workers, and state and municipal employees—actively supported civil rights initiatives. Americans for Democratic Action, the American Civil Liberties Union, the Japanese-Americans Citizens League, the American Veterans Committee and similar groups lobbied for civil rights legislation in 1963–1964 and were joined by a large number of church groups; some nine Protestant associations, seven Jewish councils, and the National Catholic Conference for Interracial Justice played an important role in generating political support for congressional action.[4]

These organizations strengthened the position of the old, established civil rights groups as well as of the new direct action groups formed during this period. The National Association for the Advancement of Colored People (NAACP) concentrated on legislative initiatives; the NAACP Legal Defense and Education Fund (which had no official ties to the NAACP itself) focused on litigation. The National Urban League was particularly interested in legislation to improve housing and employment opportunities for blacks. The boycotts, demonstrations, sit-ins, and protests organized by the Southern Christian Leadership Conference were of primary importance in generating public support for civil rights legislation. Assassinations of civil rights workers, shootings of black children, news reports and pictures of fire hoses and guard dogs unleashed on peaceful demonstrators all produced widespread sympathy for the movement.

This outpouring of support for civil rights combined with lobbying and political activities under the umbrella of the Leadership Conference on Civil Rights, founded in 1949 to coordinate such efforts, resulted in significant civil rights planks in the platforms of both parties in 1960. For example, the Democrats called for a fair employment practices commission and a permanent status for the U.S. Civil Rights Commission, while the GOP platform recommended the formation of a commission on equal job opportunity and an end to discrimination in public transportation, public housing, and other services "authorized" by government.[5]

President John Kennedy did not actively pursue civil rights legislation until 1963; his hesitation has been attributed to concerns that opposition to such initiatives by southern chairmen of important committees would spill over to defeat his other New Frontier programs. Congress began seriously considering legislation aimed at ending employment discrimination in 1963, when a House committee passed a bill that would have prohibited discrimination in employment and labor union decisions and would have established a five-member equal opportunity commission empowered to initiate suits against employers and unions guilty of discriminatory practices. The bill, however, was never considered by the full House.

Much of the basis for legislative initiatives arose from the recommendations of the Civil Rights Commission, which had been established in 1957. In its 1961 report, the commission recommended that Congress create a new agency similar to the President's Committee on Equal Employment Opportunity or empower that agency to enforce a policy of nondiscrimination in all employment decisions where federal funds or contracts were involved. Unions would be prohibited from discriminatory practices in accepting or discharging members or in segregating them. Congress also was 'encouraged to provide for job training programs that would assure members of minority groups, and especially teenagers, vocational education and apprenticeship opportunities. In 1963, the commission recommended that fair employment legislation be extended to employment practices related to interstate commerce and that all employment resulting from federal grants, loans, and other spending take place in a nondiscriminatory manner.[6]

The Civil Rights Act of 1964

By the middle of 1963, debate in Congress focused on the public accommodations provisions of the civil rights bills that were before it because great attention had been generated by the sit-ins and demonstrations directed at restaurant and hotel operators who refused to serve black customers. Democratic sponsors of civil rights legislation actively courted Republicans in order to build sufficient bipartisan support to overcome southern Democratic opposition. In the Senate, Republican minority leader Everett Dirksen (R-Ill.) called for voluntary measures to end discrimination; the Senate Judiciary Committee, chaired by James O. Eastland (D-Miss.), held hearings on various bills but took no action. However, supporters of civil rights in the Senate, fearing a southern-led filibuster against any civil rights bill brought to vote, decided to wait until the House took action.

In the House, Democrats split between the administration's position on civil rights bills and that of liberals on the Judiciary Committee, who called for much greater federal involvement in state affairs. A bill specifying greater federal involvement in regulating states' discriminatory practices was reported by the committee but did not reach the floor before President Kennedy's assassination. Lyndon Johnson, five days after Kennedy's death, addressed Congress and urged passage of this civil rights bill: "No memorial oration or eulogy could more eloquently honor President Kennedy's memory than the earliest possible passage of the civil rights bill for which he fought so long."[7] The assassination was perhaps more responsible than anything else for the passage of the bill at that time, although Lyndon Johnson also probably saw it as an opportunity to extend his constituency because he had no real record for civil rights and some civil rights leaders believed he was unsupportive of earlier legislative efforts.[8]

The House version of the legislation passed in 1964, however, was rejected as too extreme by Republican leaders, who negotiated with leaders of both parties and with Justice Department officials and eventually softened the bill enough to gain solid bipartisan support and overcome southern opposition. Some compromises led to less federal involvement than had been proposed and permitted local governments to attempt solving problems before federal authorities intervened. There was particular opposition to the equal employment opportunity and access to public accommodations sections, both of which were amended. In the House, proponents of the legislation were well organized—lobbying by the White House, the Democratic Study Group, and some seventy groups allied with the Leadership Conference on Civil Rights assured strong support, while the southern Democrats were ill-prepared for the fight and sought vainly to block the legislation by offering some 122 amendments. The amendment that prohibited discrimination on the basis of sex eventually became the most important change from the original bill. Contrary to the hopes of the amendment's sponsor (Representative Howard Smith [D-Va.]), who saw the proposal as an opportunity to generate opposition to the whole package, the amendment passed, as did the entire bill.

In the Senate, opponents blocked legislative action through a filibuster conducted by eighteen southern Democrats and one southern Republican that featured a twenty-four-hour-long speech by Strom Thurmond (D-S.C.). The filibuster was organized into a three-platoon system to assure continual control over Senate proceedings. Southern opposition focused mainly on the sections of the proposed legislation that provided for a cut off of federal funds for discriminatory practices and that set up a fair practices commission. At the same time that southern Democrats tried to block the legislation, Republicans worked to gain concessions on the provisions they were most concerned about—access to public accommodations and fair employment practices. Ultimately, the negotiators agreed to provisions that permitted government suits only for egregious cases of discrimination (where there was a clear "pattern or practice" of discriminatory behavior), that required the administrative agency created to enforce the law to seek *voluntary* compliance with the law, and that permitted individuals to sue in federal courts for redress.

Once an agreement was struck, Republicans supported efforts to end the filibuster. Congress also was spurred to action by increasing urban unrest and violence. The filibuster finally was cut off by a vote of 71–29 on June 10: Republicans voted 27–6 in favor of cloture; Democrats voted 44–23 (northern Democrats voted 41–3 while Southern Democrats voted 3–20). Southerners then presented a large number of amendments that were resoundly defeated; northern Democrats grew weary and decided not to call up strengthening amendments as planned. The bill was passed, 73–27, with 6 Republicans and 21 Democrats (20 of them southerners) opposing passage. The House agreed not to tamper with the fragile Senate compromise and passed the bill by a vote of 290–130. The vote was 138–34 by Republicans and 152–96 by Democrats (with northern Democrats voting in favor 141–4 and southern Democrats opposing the bill 11–92). President Johnson signed this legislation July 2.[9]

Title VII of the Civil Rights Act of 1964, the fair employment practices section of the act, contained five major provisions. First, it prohibited hiring, firing, disciplinary, and other employment and union practices on the basis of race, color, religion, national origin, or sex. Second, Title VII extended coverage to those employees and union members in organizations of greater than twenty-five individuals. (The act eventually was amended to reach organizations with fifteen or more members.) Third, Title VII provided exemptions from coverage for individuals who required security clearances for government employment; for individuals who were hired for educational functions by educational institutions or religious activities by religious groups; for cases where employees of a particular religion, national origin, or sex were part of a bona fide occupational qualification; and for Native Americans hired on or near reservations. Fourth, Title VII created an independent agency, the Equal Employment Opportunity Commission, and charged it with the responsibility to investigate claims brought by aggrieved individuals; to attempt negotiating resolutions; and to provide technical assistance to employers and unions seeking to comply with the law. The attorney general was empowered to bring suits for widespread (pattern or practice) discrimination, and individuals also could bring suit should EEOC conciliatory efforts fail. Finally, the title defined as permissible seniority systems, merit systems, tests used in application procedures, and different standards of compensation or work responsibilities as long as these practices were not used with the intent to discriminate.

Title VII also expressly rejected the imposition of quotas in the hiring of members of minority groups or women. Section 703(j) of the act was added in response to criticisms that the law would require hiring quotas; this section prohibited "preferential treatment to any individual or group . . . on account of an imbalance which may exist with respect to the total or percentage of persons of any race, color, religion, sex, or national origin employed . . . in any comparison with the total number or percentage in any community, state, section or other area or in the available workforce in any community."

Sponsors of the bill emphasized that this addition would prohibit "reverse discrimination," "quotas," and other "preferential treatment." Sponsors maintained that the law "does not require an employer to achieve any sort of racial balance in his workforce by giving preferential treatment to any individual or group." "What the bill does," explained one sponsor, "is to simply make it an illegal practice to use race as a factor in denying employment."[10]

Once Title VII was enacted, proponents of the legislation began pressing for action to strengthen the Equal Employment Opportunity Commission. Legislation was introduced in 1965 that would have given the EEOC the authority to bring charges against employers who discriminated, to issue cease-and-desist orders in order to end prohibited practices, and to order employers to hire or reinstate victims of discrimination. In the House, the proposal won broad bipartisan support. In the Senate, however, southern Democrats teamed with other members who responded to lobbying by business groups that feared increased governmental intervention in their decisionmaking to defeat the proposal.[11]

In 1969, the Nixon administration began lobbying for legislation that would authorize the EEOC to bring suits in federal district courts against employers; the administration argued that the courts, not administrative proceedings, were the most appropriate forum for hearing civil rights disputes. Attention concerning this issue was sidetracked in Congress when the administration announced the Philadelphia Plan, a Labor Department program for goals and timetables for increasing minority employment in the construction industry named after the city in which it was first applied. Congressional criticism of the plan was triggered by a study conducted by the comptroller general that had concluded that the plan violated Title VII's prohibition against discrimination on the basis of race.

Organized labor found sympathetic allies in the Senate who attached a rider to a fiscal year 1970 appropriations bill that would have prohibited spending for any program or contract found in violation of federal law by the comptroller general, thus killing the Philadelphia Plan. The rider passed in the Senate but was rejected by the House where a majority (115–84) of Democrats (with southern Democrats voting 61–6 and northern Democrats voting 54–78) supported the rider, thus opposing the plan, while a majority of Republicans (41–124) sided with the Nixon administration against the rider.[12]

In 1970, Congress was on the verge of significantly strengthening the powers of the EEOC. In a reversal of earlier roles, the Senate passed a bill that gave the EEOC cease-and-desist powers, authority to sue employers for a "pattern or practice" of discrimination, and jurisdiction over the employment practices of state and local governments. The Nixon administration opposed the measure, preferring instead to provide for court enforcement of Title VII. The House Committee on Labor and Education reported a similar bill, but the Rules Committee failed to bring it to a vote.[13]

Equal Employment Opportunity Act of 1972 (P.L. 92-261)

In late 1971, legislation to amend Title VII of the 1964 Civil Rights Act was passed by a Senate committee; this legislation granted to the EEOC cease-and-desist powers. The Nixon administration opposed the transfer of power from the Justice and Labor Departments to the EEOC, while the NAACP, Commission on Civil Rights, and the AFL-CIO backed the transfer. The opposition was led by Sam Ervin (D-N.C.) and James Allen (D-Ala.), who argued that such authority would render the EEOC "prosecutor, judge and jury" and would prevent employers from enjoying the rights of due process. Ervin and Allen favored the Nixon administration's proposal for empowering the EEOC to bring suits against violators of Title VII provisions. Three times the Senate voted, by slim margins, to reject the Ervin-Allen alternative; Senator Allen threatened to filibuster in order to block a final vote on the amendments to Title VII. Proponents, failing to find sufficient votes to invoke cloture and prevent the filibuster, agreed to compromise. The court-enforcement alternative eventually was passed by the Senate along with another major point of controversy—bringing state and local government employees under Title VII, expanding coverage to firms with fifteen or more employees, and maintaining the power to bring pattern or practice suits by the attorney general rather than by the EEOC.

In the House, it became clear that organized labor favored the transfer of power to the EEOC as a way to weaken the Labor Department and the Philadelphia Plan. The labor–civil rights coalition was reformed to lobby for the proposal, yet was split over the desired outcome of the transfer. The House, by a vote of 200–195, comprised of a coalition of Republicans (131–29) and southern Democrats (163–16), defeated the northern Democrats (who voted 6–150) and the Education and Labor Committee that had supported the transfer.[14] House and Senate conferees eventually agreed on most of the Senate positions, but gave to the EEOC authority to bring pattern or practice suits against employers, brought employees of educational institutions under coverage (these employees had been exempted in the 1964 act), and created the Equal Employment Opportunity Coordinating Council to facilitate cooperation between the EEOC, the Office of Federal Contracts Compliance (OFCC), and other agencies.

The passage of the Equal Employment Opportunity Act of 1972 was a clear defeat for civil rights groups, whose major goal had been to empower the EEOC to issue cease-and-desist orders against discriminatory employment practices. One civil rights leader described the act as a "slap in the face, but not a knockout punch" for the civil rights movement.[15] It is clear from the tortuous history of the 1972 amendments to Title VII of the 1964 act that Congress as a whole was quite willing to rely on the federal courts as the primary forum for the implementation of equal employment opportunity. For southern members of Congress, this was an attractive alternative because federal judges were residents of the areas over which they presided and to some extent were screened and approved by senior members of Congress before being appointed by the president. Thus, these judges were likely to reflect the norms and values of the communities in which they lived.

For others in Congress, federal bureaucrats who were free from local prejudices were viewed as more appropriate enforcers of the law, but federal judges at least might provide some independence and would be preferable to a reliance on state and local officials to implement antidiscrimination laws. Congress also was willing to defer to judicial judgments in defining substantive provisions. In a section-by-section analysis of the 1964 Civil Rights Act and the 1972 amendments, sponsors of the legislation stated that "in any area where the new law does not address itself, or in any areas where a specific contrary intention is not indicated, it was assumed that the present case law as developed by the courts would continue to govern the applicability and construction of Title VII."[16]

Congress has reversed only one Supreme Court decision. In the case of *General Electric v. Gilbert*, 429 U.S. 125 (1976), the Court ruled that an employer's exclusion of pregnancy benefits from a disability plan was not gender-based discrimination but was motivated only by economic considerations. Women's, labor, and civil rights groups were very outspoken in their criticism of this decision and began pressuring Congress for action. Some fifty organizations, including the National Organization for Women, the Leadership Conference on Civil Rights, and the AFL-CIO formed the Campaign to End Discrimination Against Pregnant Women.

A bill in response to *Gilbert* was introduced and quickly became mired in disputes about how abortions were to be provided for. The bill eventually passed in the House and went into conference where a compromise was fashioned that permitted employers to exempt from coverage for medical payments elective abortions unless the life of the mother was threatened. But employers were required to grant disability benefits to women recovering from an abortion. Title VII thus was amended in 1978 (92 Stat. 2076) to read that all pregnancy-based distinctions were to be considered gender-based discrimination and that pregnancy was to be treated the same way as any other temporary disability in employee benefit programs.

In certain legislation passed in the 1970s, Congress began requiring affirmative action by state agencies that received federal funds to employ and promote handicapped persons and by federal agencies for veterans. In the Public Works Employment Act of 1977, Congress required 10 percent of the grants to state and local governments for public works to be directed toward "minority business enterprises," businesses owned and controlled by U.S. citizens from the following minority groups: Negroes, Spanish-speaking persons, Orientals, Indians, Eskimos, and Aleuts. Thus, except for action it took in 1978, Congress has preferred to leave untouched its delegations to agencies and the courts. Congress has shown little interest in the implementation of affirmative action, despite widespread public opinion opposing preferential treatment.

JUDICIARY

The Supreme Court assumed a major role in grappling with important issues that sprung from the implementation of Title VII. First, the Court tried to provide criteria for determining when discrimination could be adjudged to have occurred. Second, the Court sought to define appropriate remedies once discrimination had been demonstrated. Third, the Court attempted to interpret actions of employers as required by Title VII and to indicate which employees, employers, and employment practices were exempt from coverage.

Proving Employment Discrimination

Title VII specified various prohibited employment practices; these included limiting, classifying, or segregating applicants or employees on the basis of race, color, religion, sex, or national origin in making hiring decisions, determining compensation and other conditions of employment, or discharging employees. Two kinds of discriminatory employment practice became apparent: those that treated individual employees differently and thus were violations of the law and those that resulted in disparate impacts among different employee groups. Each kind of discriminatory behavior has been a major concern of the federal courts in applying Title IV to employment practices and was the subject of a number of important Supreme Court cases.

In this first area of concern, the Court tried to define, through a series of cases between 1973 and 1981, the nature of the burden of proof required in proving disparate treatment. In *McDonnell Douglas Corp. v. Green*, 411 U.S. 792 (1973), the Court ruled that the employee who claims to be a victim of discrimination must first show that "(i) he belongs to a racial minority; (ii) that he applied and was qualified for a job for which the employer was seeking applicants; (iii) that, despite his qualifications, he was rejected; and (iv) that, after his rejection, the position remained open and the employer continued to seek applicants from persons of [the employee's] qualifications." If these conditions are met, the burden then shifts to the employer to "articulate some legitimate, nondiscriminatory reason for the employee's rejection." Finally, the employee then could seek to show that the employer's justification was merely a "pretext for discrimination."

The *McDonnell Douglas* decision resulted in a variety of interpretations by lower courts in subsequent cases. These courts attempted to grapple with the question of how extensive the burden of proof had to be—what the *McDonnell Douglas* Court meant by "articulate" (rather than "prove") and whether "one" or "some" legitimate reasons were sufficient defense. Five years later, in *Furnco Construction Corp. v. Waters*, 438 U.S. 567 (1978), the Court tried to provide additional guidance for resolving these questions. Here the Court concluded that "in the absence of any other explanation it is more likely than not that those actions were bottomed on impermissible considerations." Furthermore, the employer then should be allowed "some latitude to introduce evidence which bears on his motive" for his actions.

In a subsequent case, *Board of Trustees of Keene State College v. Sweeney*, 439 U.S. 295 (1978), the Court ruled that lower courts that had required employers to rebut prima facie cases of discrimination by "articulating some legitimate, nondiscriminatory reason" and "proving absence of discriminatory motive" had erred because the former standard was sufficient. However, the lower federal courts still continued to render conflicting decisions, thus forcing the Court to try again to define clearly the issues. In *Texas Department of Community Affairs v. Burdine*, 450 U.S. 248 (1981), the Court again addressed the nature of the proof required of employers charged with a prima facie case of discrimination. The decision of a lower court, which imposed the requirement that employers "prove by a preponderance of the evidence the existence of nondiscriminatory reasons" for taking the actions in question, was rejected by the high court; an employer so charged "bears only the burden of explaining clearly the action."

In a related area of concern, the determination of whether employment decisions have resulted in a disproportionate impact on minorities or women, cases also have centered on the burden of proof. In one of its first Title VII cases, *Griggs v. Duke Power*, 401 U.S. 424 (1971), the Supreme Court ruled that employment practices resulting in an adverse impact on minority applicants were illegal. At issue here was the employer's use of a general intelligence test and the requirement of a high school diploma in determining promotions from one division of the Duke Power Company to another. Black employees, who had effectively been prevented from transferring to other divisions and the higher-paying jobs within those divisions, brought suit against their employer. The court of appeals upheld the use of the test because the court found no intent to discriminate; the Supreme Court rejected that view in arguing that "good intent or absence of discriminatory intent does not redeem employment procedures or testing measures that operate as 'built-in headwinds' for minority groups and are unrelated to measuring job capability."

The justices argued that in Title VII, Congress had authorized the use of "any professionally developed ability test" except those that were "designed, intended or used to discriminate because of race" (Section 703[h]). The Court found that because members of minority groups failed to qualify for employment positions at a greater rate than did nonminority applicants as a result of employer selection devices, the burden of proof then fell upon the employer to show that the selection devices were reasonably related to job performance and not intended to discriminate against minorities. If the employer could demonstrate that tests were job related, then the burden was shifted back to the party initiating the complaint to show that the selection devices or tests would be just as useful in choosing qualified employees without producing the disparate impact.

The Court also relied on EEOC guidelines that indicated that employers should only use tests or other selection devices where data were available to demonstrate that the device was "predictive of or significantly correlated with important elements of work behavior which comprise or are relevant to the job or jobs for which candidates are being evaluated."[17] The Court concluded that the "administrative interpretation of the Act by the enforcing agency is entitled to great deference."

In subsequent decisions, the courts have failed to come to an agreement concerning how much of a disparity is sufficient proof of a prima facie case of discrimination that then must be rebutted by employers. In 1978, the EEOC and Office of Federal Contracts Compliance Programs (OFCCP) issued guidelines for the use of selection tests that offered a four-fifths rule: If the passing rate of minorities is less than 80 percent of the rate for nonminorities, a prima facie case of discrimination has been shown, and the burden of proof then falls on the employer to demonstrate that the test measures job-related characteristics. This standard has been used by a number of courts in subsequent cases.[18]

Proving that tests and other selection devices measure job-related skills is a very difficult and expensive procedure and has caused some employers to initiate their own hiring or promotion quotas in order to avoid the cost of validating selection devices and to protect against litigation. Criticism of the *Griggs* ruling has called it inconsistent with legislative intent. Sponsors of Title VII emphasized that an intent to discriminate was to be determinative: "Inadvertent or accidental discrimination will not violate the Title. . . . It means simply that the respondent must not have intended to discriminate."[19] In response to concerns that employers might be required to achieve racial balance in their work force and thus perhaps be forced to give preferential treatment to minorities, Title VII was amended to prohibit "preferential treatment to any individual or group . . . on account of an imbalance which may exist with respect to the total or percentage of persons of any race, color, religion, sex, or national origin employed" (section 703[j]).

Congress could have done more to resolve the issues of when racially based criteria could be used or what test should be employed in determining whether or not discrimination had occurred. Debate concerning the 1972 amendments to Title VII included a claim, unchallenged by proponents of affirmative action, that "to hire a negro solely because he is a negro is racial discrimination just as much as a white only policy. Both forms of discrimination are prohibited by Title VII." At the same time, the Senate rejected an amendment that would have prohibited government agencies from requiring employers to practice reverse discrimination by hiring applicants of a particular race or sex in order to reach a quota.[20]

The Court dismissed a literal reading of Title VII as inconsistent with the underlying purpose of the title because a literal reading would require that discriminatory intent be proven. The opinion here seemed to have borrowed from a case in another area of civil rights, *United States v. Gaston*, 395 U.S. 285 (1969), where the Court found a literacy test unlawful because of its discriminatory impact on blacks. Likewise, the opinion borrowed from a 1970 decision, *Turner v. Fouche*, 396 U.S. 346, where a statistical under-representation of minorities in juries was found to be a prima facie case of discrimination. Thus, the Court seemed to be making an attempt to develop some consistency in discrimination cases for the different substantive areas of concern and litigation rather than a strict adherence to statutory intent.[21] The Supreme Court refined its *Griggs* position in a 1977 case, *International Brotherhood of Teamsters v. U.S.*, 431 U.S. 324 (1977), where the Court ruled that a statistical disparity alone was insufficient proof of discrimination and that it must be accompanied by other evidence. Yet the Court still maintained that such a standard was consistent with congressional intent and argued that a reliance on proof of intent would render Title VII useless.

In these cases, the Supreme Court has tried to balance what it sees as congressional intent, EEOC interpretative guidelines, case law in relevant areas, and the particular situations of the cases in determining what constitutes proof of discrimination. Although the Court has not provided a clear and consistent set of principles for such determination, it has narrowed down the possibilities somewhat. Yet much uncertainty remains, and attention is naturally directed toward future clarification.

Remedies for Employment Discrimination

In the second area of judicial policymaking—providing for remedies once discrimination has been shown—the Court assumed a more conservative stance relative to congressional intent. In *Albemarle v. Moody*, 422 U.S. 405 (1975), the Supreme Court ruled that once discriminatory activity was proven, back pay was generally to be awarded in order to "make whole" victims of illegal behavior. Retroactive seniority also was awarded to victims of Title VII violations in *Franks v. Bowman Transportation Co.*, 424 U.S. 747 (1976). Both decisions were justified by the Court as consistent with the power of the courts under Title VII to grant equitable relief, and specifically to award back pay, although Title VII clearly indicates that such remedies can be awarded only "if the court finds that the [employer] has intentionally engaged in or is intentionally engaging in an unlawful employment practice" (Section 706[g]).

In *Memphis Fire Department v. Stotts*, 104 S.Ct. 2576 (1984), the Supreme Court maintained its view that "bona fide" seniority systems could not be interfered with in trying to protect the jobs of minorities who, as last to be hired, were first to be fired or laid off by cities or other employers suffering from financial constraints. That decision was reinforced in *Wygant v. Jackson Board of Education*, 106 S.Ct. 1842 (1986). A collective bargaining agreement between teachers and the school board required that in the event of layoffs, teachers with the most seniority would be the last to be laid off, except that a greater percentage of minority teachers could not be laid off than the current percentage of minority personnel employed at the time of the layoffs. The Court reaffirmed the majority position taken in earlier cases that race-conscious actions must meet three conditions: There must be a "compelling state interest" that requires a response; the action taken must be "narrowly tailored"; and there must be evidence of prior discrimination. The Court rejected the argument that the value of having minority teachers as role models outweighed the commitment to the seniority system.

The Responsibilities of Employers

The third area of important judicial influence is that of determining the general extent of employer responsibility under Title VII. In *United States v. Weber*, 433 U.S. 193 (1979), the Supreme Court upheld an affirmative action agreement embodied in a collective bargaining agreement that reserved 50 percent of the openings in a training program for black employees. A nonminority employee challenged the agreement as a violation of Title VII's prohibition against preferential treatment (Section 703[j]). The plan in question here was upheld by the Court for three reasons. First, although Section 703 prohibited government from requiring preferential treatment in response to a racial imbalance, the section did not interdict a voluntary effort. Second, the plan was temporary and was "not intended to maintain a racial balance but simply to eliminate a manifest racial imbalance." Third, the plan did not "unnecessarily trample the interests of white employees," nor did it "require the discharge of white workers and their replacement with new black hirees."

In cases related to Title VII and affirmative action, the Court has provided a variety of hints at what would and would not be acceptable interpretations of affirmative action. In *Fullilove v. Klutznick*, 448 U.S. 448 (1980), the Supreme Court upheld a 1977 federal works program enacted by Congress that set aside 10 percent of the provided funds for "minority business enterprises." The Court concluded that Congress need not act in a "wholly color-blind fashion" in remedying discrimination, but that such action could be justified only under the broad remedial powers of Congress. In *United Jewish Organization v. Carey*, 443 U.S. 144 (1978), a case involving the redrawing of voting district lines, the Court ruled that the state legislature could consider the impact of redistricting on racial groups even though there had been no finding of discrimination in previous redistricting decisions. In *Regents of the University of California v. Bakke*, 438 U.S. 265 (1978), the Court rejected the university's medical school admission policy, which set aside sixteen admissions for minority applicants. The Court argued that such quotas were only appropriate in response to a clear finding of discrimination. However, the Court did uphold race as one of many factors the university could consider in trying to assure diversity in the school's student body.

In *Local 28 of the Sheet Metal Worker's International Association v. EEOC*, S.Ct. Dkt. no. 84-1656 (1986), the Court upheld race-conscious relief as a remedy for past discrimination and ruled that remedial action need not be limited to actual victims of discrimination. The lower court's imposition of a goal of 29.23 percent for black membership in the union was upheld by the Supreme Court as a narrowly tailored and reasonable response to a "history of egregious violations" of Title VII. The remedy was temporary; it did not "unnecessarily trammel the interests of white employees." It was consistent with congressional intent and was not invoked "simply to create a racially balanced work force."

In the Court's third 1986 case, *Local Number 93, International Association of Firefighters v. City of Cleveland*, S.Ct. Dkt. no. 84-1999 (1986), the Court upheld a consent decree adopted by a lower court that required a fixed number of goals for the promotion of minority employees. The city of Cleveland had been unsuccessful in defending itself in a number of other lawsuits charging it with illegal hiring practices, and it negotiated with an organization of black and Hispanic firefighters a set of promotion goals that was submitted to a federal court as a proposed consent decree. The court approved the decree in 1983, over the objections of the union. The Supreme Court found that even though the plan benefited individuals who were not actual victims of discrimination, the Congress had intended to encourage "voluntary" agreements between unions and employers to end discriminatory practices. Consent decrees were characterized by the Court as essentially voluntary, thus exempting them from the restrictions placed by Congress on judicially imposed remedies for Title VII violations.

In two key decisions issued in 1987, the Supreme Court ruled that federal courts may impose promotion quotas to bring the percentage of qualified minority employees up to the level of minority participation in the relevant labor force, given a long history of discrimination and resistance to court orders (*U.S. v. Paradise*, S.Ct. Dkt. no. 85-999 [1987]). In *Johnson v. Transportation Agency*, S.Ct. Dkt. no. 85-1129 (1987), the Court indicated that female employees who possessed the requisite qualifications for promotion could be given preferential treatment where there was an "obvious imbalance" of men and women. Even absent legal findings of past discrimination, the Court sanctioned preferential treatment that was a "moderate, flexible, case-by-case approach to effecting a gradual improvement in the representation of minorities and women in the Agency's work force."

Supreme Court decisions are expected, as the final exposition of national law, to fill in legislative gaps, reconcile differences between administrative action and congressional intent, and provide a consistent and broadly applicable set of legal guidelines for public policy. It is not surprising that such an assortment of expectations is rarely satisfied. Because clear expressions of legislative intent or constitutional principles cannot decide cases unequivocally, the Court often seeks to strike a balance among the competing views. Even though the case at hand may be resolved, the way in which the Court acts encourages other parties to bring their own cases and argue that their situations are different enough to warrant different kinds of balancing.

PRESIDENCY

The earliest attempts of the federal government to encourage fair employment practices originated in the executive branch. In the 1940s and 1950s, there was some pressure exerted by black leaders for governmental action, but the response of presidents from Franklin Roosevelt to John Kennedy was to limit efforts to the employment practices of federal contractors. Such a limited scope of coverage was politically noncontroversial; it also was consistent with general expectations of limited presidential power and with the idea that federal funds should not be used to subsidize discriminatory actions. Roosevelt issued Executive Orders 8802, 9001, and 9346, which were the first in a series of important presidential initiatives for equal employment opportunity. Under the orders, defense contractors were prohibited from discrimination in hiring and other employment practices on the basis of race, color, creed, or national origin. The Fair Employment Practices Committee (FEPC) was created to monitor compliance, but the committee had, at best, a modest impact on employment decisions given that its "mild sanctions were seldom applied."[22]

President Truman also issued a series of executive orders. The first order assured the continuance of the FEPC, subject to some conditions set for it by Congress; the second order transferred responsibility for FEPC activities to the Defense Department and granted authority to other agencies that contracted for defense-related goods and services to require nondiscrimination in the employment decisions of their contractors; and the third Truman order created the Committee on Government Contract Compliance to monitor compliance with the government's fair employment policy and to study the effectiveness of previous efforts.[23] The committee recommended that agencies be empowered to cancel current contracts and debar future contracts for employers guilty of discrimination. Such an increase in the enforcement power was politically infeasible at that time, and the committee's charter expired in 1953.

President Eisenhower issued an executive order in 1953 that established the President's Committee on Government Contracts and, for the first time, extended nondiscrimination requirements to all companies that contracted with the federal government. The committee was empowered to receive complaints concerning discriminatory employment practices of contractors and to promote nondiscrimination through educational programs. One year later, a second Eisenhower order extended coverage to subcontractors.[24] The committee also recommended to agencies that if negotiations with contractors charged with discriminatory practices failed to resolve the problem, the agency should move to debar the contractors from future contracts. There is no evidence, however, that any agency ever exercised that power.[25]

In the nearly two decades of presidential initiatives, administrative negotiations and conciliation, and a modest publicity and education campaign, the role of the federal government in assuring equal employment opportunity changed very little. Much of the effort was noncontroversial and enjoyed widespread support; there was clear consensus that government spending should not be used to continue discriminatory practices, yet there was also general agreement that agencies should not be empowered to take any action other than to try getting contractors to comply voluntarily with the executive orders outlining fair employment practices. It was not until the Kennedy administration that the executive branch began to consider taking a more vigorous and aggressive role in pursuing equal employment opportunity.

Two months after he took office, President Kennedy issued Executive Order 10925, which continued to require fair employment practices of contractors with federal agencies and created the President's Committee on Equal Employment Opportunity. Chaired by Vice President Lyndon Johnson, the committee was given jurisdiction over all complaints of discriminatory behavior by contractors, was empowered to conduct compliance reviews and to require that contractors supply hiring data and other employment records, and was authorized to cancel existing contracts and debar firms violating the executive order from future contracts.[26]

Although no new policies were announced here, for the first time there was a general acceptance of the power of agencies to cancel contracts if companies engaged in unfair employment practices. Of more importance, however, was the requirement that all contracts include the following clause: "The contractor will take affirmative action to ensure that applicants are employed, and that employees are treated during employment without regard to their race, creed, color or national origin" (Part III, Section 301 [1]). No definition for affirmative action was provided, nor was there any explanation of what exactly was required of contractors. Action eventually began to shift to Congress, and proponents of equal employment opportunity concentrated on passage of the Civil Rights Act of 1964.

One of the most important actions affecting the affirmative action efforts of the federal government was the issuance of E.O. 11246 by Lyndon Johnson in 1965. This executive order delegated to the secretary of labor authority to issue regulations implementing the order; the rules that were issued subsequently included the requirement that construction contractors and subcontractors who received federal contracts must comply with goals and timetables for female and minority employees in job categories where both groups had been "underutilized" in the past.

In 1967, the Labor Department under President Nixon announced the development of its Philadelphia Plan, a program of goals and timetables for increasing minority employment in the construction industry named after the city in which it was first put into effect. The Philadelphia Plan empowered the Department of Labor's Office of Federal Contracts Compliance to set hiring quotas for minority workers that then were to be applied to federal contractors bidding for jobs in the Philadelphia area. Labor Department officials had found that because of racial discrimination in craft trade unions, blacks had been employed in construction projects in extremely small numbers. After a series of public hearings, the Labor Department established goals for the employment of minority ironworkers, plumbers and pipefitters, electrical and other workers that would have increased black employment in these crafts from less than 5 percent to 19–26 percent by 1973.[27]

The Nixon administration defended the Philadelphia Plan against its critics in Congress, who proposed in 1969 that no funds be appropriated for efforts to require contractors to meet minority employment goals. The White House urged members of Congress to defeat this proposal as "the most important civil rights issue in a long, long time."[28] Attorney General John Mitchell defended the Labor Department's policy by arguing that "it is now well recognized in judicial opinions that the obligation of nondiscrimination . . . does not require, and in some circumstances may not permit obliviousness or indifference to the racial consequences of alternative courses of action which involve the application of outwardly neutral criteria."[29] The Labor Department hailed its policy as a "major breakthrough in the fight for equality of opportunity in employment."

Leadership of the construction trade unions and the AFL-CIO, however, condemned the Philadelphia Plan, which caused a split between labor and civil rights groups and their congressional supporters. White union members, fearing that such plans would result in lost jobs for them, pressured union leaders to oppose the Labor Department. George Meany, the head of the AFL-CIO, charged that the Nixon administration was using the quota plan, what he called "a concoction and contrivance of a bureaucrat's imagination" to "horsewhip" the unions. Critics argued that the administration was trying to gain some credit for supporting a civil rights initiative, while at the same time weakening it by driving a wedge between black and white workers. Clarence Mitchell of the NAACP condemned the action as a "calculated attempt coming right from the President's desk to break up the coalition between Negroes and labor unions. Most of the social progress in this country has resulted from this alliance."[30]

The Ford administration was roundly criticized by civil rights groups for its lack of interest in equal employment opportunity. Black leaders attacked budget cuts in health, education, and welfare programs; a lack of initiatives to combat black unemployment; and a general attitude of "benign neglect" to the concerns of blacks.[31]

The Carter administration came to office with a strong commitment to civil rights and directed much of its attention to improving the administration and enforcement of equal employment opportunity. In 1978, Carter reorganized the executive branch's equal employment opportunity efforts and consolidated power and responsibility in the Equal Employment Opportunity Commission and the Office of Federal Contracts Compliance Programs (OFCCP). Much of the controversy regarding affirmative action centered on important Supreme Court cases decided between 1977 and 1980, and the Carter Justice Department was a vigorous proponent of affirmative action in the cases it litigated as well as in those it got involved in through supporting briefs.[32]

Affirmative action was embraced strongly by Jimmy Carter and the Democratic platform in 1980 and was attacked strongly by Ronald Reagan. The 1980 Republican platform's civil rights plank contained no major initiatives aimed at blacks. Indeed, the platform contended that "our fundamental answer to the economic problems of black Americans is the same answer we make to all Americans—full employment without inflation through economic growth."[33] Civil rights was a major topic in Carter speeches, as he threatened that a Reagan victory would polarize blacks and whites and divide the country. Perhaps a more representative view of the real differences between the two candidates surfaced in one of the debates in which candidate Reagan said, "We have made great progress from the days when I was young and when this country didn't even know it had a racial problem." President Carter, on the other hand, said, "Those who suffered from discrimination . . . certainly knew we had a racial problem. We have gone a long way . . . but we still have a long way to go."[34]

The Reagan administration promised to make dramatic changes in equal employment opportunity policy from the efforts of its predecessors in at least three areas. First, the Reagan administration reversed many of the Carter administration's enforcement initiatives and ordered industry-wide targeting to be dropped and the EEOC to concentrate on cases where it could readily prove discrimination. The administration sought to drop the back pay remedy or at least to limit it to a maximum of two years. The administration also shifted away from "pattern or practice" cases, class action suits, and broad investigations of employer actions to individual claims of unfair treatment.[35] Under Reagan, officials proposed changes in administrative regulations that would reduce the number of companies required to file affirmative action plans (AAPs) with the federal government and that would mandate that only one AAP be required for each country rather than for each facility.[36]

Second, President Reagan sought to gain control of the U.S. Civil Rights Commission by replacing five of the six commissioners appointed by his predecessors and ending its criticisms of his efforts to dismantle affirmative action, busing, and other programs. Reagan was successful in restructuring the commission and in appointing commissioners and staff members sympathetic to his views. The commission ultimately was weakened, however, by splits among the commissioners and the controversy generated by the chairman of the commission, Clarence Pendleton, who vigorously attacked traditional civil rights groups and their support for affirmative action. Congressional supporters of the commission then began to call for its abolishment, charging that it no longer could function. Although the commission still was operating by the end of 1987, several Reagan appointees had left, its budget was cut dramatically by Congress, and its future remained uncertain.[37]

Third, the administration joined in litigation to overturn decisions by federal courts and state and local governments that imposed hiring and promotion goals. In 1984, after the Memphis firefighters case, Assistant Attorney General Reynolds proclaimed that the "era of racial quotas has run its course" and that EEOC and OFCCP officials no longer would require employers to develop numerical hiring goals in order to increase minority employment.[38] The Supreme Court's two 1986 decisions upholding hiring goals, however, dampened these efforts. The Reagan Justice Department also proposed that Executive Order 11246 be rewritten to prohibit the use of hiring and promotion goals. The Labor Department resisted the proposal, and by the end of 1987 no decision had been made.

The Reagan administration has sought to reverse affirmative action policy for two reasons. First, affirmative action requirements were viewed as part of the general regulatory burden imposed on business that candidate Reagan promised to reduce. Regulatory relief, through budget and personnel cuts, reduction of new regulations and review of existing ones, and changes in enforcement priorities, has been an important part of the Reagan administration's economic reform and stimulation effort.[39]

The Business Roundtable has complained that affirmative action requirements are the second most costly regulatory program (after environmental regulations). Cost of compliance with OFCCP regulations has been estimated at $1.2 billion per year by the Equal Employment Advisory Council, a trade association of one hundred fifty large companies that has criticized affirmative action as expensive, enforced through harassment by on-site inspectors, and responsible for increasing racial tension and confrontation among workers. Business groups have lobbied White House officials

for changes in the executive order mandating affirmative action for contractors.[40]

Second, administration officials have argued that affirmative action
quotas are inherently objectionable. Assistant Attorney General William
Bradford Reynolds has labeled racial quotas as "morally wrong." William
French Smith, attorney general in Reagan's first term, has argued that such
policies come "perilously close . . . to fostering discrimination." Given that
the past five administrations all have promoted affirmative action, this shift
in policy under the Reagan administration is significant.

The civil rights community has been critical of the Reagan administration's rejection of affirmative action. A number of reports have been
issued from groups such as the Citizens' Commission on Civil Rights,
headed by former U.S. Civil Rights Commission chairman Arthur Flemming,
that argue race- and sex-conscious remedies are required to have any real
effect. The Civil Rights Commission itself has been split about the issue as
a result of Reagan appointees who are opposed to quotas.

Business groups have voiced frustration at the confusion within the
administration. One corporate equal employment opportunity official complained that the "biggest problem we have is the indecision out there. It's
better to have bad guidelines that we understand than to have good guidelines
that no one can understand."[41]

BUREAUCRACY

The evolution of employment policy from equal opportunity to affirmative
action and preferential treatment has occurred within the partnership of the
courts, the Equal Employment Opportunity Commission, and the Office of
Federal Contracts Compliance (later retitled the Office of Federal Contracts
Compliance Programs). In 1965, responsibility for equal employment opportunity (EEO) in federal contracting activities was transferred to the
secretary of labor; in 1966, the OFCC was created to assure fair employment
practices. In 1967, discrimination on the basis of sex was added to the
prohibited practices.[42] Much of the current controversy regarding EEO can
be traced to actions taken by the OFCC during this time. The initial concern
during this period was to define what was required of contractors in taking
affirmative action. The director of OFCC in 1967, Edward C. Sylvester, Jr.
explained that "in a general way, affirmative action is anything that you
have to do to get results. But this does not necessarily include preferential
treatment. The key word here is 'results.' . . . Affirmative action is really
designed to get employees to apply the same kind of imagination and
ingenuity that they apply to any other phase of their operation."[43]

The OFCC issued regulations in 1968 that for the first time required
all contractors with fifty or more employees and contracts of at least $50,000
to have a written affirmative action plan. The AAP was to identify areas
where minority employment rates were less than the levels of participation
for nonminorities and to outline a plan for remedying these problems,

including goals and timetables to assure equal employment opportunity.[44] The OFCC eventually issued additional regulations, known as Order no. 4, that provided instructions for contractors in complying with Executive Order 11246. These guidelines became the basis for almost all subsequent efforts related to affirmative action.

Order no. 4 defined an affirmative action program as "a set of specific and result-oriented procedures to which a contractor commits himself to apply every good faith effort. The objective of those procedures plus such efforts is equal employment opportunity."[45] The key components of an AAP were to include an "analysis of areas within which the contractor is deficient in the utilization of minority groups, and further, goals and timetables to which the contractor's good faith efforts must be directed to correct the deficiencies and thus to achieve prompt and full utilization of minorities at all levels and in all segments of his work force where deficiencies exist."[46] The OFCC was careful to insist that preferential treatment of any kind was not required; rather, the order required action "necessary to assure that all persons receive equal employment opportunity."

During this period, the OFCC also shifted from a policy of encouraging voluntary compliance with fair employment practices to enforcement activities including debarment of contractors. In 1968, OFCC director Sylvester, testifying before Congress, described this change in emphasis: "During the past two years, this program moved steadily from an education and voluntary compliance activity to one of the enforcement of Federal contracts. This principle has taken hold within the contracting agencies and among Federal contractors, and the results in providing equal employment opportunities are impressive."[47] In 1969, for the first time, contracting agencies began reporting to Congress that they had cancelled or suspended contracts with contractors who failed to comply with EEO requirements and that some contractors had been debarred from future contracts.

The first area of contracting activity to be subjected to specific affirmative action requirements was the construction industry. Concerned about past discriminatory practices that had restricted minority membership in construction crafts, the OFCC instituted its Philadelphia Plan. This administrative shift in policy toward quotas and preferential treatment was a result of a number of factors. There was much frustration about the lack of dramatic progress in overcoming the effects of past discrimination. Requirements that there simply be no future discrimination seemed to be an inadequate response. The Civil Rights Commission pushed for more aggressive efforts:

"Volunteerism," which has characterized most of the life of contract compliance, means seeking to achieve compliance through persuasion and cooperation by the employer . . . but if any one fact emerges clearly from the history of Federal contract compliance, and indeed, civil rights generally, it is that unless constructed upon a backbone of strict enforcement, volunteerism easily becomes an excuse for inaction.[48]

Many of the bureaucrats attracted to working in the OFCC, EEOC, and other related agencies were committed to an aggressive effort to do whatever was necessary to bring about an end to discriminatory practices. These bureaucrats were in considerable contact with other civil rights advocates who served as an important constituency for the OFCC and supported actions such as goals and timetables and other elements of affirmative action. There were bureaucratic incentives that encouraged growth in agency jurisdiction and involvement, as had been true of most agencies.

Enforcement efforts could not rest on findings of discriminatory intent, as some had argued they should, because evidence for such motivations was so difficult to uncover. The reliance on statistical disparity as evidence of discrimination was an extremely important development in the shift toward preferential treatment, as proponents argued that enforcement activity in response to such disparities was

> grounded on the common-sense proposition that the underrepresentation of minority and women in any area of economic or professional enterprise is an indication that discrimination may exist. . . . Apparently rational arguments can mask discriminatory behavior and even neutral efforts can unintentionally cause discriminatory results. In such circumstances, the best available means for detecting the possible presence of discriminatory processes is to examine their statutory outcome.[49]

Proponents argued that the nature of discrimination itself required aggressive action.

> By presuming on the basis of statistical data showing unequal results that illegal discrimination has occurred, [the Supreme Court] has recognized the existence of a pervasive and interlocking process of discrimination in education, employment and other areas. Neutrality—the presence of a "good" or the absence of "bad" intent—in such a context will only perpetuate inequalities. To prevent the perpetuation of discrimination the [Court] imposes a legal duty on employers and unions not to compound the discriminatory acts of others.[50]

Underlying this reliance on statistics was the assumption that the distribution of jobs among members of minority groups would parallel the distribution of these groups in the general population. Although there was little labor market evidence to support such an assumption, it nevertheless formed the basis for evaluating employment practices and fashioning remedies for illegal conduct.

Perhaps the most important factor in this shift, however, was the difficulty in recognizing and measuring progress in gaining compliance. Congress had faced a similar problem in the area of voting rights. After great frustration about a lack of progress in getting state and local officials to comply with voting rights, Congress imposed a simple statistical test in the Voting Rights Act of 1965 (P.L. 89-110). In any area where black voting rates in the 1964 presidential election were less than 50 percent, federal inspectors would be dispatched to investigate possible discrimination in registration practices.

A related difficulty was the use of data to demonstrate progress in achieving policy objectives. For equal employment opportunity, the number of suspended contracts or debarred contractors became convenient indicators of policy effectiveness, even though there was no clear correlation between such figures and increased opportunities for minorities. The director of OFCC in the Nixon administration, John Wilks, observed that

> the [OFCC] program, at present, does not have the means to evaluate accurately the extent to which equal opportunity is being accomplished. Additionally, the minority community and the general public tend to assess the progress or lack of progress of Government's equal employment opportunity program by such factors as the number of contract cancellations or the number and magnitude of public demonstrations, riots and other forms of racial unrest.[51]

Thus, political and bureaucratic incentives directed attention toward bureaucratic activity that was easiest to measure rather than toward what was most likely to achieve the program's objectives.

Finally, it should be noted here that the OFCC rather than the EEOC was primarily responsible for bureaucratic initiatives for affirmative action. During much of the late 1960s and into the 1970s, the Equal Employment Opportunity Commission spent much of its time trying to get organized. During the EEOC's first three years of operation, one or two of the five commissioner slots were vacant for more than half the time. There was no chairperson for four months in 1966, and there was a high turnover because the first five commissioners were appointed for terms of five, four, three, two, and one years to assure a future distribution of appointments.[52]

The EEOC also suffered from management problems, which resulted in a severe backlog of cases. Therefore, in 1977, managerial reforms were made by staff that reduced the backlog in cases from more than 120,000 to 33,000, reduced the average time to process a case from two years to less than three months, and produced a much more vigorous enforcement effort in the EEOC by the end of the Carter administration. A 1978 reorganization consolidated responsibility for the development and enforcement of equal employment opportunity policy in the federal government, and the EEOC took the lead in developing guidelines for voluntary affirmative action by employers.[53] The OFCCP, however, continued to play a major role in the development of affirmative action policy because of the agency's authority over government contractors and the belief of agency personnel that more expansive requirements could be placed on employers who voluntarily accepted federal contracts than could be placed on private employers as a whole.

During the Reagan administration, however, there was a dramatic shift in enforcement activities. In 1980, the administration reduced by 16 percent the number of full-time employees in the EEOC, and fewer complaints were processed in the years after 1980 than occurred before. While total spending for all civil rights–related activities increased during the Reagan era, the EEOC's budget, after inflation, was reduced (Table 5.1). Most importantly,

TABLE 5.1 U.S. Budget and Administrative Activity for Civil Rights and the EEOC, 1971-1985

Year	Total Outlays for all Civil Rights ($ millions)	EEOC Outlays ($ millions)	EEOC Full-time Personnel	Administrative Complaints Processed by EEOC	
				Filed	Resolved
1971	120	16	910	na	
1972	197	21	1,325	na	
1973	262	28	1,909	na	
1974	291	42	2,416	na	
1975	346	56	2,384	na	
1976	375	59	2,584	77,400	56,600
1977	428	72	2,487	79,800	62,973
1978	448	74	2,837	74,800	80,800
1979	464	93	3,627	67,800	81,700
1980	513	131	3,433	56,425	57,327
1981	544	134	3,412	58,754	71,690
1982	568	138	3,137	54,590	68,890
1983	590	143	3,000	66,461	68,058
1984	633	153	3,100	na	
1985 est.	643	160	3,100	na	

Source: Budget of the U.S. Government, Special Analyses, FY 1973-85;
Budget of the U.S. Government, Appendix, FY 1972-84 (Washington, D.C.:
U.S. Government Printing Office).

the top appointees in the Justice Department assumed leadership for equal employment policy and pushed for less aggressive enforcement in order to encourage employers to comply voluntarily with fair employment statutes and regulations. Department of Justice officials also began reversing efforts of federal agencies to impose hiring goals and ratios. The Labor Department, however, continued to support goals and ratios and resisted Justice Department pressure to have the president rewrite Executive Order 11246 in order to forbid numerical goals. White House advisers, especially Chief of Staff Donald Regan, apparently refused to have the president resolve the issue, preferring instead to have staff settle disputes, and the two sides reached a stalemate. At the end of 1986, the executive order remained in place, and the Labor Department and the EEOC continued to enforce affirmative action guidelines, largely due to the persistence of the Labor Department and the decisions of the Supreme Court.

In January 1987, Joseph N. Cooper announced his resignation as director of OFCCP. Cooper, a black, alleged that Attorney General Edwin Meese, among others, wanted to thwart federal rules now requiring numerical hiring quotas for companies with federal contracts. Cooper was appointed by labor secretary Bill Brock, a supporter of affirmative action, but, said Cooper, the "vocal dissenters promote the idea that goals and timetables are quotas, and that reverse discrimination is a reality."[54]

INTEREST GROUPS

The civil rights movement was instrumental in awakening the nation to racial injustices and forcing the Congress to consider major legislation, including the Civil Rights Act of 1964. At that time, affirmative action was not mandated by any law, and Congress had disavowed any intention to require racial quotas. The controversy regarding affirmative action came later. By the early 1970s, when affirmative action programs became firmly entrenched in the federal bureaucracy and courts, group opposition to the programs began to mount. Litigation in the federal courts by "victims" of "reverse discrimination" and other opponents came to light. This development caused a deep split among groups that had been allies in the civil rights movement. Organized labor, which had banded together behind civil rights legislation, now was divided about affirmative action. Affirmative action was rejected by virtually all major Jewish groups.[55] A third source of opposition came from groups representing "white ethnic" voters, who believed that they, too, suffered from discrimination but now had to cope with the special advantages being given to minorities.

This conflict was illustrated by the organizations filing *amicus* briefs in the major affirmative action cases to reach the Supreme Court during the late 1970s. This pattern was best illustrated by the case of *Regents of the University of California v. Bakke*, 438 U.S. 265 (1978), which addressed the constitutionality of quotas aimed at increasing minority student enrollment in medical school. Some 116 organizations submitted *amicus* briefs in this case (see Table 5.2). The most important division reflected in these data was between groups representing blacks, Spanish-speaking persons, Orientals, and Native Americans and those speaking for the Jewish community and "white ethnic" nationalities. Racial minorities are the protected groups under most affirmative action programs, whereas religious and ethnic minorities do not benefit from such programs even though religion is mentioned along with race, color, and sex in the 1964 Civil Rights Act. No Jewish or white ethnic group (for example, those with Italian, Ukrainian, Greek, or Polish memberships) endorsed affirmative action in an *amicus* brief; and no black, Spanish-speaking, Oriental, or Native American group allied itself with Bakke's position.

Although no single-issue group filed *amicus* briefs, it is noteworthy that racial and ethnic groups within multi-interest organizations from the

TABLE 5.2 *Amicus Curiae* Briefs to the Supreme Court by Interest Groups
Supporting and Opposing Affirmative Action in the *Bakke* Case

Type of Group Filing Brief	Number Supporting Affirmative Action	Number Opposing Affirmative Action
Black/Spanish/Oriental/Native American	30	0
White ethnic	0	8
Jewish	0	6
Unions	5	2
Business[a]	0	2
Law enforcement	0	4
Political	1	1
Academic[a]	20	1
Legal[a]	12	3
Medical/health[a]	2	1
Religious	2	0
Women's[a]	4	0
Government	7	0
Other	5	0
Totals	88	28

[a]Any business, academic, legal, medical/health, or women's group that represents a racial or white ethnic or Jewish minority was *omitted* from these categories and included under black/Spanish/Oriental/Native American, white ethnic, or Jewish headings.

Source: Law Reprints' Microfiche Edition of the Supreme Court Records and Briefs in the *University of California v. Bakke* (1978).

legal, health/medical, and academic sectors were mobilized on this question. These groups included the American Indian Bar Association, the Puerto Rican Legal Defense and Education Fund, the Hellenic Bar Association of Illinois, and the black National Medical Association.

Arguments Opposing Affirmative Action

Critics of preferential treatment contend that it is unjust and unfair; that it fails to assure that compensation is given only to actual victims of discrimination; and that it is too imprecise because it gives special benefits to some women and minorities who have not been actual victims of employment discrimination. The Reagan Justice Department has invoked the Constitution in opposing quotas: "We have profound doubts whether the Constitution permits governments to adopt remedies involving racial quotas to benefit persons who are not themselves the victims of discrimination."[56]

Other critics charge that affirmative action perpetuates racism and sexism and further divides society. Jewish groups have been particularly critical of the use of quotas, benign as they may appear to be. Morris Abram, a Reagan appointee to the U.S. Civil Rights Commission, has argued that "equal means equal," that "equal does not mean you have separate lists of blacks and whites for promotions, any more than you have separate accommodations for blacks and whites for eating. Nothing will ultimately divide a society more than this kind of preference and this kind of reverse discrimination."[57]

Affirmative action is rejected by others, including some blacks, for undermining the self-respect of those who are the action's intended bene- ficiaries and denigrating the progress and advancement achieved by blacks. Thomas Sowell has contended that the primary harm of quotas is done to blacks themselves: "What all the arguments and campaigns for quotas are really saying loud and clear, is that black people just don't have it, and that they will have to be given something in order to have something. The devastating impact of this message on black people—particularly black young people—will outweigh any few extra jobs that may result from this strategy."[58] Sowell has sought to demonstrate, through comparative studies of the participation of different ethnic groups in the labor market, that statistical disparities are not simply a result of discrimination, but are also a function of age, education, culture, and other differences among different groups.[59]

But critics allege, to the contrary, that such statistics are evidence that affirmative action has not worked and should be abandoned. Some argue further that economic growth holds the greatest promise for improved employment opportunities for blacks, while other critics reject affirmative action as failing to address the problems of the black "underclass," which appears to be unaffected by those policy initiatives.[60]

There are also practical objections to affirmative action. Blacks, His- panics, Native Americans, veterans, handicapped persons, and women all lay claim to preferential treatment under judicial, administrative, and statutory provisions. Choices must be made among members of various minorities in offering limited opportunities.

Arguments Supporting Affirmative Action

Affirmative action has been championed by many groups as a way of exorcising guilt about the history of race relations in the United States. From that perspective, too much cannot be done to compensate blacks for what their ancestors suffered. Civil rights activists view discrimination as a result of working-class and middle-class racism and insensitivity to the poor, which can be remedied only through drastic action. Supporters of equal opportunity who are opposed to preferential treatment find themselves

TABLE 5.3 Percentage of Blacks Employed in Various Occupational Groupings

Occupational Grouping	1960	1972	1982
Professional/technical/kindred	4.7%	9.5%	9.2%
Managers/administrators	2.5	3.0	3.9
Sales workers	1.6	3.0	3.8
Craftspersons and kindred	5.9	6.2	6.7
Operatives	20.1	12.2	13.5
Transportation	--	14.2	13.1
Laborers	13.8	18.6	15.1
Service workers	17.5	17.1	15.7

Source: U.S. Department of Commerce, Statistical Abstract of the United States (Washington, D.C.: U.S. Department of Commerce, Bureau of the Census, 1962), p. 382, and 1986 edition, pp. 419-420.

in an awkward position, as criticism of these race-conscious remedies are equated with opposition to civil rights. For others, preferential treatment was the norm rather than the exception: Universities gave it to athletes and children of influential alumni; employers gave it to relatives and social acquaintances. Affirmative action meant that blacks and women were more likely to be included in a system that was highly dependent on considerations other than merit.

Proponents of affirmative action reject the argument that civil rights are individually based. Discrimination, these groups argue, is a result of group characteristics and thus requires group-based remedies. For others, affirmative action seeks to remove the "unfair advantage that white males as a class enjoy due to past discrimination." According to this view, group characteristics were the appropriate target of action: "Individuals are discriminated against because they belong to groups, not because of their individual attributes. Consequently, the remedy for discrimination must respond to these group wrongs."[61]

Statistical measures of employment patterns among blacks often are cited by advocates of affirmative action as evidence that such efforts have borne fruit. While there is still a black-white wage gap and inadequate black representation in some professions, some progress has been made, advocates claim, and affirmative action must continue. Table 5.3,[62] for example, cites the employment percentages of blacks in major occupational groupings during two decades. Although increased numbers of blacks have joined the ranks of professional/technical/kindred employees (for example, accountants, engineers, lawyers) as well as (sales) managers and (school) administrators,

TABLE 5.4 Smith/Sheatsley index of racial tolerance[a]

Year	Northern Whites	Southern Whites
1963	2.45	1.11
1970	2.88	1.47
1976	3.35	2.40
1980	3.47	2.66
1984	3.70	3.02

[a]A higher score denotes greater racial tolerance.

Source: Tom W. Smith and Paul B. Sheatsley, "American Attitudes Toward Race Relations," *Public Opinion* (October-November 1984): p. 15. Reprinted wth permission of American Enterprise Institute for Public Policy Research.

the bulk of black employment remains in the nonprofessional categories of operatives (assemblers, garage workers, welders, and the like), transport workers (bus, taxi, and truck drivers), laborers, and service workers in such industries as cleaning and food establishments and health services.

PUBLIC OPINION

Surveys point to three conclusions about how the public views equal employment opportunity and affirmative action. First, there has been a gradual shift during the past two decades toward more racial tolerance among both northern and southern whites. One study by Tom W. Smith and Paul B. Sheatsley constructed a racial tolerance index that tabulated the responses of northern and southern whites to questions related to access to parks, restaurants and hotels; bringing a black friend home for dinner; integrating neighborhoods; interracial marriages; and efforts by blacks to "push themselves where they're not wanted."[63] Response ranged from 0 (intolerant) to 5 (very tolerant) and demonstrated a gradual shift in public opinion, as indicated in Table 5.4.

Smith and Sheatsley also found that there has been a significant evolution in opinion concerning employment opportunity, as demonstrated in opinion surveys between 1942 and 1972. In response to the question, "Do you think (Negroes/Blacks) should have as good a chance as white people to get any kind of job, or do you think white people should have the first chance at any kind of job?" 42 percent of the respondents in 1942 indicated that there should be equal treatment. By 1963, 83 percent favored equal treatment, and by 1972, the figure was 96 percent.

A second characteristic of public opinion is that there is a tremendous gap between the opinions of whites and blacks. Table 5.5 reports the findings of five election surveys by the University of Michigan on whether the primary responsibility for uplifting the social and economic position of blacks and other minorities depends upon government help or upon the minorities themselves. The majority of blacks favored government intervention, but most whites believed that minorities should help themselves. Table 5.6 focuses on fair employment practices. The Survey Research Center in 1956 and 1960 found virtually a consensus among blacks that government should assure "fair treatment in jobs and housing," and a series of questions posed in 1964, 1968, and 1972 found blacks looking toward the federal government to monitor "fair treatment in jobs," whereas whites tended to give that responsibility to the states and localities.

A third important element of public opinion is that there is overwhelming opposition to preferential treatment among all groups of citizens, even blacks, although preferential treatment continues to be a part of equal employment opportunity policy. This sentiment was analyzed by Gallup Polls taken in 1977, 1980, and 1984 (Table 5.7) that asked, "Some people say that to make up for past discrimination, women and members of minority groups should be given preferential treatment in getting jobs and places in college. Others say that the ability, as determined by test scores, should be the main consideration. Which point of view comes closer to how you feel on this subject?"[64]

In addition, a 1984 Gallup Poll found that 87 percent of whites and 63 percent of blacks favored ability, although three times as many blacks backed preferential treatment. Here the results of this survey may have been strongly influenced by the choice of wording, insofar as preferential treatment versus ability congers up the idealized view that employment decisions always are made on the basis of merit when, in actuality, a variety of subjective as well as objective criteria are applied to the recruitment process. After reviewing the survey data on this issue, Seymour Lipset and William Schneider concluded:

> Policies favoring quotas and numerical goals for integration . . . violate traditional conceptions of the meaning of equality of opportunity. Americans will accept the argument that race and sex are disadvantages deserving of compensation. . . . They will go along with special compensation up to the point where it is felt that resources have been roughly equalized and the initial terms of competition are once again fair. But the data show that every attempt to introduce any form of absolute preference . . . meets with stiff and determined resistance from the vast majority of Americans.[65]

More support for affirmative action came from business executives who developed such programs in response to OFCCP regulations on contractors. The director of public affairs for Time, for example, indicated that

TABLE 5.5 Attitudes on Whether the Federal Government Should Help Minorities[a]

Year	Government to Help Minorities				Minorities to Help Themselves		
	1	2	3	4	5	6	7
1970							
Total		31.2%		25.1%		43.8%	
Whites		25.0		26.8		48.1	
Blacks		83.3		10.1		6.1	
1974							
Total		32.2%		24.3%		43.4%	
Whites		27.4		25.6		46.9	
Blacks		79.2		11.4		9.3	
1978							
Total		27.1%		24.9%		47.9%	
Whites		23.0		25.9		50.9	
Blacks		65.4		15.4		19.1	
1980[b]							
Total		21.7%		29.4%		48.9%	
Whites		18.0		30.0		52.0	
Blacks		51.1		24.4		24.5	
1982							
Total		25.0%		29.6%		45.4%	
Whites		21.1		30.3		48.6	
Blacks		58.1		23.8		18.1	

[a]Respondents were asked the following question: "Some people feel that the Government in Washington should make every possible effort to improve the social and economic position of blacks and other minority groups. Suppose these people are at one end of the scale, at point 1. Others feel that the government should not make any special effort to help minorities because they should help themselves. Suppose these people are at the other end, at point 7. And, of course, some other people have opinions somewhere in between. Where do you place yourself on this scale?"

[b]In 1980 the phrase "even if it means giving them preferential treatment" was inserted at the end of the first sentence, above.

Source: The 1982 data were derived from the *American National Election Study, 1982: Post-Election Survey File* (machine-readable data file). Conducted by the Center for Political Studies of the Institute for Social Research, The University of Michigan, and the National Election Studies, under the overall direction of Warren E. Miller. 1st ICPSR ed. Ann Arbor, Mich.: Inter-University Consortium for Political and Social Research, 1983. Data for 1970, 1974, 1978, and 1980 derived from the National Election Surveys for those years.

TABLE 5.6 Attitudes on Government Responsibility for Fair Employment Practices for Blacks

| Year | Government Is Responsible for Fair Practices | | |
	Strongly Agree or Agree	Not Sure	Strongly Disagree or Disagree
1956[a]			
Total	70.2%	7.5%	22.3%
Whites	67.5	8.1	24.5
Blacks	97.1	2.1	0.7
1960[a]			
Total	71.5%	8.3%	20.2%
Whites	68.8	9.1	22.1
Blacks	97.6	0.0	2.4

| Year | Who Is Responsible for Ensuring Fair Practices? | | |
	Responsibility of Government in Washington	Do Not Know/ No Interest	Responsibility of States/Local Communities
1964[b]			
Total	44.9%	8.4%	46.6%
Whites	39.0	9.1	51.9
Blacks	91.4	3.3	5.3
1968[b]			
Total	43.5%	7.4%	49.1%
Whites	38.3	8.0	53.7
Blacks	88.4	2.2	9.4
1972[b]			
Total	50.0%	7.3%	42.7%
Whites	44.9	8.2	46.9
Blacks	91.0	0.0	9.0

[a]Respondents were asked, in 1956 and 1960, "If Negroes are not getting fair treatment in jobs and housing, the government should see to it that they do. Do you think the government should do this?"

[b]In 1964, 1968 and 1972, the question was altered somewhat: "Some people feel that if Negroes (colored people) are not getting fair treatment in jobs the government in Washington ought to see to it that they do. Others feel that this is not the federal government's business. . . . How do you feel? Should the government in Washington: See to it that Negroes get fair treatment in jobs or leave these matters to the states and local communities?"

Source: Data derived from American National Election Study for various years, Survey Research Center, The University of Michigan, Inter-University Consortium for Political Research, Ann Arbor, Michigan 48106.

TABLE 5.7 Gallup Polls on Job Hiring:
Preferential Treatment Versus Ability

Year	Preferential Treatment	Ability
1977	11%	81%
1980	10	83
1984	10	84

Source: Adapted from The Gallup Report
(May 1984): p. 29.

Time's affirmative action efforts "didn't change when Reagan came to power" and that efforts "have redoubled in the last four years."[66] Companies reported satisfaction with the more diverse work forces resulting from affirmative action and maintained that it was "good business sense" to develop such plans. A Mountain Bell executive stated that its minority and female work force was a "gold mine" for good managers, but were it not for hiring goals imposed on the company by a court decree, Mountain Bell would not have made such efforts on its own.[67]

SUMMARY

The increased focus on affirmative action has altered considerably the political relationships in the area of equal opportunity policy. What was once a policy with bipartisan support that united the Democratic party has come to pit unions against minority advocates and to alienate Jewish and white ethnic groups. The 1964 Civil Rights Act did not mandate racial quotas, and public opinion is against preferential hiring. But Congress has found this issue too controversial and thus has delegated to judges and administrators the responsibility (and blame) for making difficult choices.

Federal courts and federal agencies have played major roles in the development of affirmative action programs, as shown by the far-reaching 1987 Supreme Court rulings. Both the courts and the agencies have been staffed by people sympathetic to arguments that women and blacks face employment barriers, and these bureaucrats have been impatient with the perceived intransigence by state and local officials. The Reagan administration has taken an unprecedented stand against racial quotas and preferential treatment. But despite the administration's harsh rhetoric and the lobbying of business groups, it has neither rescinded nor modified the executive orders providing for affirmative action. President Reagan seemed content to pursue retrenchment through budgetary and personnel cuts rather than through more formal, permanent arrangements.

Moral policies are enveloped by a political discourse that emphasizes absolutes—clear positions that are enshrined in simple slogans such as "the Constitution is colorblind." We generally applaud principled policymaking and often equate it with diplomatic skill, but this emphasis fails to appreciate the lack of absolutes in reality. Preferential treatment cannot be contrasted with hiring and promotion decisions that are strictly based on objective standards of merit, for such decisions rarely occur. It ought to be compared with the variety of existing criteria used in making employment decisions. They must be examined in tandem with the real barriers women and minorities face in employment. The effects of affirmative action plans on women and minorities also should be assessed. Quotas have dominated the policy debate about affirmative action, with too little attention on educational programs, job training, and employer outreach designed to help blacks and other minorities compete more effectively in the job market. What is needed is more attention to the costs and benefits of affirmative action and an examination of policy alternatives, not a continued debate about moral absolutes.

✑ Chapter Six ✑

ABORTION
Prochoice Versus Prolife

Raymond Tatalovich

On January 22, 1973, the Supreme Court delivered its landmark ruling in *Roe v. Wade, District Attorney of Dallas County*, 410 U.S. 113 (1973), and the companion case *Doe v. Bolton*, 410 U.S. 179 (1973). This decision legalized abortion during the first trimester of a pregnancy and thus required forty-six states and the District of Columbia to rewrite their abortion laws. *Roe* was one of the most sweeping decisions ever rendered by the high court. It overrode states' rights, which had regulated abortions since the mid-1800s. It relied heavily on an eight-year-old precedent based on "privacy" rights to extend to women the constitutional right to terminate their pregnancies without interference by government. *Roe* outstripped public opinion on abortion and disrupted an emerging consensus in favor of abortions for "therapeutic" or medical reasons. Finally, *Roe* caused a massive political backlash. More than a decade later, there is every sign that the abortion controversy will worsen before it diminishes because today the debate is polarized between proabortion ("prochoice") and antiabortion ("prolife") movements. This dispute has effectively destroyed the political middle, and both sides judge candidates for political office in terms of their views on abortion. Although most members of the U.S. public do not subscribe to a rigid prolife or prochoice position when they evaluate abortion policy, the moderate tenor of public opinion has simply been ignored as the abortion controversy has developed in the United States.[1]

Abortion was not regulated in the United States until 1821 when Connecticut enacted the first statute outlawing abortion after quickening (when recognizable movement of the fetus occurs). That was followed in 1829 by a New York state law that added the first "therapeutic" qualification. This law legalized abortions necessary to preserve the mother's life. This "therapeutic" exception was included by the majority of states when they

TABLE 6.1 States Reforming Abortion Laws, 1966-1972

Mississippi (1966)	Delaware (1969)
Colorado (1967)	Kansas (1969)
California (1967)	New Mexico (1969)
North Carolina (1967)	Oregon (1969)
Georgia (1968)	South Carolina (1970)
Maryland (1968)	Virginia (1970)
Arkansas (1968)	Florida (1972)

Source: Raymond Tatalovich and Byron W. Daynes, *The Politics of Abortion: A Study of Community Conflict in Public Policymaking* (New York: Praeger, 1981), p. 24. Reprinted by permission of Praeger Publishers.

revised their laws governing abortion policy during the late 1800s and early 1900s.

The historical record is very important to the modern debate about abortion policy. One basic disagreement between the prolife and prochoice advocates involves the rationale for those "original" antiabortion laws. Proabortionists contend those laws were designed to protect the mother during an era when surgical techniques were very risky and often fatal. The *Roe* opinion made reference to "some scholarly support for this view of original purpose" and specifically cited research by Cyril Means.[2] Means was an attorney active in abortion reform, and it has been alleged that his research was published to influence the Supreme Court on that question.[3] After *Roe* was decided, the definitive study of those "original" nineteenth century abortion laws refuted Means's allegation that they were intended to protect the mother and not the fetus.[4] The heart of the antiabortionist position is that those original laws were intended to protect the unborn child during an era when medical evidence showed that quickening was an unreliable guide to the stage of fetal development. As David Louisell and John Noonan argued, "The quickening requirement often was abolished so that the fetus was protected from the moment of conception throughout the entire period of gestation."[5] What especially outraged the antiabortionists was the Supreme Court's willingness to accept the proabortion view of original purpose coupled with the Court's apparent disregard for the notion that the fetus is a human being.

There was no popular agitation to reform the state abortion laws, which outlawed abortions except where necessary to save the mother's life. Beginning in 1966, however, the "original" restrictive state abortion laws were reformed by fourteen states (see Table 6.1). In addition, Alaska, Hawaii,

New York, and Washington went beyond reform to "repeal" their existing laws, thus making abortion an elective procedure.

During the 1960s, a movement to liberalize the nation's abortion laws was begun by physicians and health care professionals working through ad hoc groups. These professionals were alarmed by the illegal abortions being performed by untrained abortionists in unsanitary conditions, and the mass media dramatized the tragic deaths that sometimes resulted. An important milestone came in 1959 when the American Law Institute (ALI) recommended a model penal code sanctioning "therapeutic" abortions whenever the pregnancy involved substantial risk of grave and irremediable physical or mental impairment to the mother or child and in cases of rape. The ALI Model Penal Code had substantial legislative impact in a relatively short period of time. Taken together, these eighteen states authorized abortion to save the mother's life and in cases of rape; all except Mississippi made reference to the mother's physical or mental health as well; and all but Mississippi and California included fetal abnormalities as grounds for therapeutic abortion. A consensus was emerging behind abortion reform because abortion was viewed primarily as a *medical* issue.

Nevertheless, the problematic nature of existing antiabortion laws was dramatized in 1962 by the plight of Sherri Finkbine of Phoenix, Arizona.[6] Finkbine had taken the drug thalidomide but later discovered that it caused grossly deformed fetuses. She petitioned a hospital in Arizona to grant her an abortion. Physicians heretofore had interpreted the state law liberally to allow such abortions where the prospect of a grossly deformed fetus would cause emotional trauma and pose a mental health problem for the mother. But her story made the front page of local newspapers and quickly spread across the country. As a consequence, the local prosecutor threatened to arrest the attending physician, the hospital then cancelled the scheduled abortion, and eventually Sherri Finkbine had to travel to Sweden for that operation (which revealed a badly deformed fetus). The onslaught of intense publicity (even the Vatican condemned Finkbine's abortion in Sweden) transformed a purely medical question into a heated political debate, and thus the ability to achieve a working consensus was rendered impossible.

Early efforts to reform state antiabortion laws were spearheaded by activists who formed single-issue groups. Dr. Robert Hall, a physician, was prominent in this movement, as was Lawrence Lader, a long-time abortion activist. Initially, their activities focused on New York state and on California, where such groups as the Association for the Study of Abortion (New York), Society for Humane Abortion (San Francisco), and California Committee on Therapeutic Abortion (Los Angeles) were formed. In 1965, the umbrella group, the National Association for Humane Abortion, held its organizational meeting. The critical role of such ad hoc groups was illustrated by case studies of how specific states repealed their antiabortion laws. In Hawaii, for example, a state senator joined a leader of the Honolulu Chapter of the American Association of University Women to mobilize a grass-roots coalition behind abortion liberalization.[7]

The founding of the National Association for Repeal of Abortion Laws (NARAL) in 1969 was the work of a small cadre of activists now motivated to promote the feminist goal of abortion as a woman's personal right. Lawrence Lader was a key figure in organizing NARAL, and he described how a few people met in Chicago in July 1968 to discuss convening a national conference.[8] During the next six months these founders of NARAL built an organization, attracted elites with reputation and influence, and obtained endorsements from established groups. NARAL targeted New York state as an early battleground to focus proabortion energies around repeal, not just reform. From February 14–16, 1969, the First National Conference on Abortion Laws was held in Chicago, and NARAL forged a consensus behind the "repeal" of abortion laws. By this action, NARAL moved far ahead of prevailing medical opinion and public opinion, which was beginning to accept abortion as a medical necessity but not a woman's constitutional right. This shift in goals was accompanied by a new strategy that focused on judicial intervention instead of legislative lobbying. Lawsuits were brought against state antiabortion statutes in the hope that a court decision would bring immediate and complete victory.

JUDICIARY

In a 1968 article, Roy Lucas determined that "the constitutional issues implicit in the enactment and application of abortion laws have received scant judicial attention."[9] However, by the time *Roe* was decided in 1973, there were several abortion rulings by various federal and state courts. In these cases, the abortion advocates had based their lawsuits on such grounds as women's rights, statutory vagueness, the question of personal privacy, and equal protection of the law. In support of their cases, abortion rights advocates were able to cite a precedent established by the Supreme Court in *Griswold v. Connecticut*, 381 U.S. 479 (1965).

Griswold provided a unique opportunity to challenge state antiabortion laws. The concept of privacy rights was fundamental to the *Griswold* decision. The Supreme Court relied heavily on the Ninth Amendment, which holds that the enumeration of rights in the Constitution "shall not be construed to deny or disparage others retained by the people." Privacy was interpreted to be a "retained" although unwritten right. Griswold had been prosecuted for violating a Connecticut law that prohibited the use of contraceptives by married couples. That statute was nullified by the Supreme Court in a 7–2 vote, and abortion proponents reasoned that "privacy" in marital sex could be extended on similar legal grounds to abortion.

The first case to test the constitutionality of any state antiabortion law was *People v. Belous*,[10] which was decided by the California Supreme Court in 1969. Dr. Leon Belous was convicted of referring a patient to an abortionist. But in its 4–3 ruling, the supreme court nullified that law by saying that the therapeutic exception "necessary to preserve life" was unconstitutionally vague. The court further argued that the law denied the woman her fundamental right to have children or not and that the state had no compelling interest in regulating abortions. The first ruling by a federal court also came in 1969, *United States v. Vuitch*,[11] where district court judge Gerhard Gesell affirmed the legal principles expressed in the *Belous* case. The therapeutic exception "allowing abortions to preserve the mother's life or health" was ambiguous and violated due process; the woman has a right of privacy in the area of family, marriage, and sex; and the government showed no compelling interest why it should infringe upon a woman's rights. The court also said that the District of Columbia law discriminated against the poor. Judge Gesell recommended that his decision be appealed to the Supreme Court, which the U.S. government did.

In its first abortion decision, the Supreme Court in 1971 upheld the District of Columbia abortion law but expanded the meaning of a mother's "life or health" to include "psychological as well as physical well-being." In *United States v. Vuitch*, 402 U.S. 62 (1971), the high court extended the meaning of therapeutic abortion but did not accept lower federal court rulings that abortion was a fundamental right. On at least eight previous occasions, the Supreme Court had declined to review state court decisions on abortion, including the *Belous* case, but in 1971, with seventeen abortion cases pending, the Supreme Court agreed to hear arguments on a century-old Texas statute (*Roe v. Wade*) and the 1968 "reformed" Georgia abortion law (*Doe v. Bolton*). The Court decided both cases at the same time.

Roe v. Wade

The majority opinion in this landmark case was drafted by Justice Harry Blackmun, who apparently labored many months trying to fashion a majority on this question. The case dealt with Jane Roe (a pseudonym), a pregnant and unmarried woman who appealed to the Supreme Court because she was unable to get a legal abortion in Texas and could not afford to travel elsewhere to obtain a legal abortion. Her "class action" suit on behalf of all women in this situation claimed that her privacy rights were violated. The state of Texas countered that it held control over fetal life from the time of conception. Roe eventually appealed to the Supreme Court along with John and Mary Doe, a married couple desiring abortion as a birth control method, and Dr. James H. Hallford, a physician and abortionist who sought protection from prosecution. Only Roe was declared to have standing to sue. The Supreme Court ruled in her favor, applying "privacy" rights from *Griswold* and other precedents to give freedom of choice to the pregnant mother.

In his majority opinion, Justice Blackmun distinguished among the three trimesters of pregnancy. Because abortions during the first three months (trimester) are safer than childbirth, he argued that "the attending physician, in consultation with his patient, is free to determine, without regulation by the State, that, in his medical judgment, the patient's pregnancy should be terminated. If that decision is reached, the judgment may be effectuated by an abortion free of interference by the State."

During the second trimester, government may regulate abortions to preserve the mother's health, thus furthering a legitimate state interest, and during the third trimester the state can prohibit abortions unless necessary to protect the mother's life or health. The Supreme Court thereby judged the woman's privacy rights to be fundamental during the first trimester, whereas the state's interest in protecting "potential" life becomes compelling during the last three months when the fetus "presumably has the capacity for meaningful life outside the mother's womb." But Texas also contended that government had a compelling interest to protect the fetus regardless of whether it was legally a person, so the majority opinion in *Roe* was obliged to add this caveat: "We need not resolve the difficult question of when life begins. When those trained in the respective disciplines of medicine, philosophy, and theology are unable to arrive at any consensus, the judiciary at this point in the development of man's knowledge, is not in a position to speculate as to the answer." Nonetheless, the Court then proceeded to say that there "has always been strong support for the view that life does not begin until live birth."

Roe v. Wade did not resolve the abortion controversy. The decision was hailed by women's rights advocates. Lawrence Lader called it "so sweeping that it seemed to assure the triumph of the abortion movement."[12] *The Christian Science Monitor* editorialized, "No victory for women's rights since enactment of the 19th Amendment has been greater than the one achieved Monday in the Supreme Court."[13] But the reaction among Catholics was decidedly negative. John Cardinal Krol of Philadelphia said *Roe* would permit "the greatest slaughter of innocent life in the history of mankind."[14] To antiabortionists, *Roe* was a singular defeat, and they began to exert political pressure on local, state, and federal governments through elected officials to limit the impact of the Court's decree. In turn, proabortion defenders returned to the courts to safeguard a woman's fundamental right to an abortion against interference by government. The evolution of the abortion controversy, therefore, spotlights the activist role of the federal judiciary both in initiating legalized abortion and in monitoring its implementation by state governments.

Post-Roe Cases

Including the *Roe* and *Doe* decisions of 1973, seventeen abortion cases reached the Supreme Court through 1986.[15] With the exception of four rulings on government funding of abortions, the Supreme Court has yielded little ground to the prolifers. The judiciary has not reneged on abortion as a woman's constitutional right. At the same time, the Court has nullified obstacles designed to prevent women from getting abortions and has refused to acknowledge that the unborn is a "person" in any legal sense.

In *Planned Parenthood of Central Missouri v. Danforth*, 428 U.S. 52 (1976), the Supreme Court invalidated state requirements that a woman gain the consent of her husband and that a minor have the consent of her parent before obtaining an abortion, and the Court disallowed the law's prohibition on the commonly used saline amniocentesis method of first trimester abortions. By deciding *Colautti v. Franklin*, 439 U.S. 379 (1979), the Supreme Court nullified provisions of the Pennsylvania Abortion Control Act that imposed criminal liability on a physician who did not try to preserve the life of a fetus that was "viable" or when there was "sufficient reason to believe that the fetus may be viable." In this 6–3 ruling, the high court held that the statute was unconstitutionally vague and interfered with the physician's medical judgment. In *Bellotti v. Baird*, 443 U.S. 622 (1979), the Supreme Court declared unconstitutional a Massachusetts law requiring a pregnant minor to seek permission of her parents before getting an abortion. This requirement also was viewed as an intrusion on the woman's privacy.

A very important case to reach the Supreme Court in 1983 was *Akron v. Akron Center for Reproductive Health, Inc.*, 103 S.C. 2481 (1983). An Akron, Ohio, ordinance was the most restrictive antiabortion law by any municipality in the nation. The law required that abortions after three months be performed in a hospital, that abortions on unmarried minors under age fifteen require parental consent or a court order, and that the patient be informed about fetal development and alternatives to abortion. The prochoice advocates were especially alarmed about the requirement for hospital-based abortions after the first trimester because the vast number of abortions are performed today in specialized clinics.

The majority opinion in this case was written by Justice Lewis Powell, who argued that no city or state regulation could "interfere with physician-patient consultation or with the woman's choice between abortion and childbirth." Nor would any regulation be upheld by the Court unless the government could show that the regulation promotes a legitimate state interest in preserving fetal life. In this case, the requirement for hospital-based abortions imposed a heavy and unnecessary burden on a woman's access to a relatively inexpensive, otherwise accessible, and usually safe procedure. That restriction, said Powell, was therefore an "unreasonable" infringement on a woman's constitutional right to an abortion.

The only, but not inconsequential, concession by the Supreme Court to prolife advocates has been its rulings on government funding of abortions. Three of these decisions came in 1977. In *Beal v. Doe*, 432 U.S. 438 (1977), the Supreme Court agreed with Pennsylvania that the Social Security Act does not require that state to fund nontherapeutic abortions from Medicaid funds as a condition for participation in this federal-state funded medical care program for the indigent. In *Maher v. Roe*, 432 U.S. 464 (1977), the Supreme Court ruled that Connecticut did not violate the "equal protection" clause of the Fourteenth Amendment by choosing to fund childbirths but not nontherapeutic abortions under its Medicaid program. In both cases the majority opinion was drafted by Justice Powell. He stated that abortion was not an "unqualified" right under the Constitution. Moreover, "there is a basic difference between direct state interference with a protected activity [abortion] and state encouragement of an alternative activity [childbirth] consonant with legislative policy."

The third case, *Poelker v. Doe*, 432 U.S. 519 (1977), found the high court upholding a ban on nontherapeutic abortions in city-owned hospitals in St. Louis, Missouri. A directive by Mayor John Poelker barred abortions in public hospitals unless the mother faced serious physical injury or death. The plaintiffs in this case sued on the grounds that because women were denied access to publicly funded hospitals, they were denied equal protection of the law. But the Supreme Court was not convinced. It held that the citizenry of St. Louis, by electing Mayor Poelker to office, expressed its collective preference for childbirths rather than for abortions. That policy might obstruct a woman seeking an abortion, said the Court, but the policy did not interfere with her fundamental right to have an abortion.

None of these cases addressed the question of whether Congress could ban the use of federal funds, such as Medicaid moneys, for abortions, but the Hyde amendment, sponsored by Congressman Henry J. Hyde (R-Ill.) and passed in 1977, did: "None of the funds contained in this Act shall be used to perform abortions except where the life of the mother would be endangered if the fetus were carried to term." Some version of this prohibition on federal Medicaid funds has been approved by Congress ever since. In June 1980, the Supreme Court ruled 5–4 in *Harris v. McRae*, 448 U.S. 297 (1980), that the Hyde amendment was constitutional. In his majority opinion, Justice Potter Stewart argued that the law did not violate the First or Fifth Amendments, and he affirmed the Court's reasoning in *Maher* and *Beal* that *Roe* did not establish an "entitlement" guaranteeing women—rich and poor— equal access to abortions. As he wrote, "It simply does not follow that a woman's freedom of choice carries with it a constitutional entitlement to the financial resources to avail herself of the full range of protected choices."

By this logic the Supreme Court chose not to directly confront the Congress because one *amicus curiae* brief submitted to the Court was filed by 238 members of the House of Representatives. In this brief, the separation-of-powers principle (wherein Congress retains the "power of the purse") was invoked to support the Hyde amendment. The high court made no reference to that statement, but undoubtedly this brief weighed on the Court's deliberations. In his majority opinion in *Maher*, Justice Powell showed an awareness of the separation-of-powers argument by noting, "When an issue involves policy choices as sensitive as those implicated by public funding of nontherapeutic abortion, the proper forum for their resolution is the legislature."

After a three year hiatus, in 1986 a deeply divided Supreme Court rendered its decision in *Thornburgh v. American College of Obstetricians and Gynecologists*, 106 S.Ct. 2169 (1986). At issue was Pennsylvania's Abortion Control Act of 1982, which required that doctors provide women seeking abortions with information about risks and alternatives; that detailed records be kept by physicians; that two doctors be present during late-term abortions; and that an abortion method be used that would most likely produce a live birth unless the method posed a "significantly greater" risk to the mother. The 5–4 majority opinion was authored by Justice Harry Blackmun, joined by Justices William Brennan, Thurgood Marshall, Lewis Powell, and John Paul Stevens. A review of those provisions, said Blackmun, "shows they wholly subordinate constitutional privacy interests and concerns with maternal health in an effort to deter a woman from making a decision that, with her physician, is hers to make."

In sharply worded dissents, Justices Byron White, William Rehnquist, Sandra Day O'Connor, and Chief Justice Warren Burger charged that the Court's abortion rulings had run amuck of the Constitution. O'Connor said these rulings "have already worked a major distortion in the Court's constitutional jurisprudence." In asking that the high court "re-examine" Roe, Burger asserted that "we may have lured judges into roaming at large in the constitutional field." Contrary to Burger's original expectation in Roe, the Court had extended that decision to require "abortion on demand" and, furthermore, had abandoned its view that states could regulate late-term abortions to protect "the potentiality of human life." The dissent filed by Justice White (joined by Rehnquist) said that Thornburgh "carries forward the difficult and continuing venture in substantive due process that began with . . . Roe v. Wade (1973), and has led the Court further and further afield in the 13 years since that decision was handed down." Having dissented in that original decision, White now "would return the issue to the people by over-ruling Roe v. Wade." By the time that Thornburgh was decided, Justice Potter Stewart—who voted with the majority in Roe—had been replaced by Sandra Day O'Connor, who now expressed reservations about legalized abortion. The fact that Chief Justice Burger reversed his Roe position in the Thornburgh case suggested that the Court was beginning to rethink its position on this controversy.

The reelection of President Reagan in 1984 was crucial for the prolife agenda because Justices Marshall, Brennan, Blackmun, Powell, and Burger were at or nearing eighty years of age. Included in this group of elderly justices were three who had been consistent in voting prochoice. (Roe was decided by a 7–2 vote, with only White and Rehnquist dissenting.) In sixteen abortion cases, the Supreme Court opinion differentiated cleanly between the prochoice and prolife positions.[16] (The one case excluded here is Connecticut v. Menillo, 423 U.S. 9 [1975].) The percentage and number of prochoice votes cast by each justice in those decisions are as follows.

Blackmun	100%	(16 of 16)
Marshall	100%	(16 of 16)
Brennan	100%	(16 of 16)
Douglas	100%	(3 of 3)
Powell	62%	(10 of 16)
Stevens	61%	(8 of 13)
Stewart	50%	(6 of 12)
Burger	44%	(7 of 16)
O'Connor	25%	(1 of 4)
Rehnquist	13%	(2 of 16)
White	6%	(1 of 16)

Blackmun, Marshall, and Brennan (and Douglas on three cases when he voted) had perfect prochoice voting records. White and Rehnquist showed very consistent prolife voting, and Sandra Day O'Connor supported prolife in three of four cases to date.

No sooner had the Supreme Court decided the *Thornburgh* case when important changes in its personnel were made. Following the resignation of Chief Justice Warren E. Burger on June 17, 1986, President Reagan nominated William E. Rehnquist (age 61) to be Burger's successor and Antonin Scalia (age 50) to be an associate justice. By mid-September, both men were confirmed by the Senate, although the 65–33 vote on Rehnquist had the largest number of negative votes ever cast on a Supreme Court confirmation.

Rehnquist has been decidedly more conservative than Burger in his opinions and the intellectual force behind the Court's conservative faction. Burger voted with the majority in *Roe* where Rehnquist dissented and has sided with the prochoice position more often than has Rehnquist. Scalia is a legal scholar who was appointed by President Reagan in 1982 to the U.S. Court of Appeals for the District of Columbia. In his articles, opinions, and debates, Scalia (who is Catholic) has argued that the Supreme Court was wrong to recognize a constitutional right to abortion. Thus, the stage is set for a major reversal in abortion policy should President Reagan, or his successor, appoint another conservative to the high court.

PUBLIC OPINION

During the 1960s, there was Catholic resistance to abortion reform, although this resistance was sporadic and disorganized. However, *Roe* galvanized that opposition into a nationwide prolife movement. In reaction, the defenders of legalized abortion intensified their organizational efforts and political vigilance. What has emerged therefore is a situation of two "intense minorities" on each side of public opinion. The majority of the population stands to the right of the prochoice position but to the left of the prolife position. While most people generally oppose the strident tactics used by prolifers in their attempts to overthrow *Roe*, the former seem to resist the logic of the prochoice position. At the heart of the prochoice dilemma is that abortion on demand has not gained widespread acceptance despite the Supreme Court ruling. Writing in 1980, Eric Uslaner and Ronald Weber explained, "The abortion policies of *Roe* and *Doe* have not been legitimized. We have not seen substantial increases in public support for abortion after the Court decisions; instead, we have witnessed a hardening of positions by many who were opposed to abortions."[17]

There is much longitudinal opinion data on how the U.S. populace views abortion. In one respect, public opinion on abortion has remained stable since *Roe*. The abortion reformers of the 1960s advocated therapeutic medical abortions, and this goal is now accepted by virtually everyone. A Gallup Poll in June 1983 found that only 16 percent favored an absolutist

TABLE 6.2 Gallup Polls on Legal Conditions for Abortion, 1975-1983

Year	Legal Under any Circumstances	Legal Under Only Certain Circumstances	Illegal in all Circumstances
1983	23%	58%	16%
1981	23	52	21
1980	25	53	18
1979	22	54	19
1977	22	55	19
1975	21	54	22

Source: Data adapted from *The Gallup Report* (August 1983): p. 18. The question was, "Do you think abortions should be legal under any circumstances, legal under only certain circumstances, or illegal in all circumstances?"

prolife prohibition against all abortions, 23 percent endorsed legalized abortion for any reason, but the majority (54 percent) approved abortions only under certain circumstances. This Gallup Poll confirmed a trend dating back to at least 1975 (Table 6.2). Surveys taken by the University of Chicago's National Opinion Research Center (NORC) also showed that pattern.

NORC asked whether abortions should be legal under various conditions, including when the woman wants one for "any reason" (Table 6.3). Even before *Roe*, a consensus existed in favor of therapeutic abortions for so-called hard or medical reasons (mother's health, rape, defective child), but when soft or socioeconomic reasons were cited (unmarried mother, unwanted child, poverty), the public was more reticent to give its approval. In 1985, only 36 percent favored abortions for any reason, and this data suggested that since 1982 there had been a retrenchment in public support for nontherapeutic abortions.

On the other hand, prochoice advocates can cite parallel questions by Harris and Gallup showing plurality or majority support for the Supreme Court decision that legalized abortions in the first trimester. These data are given in Table 6.4.[18] This survey must be weighed against the previous Gallup and NORC findings because public opinion toward abortion is influenced by the questions posed. Acceptance of abortion tends to increase when its legality is cited, for example by references to the Supreme Court, or when couched in terms of being a medical decision between a woman

TABLE 6.3 NORC Surveys on Medical and Socioeconomic Reasons for Abortion, 1972-1985 (percent approval)

Reason	1972	1973	1975	1977	1980	1982	1984	1985
Mother's health	83%	91%	88%	88%	88%	89%	87%	87%
Rape	74	81	80	80	80	83	77	78
Defect in child	74	82	80	83	80	81	77	76
Mother unmarried	41	47	46	47	46	47	43	40
Family too poor	46	52	51	52	50	50	44	42
No more children	38	46	44	44	45	46	41	39
Any reason				36	39	39	37	36

Source: Data based on the National Opinion Research Center, General Social Surveys (July 1982): pp. 154-155, and (July 1986): pp. 227-229. The question was, "whether or not you think it should be possible for a pregnant woman to obtain a legal abortion if (a) there is a strong chance of a serious defect in the baby? (b) if she is married and does not want any more children? (c) the woman's own health is seriously endangered by the pregnancy? (d) the family has a very low income and cannot afford any more children? (e) she became pregnant as a result of rape? (f) she is not married and does not want to marry the man? (g) the woman wants it for any reason?"

and her doctor. Even with this caveat in mind, however, these Harris/ Gallup polls revealed that 37–45 percent of their respondents opposed the high court's abortion ruling.

The Supreme Court in Roe presumed that life begins at birth, but the public feels otherwise. Gallup Polls in 1973 and 1975 were analyzed by Judith Blake, who found "considerable error in the Supreme Court's assessment of non-Catholic opinions on this subject."[19] Fewer than 10 percent of the women surveyed and no more than 20 percent of the men supported the view that life begins at birth. The majority of men and women as well as Catholics and Protestants believed that human life starts either at conception or at quickening.

Public opinion departs from the prolife agenda when the agenda's legislative proposals aimed at restricting abortions are evaluated. In 1976, a New York Times/CBS national survey found 56 percent against a constitutional amendment making all abortions illegal.[20] A 1980 survey by Time/ Yankelovich, Skelly, and White found 63 percent opposed to such an

TABLE 6.4 Harris/Gallup Surveys on Supreme Court Ruling
Legalizing Abortions, 1973-1986

		Favor	Oppose
1973	(Harris)	52%	41%
1974	(Gallup)	47	44
1975	(Harris)	54	38
1976	(Harris)	54	39
1977	(Harris)	53	40
1979	(Harris)	60	37
1981	(Gallup)	45	46
1983	(Gallup)	50	43
1985	(Gallup)	45	45
1986	(Gallup)	45	45

Source: Data based on the Harris Survey News Release
(May 26, 1975), (April 18, 1977), (March 6, 1979); and
The Gallup Report, nos. 244-245 (January-February 1986):
pp. 17-18. The question asked by Harris was, "In general,
do you favor or oppose the U.S. Supreme Court decision
making abortions up to three months of pregnancy legal?"
The Gallup Poll asked, "The U.S. Supreme Court has ruled
that a woman may go to a doctor to end pregnancy at any
time during the first three months of pregnancy. Do you
favor or oppose this ruling?"

amendment,[21] and a 1982 Harris Survey found 62 percent against a constitutional amendment "to ban legalized abortion."[22]

There is more support for restrictions on abortion so long as its
therapeutic use is assured. A 1976 Gallup Poll, for example, found the public
more divided—49 percent favoring and 45 percent opposing—an amendment
banning abortions except when the mother's life is endangered.[23] This also
is shown by two polls taken by the *New York Times*/CBS in 1984.[24] One
poll found 63 percent opposed to an amendment "that would make all
abortions illegal," whereas only 48 percent disapproved of an amendment
permitting abortions "only in order to save the life of the mother." A
comparison of these results indicates a 15 percent shift in public opinion
toward a constitutional amendment permitting a therapeutic exception for
abortion.

INTEREST GROUPS

Unfortunately, the debate about abortion is not defined by public opinion but by prolife versus prochoice advocates. These antagonists do not "agree to disagree"; they represent different political constituencies as well as divergent moral positions. The prochoice and prolife groups are as different as are their rallying cries.

Prochoice Coalition

The prochoice movement emerged from those single-issue groups that rallied behind abortion reform in the 1960s. Today, a broad-based coalition supports legalized abortion, although these groups are not held together by a singular focus. Women's groups, health care associations, religious denominations, and traditional "liberal" groups constitute the prochoice coalition. Its leadership tends to exaggerate the endorsements made by such organizations to imply that everybody favors abortion on demand when, in reality, some groups only endorsed abortion reforms. But an impressive number of national organizations belong to the prochoice coalition, and they generally are opposed to Hyde amendment restrictions on Medicaid funding of abortions.

A large number of liberal Protestant churches and reformed Jewish synagogues have joined the cause, plus a tiny splinter group among Catholics— Catholics for Free Choice—who oppose their church's position on abortion. These denominations are mobilized under an umbrella, single-issue organization known as the Religious Coalition for Abortion Rights (RCAR). Its twenty-eight groups represent fourteen denominations and are organized nationally into twenty-five state and local coalitions. RCAR was established in 1973 to oppose a constitutional amendment outlawing abortions. RCAR tries to influence members of Congress and their staff by lobbying them directly during "clergy/Congress breakfasts."

More than other interest groups in the prochoice coalition, the American Civil Liberties Union (ACLU) has taken a leadership role in defending *Roe* against encroachment by local, state, and federal governments. The ACLU's Reproductive Freedom Project is a nonprofit organization whose purpose is to educate the population on abortion and to participate in litigation. Unlike most prochoice groups, the ACLU relies almost exclusively on litigation to promote its abortion agenda.

The nationwide "single-issue" prochoice organization is the National Abortion Rights Action League (NARAL), which was established in 1969 as the National Association for the Repeal of Abortion Laws. NARAL focuses more energy on the political process, electioneering, and legislative lobbying and, toward those ends, in 1978 created the Political Action Committee. NARAL's membership of seventy thousand is organized into national, state, and local affiliates. NARAL conducts research, monitors legislation, keeps its membership informed, provides testimony to Congress, supports demonstrations and debates, and contributes to election campaigns. Since 1980, in light of the countermobilization of prolife forces, NARAL has given more attention to strengthening its grass-roots organization.

Because prochoice groups see an ally in the federal judiciary, they press their legal advantage in the courtroom. An analysis of the seventeen abortion cases to reach the Supreme Court during 1973–1986 was done to determine which groups submitted *amicus curiae* briefs to influence its deliberations (see Table 6.5). A total of 157 different prochoice groups authored or co-authored 309 *amicus* briefs, and the majority (55 percent) were filed by women's groups, church organizations, and health care associations. The most active prochoice groups in this regard were the Planned Parenthood Federation of America (9), the American Public Health Association (8), the Association of Planned Parenthood Physicians (7), and the National Organization for Women (6).

Prochoice Arguments

Prochoice literature warns its readers that prolife activities are an attack on religious freedom, civil liberties, minority rights, and a fundamental assault on the establishment clause of the First Amendment, which guarantees church-state separation. The ACLU ardently opposes the Hyde amendment because that law "serves no secular purpose. It does not promote health, or save public funds. Its only purpose is to promote a particular religious view on the question of when life begins."[25] The Religious Coalition for Abortion Rights is against any prolife amendment to the Constitution because "it would enact into civil law one particular theology—a theology that is not shared by the majority of western denominations."[26] RCAR also generalizes the threat prolifers pose to other U.S. freedoms. One pamphlet states, "American liberties have been secure in large measure because they have been guaranteed by a Bill of Rights. . . . If the first clause of the Bill of Rights, which protects religious freedom, should prove so easily susceptible to amendment, none of the succeeding clauses would be secure."[27] For this reason, prochoice advocates fear the convening of a constitutional convention to add a prolife amendment. As the ACLU makes the argument, "A 'runaway' convention, controlled by right wing groups opposed to abortion, could pass amendments eliminating the right of privacy, due process, equal protection of the laws, and freedom of expression and inquiry—every one of the civil liberties we now enjoy."[28]

Prolife Lobby

To date, the prolifers have not forged a broad-based coalition with established interest groups, but compared to the prochoice coalition, the prolifers are more homogeneous and single-minded in their political objectives. This fact is illustrated by the prolife groups that were most active in submitting *amicus curiae* briefs to the Supreme Court during 1973–1986. These groups were the Legal Defense Fund for Unborn Children (9), Americans United for Life (8), and the U.S. Catholic Conference (5). The prolife lobby depends more heavily on single-issue groups to promote its cause, and this feature

TABLE 6.5 *Amicus Curiae* Briefs to the Supreme Court by Interest Groups in Seventeen Abortion Cases

		Classification of Interest Groups Filing Briefs[a]		
No. of pro life groups	No. of pro life briefs	Group category	No. of pro choice groups	No. of pro choice briefs
7	13	Religious	36	75
4	5	Health/medical	26	61
5	15	Civil liberties/law	24	53
3	5	Social welfare	13	23
5	7	Women's groups	26	46
18	30	Single-issue	12	27
12	17	State/federal governments	3	4
--	--	Ethnic	8	8
--	--	Labor unions	5	6
1	1	Other groups	4	6
Total 55	93		157	309

Most Active Interest Groups Filing Briefs

	Number of Briefs Filed		Number of Briefs Filed
Legal Defense Fund for Unborn Children	9	Planned Parenthood Federation of America	10
Americans United for Life	8	American Public Health Association	9
U.S. Catholic Conference	6	Association of Planned Parenthood Physicians	7
National Right to Life Committee	4	National Organization for Women	7
Lawyers for Life	3	National Emergency Civil Liberties Committee	6
Solicitor General	3		

[a]Listed below are the number of *different* groups involved in amicus curiae activity; the number of briefs is the number of times each different group either submitted an amicus curiae brief on its own or joined with other groups in authoring a friend-of-the-court brief. In a sense the number of "single-issue" groups is underestimated insofar as pro-life or pro-choice factions within a larger classification (for examples, Missouri Nurses for Life or Feminists for Life) are included with the latter (respectively health/medical and women's groups in these examples).

is shown by the *amicus* activities of the Legal Defense Fund for Unborn Children and Americans United for Life. However, the prolife lobby does not pin its hopes for fundamental change in abortion policy on the Supreme Court, and each year—as a sign of their continuing protest—on the anniversary of *Roe* (January 22) thousands of prolifers stage a March for Life around the Supreme Court building.

The Roman Catholic church remains in the forefront of the prolife movement. In a celebrated move in November 1975, the National Conference of Catholic Bishops announced its Pastoral Plan for Pro-Life Activities, which advocated a three-pronged strategy: an educational and public relations campaign, pastoral work dealing with pregnancy-related problems, and a public policy effort to lobby the legislative, judicial, and executive branches. The most controversial goal was "the development in each congressional district of an identifiable, tightly-knit and well-organized pro-life unit."[29] One cannot assume that all lay Catholics agree with their church's position on abortion (and polls show that many do not), but Catholics are 27 percent of the U.S. population, which assures a potent grass-roots constituency behind prolife objectives.

The intimate relationship between the Roman Catholic church and the Right-to-Life (RTL) Committees causes prochoice spokespersons to raise the specter that the First Amendment separation of church and state is threatened. According to this view, the RTL movement is a "secular" arm of the Roman Catholic church: "There is convincing evidence that Catholics and the Catholic Church overwhelmingly dominate the RTL movement. Not only do Catholics comprise the bulk of RTL rank-and-file organizations, but the Church provides the movement's financial and institutional base."[30]

In fact, the Women's Lobby took the Roman Catholic church to court for its failure to register as a political lobby. That action forced the National Conference of Catholic Bishops in 1973 to establish the National Committee for a Human Life Amendment (NCHLA) for lobbying purposes. To further mute criticism of its activist political role, in 1976 the bishops issued a statement, "Political Responsibility: Reflections on an Election Year," that contended that no violation of the church-state separation had occurred and that, to the contrary, they had every right in a democracy to speak out for social justice and for human rights.

Catholics are allied in the prolife struggle with fundamentalist Protestant denominations, religious crusades, ultraconservative political groups, and organizations tied to the Roman Catholic church. The Mormon church is solidly opposed to abortions, and the church exerts dominant political influence in the intermountain West. Southern Baptists, with 13.4 million members, are the largest non-Catholic denomination to endorse prolife objectives. Fundamentalist religious crusades oppose abortions as part of their rightist social agenda. The Christian Action Council, founded by Reverend Billy Graham, opposed abortion along with fetal experimentation, euthanasia, and infanticide. The Christian Crusade led by fundamentalist preacher Billy Jean Hargiss is against abortion, as is the Moral Majority.

The Right-to-Life Committees are single-issue groups essential to the prolife lobby. Organized at the local, state, and national levels, the RTL movement claims a membership of 11 million. When first established, the primary goal of the RTL was to enact a constitutional amendment banning abortions, but RTL has attributes of a social movement. For example, in New York state in 1978, the RTL Committee displaced the Liberal party as the fourth largest political party; the RTL's gubernatorial candidate received 130,193 votes.[31] RTL groups also participate in July 4th parades, disseminate books and newspapers detailing the horrors of abortion, and utilize "hit lists" to target proabortion members of Congress for defeat. These RTL Committees are the pristine single-issue group, as described by political scientist Walter Dean Burnham: "The right-to-lifers *are* doing what others have done, but with a major difference in intensity. The emotional charge coming from opposition to abortion is greater than from civil rights or the right to bear arms or any similar cause. The people who are dedicated right-to-lifers really believe that, in a special religious sense, they are doing the Lord's work."[32]

In addition, there are smaller single-issue groups in the prolife lobby. The U.S. Coalition for Life was founded in 1972 and serves one thousand two hundred groups in seventeen countries. The American Citizens Concerned for Life has an advisory committee that includes members of Congress. The American Life Lobby (ALL) is very aggressive in its opposition. With 70,000 members, ALL prides itself on being the organization most steadfastly opposed to the Planned Parenthood Federation of America on many questions, including sex education in the schools and abortion. Of lesser importance are the Citizens United for Life, the Society for Protection of Unborn Children, and the National Youth Prolife Coalition. Despite the official stands of the AMA and the ANA, Doctors and Nurses for Life oppose abortions. Most feminist groups are proabortion, except for STOP ERA, Feminists for Life, and Women Concerned for the Unborn Child.

Prolife Arguments

Although both sides try to generalize the threat posed by the enemy to sacred U.S. values, prolifers took the offensive in this regard by drawing analogies between abortion and slavery, the Nazi genocide, and moral decay. Prolifers say that legalized abortion reflects a developing, selective morality in the United States that condones the destruction of human life simply for convenience. Unchecked, this amorality will lead to more barbarious actions against people. The bottom-line argument by prolifers is simply that abortion is murder. The latter argument has been exploited fully by antiabortionists, and a major symbolic victory came to the prolifers when Dr. Bernard Nathanson, a founder of NARAL and owner of an abortion clinic, was transformed into an avid prolife spokesperson. His new outlook was publicized in a book entitled *Aborting America*, where he contended that advances in medical knowledge proved beyond a doubt that the fetus is a living being.

The prolifers widely propagandize the fact that by 1984 more than 15 million abortions have been performed in the United States. That statistic was responsible for Vice President George Bush's about-face on abortions. In his 1984 debate with Geraldine Ferraro, the Democratic challenger, Bush admitted that his earlier views on abortion had hardened: "So, yes, my position's evolved, but I'd like to see the American who faced with 15 million abortions isn't re-thinking his or her position."[33] This point was made more forcefully by President Reagan in his October 7, 1984, debate with Democrat Walter Mondale. Reagan told the story of a man in California who beat a pregnant woman so savagely that her child was born dead, which prompted the state legislature to enact a law making that a crime. He added, "Now isn't it strange that the same woman could have taken the life of her unborn child and it was abortion and no murder but if somebody else does it, that's murder."[34]

This ethical dilemma causes problems for Catholic politicians who endorse abortion. Geraldine Ferraro's prochoice record in the Congress stalked her during the presidential campaign of 1984 after she was involved in a much publicized exchange with Archbishop John H. O'Connor of New York City. She had co-signed a letter with other congresspersons stating that the Catholic position on abortion was not "monolithic" and thus allowed personal interpretation. The archbishop countered that Ferraro's views misrepresented the church and that on abortion "there is no variance, there is no flexibility, there is no leeway."[35] This confrontation brought Governor Mario Cuomo (D-N.Y.) and Senator Edward Kennedy (D-Mass.), both prochoice Catholics, to Ferraro's defense. They, too, disapproved of abortion but said that Catholic politicians could legislate in ways contrary to church doctrine. This episode focused attention on the double standard that plagues prochoice advocates in the Catholic church.

The Seamless Garment

Ideological appeals are intended to discredit the opposition and to rally supporters behind a political cause. But ideology can be a double-edged sword. Ideological rigidity may be attractive only to very few true believers, thus alienating the mass of potential allies. This problem may be confronting the prolife forces in light of a change in strategy by the Roman Catholic church. In a major address at Fordham University on December 6, 1983, Joseph Cardinal Bernardin, archbishop of Chicago, called upon his parishioners to oppose abortion as well as capital punishment and nuclear escalation in a "comprehensive ethic of life." He said that the antiabortion movement would be strengthened by this linkage: "The issues I have raised are all different, but the same principle—the sanctity of life—underlies them all. And I hope, as the result of my insistence on this point, that groups who have not been talking to each other before will begin to talk with each other now."[36] This allusion to a "seamless garment" wherein a prolife thread ties together opposition to abortion, death penalty, and nuclear weapons concerns many prolifers that the antiabortion agenda will suffer. The prolife movement no longer would have its single goal; instead the movement's energies would be diffused among several objectives that most of the population does not view as interrelated.

What probably would happen is indicated by a special analysis I commissioned of three Gallup Polls taken on September 17–20, 1982. Respondents were asked whether they favored or opposed (1) a ban on federal financing of abortions, (2) the death penalty for convicted murderers, and (3) a unilateral freeze on the production of nuclear weapons. The original results found that the majority opposed a ban on abortion funding (56 percent), favored the death penalty (72 percent), and opposed the nuclear freeze (55 percent). I requested a reexamination of these questions in terms of how many respondents gave a consistently "prolife" answer to all three questions. The reexamination found that only 3 *percent* of the national sample (including 3 percent of the Catholics) held a consistently prolife stance on the matters of abortion, capital punishment, and the nuclear freeze.[37] Thus, it is very likely that a strategy proclaiming a prolife ideology will offend antiabortion allies and reduce the prolife constituency rather than attract prochoice advocates or political liberals as supporters of the Roman Catholic church.

Prochoice/Prolife Activists

The antagonists in the abortion struggle represent distinctive socioeconomic and ideological constituencies. While most members of the public know about the abortion controversy and hold opinions on the subject, only a small number are activists on either side. A 1981 Gallup Poll determined that 1 percent of the respondents were members of prolife or prochoice groups, and only slightly more people made contributions to prolife organizations (3 percent) than gave money to prochoice groups (1 percent).[38]

There is evidence that abortion divides the population into classes based upon cultural values. Peter Skerry made this argument in a compelling way: "Abortion is part of a larger cultural conflict between certain strata of the upper-middle class—the highly educated professionals, scientists, and intellectuals—and the mass of Americans who comprise the working and lower-middle classes."[39] That hypothesis was verified to some extent by Donald Granberg's research, which demonstrated that education was the strongest "class" predictor of attitudes toward abortion and that both occupation and income were interrelated with education. Upper socioeconomic status (SES) people favored abortions; lower SES people opposed them. But Granberg went further than had most researchers by studying whether prolife and prochoice activists held divergent views on related issues. The antiabortionists did *not* express consistently prolife opinions compared to the prochoice advocates. More significant was the discovery that questions of "personal morality" polarized the two sides. Opposition to abortion correlated with a conservative view towards sex education, family size, birth control, premarital sex, and pornography.

PRESIDENCY

The abortion controversy has become a partisan issue between Democrats and Republicans. It has been exploited by Richard Nixon and especially Ronald Reagan to attract working-class and Catholic voters away from their traditional allegiance to the Democratic party. But abortion has troubled liberal Democrats seeking the presidential nomination, and election, because their firmly prochoice stance deeply offends prolifers. The right-to-lifers targeted liberal Democrats, such as Edward Kennedy in the 1980 primaries and Geraldine Ferraro in the 1984 general election, for political harassment and defeat. In the middle of all this party turmoil was Jimmy Carter, who tried to accommodate both prolife and prochoice positions and ended by alienating both sides.

In the 1972 presidential campaign, Richard Nixon used the abortion controversy, just emerging at the time, to lure Catholic voters to his candidacy. When the President's Commission on Population Growth endorsed abortion on demand, President Nixon repudiated its recommendation and sided with Terrance Cardinal Cooke of New York City, a well-known prolife spokesperson. At the same time, George McGovern, who was nominated by a Democratic party dominated by very liberal activists, was upset by the persistence of the abortion issue. He tried to be ambivalent. McGovern believed that abortion was "a private matter" between a woman and her doctor and that no law should interfere. But he added this qualification: "I do believe, however, that abortion is a matter to be left to the state governments."[40] Neither view satisfied the prolifers. By 1976, abortion was important enough to be considered by the parties' convention platforms. The Democratic party was more cautious then. It acknowledged "the religious and ethical nature" of the controversy and also added, "We feel, however, that it is undesirable to attempt to amend the U.S. Constitution to overturn the Supreme Court decision in this area."[41] The Republican party platform had two, wordier references to abortion. In expressing its "concern for family values," the GOP recommended "a position on abortion that values human life." This position was affirmed elsewhere in the platform, although in a moderate way: "The Republican Party favors a continuance of the public dialogue on abortion and supports the efforts of those who seek enactment of a constitutional amendment to restore protection of the right to life for unborn children."[42]

President Ford was uneasy with the GOP platform; he personally preferred an amendment to return abortion policy to the states. Ford was challenged in the primaries by Ronald Reagan, who was firmly behind a prolife amendment, a view he has held ever since. Jimmy Carter, the "outsider" who won the Democratic party nomination in 1976 and who proceeded to narrowly defeat Ford in the election, equivocated on abortion. Because Carter was a born-again Christian, a man with deeply held moral convictions, he could hardly take abortion lightly. Given his southern Baptist roots, moreover, Carter was suspect by Catholic white ethnic voters, so he had to deal with their estrangement from the Democratic party. During the 1976 campaign, in Ohio, Carter said that government should not encourage abortions, but, on the other hand, he was opposed to any amendment overturning *Roe*. Carter's ambivalence plagued his campaign from then on, and he met with six Catholic bishops in August in an effort to clarify his position. But the bishops left that meeting unconvinced.

Jimmy Carter was elected president, but the abortion controversy did not go away. Instead, Carter's efforts to placate both sides backfired; he lost any support he may have hoped for from the prolifers, and he deeply offended some feminists (the National Organization for Women refused to endorse Carter in 1980, for many reasons). A comment he made as president really angered prochoice advocates. In July 1977, President Carter and Joseph Califano, secretary of health, education, and welfare, stated their opposition to federal funding of abortions. When asked if that discriminated against poor women who desired abortions, Carter replied, "Well, as you know, there are many things in life that are not fair, that wealthy people can afford and poor people can't. But I don't believe that the federal government should take action to try to make these opportunities exactly equal particularly when there is a moral factor involved."[43] Thus, President Carter was personally opposed to abortions, but he was against any prolife amendment to the Constitution. He supported the *Roe v. Wade* decision as the law of the land, but stood behind the Hyde amendment as policy despite its obvious discriminatory impact. Without doubt, Jimmy Carter's position on abortion was an ambivalent one.

By 1980, when Ronald Reagan defeated President Carter's reelection bid, abortion was a partisan issue that cleanly divided the Republicans and Democrats. The 1980 Republican platform reflected Ronald Reagan's well-known antiabortion views. Reagan had referred to *Roe* as "an abuse of power as bad as the transgressions of Watergate and the bribery on Capital Hill."[44] The 1980 GOP platform agreed and called for "support of a Constitutional amendment to restore protection of the right to life for unborn children . . . [and] Congressional efforts to restrict the use of taxpayers' dollars for abortion."[45] To further strengthen the prolife commitment, right-wingers in the Republican party got a very controversial plank added to the platform that called for "the appointment of judges at all levels of the judiciary who respect traditional family values and the sanctity of innocent human life." This armed the prochoice side with new propaganda that added credibility to its arguments that abortion was a right-wing plot. Now the right wing was attacking the "independent" judicial system. But these commitments earned Ronald Reagan the formal endorsement of the National Right-to-Life Committee in 1980 and again in 1984.

Jimmy Carter's caution on abortion was not reflected in the 1980 Democratic party platform. Carter was challenged by Edward Kennedy for the nomination, and although Kennedy faltered in the primaries, the liberal wing under his leadership forced Carter to accept "minority" planks in the 1980 platform including one denying party funding to Democratic candidates who opposed the Equal Rights Amendment. A strong prochoice plank also reflected the feminist pressures on the Democratic party:

> We fully recognize the religious and ethical concerns which many Americans have about abortion. We also recognize the belief of many Americans that a woman has a right to choose whether and when to have a child. . . . The Democratic Party supports the 1973 Supreme Court decision on abortion rights as the law of the land and opposes any constitutional amendment to restrict or overturn that decision.[46]

The die was cast for the 1984 presidential contest when the Democratic party offered the electorate a real policy choice on abortion. President Reagan stood for reelection upholding the antiabortion policies, and symbolism, of his administration. The Democratic presidential candidate, Walter Mondale, was a life-long liberal who championed social causes; he was firmly prochoice. But his record did not satisfy feminists at the party's convention, who threatened to nominate Congresswoman Geraldine Ferraro (D-N.Y.) should Mondale not choose a woman to be his running mate. Mondale did select Ferraro, a Catholic from New York City who had a consistently prochoice voting record in Congress. That decision proved to be costly to the extent that Ferraro became embroiled in the abortion controversy, was harassed by prolifers, and was harangued by Catholic bishops.

The 1984 platform of the Democratic party expanded upon its 1980 commitment to prochoice objectives. A long statement in the platform called "reproductive freedom" a "fundamental human right" and opposed government interference, especially that "which denies poor Americans their right to privacy by funding or advocating one or a limited number of reproductive choices only" (an obvious reference to the Hyde amendment). The platform reaffirmed the party's support for *Roe* and opposition to any constitutional amendment overturning it. In a reference to direct action against abortion clinics, the platform added: "We deplore violence and harassment against health providers and women seeking services, and will work to end such acts."[47] The platform made no mention of the unborn; that was reserved to the Republican party.

As almost a rebuttal to the Democratic party, the 1984 GOP platform took issue with everything supported by the opposition.

> The unborn child has a fundamental individual right to life which cannot be infringed. We therefore reaffirm our support for a human life amendment to the Constitution, and we endorse legislation to make clear that the Fourteenth Amendment's protections apply to unborn children. We oppose the use of public revenues for abortion and will eliminate funding for organizations which advocate or support abortions. We commend the efforts of those individuals and religious and private organizations that are providing positive alternatives to abortion by meeting the physical, emotional, and financial needs of pregnant women and offering adoption services where needed.[48]

CONGRESS

The prime mover behind the organization of a policy response to *Roe* has been the Congress, although President Reagan has joined the battle since 1981. But Reagan's activism has not matched his rhetoric against abortion, according to the ultraconservatives in his party, because the president focused primarily on economic policy and budgeting during his first term rather than on the "social" agenda promoted by the political right. The fact that Reagan has concentrated on the economy, which is more a "consensus" issue to the citizenry, is interpreted by moderates inside and outside the Republican party to mean that the president is less conservative on many questions, such as abortion, than his speeches and symbolism might indicate. It often is pointed out, for example, that President Reagan has not mobilized the resources of his office or his immense popularity behind a prolife amendment, which consequently remains bogged down in the Congress.

Legislative Backlash

Since *Roe v. Wade*, there has been a surge in abortion legislation proposed by members of the Congress. According to an analysis by Lynn D. Wardle (updated by this author), no substantive abortion legislation was introduced to Congress during 1963–1969.[49] In 1970, there was one bill; in 1971, six bills; and in 1972, three bills. Beginning in 1973, however, a tremendous number of abortion bills were sponsored (Table 6.6). During the thirteen-year period 1973–1985, 525 bills or resolutions were sponsored in Congress, of which 498 (95 percent) promoted prolife objectives in some way. The proposals were of two types: a constitutional amendment overturning *Roe* (55 percent of the prolife bills) and limits on government funding of abortions (17 percent). Among the other antiabortion provisions were bills to allow "right of conscience" to hospitals and health-care personnel so they are not required to do abortions; investigations on the impact of *Roe;* statutory definitions of "personhood" under the Fourteenth Amendment to include the unborn; and prohibitions on abortion-related activities by particular federal agencies.

These findings on legislation contrast sharply with the data on *amicus* briefs before the Supreme Court. Whereas prochoice groups predominated in using a litigation strategy, for the most part they left the legislative arena to the prolife forces. Prochoice groups are not likely to get involved in the legislative process, given that their chances of success have been quite slim. There is a solid phalanx of prolife votes in Congress, especially in the House of Representatives.

Voting Behavior

The acknowledged prolife leader in the House is Congressman Henry J. Hyde (R-Ill.), a Catholic and conservative, but he is not alone. Three votes on the Hyde amendment in 1976 were analyzed by Maris Vinovskis, who found that party was not a strong predictor of how representatives voted.[50]

TABLE 6.6 Legislation on Abortion Introduced in Congress 1973-1986

Congress	Pro Life Legislation				Total Pro choice	Total Bills	Number Enacted
	Total Pro life	Constitutional Amendments	Restrictions on Abortion Funding	Other Legislation			
93rd 1973-1974	93	46	1	46	1	94	0
94th 1975-1976	100	78	4	18	0	100	2
95th 1977-1978	108	65	21	22	18	126	9
96th 1979-1980	72	36	20	16	2	74	8
97th 1981-1982	81	26	34	21	2	83	8
98th[a] 1983-1984	27	16	3	8	1	28	0
99th[a] 1985 (only)	17	8	1	8	3	20	0
Totals	498	275	84	139	27	525	27

[a]Data for 1983, 1984, and 1985 collected by this author from the *Congressional Record* for each year.

Source: Lynn D. Wardle, "Restoring the Constitutional Balance: The Need for a Constitutional Amendment to Reverse *Roe v. Wade*," in U.S. Senate, *Hearings Before the Subcommittee on the Constitution of the Committee on the Judiciary*, 98th Cong., 1st sess., on S.J.Res. 3, Joint Resolution to Amend the Constitution to Establish Legislative Authority in Congress and the States with Respect to Abortion, February 28 and March 7, 1983, pp. 70-77. The foregoing classification scheme is based on these data.

The most important variable was the representative's degree of liberalism; liberals voted three to four times more often against the Hyde amendment than did conservatives. A second variable was religion. Seventy-five percent of the Catholics and 57 percent of the Protestants but only 11 percent of the Jewish congresspersons supported the Hyde amendment. A follow-up statistical analysis by Barbara Bardes and Raymond Tatalovich of the 93rd, 94th, 95th, and 96th Congresses verified Vinovskis's findings.[51] Ideology was the strongest predictor of voting on abortion; religion was the second. When multivariate controls were imposed, party had no independent effect on voting primarily because Catholic Democrats deviated from party loyalty to support prolife policies. Consequently, the Republicans were more unified around prolife legislation than were the Democrats.

Voting patterns in Congress, especially in the House of Representatives, indicate that the majority opinion on abortion is prolife, which explains why Congress has enacted antiabortion curbs since the 1970s. Under P.L. 93-45, judges or public officials are barred from ordering recipients of federal funds to perform abortions or to make facilities available for this use where the moral convictions or religious beliefs of these persons are violated. In 1978, Title VII of the 1964 Civil Rights Act (P.L. 95-555) was amended so that employers are not required to fund health insurance benefits for abortion except to save the mother's life.

The most famous of many prohibitions on the use of federal funds for abortions or abortion-related services is the Hyde amendment. Legal challenges to this legislation (P.L. 94-439), which was to take effect in 1976, stopped its implementation until August 4, 1977. Originally the Hyde amendment barred Medicaid funds for abortions except to save the mother's life. In subsequent years, funding for abortions was allowed in cases of rape and incest and when two physicians determined that the woman might suffer serious, long-term physical problems should her pregnancy be carried to term. But in June 1981, the Hyde amendment was tightened again, with abortions now permitted only to save the mother's life.

The ultimate prolife threat to *Roe* is a constitutional amendment to protect the unborn. There have been 275 proposals introduced to Congress since 1973 (through 1985), but until 1983 none was approved by a standing committee to allow a floor vote in either house. On June 28, 1983, the Senate defeated on a 49–50 vote the so-called Hatch-Eagleton amendment, which read, "A right to abortion is not secured by this Constitution." The amendment's intent was to return abortion policy to Congress and to the states, but this outcome was far short of the needed two-thirds vote for approval. Analysis of this key vote by Donald Granberg found that "the probability of a *pro-HEA* [Hatch-Eagleton amendment] vote increased . . . if the Senator was a *Catholic*, if the Senator was a *Republican*, if the Senator's state had a relatively *low income*, and if the Senator represented a state *not* in the *New England, Pacific*, or *Middle Atlantic* region."[52] Another proposal authored by conservative senator Jesse Helms (R-N.C.) is the Human Life Statute, which only requires a majority vote for enactment. It would define a fetus as a person and the beginning of human life at conception, but this bill has not commanded much support either in the Senate or in the House.

BUREAUCRACY

By statutory means the Congress has forced the executive branch to act, in some instances, and curbed its discretion to act in other areas. Abortion policy finds deep intervention by Congress in the administration of law. The *Roe* decision came in 1973, during Richard Nixon's tenure, and was implemented under the Medicaid program without interruption during the Nixon/Ford administration. Congressman Henry J. Hyde was prompted to amend the appropriations bill for the Department of Health, Education, and Welfare with an antiabortion "rider" by his discovery that the federal government was paying for more than two hundred fifty thousand abortions yearly under Medicaid at a cost of $45 million.[53]

Before Congress acted, Medicaid coverage for abortions was technically available without restriction to women in forty-five states and the District of Columbia. Arizona had (and still has) no Medicaid law, and four other states funded abortions under Medicaid with certain restrictions. The Hyde amendment would have been implemented on October 1, 1976, had it not been enjoined by the Federal District Court for the Eastern District of New York. On June 29, 1977, the Supreme Court instructed that district court to reconsider its injunction against Medicaid funding in light of recent Supreme Court decisions (*Beal* and *Maher*) upholding the states' authority not to spend Medicaid moneys for nontherapeutic abortions. On August 4, 1977, therefore, the injunction was lifted. During much of fiscal year 1977 (October 1, 1976 to September 30, 1977), the Hyde amendment was under court challenges, so the federal government was not restricted in what abortions could be funded under Medicaid. As a result, the federal government paid for medically necessary abortions, which totalled 294,600 that year.[54]

On February 14, 1978, the Health Care Financing Administration implemented regulations based upon the Hyde amendment, including a system to report Medicaid-financed abortions. As a result, federally funded abortions plummeted during fiscal year 1978. Only a fraction of the previous number of abortions were funded under Medicaid, and the financial burden shifted to those few states willing to pay for nontherapeutic abortions.

In 1980, Judge John F. Dooling, Jr. of the Eastern District of New York again intervened in the controversy. From February 19 until September 19, 1980, he issued a permanent injunction barring the enforcement of the Hyde amendment. The Supreme Court refused to stay his injunction, and the Department of Health, Education, and Welfare then notified the states that the federal government would resume paying for medically necessary abortions under Medicaid. As a consequence, Medicaid-funded abortions sharply increased in 1980. This trial adjudicated by Judge Dooling was the only suit to challenge the constitutionality of the Hyde amendment. This suit was a nationwide class action brought in 1976 by women needing

Medicaid abortions, affected physicians, the Women's Division of the Board of Global Ministries of the United Methodist Church, Planned Parenthood of New York City, and the New York City Health and Hospitals Corporation. The trial lasted more than a year, when Judge Dooling finally ruled that the Hyde amendment in fact was unconstitutional. The U.S. government appealed that ruling, and in the landmark *Harris v. McRae* decision, the Supreme Court upheld the Hyde amendment.

Given the enactment of the Hyde amendment in varying forms plus federal court injunctions against its implementation, the Code of Federal Regulations specified differing criteria for funding Medicaid abortions from 1977 to 1986, as follows.[55]

Oct. 1, 1976–Sep. 30, 1977: medical necessity
Oct. 1, 1977–Dec. 4, 1977: mother's life
Dec. 5, 1977–Oct. 11, 1979: mother's life; mother's physical health; rape; incest
Oct. 12, 1979–Feb. 18, 1980: mother's life; rape; incest
Feb. 19, 1980–Sep. 19, 1980: medical necessity
Sep. 20, 1980–June 4, 1981: mother's life; rape; incest
June 5, 1981–Sep. 30, 1981: mother's life
Oct. 1, 1981–Sep. 30, 1986: mother's life

As of 1986, the Code of Federal Regulations reflected the most restrictive version of the Hyde amendment (enacted June 1981), which allowed Medicaid abortions only when the mother's life is threatened.

P.L. 91-572 (Family Planning Services and Population Research Act of 1970) prohibited the use of federal funds for any program where abortion is a method of family planning. As a result, since 1972 the Code of Federal Regulations has had an absolute ban on the use of funds under this program for abortion. Under Title X of this statute, grants are made to public and private nonprofit organizations that operate voluntary family planning projects and clinics. A 1982 report by the General Accounting Office (GAO) found no evidence that Title X moneys were used directly for abortions or to advise clients to have abortions.[56] The GAO did advise Congress, however, about questionable practices due to ambiguous Department of Health and Human Services or Office of Management and Budget guidelines. This investigation was requested by Senator Orrin Hatch (R-Utah), a well-known prolife spokesperson, and Senator Jeremiah Denton (R-Ala.), but the GAO findings did not satisfy the prolifers. At the end of 1985, as the fiscal year 1986 budget was debated, Senator Hatch and Congressman Jack Kemp (R-N.Y.) collaborated on amendments to further restrict discretion under Title X. Hatch's and Kemp's intent was to stipulate that no Title X funds could be used for abortion referral or counseling except where the mother's life was endangered and that no Title X funds could be awarded by grant or contract to any organization involved with abortions. This antiabortion legislation remained buried in a House committee through 1986, but the following year the Reagan administration moved to achieve this objective through executive action. Such intervention in the absence of enabling legislation, however, is likely to be overturned by the courts.

The leadership of Congressman Jack Kemp in these deliberations as well as in other antiabortion legislation has political significance. Because he was an acknowledged contender for the 1988 Republican presidential nomination, Kemp already has established his credentials with the prolifers.

In two celebrated instances, the Congress curbed discretionary authority by federal agencies on abortion policy. On July 25, 1974, President Nixon quietly signed P.L. 93-355, which transferred the legal services program from the Office of Economic Opportunity to an independent corporation, the Legal Services Corporation (LSC), managed by an eleven-member board of directors. This action resulted after three years of difficult negotiations by the House, Senate, and the Nixon administration because throughout its history conservatives have attacked this program. The LSC is charged with giving legal services to the poor and is an activist, liberal agency that has sued local governments and agencies on behalf of its clients. (President Reagan has tried to eliminate funding for LSC programs.) One amendment included in P.L. 93-355 was offered by Representative Lawrence J. Hogan (R-Md.) in 1973 to prohibit "legal assistance with respect to any proceeding or litigation relating to abortion." His absolute ban was modified by a substitute amendment from Congressman Harold V. Froehlich (R-Wis.) that prohibited LSC lawyers from helping women procure nontherapeutic abortions or forcing hospitals, institutions, or doctors to participate in abortions if doing so offended their policy or convictions. The Froehlich substitute was accepted on a 316–53 vote whereupon the House of Representatives approved, by a lopsided 301–68 margin, the Hogan amendment. Congressman Hogan was prompted to introduce his amendment by Office of Economic Opportunity (OEO) reports in which officials said that despite Congress's 1970 ban on family planning grants for abortion (Title X), legal services attorneys in community action agencies should help their clients obtain abortions. The OEO also was encouraging its lawyers to oppose state laws that restricted abortions. Hogan gave examples of those actions and, along with his sponsorship of a prolife amendment, defended his amendment as "another small step toward the protection of those least able to defend themselves, the unborn."[57]

In 1978, Congress approved P.L. 95-444, which, in addition to extending the life of the United States Commission on Civil Rights, forbade the commission from collecting and analyzing abortion laws and policies of government. This antiabortion "rider" was sponsored by Congressman David C. Treen (R-La.) and stated, "Nothing in this or any other Act shall be construed as authorizing the Commission, its Advisory Committees, or any person under its supervision or control to appraise, or to study and collect information about, laws and policies of the Federal Government, or any other government authority in the United States, with respect to abortion."

This reaction was triggered by an April 1975 report of the U.S. Civil Rights Commission entitled "Constitutional Aspects of the Right to Limit

Childbearing." Although this was the only study on abortion the commission conducted in its twenty-one year existence, nonetheless opponents argued that the commission had overreached its jurisdiction in dealing with this subject. In the view of the commission, because minority women very often are poor, abortion involves their rights to equal protection. But Treen countered that abortion "is not a civil rights matter" and furthermore that "no one denies that, unfortunately, minorities are disproportionately represented among the poor. But that analysis surely does not authorize the commission to appraise every law . . . that may impact poor persons." He also charged that the commission "does not have the mission of advising Congress that it must spend public funds on services of one sort or another for the poor, because not to do so denies 'equal protection' to racial and ethnic minorities."[58] Treen's arguments carried the day. The House of Representatives approved his amendment 234–131, and given the strength of that vote, House conferees told the Senate that no final legislation would be enacted unless this antiabortion rider was upheld. It was.

Ronald Reagan has promoted the prolife agenda more than has any previous chief executive. During his tenure, Reagan met with prolife groups, filmed an address to the 1982 National Right-to-Life convention, sent an aide to the 1984 Americans United for Life convention, and even authored *Abortion and the Conscience of the Nation*. He also endorsed antiabortion legislation and a prolife amendment to the Constitution, and in 1985 he composed a eulogy that was read in Los Angeles at the burial of 16,433 aborted fetuses. Many of these actions are rhetorical and symbolic, but the Reagan administration has taken administrative actions as well. The president nominated, and the Senate in 1985 confirmed, Charles Fried as solicitor general of the United States. A law professor at Harvard, Fried is a foe of abortion like his predecessor Rex E. Lee, but, unlike Lee, Fried shares the viewpoint of Attorney General Edwin Meese that the solicitor general should more aggressively promote the administration's social agenda before the Supreme Court.[59] Even before he was confirmed, Acting Solicitor General Charles Fried submitted the *amicus* brief in *Thornburgh* asking that *Roe v. Wade* be overturned by the Supreme Court.

Unlike his predecessors, President Reagan authorized the Office of Personnel Management to disallow the use of the Combined Federal Service Campaign, a nationwide program for obtaining tax-deductible donations from federal employees for charities, to solicit funds for the Planned Parenthood Federation of America.[60] The Reagan administration also moved to cut funds flowing to Planned Parenthood's international affiliate. In Mexico City, in August 1984, James Buckley (formerly a conservative, prolife senator from New York state) spoke to the U.N. World Population Conference as the chief U.S. delegate. He said that the United States would stand by the $240 million appropriated by Congress for this work, but that money could not go to projects or organizations that use abortion as an acceptable means of population control. Governments that condone abortions would have to use those funds through "segregated accounts" in order to assure that abortions are not subsidized. Nor would the United States contribute moneys to the United Nations Fund for Population Activities until assurances are received that it "is not engaged in, or does not provide funding for, abortion or coercive family planning programs."[61] With this policy change, the big loser was the International Planned Parenthood Federation, which subsequently announced a 30 percent reduction in its $55 million budget due to the Reagan administration's threat to cut $17 million in assistance.[62] (Since 1974, the use of U.S. foreign aid for abortions has been prohibited, but by its latest decision the Reagan administration would stop aiding organizations that promote or perform abortions whether or not U.S. funds are used directly for abortions.)

FEDERALISM

In the post-*Roe* era, state governments had to rewrite their abortion statutes, but were in no hurry to do so. Immediately following *Roe*, in protest, Idaho and South Dakota enacted laws saying that should the states regain the authority to prohibit abortions, Idaho and South Dakota would do so. In 1976 testimony before Congress, a University of Chicago law professor observed, "Many legislatures have not amended their pre–*Roe v. Wade* abortion statutes. Often the reason for this is a conscious decision by the legislative body to let the courts now regulate the abortion mess they have created."[63] Moreover, when those antiabortion laws were revised, state legislatures took the opportunity to impose restrictions and procedural safeguards on the implementation of *Roe*, actions that precipitated subsequent Supreme Court challenges.

State governments generally have regulated abortions in three ways. First, "right of conscience" legislation permits physicians, medical personnel, and hospitals to refuse to do abortions. Second, "protection of fetus" laws declare that a live-born fetus resulting from an abortion has the right to medical care like any premature baby and that reasonable steps must be taken to sustain the fetus's life. Third, most states require that physicians report all abortions to a state agency. The enactment of the Hyde amendment afforded yet another opportunity for states to reassert some authority over abortions, and since 1977 the trend has been clear. In the absence of federal funds, the majority of state governments are unwilling to subsidize non-therapeutic abortions using state revenues.

By December 31, 1978, only ten states funded all abortions *or* all medically necessary abortions. Eighteen paid for abortions to protect the mother's life, in cases of rape or incest, and where the woman might suffer lasting physical damage; sixteen states funded abortions only when the mother's life was endangered; five did so to protect the mother's life and when rape or incest had occurred; and Arizona had no Medicaid statute.[64] This uneven funding pattern results in relatively few states paying for most abortions. During fiscal year 1981, for example, the thirty-five states with restrictive Medicaid regulations funded only 6,999 abortions from their own revenues, whereas the District of Columbia and fourteen states with liberalized standards funded 185,359 abortions, or 90 percent of the total 210,341 abortions paid for under *both* federal and state programs that year.[65] (These fourteen states paying for all or medically necessary abortions include nine of the previous ten—except Idaho, which moved into the restrictive category— plus five more states under court orders to do so.)

The other major avenue of redress taken by states is to petition the Congress to call a constitutional convention in order to reverse *Roe*. To date, nineteen states have approved resolutions for that purpose. This number is short of the required two-thirds, but what concerns proabortionists is the location of these states in every region of the nation. Included among these states that petitioned Congress are Massachusetts, Pennsylvania, and New Jersey.[66]

These actions strongly indicate that most states remain opposed to legalized abortion. To what extent do such antiabortion policies reflect public opinion within the states? This question was evaluated in terms of a simulation by Uslaner and Weber that estimated public opinion toward abortion in each state for 1969 and 1972.[67] The question was, "Would you favor or oppose a law which would permit a woman to go to a doctor to end pregnancy at any time during the first three months?" The fifty states were ranked according to the estimated percentage favoring legalized abortions. Uslaner and Weber generally found that support for abortions increased between 1969 and 1972 in most states, but nonetheless in 1972 only fourteen[68] states were estimated to have majority support for first trimester abortions.

During the period 1966–1972, eight of these fourteen states (57 percent) had "reformed" or "repealed" their original antiabortion laws compared to only ten among the other thirty-six states (28 percent). The pattern of Medicaid funding in 1978 shows that ten states paid for all or medically necessary abortions. Of these, seven[69] are included in the fourteen (50 percent) versus only three among the remaining thirty-seven states (or 8 percent). Whereas three[70] of the fourteen states with liberal opinion on abortion (21 percent) have petitioned Congress for a constitutional convention on abortion, this action was taken by sixteen of the other thirty-six states (or 44 percent).

To generalize, among the fourteen states estimated to have more liberal opinions on abortion as early as 1972, a larger proportion had liberalized their abortion laws prior to *Roe* and afterward had more generous funding of abortions under Medicaid, but proportionately fewer have called upon the Congress to convene a constitutional convention against abortion.

SUMMARY

Before *Roe v. Wade*, a political consensus was emerging behind abortion reform, a goal supported by the U.S. population. That 1973 Supreme Court ruling polarized the abortion debate into non-negotiable prolife versus prochoice positions, although the majority were, and still are, opposed to both extremes. The persistence of the abortion controversy, therefore, stems from the failure of public opinion to rally behind abortion on demand.

The abortion debate now divides political parties and envelops their presidential candidates, although Ronald Reagan has supported the prolife cause more than did any of his predecessors in the White House. But the political backlash against *Roe* is centered in Congress and in the state legislatures. The Hyde amendment bars the use of Medicaid funds for nontherapeutic abortions, and in its wake, the majority of states have chosen not to pay for elective abortions. Since the 1970s, antiabortion riders have been attached to various bills, and each provoked renewed legislative conflict.

The next chapter in the abortion controversy already is shaping up. The federal judiciary remains a staunch prochoice ally, but prolifers are pinning their hopes on President Reagan. So far, he has appointed William Rehnquist as chief justice as well as Sandra Day O'Connor and Antonin Scalia as new associate justices, all of whom are prolife sympathizers. In 1987, William F. Powell suddenly announced his resignation from the high court, and as his successor President Reagan nominated Robert Bork. Bork is a jurist, but his ultraconservative opinions mobilized a phalanx of civil rights, libertarian, and women's groups to rally public opinion against his confirmation. People for the American Way took the unprecedented step of putting ads on television and in newspapers opposing Bork's appointment. After a sharply partisan battle in the Senate, he was rejected 58–42, whereupon President Reagan nominated another judge, Douglas H. Ginsburg, who lacked the "paper trail" of controversial opinions that plagued Bork. But Ginsburg withdrew his name from consideration when a story surfaced in the media that he occasionally had smoked marijuana during the 1970s.

Bork and Ginsburg were strongly backed by White House conservatives led by Attorney General Edwin Meese, who wanted an appointee who would turn the Supreme Court decisively to the right. On the third round, however, Reagan followed the preference of White House chief of staff Howard Baker, a political moderate, by nominating Anthony M. Kennedy. Alongside Bork and Ginsburg, Kennedy was called a moderate, although his more than four hundred opinions as an appellate judge on the ninth circuit show a conservative bent. Although Kennedy's nomination was confirmed, there were few clues about his views on abortion, and some prolifers were alarmed that he might not vote to overturn *Roe*. Kennedy's appointment may or may not be a turning point in the battle about abortion. But until a decisive change in the Supreme Court membership does occur, we can expect the political stalemate between the judiciary, backed by prochoice defenders, and the Congress, aligned with the Right-to-Life movement, to continue.

CONCLUSION
Social Regulatory Policymaking

Raymond Tatalovich and Byron W. Daynes

There are remarkable similarities in how the six controversies about social regulatory policy (school prayer, pornography, crime, gun control, affirmative action, and abortion) are handled by the political system. What are the common characteristics of these types of social regulatory policymaking? We will outline these attributes as fourteen propositions that summarize the roles played by the president, Congress, the judiciary, interest groups, public opinion, the federal bureaucracy, and federalism.

Our previous research on abortion suggested to us that the political process affecting such issues would be distinguished by conflict about *noneconomic, moral values,* militant *single-issue groups,* and an activist *judiciary.* These case studies generally affirm the validity of that hypothesis. To begin this conclusion, therefore, we first discuss these critical variables of social regulatory policymaking and then proceed to evaluate the president, Congress, public opinion, the federal bureaucracy, and federalism. In doing so, we also will integrate the findings from these case studies with whatever existing research seems relevant to developing more fully our characterization of the "arena of power" of social regulatory policymaking.

Self-interest is the overriding motivation that politicizes the antagonists when economic regulations are debated. Such regulations usually divide the business community from those consumer advocates, workers, or environmentalists who seek greater government vigilance. Since the New Deal, it has been commonplace to label the proponents of economic regulation as liberals, whereas conservatives argue against more infringements on free enterprise and private property. But when social regulatory policy is debated the reverse applies. Liberals defend personal liberties from government regulation, and conservatives want individual freedoms subordinated to community norms. Liberals also will accommodate social change, whereas conservatives seek to protect traditional norms and the status quo. Social regulatory policy cannot be understood except in terms of this liberal-conservative cleavage, which is why ideology plays a significant role in this arena.

The normative underpinnings of social regulatory policy give rise to intellectual debates about the political, philosophical, and legal reasoning of previous generations. When existing values are being challenged, advocates of social change must argue that traditional norms are irrelevant if not dangerous today. The debate about gun control, for example, finds the National Rifle Association (NRA) asserting that the Second Amendment grants the individual a "right to bear arms" while the antigun lobby counters that the amendment's original intent was to arm a militia.

Ideology is used as a political weapon to allege that an issue portends a more ominous threat to U.S. life. Ideology is used to draw into the conflict people who otherwise might remain uninvolved because their economic self-interest is not directly affected. Self-interest cannot be the motivating force behind social regulatory policymaking because these conflicts focus on noneconomic, normative, and symbolic goals. Activists do not get involved for tangible benefits, which is why Roger Cobb and Charles Elder referred to activists as "do-gooders."[1] Thus, most advocates of legalized abortion do not intend to have abortions, and most opponents of capital punishment do not reside on death row. Whenever people are activated to join causes offering no tangible economic benefits, then we must assume such people are driven by values that give meaning to their lives.

Proposition 1a: Single-issue groups are the lobbies that most increase public awareness and the political significance of social regulatory policy.

Different kinds of interest groups influence policymaking in each of Theodore Lowi's functional arenas. Because distributive policy gives benefits to recipients, these "clientele" groups lobby for such programs. Redistributive policy is shaped by huge "peak" associations, such as the AFL-CIO, that achieve substantial unity due to their "class" implications. These groups are not important to social regulatory policymaking for two obvious reasons. First, peak associations exist to defend their economic self-interest, not to champion moral crusades. Second, moral disputes would fracture the internal unity of these associations and thus jeopardize their political effectiveness. The same reasons also explain why trade associations, which represent particular industries such as steel or agriculture, played no role in our six case studies.

Political scientists assume that interest groups stand ready to engage in political combat in order to protect their self-interest, and this view does hold for most "economic" interests in the United States. But there are exceptions. Mancur Olson noted that some groups promote noneconomic objectives; for example, philanthropic organizations, religious lobbies, and people committed to "lost causes."[2] Our case studies indicate that this kind of grass-roots activism is linked to single-issue groups where moral conflict is involved. Right-to-Life Committees are the foremost antiabortion lobby, just as the National Rifle Association singlehandedly has prevented gun controls. School prayer is back on the political agenda due mainly to the pressure of southern fundamentalists.

An approach that gives theoretical support for our position is drawn from the sociological literature on collective behavior. According to Neil Smelser, one type of collective behavior is the "norm-oriented" movement, which is "an attempt to restore, protect, modify, or create norms" and is supported by persons who "may demand a rule, a law, a regulatory agency, designed to control the inadequate, ineffective, or irresponsible behavior of individuals."[3] Such movements are generated by a structural "strain" that results from four conditions. Two seem relevant to our analysis: (1) a disharmony between normative standards and actual social conditions and (2) the real or apparent loss of wealth, power, or prestige by groups.

The first condition would seem highly significant as a prerequisite for activating groups that promote social change. This "strain" explains the rise of civil rights agitation for equal employment after World War II, and obvious parallels account for the women's rights movement of the 1970s. Those opposed to social change will establish organizations to defend existing norms. The rise of single-issue groups in the social regulatory arena may be linked to the second condition of "strain"—the loss of power or prestige by groups.

During the 1950s, social scientists hypothesized that people with psychological insecurities and without social ties to established institutions were attracted to radical causes and charismatic leaders offering solutions to what such people perceived to be harmful changes in society.[4] Historian Richard Hofstadter used the term *status politics* to explain the rise of the Radical Right at that time.[5] This concept originated with sociologist Max Weber, who theorized that politics may reflect conflict based on social status and prestige rather than on economic class.[6] Groups with divergent life-styles or social norms clash about whose values should be reflected in public policy. These controversies often erupt when social changes bring new groups, perceived to be outsiders, into a community, and the outcome of these political conflicts defines the relative "status" of new or old groups in the community.

Joseph Gusfield applied Weber's theory in his research on the Women's Christian Temperance Union.[7] Alcohol triggered a life-style conflict between the "old middle class" and the "new middle class," which was why the temperance movement was a moral crusade. This approach was used in a study of antipornography campaigns by Louis Zurcher, George Kirkpatrick, Robert Cushing, and Charles Bowman, who concluded that "a primary function of the symbolic crusade is to provide those individuals whose life style is being threatened by social change with a way to reinforce that style."[8] Our case studies do not support this allegation that symbolic politics is purely "expressive" and without impact on substantive policy. Not only does that view belittle the value of symbols in political combat, but symbols also shape the distribution of scarce resources in society.[9] Nobody can conclude that the National Rifle Association's opposition to gun controls has been purely symbolic or that prolife lobbying for the Hyde amendment has not restricted legalized abortion. Social regulatory policy goes beyond symbolism to substance.

An analysis by Ann Page and Donald Clelland of the Kanawha County, West Virginia, textbook controversy found that "the protestors are adherents of a life style and world view which are under threat from . . . the educational system, the mass media, the churches—fundamentally from every social-ization agency beyond their immediate control which impinges on their lives."[10] Matthew C. Moen turned his attention to the school prayer con-troversy and also determined that status politics had much explanatory power: "People support prayer because they are religious, but even more so because they see in modern society a threat to their cherished values and their established way of life."[11] Status politics is apparently linked to why people opposed the Equal Rights Amendment.[12]

This theory of collective behavior, however, does not adequately explain public opinion on social regulatory policy. It stretches the imagination to believe that status insecurities preoccupy the thinking of the majority of citizens who express traditional values toward school prayer, crime control, and affirmative action. But status politics and life-style concerns seem relevant to explaining why grass-roots activists and single-issue groups emerge to defend community norms against social change. An important consequence flowing from this intense political activism is that a degree of freedom is denied to political leaders who may desire to resolve these thorny issues by compromise and moderation.

Proposition 1b: Single-issue groups promote absolutist positions on social regulatory policy that polarize the debate as one of non-negotiable, moral alternatives.

Writing in 1958, Eric Hoffer characterized the "true believer" as a zealot, someone entirely committed to one cause.[13] He or she will expend tremendous energy and resources to win the battle; thus, to compromise or negotiate a settlement is tantamount to betraying his or her principles. This is shown by prolife congressman Henry J. Hyde's (R-Ill.) view of abortion: "You don't compromise on this issue of abortion. How do you compromise when the issue is a human life—not your life, somebody else's life."[14] Likewise, the tenacity with which the NRA opposes any curbs on the right to bear arms also illustrates this point. Gun owners are more passionate about this issue than are most citizens, which is why the NRA membership is so readily mobilized whenever Congress considers antigun legislation.

This attribute of single-issue groups brings a disruptive influence to normal political discourse and undermines political stability and consensus building. Social regulatory policymaking on the national level is analogous to episodes of community conflict at the local level.[15] As T. Alexander Smith pointed out, although public officials would not ordinarily take positions on "emotive symbolic" controversies, public opinion would "insist on getting its own way," and thus legislators would have to address those demands.[16] Single-issue politics, therefore, is a no-win situation for most politicians. However, in this milieu, outspoken mavericks assume leadership positions on such issues. In the 1980s, Senator Jesse Helms (R.-N.C.) was the acknowledged spokesperson for New Right causes, including prolife and school prayer. The political dynamics of the social regulatory arena suggest also that liberal groups will prefer litigation to legislation as their primary strategy to effect change.

Proposition 2a: Courts promote legal change in social regulatory policy by asserting individual rights and liberties against traditional social values.

Lowi did not give a role to the judiciary in his policy arenas, but the courts historically have made policy that "legitimates" certain private behaviors. This aspect is crucial to the social regulatory arena. The degree to which the individual's social behavior in the community ought to be regulated is a public consideration that must be balanced against the individual's desire that he or she enjoy the greatest freedom from government interference. How society defines this balance at any point in time is the essence of social regulatory policy.

A feature of social regulatory disputes is that they involve questions of civil liberties and civil rights. Redress to the courts provides a mechanism for promoting legal changes in social regulations that are beyond the immediate control of the political leadership. In recent years, questions of women's rights, race relations, obscenity, school prayer, gay life-styles, birth control and abortion, and the rights of criminal defendants have jammed the Supreme Court docket. The Court's concern for civil liberties and minority rights has displaced its previous involvement in economic disputes.[17]

The degree of oversight by federal courts in these matters points to an activist judiciary in social regulatory policymaking. Donald Horowitz argued that judicial intervention has changed radically from the time courts simply resolved grievances between litigants. Today the judiciary is engaged in problem solving and administrative oversight to assure the compliance of government agencies and private institutions with legal standards of behavior.[18] The federal courts oversee social regulations much like federal agencies implement the "new" social policies of the 1970s.

Judicial activism was legitimized by the school desegregation ruling in *Brown v. Board of Education* (1954), but the trend was accelerated when disaffected minorities turned increasingly to the courts for redress. The aggrieved claim that their civil liberties or rights are being violated by state action, thus opening the door to judicial intervention. In our six case studies, new social regulations were mandated by the Supreme Court. Beginning with a 1957 ruling, the Court interpreted state antipornography laws to be unconstitutional infringements on free press, and through three rulings in 1962–1963 the Court declared school prayer a violation of the establishment clause of the First Amendment. Since 1964, the high court has ruled in landmark cases that most "procedural" rights in Amendments Four through Eight must be adhered to by states when dealing with criminal defendants. In 1973, the Supreme Court upheld legalized abortion during the first trimester of a pregnancy, and in 1987 the Supreme Court required a state government to rectify a history of discriminatory hiring against blacks through the use of explicit racial quotas. Although no Court decision mandates that firearms be regulated, the Supreme Court has ruled that gun controls by state or federal governments are constitutional.

Proposition 2b: Federal courts have expanded the opportunities for using litigation to change social regulatory policy outside the normal political process.

The debate about judicial activism versus judicial restraint has gained new prominence as a result of the Supreme Court's intervention in sensitive disputes about social regulations. The Court's ruling on abortion, in particular, revived a lively debate about "fundamental rights" adjudication. In his review of the Court's application of "substantive due process," Paul Brest observed:

> The judges and scholars who support judicial intervention usually acknowledge that the rights at stake . . . are not specified by the text or original history of the Constitution. They argue that the judiciary is nonetheless authorized, if not duty-bound, to protect individuals against government interference with these rights, which can be discovered in conventional morality or derived through methods of philosophy or adjudication.[19]

The cases Brest had in mind involved the Supreme Court's discovery of "privacy" rights, beginning with Griswold v. Connecticut (1965), but his point has relevance to many social regulations. Because social regulatory policy involves a clash between community norms and social behavior, a reading of these cases by judges often will result in support for individual rights. The dilemma is that litigants who petition the courts argue that certain persons are being denied liberties in the concrete situation, whereas the defense generally alleges that long-term and indirect dangers may confront society if social behavior that deviates from community norms is permitted. Given this choice, judges can easily side with the plaintiff. Censorship that violates freedom of the press seems more immediate and paramount than the possible adverse reactions of unregulated pornography on society. A woman desiring to abort her pregnancy is more at risk than the potential life that may or may not be realized. Given the judiciary's case-by-case approach, the legal system's reliance on adversary proceedings, the courts' inability to research policy questions themselves, and the complexity of social science findings, there is a natural bias that leads the judiciary to tilt social regulatory policy in favor of civil liberties and minority rights.

Because the Supreme Court's 1973 decision required forty-six states and the District of Columbia to abandon their existing antiabortion statutes in favor of legalized abortions, law professor John T. Noonan, Jr., who also championed the pro-life agenda, said that "Roe v. Wade and [its companion case] Doe v. Bolton may stand as the most radical decision ever issued by the Supreme Court."[20] Although this decision may be radical, it is not so unusual because since 1925 the Supreme Court has argued that a substantial portion of the Bill of Rights applies to the states as well. This doctrine of "incorporation" is not found in the Constitution nor in the original intent of the Framers, but is based on an interpretation of the Fourteenth Amendment that has inspired a strong dissent among conservatives.[21] Whether this jurisprudence is valid or not is beyond the scope of our discussion, but the allegation that incorporation is illegitimate certainly intensifies the political controversy surrounding judicial activism.

Proposition 3a: Presidents generally do not exert decisive leadership to change social regulatory policy although they may make symbolic gestures.

What preoccupied the nation during the first fifty years of this century were World War I, the Great Depression, and World War II. Periods of foreign and domestic crisis normally tilt social regulatory policy toward public order.[22] President Franklin Roosevelt gave the nation a New Deal but also Executive Order 9066, which interned 112,000 Japanese-Americans. Harry S Truman desegregated the armed forces and led his Democratic party to disavow its segregationist wing in 1948, but he also began a loyalty-security program to head off more repressive legislation during the emerging Red Scare. President Dwight Eisenhower disapproved of the *Brown* school desegregation decision and did little to aid its implementation until forced to do so when Little Rock High School erupted over racial integration. Civil rights was not high on President John Kennedy's domestic agenda until attacks on blacks in the South telegraphed to the nation how serious that problem was.

All presidential overtures in social regulatory policy cannot be summarized here, but we hypothesize only modest leadership from the White House. The political constraints on strong presidential leadership seem obvious. How aggressively would any president dare to promote legalized abortions, pornography, or racial quotas in hiring? How often would a president disparage religion in public and glorify the ban on school prayer? Has any president since the 1960s demanded the enactment of strict gun control laws? Whenever presidents do enter the social regulatory arena and politicize these disputes, their actions carry a strong partisan motivation.

Proposition 3b: Republicans exploit social regulatory policy to mobilize conservative voters whereas Democrats are constrained not to abandon liberalism.

In the Lowi framework, presidents play a predominant role in redistributive policymaking but have very little impact on distribution. In the regulatory arena, a president throws his support behind one side in the dispute to influence the legislative outcome. This pattern applies to social regulations also, but whether a president becomes embroiled in these controversies depends largely upon his party affiliation. The optimal strategy for a Democrat is to say little in order not to offend a conservative public opinion or to alienate his party's liberal constituency. A Republican can be outspoken on social regulations given the policy preferences of *both* his party constituency and the electorate. Richard Nixon and Ronald Reagan were opposed to abortion and pornography and campaigned against crime and lawlessness.

Because Democrats still hold the edge in partisan identification among voters, Republicans need issues that can attract Democrats and Independents to support Republican presidential candidates. Historically, the Democratic party was perceived as the better provider of social-welfare benefits and a stronger guardian of the nation's prosperity. Focusing on social regulatory policy gives the GOP an opportunity to attract working-class, southern, and Catholic voters from the Democratic party because these groups often are more conservative on social regulatory questions.

The Supreme Court decisions expanding procedural rights of criminal defendants caused a political backlash that Nixon exploited in the 1968 presidential campaign. President Reagan has renewed the cry for school prayer as well as an amendment banning abortions while encouraging a strident attack, notably by Attorney General Edwin Meese, on judicial activism.[23] But the New Right has been impatient with President Reagan because he gave more attention to economic policy and budgeting than to the Right's social agenda. When the politics of Reaganomics ends, many liberals may breathe easier knowing that his advocacy of social regulatory policy has been mainly symbolic and no more substantive than that of his predecessors.

Proposition 4a: Congress usually opposes the federal judiciary and aligns itself with the state legislatures on social regulatory policy.

Conflict between the high court and the popular branches of government is not uncommon, and sometimes the Supreme Court is forced to yield to democratic pressures. Walter Murphy described the stages affecting this political relationship.[24] There is no serious tension until the judiciary renders a controversial ruling. Murphy concluded that in the face of a prolonged and intense outcry from public opinion and Congress, "judiciary retreat" is the usual Supreme Court response. Lowi found that Congress is the dominant policymaker in the arena of economic regulations. However, in the case of social regulation, Congress usually reacts against whatever policies the Supreme Court has initiated.

After the Court announced its ban on school prayers in 1962, Congress was flooded with amendments to overturn that decision, and since *Roe v. Wade*, several antiabortion bills have been enacted, the most famous being the Hyde amendment. In this arena, Congress is likely to agree with the states, especially the state legislatures, because they originally held jurisdiction over these policies. To uphold federalism by recommending that social regulations be returned to state control also is a favored strategy by which national leaders can displace these conflicts onto subnational political elites. The fundamental reason why Congress and state legislatures often agree on social regulatory policy is that political forces constrain them to affirm community norms.

Proposition 4b: Electoral pressures encourage Congress to represent traditional values in social regulatory policy.

Following the 1968 urban riots, Congress passed the Omnibus Crime Control and Safe Streets Act; in the 1970s, Congress approved tough restrictions on child pornography; and Congress rushed to pass antidrug legislation (the House even voted the death penalty for drug dealers) in time for the 1986 elections.[25] The public is largely in agreement about what social regulatory policies should be enacted, and, with the possible exception of gun control, most people want a conservative resolution of those questions.

Whenever the citizenry is aroused by conflict regarding social regulatory policy, public opinion weighs heavily in congressional deliberations. The best evidence for this is drawn from civil rights. During the 1950s, research found that large numbers of blacks in southern districts made those white populations fearful and thus mandated that their congresspersons vote a segregationist position on civil rights bills.[26] A well-known study by Warren Miller and Donald Stokes found the strongest linkage between legislators' perceptions of constituency opinion and their voting behavior on civil rights legislation.[27] Aage Clausen determined that constituency was a stronger predictor of congressional voting on international affairs and civil liberties than was party affiliation.[28] Although members of Congress normally enjoy discretion in voting on many questions, when disputes about social regulatory policy become highly visible, the odds increase that the members will represent constituency opinion and thus affirm community norms.

Proposition 5a: Public opinion is not readily mobilized behind legal change in social regulatory policy, especially change that undermines community norms.

It is commonplace to assert that most citizens are apolitical until aroused to defend their economic self-interest. This viewpoint finds support in the psychological research on human behavior, notably the work of A. H. Maslow.[29] He defined a hierarchy of needs based on physical, safety, love, self-esteem, and self-actualization needs. Only after immediate physical needs are fulfilled are people motivated to satisfy the next levels of need. Social science assumes that economic well-being is the primary determinant of behavior, but sometimes safety concerns (the domain of social regulatory policy) gain prominence in the public consciousness.

The theory of status politics, for example, argues that economic conflicts emerge during periods of recession, whereas prosperity forces status discontents to the forefront.[30] Gallup Poll trend data on the "most important problem" facing the nation verify that "social" concerns are not paramount. During the past four decades, worries about the economy or international affairs were uppermost in the public's mind, although race relations/civil rights and crime surfaced during the turbulent 1960s.[31] This period marked the beginning of a "social issue" in U.S. politics. Issues such as racial tensions, student demands and campus disorders, crime in the streets, drug usage, dress patterns, and sexual behavior, as Richard Dawson pointed out, "affect both political authorities and the general population very differently from the traditional issues of economic distribution and security."[32]

Gallup, NORC, and Harris regularly survey the public mood on certain social regulatory policies. Looking back to our cases, the majority favors school prayer, capital punishment, gun control, and restrictions on child pornography; on the other hand, most people oppose preferential hiring based on race or abortions on demand. Public opinion on the range of social regulations has not been analyzed systematically, but one policy domain that has received much attention is political tolerance. The early work on this subject found that elites were more tolerant of civil liberties than were the masses, and Seymour Lipset attributed this finding to a "working-class authoritarianism." In 1963, he observed, "The poorer strata everywhere are more liberal or leftist on economic issues. . . . But when liberalism is defined in non-economic terms . . . the correlation is reversed. The more well-to-do are more liberal, the poorer are more intolerant."[33] While the public's tolerance of groups deemed extremist in the 1950s (atheists and communists) had increased, the majority found newer minorities such as the Black Panthers on which to vent anger. Thus, John Sullivan, James Pierson, and George Marcus concluded that "intolerance has not necessarily declined much over the past 25 years, but merely has been turned toward new targets."[34]

Even when public opinion endorses legal changes in social regulatory policy, the public's commitment weakens once political conflict ensues. Citizens often hold contradictory opinions on these questions, which single-issue groups can exploit to their political advantage. This explains why the final outcome of any controversy will depend less on the force of public opinion than on the role of single-issue groups and their ability to manipulate the uninformed majority. The "intense minorities" who battle about social regulatory policy are driven by moral concerns that do not excite mass political behavior in most cases.

On gun control, apparently Congress can safely ignore majority opinion so long as the National Rifle Association is content. Public opinion is not a reliable ally for the antigun lobby. Although most people express a desire for stronger gun controls, they also accept the NRA view that the Constitution guarantees individuals the right to bear arms. The antigun lobby simply cannot mobilize public opinion the way the NRA can activate its membership.

School prayer illustrates the failure of public opinion to force a reversal in social regulatory policy. Since 1962, a considerable majority has opposed the Supreme Court ruling that prohibited school prayer, but during these twenty-five years Congress never approved an amendment to restore the practice. Although school prayer was more important to the Bible Belt, during the 1960s the South was viewed as a cultural backwater and its leadership lacked the political muscle to force the issue. The reemergence of school prayer in the 1980s partly reflects the population shift toward the Sun Belt accompanied by a changed balance of power in Congress.

Proposition 5b: Legal changes in social regulatory policy that require major revisions in community norms will not be easily accepted by public opinion.

Our case studies indicate that public opinion toward social regulatory policy is quite stable. Citizens seem to have a mind-set on these issues that resists major fluctuations. The majority view of abortion, school prayer, gun control, and capital punishment, as shown, changed little since Gallup began surveying the public on these topics. Public resistance to radical changes in social regulatory policy also is illustrated by opinion research on race relations and political tolerance.

While there has been growing acceptance of racial integration in U.S. society, these changes in public attitudes have been gradual. The 1968 Kerner Commission was so unimpressed by the record of integration that it alleged that two Americas existed, one black and one white.[35] Fourteen years later, Michael Corbett reviewed the data but now concluded that "there has been a tremendous change in public attitudes toward greater support for equality for black Americans during the last *twenty or thirty years*" (emphasis added).[36] Research in the 1950s also found much intolerance toward political non-conformists. The classic work by Samuel Stouffer determined that only a minority would permit free speech for communists or atheists,[37] whereas research done in the late 1970s showed much greater tolerance for dissenters.[38] But even if these findings are valid, the time frame for these changes in public opinion extended through two decades.

Whenever major revisions in community norms are mandated by law, our case studies suggest that public opinion will not readily accept those changes. The vast majority still favors school prayer despite the Supreme Court's ruling, and abortion on demand has not been legitimized in public opinion, the high court's 1973 decision notwithstanding. The public's perception of the legitimacy of official acts has implications for the consensus-building process and can affect compliance with the law. Although social regulatory policy is not a paramount concern of most citizens, the cooperation of a target population often is necessary for effective implementation. But this population most likely comprises the people who were most opposed to legal changes in the first place. Prohibition shows the enforcement nightmare when a significant minority with divergent social mores do not abide by a law. The tremendous resistance to *Brown* resulted because the vast majority of white southerners deemed that ruling to be unacceptable. Would Catholic physicians and hospitals be willing to perform abortions, and how likely would gun owners be to register their firearms voluntarily? The compliance problem in social regulatory policymaking involves the administrative process at both the federal and subnational levels.

Proposition 6a: Agencies of the federal government usually will have limited jurisdiction over social regulatory policy.

Although the enactment of civil rights laws increased the role of federal agencies in social regulatory policy, the absence of comprehensive national legislation in other areas means that the impact of the central government on policy implementation will be marginal compared to states and localities. Five of our case studies show this pattern.

Responsibility for the enforcement of federal gun laws lies with the Bureau of Alcohol, Tobacco, and Firearms (BATF), but the statutes are ineffectual. Abortion policy mainly involves federal funding and those agencies dealing with medical care, family planning, and even foreign aid. The thrust of national implementation hinges on Medicaid grants to the states and thus the Health Care Financing Administration (HCFA). Anti-pornography laws draw upon the resources of the Federal Communications Commission (FCC) but more importantly the FBI, the U.S. Customs Service, and the U.S. Postal Service. Most crimes are under state jurisdiction, but in response to the 1968 civil disturbances Congress enacted the multifaceted Omnibus Crime Control and Safe Street Act, which distributed federal moneys to states and localities through the (now defunct) Law Enforcement Assistance Administration (LEAA).

Two small agencies, the Equal Employment Opportunity Commission (EEOC) and the Office of Federal Contracts Compliance (OFCC), are charged with implementing affirmative action programs that impact thousands of governmental, business, and nonprofit organizations. On the other hand, there is no administrative agency charged with the enforcement of the school prayer ban. Here the compliance effort depends entirely upon the voluntary action of local school boards and judicial intervention resulting from private lawsuits.

Apart from the modest role given to federal agencies, the vigilance with which they discharge their duties will depend largely upon external political constraints. The administrative process that shapes social regulatory policy is a microcosm of the legislative arena of power.

Proposition 6b: The ability of federal agencies to implement social regulatory policy depends on the liberal versus conservative pressures exerted by the Congress, presidency, judiciary, clientele groups, and regulated interests.

This proposition closely follows the standard analyses of the implementation process. The administrative arena is circumscribed by the president, who sets policy, and by Congress, which appropriates funds, initiates legislation, and exercises oversight. There also are pressures exerted by clientele (beneficiary) groups and regulated interests. The judiciary also has a decisive role because beneficiary groups often use the courts to assure faithful implementation of the law. For example, an analysis by Jeremy Rabkin showed how the Office for Civil Rights in the Department of Education had become a "captive" agency of the federal judiciary due to the ongoing court orders instigated by pro–civil rights advocacy groups.[39]

We assume that federal agencies are dedicated to carrying out their legislative mandates. The literature on public administration agrees that the recruitment, socialization, and career motivations of federal bureaucrats are agency centered.[40] But the implementation of social regulatory policy depends on the agency's political relationships with significant outsiders as well as the role orientations of its personnel. Most bureaucrats are "careerists" who seek foremost to assure their agency's survival, although some may be "zealots" who are committed to achieving the agency's legislative mission. We cannot diagnose the motivations of agency officials in this research, but we would assume that new agencies with change-oriented mandates are more dedicated to goals as compared to older agencies that already have accommodated their political environments.

The Bureau of Alcohol, Tobacco, and Firearms is probably best characterized by a concern for survival. The antigun lobby is weak and is no match for the ongoing and strident criticism of this agency by the NRA (the agency's regulated interest), the NRA's allies in Congress, and by President Reagan, who once advocated the agency's abolishment. The enforcement of antipornography laws also has been lackluster, but this mainly is due to the Supreme Court's defense of free expression. Although the Court never defined obscenity as "protected" speech under the Constitution, the Court's very permissive rulings in the 1960s virtually precluded government censorship. However, since then, Congress has enacted anti–child pornography laws, and the Supreme Court has agreed to such prohibitions. Because public opinion is solidly behind a ban on child porn, the stage now is set for more rigorous enforcement by the U.S. Postal Service and other agencies.

A political backlash by a Congress fortified by the prolife movement resulted in curbs being placed on some federal agencies involved with abortion. The U.S. Civil Rights Commission was banned from studying the abortion policies of any government, and the Legal Services Corporation (LSC) was barred from litigating any abortion case. When Congress enacted the Hyde amendment in 1976, HCFA was restricted to funding Medicaid abortions only for specific therapeutic reasons. But acting on a lawsuit filed by women and doctors who benefit from liberalized abortion funding under Medicaid, a district court issued a permanent injunction against the Hyde amendment in order to allow HCFA to pay for all medically necessary abortions. This legal battle ended when the Supreme Court upheld the constitutionality of the Hyde amendment.

The experience of the LEAA shows how powerful clientele groups can distort policymaking once implementation begins. Congress wanted to show its resolve against crime; the LEAA obliged by acting swiftly in the face of a supportive public opinion; and police departments eagerly awaited this new infusion of funds. The LEAA allocated moneys to state and local anticrime programs, but due to ambiguous statutory language those funds were skewed toward law enforcement agencies rather than toward supporting long-term structural improvements in the criminal justice system.

Affirmative action illustrates how federal agencies can shape policy implementation in decisive ways. Although Congress never mandated racial quotas in hiring and actually disavowed "reverse discrimination" by amending the 1964 Civil Rights Act, the use of numerical quotas resulted because no other approach seemed likely to achieve an integrated work force. No president until Ronald Reagan meddled with this policy strategy, which shows the political clout generated when clientele groups (minorities), an agency likely controlled by zealots, and the federal judiciary join forces. This is the story of the Equal Employment Opportunity Commission.

Even more revealing is the experience of the Office of Federal Contracts Compliance (OFCC). Its administration of the minority set-aside program of the federal government seemed to have accommodated all parties involved. The program was mandated by executive order, implemented by OFCC, backed by the clientele (minority contractors), and tolerated by the regulated interest (big business). A modus vivendi had been achieved, so when President Reagan proposed terminating this program there was a much publicized dispute within his cabinet. Thus far, the program has survived the Reagan administration, despite the hostility by ultraconservatives on the presidential staff.

Proposition 7a: Federalism is important to social regulatory policy because historically the states had jurisdiction over most of these issues.

With the exception of those laws enacted during the Populist and Progressive eras, notably the Interstate Commerce Act and the Pure Food and Drug Act, almost all economic regulations date from the 1930s. This "Roosevelt revolution" was consummated when the Supreme Court acquiesced to a loose construction of the commerce clause of the Constitution, which empowers Congress to regulate interstate and foreign commerce.[41] But economic regulatory policy by the federal government did not displace state activity because previously the states had practiced very little intervention in the marketplace.[42] Because the Great Depression unified the nation around economic reforms, there were few dissenters to this historical shift of political power toward the national government.

Social regulatory policy, in contrast, showed a pervasive role by states long before the agitation for federal intervention began. Even today, the states' "police powers" assure that states will be more than equal partners in this federal relationship. The outcry about states' rights being violated was heard very loudly when the federal government began to strengthen civil rights legislation; for example, by the 1948 Dixiecrat revolt from the Democratic party. The advocates of racial progress had turned to the federal government because so little improvement was accomplished by Southern states. Although the contemporary debate about affirmative action may symbolize the latest chapter in the civil rights struggle, fundamentally this movement has sought to redefine state laws regulating the role of blacks in a white society.

Each case study points to a decisive role by state government. Beginning in the mid-1800s, the states prohibited abortions except to save the mother's life, while state antiobscenity laws date back to the founding of the Republic. The enforcement of criminal laws is almost entirely a state responsibility. Since the eighteenth century, the states have legitimized religion in many public ceremonies and later added school prayer laws. During most of U.S. history, gun controls by state governments have been weak or nonexistent. In numerous other ways, the states safeguard public order, safety, health, and moral character. Whether gambling is a vice to be discouraged or a virtue to be exploited through state lotteries depends upon how state legislatures view the matter. How the age of adulthood is defined for the purposes of alcoholic consumption, driving, or reading sexual materials varies by state. Most states have "blue laws" regulating Sunday sales, and the vast majority refuse to legalize marijuana use, prostitution, or homosexual relations. Family law affecting marriage, divorce, child care, and adoption also fall under state jurisdiction. Whether felons are imprisoned, employed on road gangs, or rehabilitated depends on state policy, just as the mentally ill, who once were confined to state hospitals, now are being deinstitutionalized to live in their communities. The imposition of capital punishment varies according to state as well.

The states have no policymaking role in Lowi's economic regulatory arena, but federalism is an important variable in social regulatory policy. There is a zero-sum quality to these disputes, moreover, because what legal authority resides with the Congress or the federal courts is lost to the states. This outcome is favored by proponents of social change who view the states as being overly protective of community norms. Social regulatory policy also involves federalism insofar as policy implementation may be obstructed, delayed, or undermined by state and local officials.

Proposition 7b: The enforcement of social regulatory policy often depends on the compliance of state and local officials as well as on decisionmakers in the private sector.

No federal law is as easy to implement as one might assume, and there are unique problems with social regulatory policy. One problem is that federal enforcement may not get top priority or have enough resources. Another is the sheer number of persons affected by social regulations. The school prayer ban involved thousands of local school boards; affirmative action guidelines affect hundreds of thousands of employer organizations; gun control focuses on millions of U.S. citizens. This complication explains why the OFCC is more effective than the EEOC. Where the federal minority set-aside program rests entirely under the jurisdiction of OFCC and involves several thousand contractors, the EEOC is supposed to oversee the employment practices of a greater number and variety of business, nonprofit, and government organizations.

As in the case of the school prayer ban, implementation may depend wholly on voluntary compliance. Other social regulatory policies are implemented by state and local authorities as well as by target populations, who are permitted much discretion. The slow progress toward equal employment as well as voting rights and open housing resulted from the inaction of local decisionmakers, as Charles Bullock and Charles Lamb explained: "Attempts to implement civil rights depend to a large degree on the response of various state and local officials and, sometimes, of private citizens. . . . It is not uncommon, therefore, for national policy objectives to depend on a number of people not directly answerable to the decision makers who propounded the policy."[43] The weak enforcement of federal gun laws by the BATF stems largely from its reliance on voluntary compliance by gun dealers.

The ultimate problem of social regulatory policy is that consensus building is more difficult to achieve compared to any other policy arena. With Social Security, the income tax, or other redistributive policies, their conflict potential can be reduced through implementation. But there is no obvious way to mute moral disagreements either at the policymaking stage or during administration. The antagonists view these disagreements as nonnegotiable, and the fact that Congress or the Supreme Court promulgates law does not automatically bring the matter to a close. It has been several years since new policies on school prayer and abortion were announced. Even a constitutional amendment is no assurance that controversy will end. The only amendment to be repealed was the Eighteenth—prohibition— which is the classic example of social regulatory policy at the federal level. Given that experience, we might conclude that conflicts about social regulatory policy will persist until they simply become irrelevant with the passage of time, when a de facto settlement in public opinion is achieved. At that juncture, once again the social mores of the U.S. people and the law of social regulatory policy will reinforce one another.

ACKNOWLEDGMENTS

We are grateful to Dr. John Williams of Loyola University of Chicago, whose editorial comments were incorporated in this final draft.

NOTES

Foreword

1. Theodore J. Lowi, "The Welfare State, The New Regulation and the Rule of Law," in Allan Schnaiberg et al., *Distributional Conflicts in Environmental Resource Policy* (London, England: Gower Publishing Co., Ltd., 1986), p. 113. My thanks to Schnaiberg for suggesting, albeit for different purposes, the first antinomy between error and sin.

2. George Will, *Statecraft as Soulcraft* (New York: Simon and Schuster, 1983), p. 20.

3. A formulation of mine in *The End of Liberalism* (New York: W. W. Norton, 1979).

Introduction

1. Theodore J. Lowi, "American Business, Public Policy, Case Studies, and Political Theory," *World Politics* 16 (July 1964):677–715. In later writings, Lowi added the fourth category—"constituent" policy. The Lowi framework of analysis has been expanded and modified by other scholars, including our own previous work. See, for instance, Raymond Tatalovich and Byron W. Daynes, *The Politics of Abortion* (New York: Praeger, 1981), Chapter 6, and "Moral Controversies and the Policymaking Process: Lowi's Framework Applied to the Abortion Issue," *Policy Studies Review* 3 (February 1984):207–222. Also see Robert J. Spitzer, *The Presidency and Public Policy: The Four Arenas of Presidential Power* (University: University of Alabama Press, 1983), and "Promoting Policy Theory: Refining the Arenas of Power," *Policy Studies Journal*, (June 1987):675–689; William Zimmerman, "Issue Area and Foreign-Policy Process," *American Political Science Review* (December 1973):1204–1212.

2. Lester M. Salamon, "Federal Regulation: A New Arena for Presidential Power," in Hugh Heclo and Lester M. Salamon, eds., *The Illusion of Presidential Government* (Boulder, Colo.: Westview Press, 1981), p. 150.

3. W. Lilley and James C. Miller, III, "The New 'Social' Regulation," *The Public Interest* 47 (1977):49–61, especially p. 52. Also see James Q. Wilson, *The Politics of Regulation* (New York: Basic Books, 1980).

4. Salamon, "Federal Regulation," p. 150.

5. Randall B. Ripley and Grace A. Franklin, *Bureaucracy and Policy Implementation* (Homewood, Ill.: Dorsey Press, 1982), p. 132.

6. Charles Murray, *Losing Ground: American Social Policy, 1950–1980* (New York: Basic Books, 1984), p. 13; Donald L. Horowitz, *The Courts and Social Policy* (Washington, D.C.: The Brookings Institution, 1977), p. 56.

7. T. Alexander Smith, *The Comparative Policy Process* (Santa Barbara, Calif.: CLIO Press, 1975).

8. James B. Christoph, *Capital Punishment and British Politics* (London: George Allen and Unwin, 1962).

9. Smith, *The Comparative Policy Process*, p. 90.

Chapter 1

1. See Willmoore Kendall, "American Conservatism and the 'Prayer' Decisions," *Modern Age* 8 (Summer 1964):245–259.

2. U.S. Senate, Subcommittee on the Constitution of the Committee on the Judiciary, *Hearings on S.J. Res. 73, A Joint Resolution Proposing an Amendment to the Constitution of the United States Relating to Voluntary School Prayer and S.J. Res. 212, A Joint Resolution Proposing an Amendment to the Constitution of the United States Relating to Voluntary Silent Prayer or Meditation*, 98th Cong., 1st sess., April 29, May 2, and June 27, 1983, pp. 617–619.

3. "School Prayer Amendment: House Vote Defeats Move," *1971 Congressional Quarterly Almanac* (Washington, D.C.: Congressional Quarterly, 1972), p. 624. See discussion pp. 624–629.

4. *Encyclopedia of Associations*, 19th ed. (Detroit: Gale Research Company, 1985), p. 1160.

5. Ibid., p. 1416.

6. Ibid., p. 1161.

7. George McKenna, *The Constitution: That Delicate Balance* (New York: Random House, 1984), p. 269.

8. J. Elliot, ed., *The Debates in the Several State Conventions on the Adoption of the Federal Constitution*, 2nd ed., 5 vols. (Philadelphia: J. B. Lippincott Company, 1941). See vol. 3, p. 659 (Virginia Res.), and vol. 4, p. 244 (North Carolina Res.).

9. *I Annals of Congress. The Debates and Proceedings in the Congress of the United States: The First Congress, 1789–1791* (Washington, D.C.: Goles and Seaton, 1834), pp. 730–731.

10. Joseph Story, *Commentaries on the Constitution of the United States*, vol. 3 (Boston: Little, Brown, 1833), p. 731.

11. George Anastaplo, "The Religion Clauses of the First Amendment," *Memphis State University Law Review* 11 (Winter 1981):189–190.

12. Edward Dumbauld, *The Bill of Rights and What It Means Today* (Norman: University of Oklahoma Press, 1957), p. 104.

13. Gerald Gunther, *Cases and Materials on Constitutional Law* (Mineola, N.Y.: Foundation Press, 1980), p. 1553, fn. 1.

14. N. Dorsen, P. Bender, and B. Neuborne, *Political and Civil Rights in the United States*, 4th ed. (Boston: Little, Brown, 1976), p. 1170.

15. Jesse Choper, "Religion in the Public Schools: A Proposed Constitutional Standard," *Minnesota Law Review* 47 (1963):371.

16. The three-prong test in *Lemon v. Kurtzman* was the following: "First, the statute must have a secular legislative purpose; second, its principal or primary effect must be one that neither advances nor inhibits religion; . . . finally, the statute must not foster 'an excessive government entanglement with religion.'"

17. *The Gallup Poll, Public Opinion, 1935–1971* (New York: Random House, 1972), p. 1837.

18. James Allan Davis, *General Social Surveys, 1972–1982* (Chicago: National Opinion Research Center, 1982), p. 100; James Allan Davis and Tom W. Smith, *General Social Surveys, 1972–1986* (Chicago: National Opinion Research Center, 1986), p. 149.

19. See *The Gallup Opinion Index*, no. 177 (April-May 1980):9–10; *The Gallup Report*, no. 206 (November 1982):18; *The Gallup Report*, no. 229 (October 1984):7.

20. William C. Adams, "American Public Opinion in the 1960s on Two Church-State Issues," *Journal of Church and State* (1975):477–494.

21. Ibid., p. 494.

22. Kirk W. Elifson and C. Kirk Hadaway, "Prayer in Public Schools: When Church and State Collide," *Public Opinion Quarterly* (Fall 1985):317–329.

23. Ibid., p. 328.

24. William M. Beaney and Edward N. Beiser, "Prayer and Politics: The Impact of *Engel* and *Schempp* on the Political Process," *Journal of Public Law* 13 (1964):478.

25. Ibid., pp. 478–479.

26. Cited in ibid., pp. 494–495.

27. See "Senate Fails to Amend School Prayer Ruling," *1966 Congressional Quarterly Almanac* (Washington, D.C.: Congressional Quarterly, 1967), pp. 512–516.

28. See "School Prayer Amendment," pp. 624–629.

29. See "Supreme Court Jurisdiction," *1979 Congressional Quarterly Almanac* (Washington, D.C.: Congressional Quarterly, 1980), pp. 396–398.

30. See "State, Justice, Commerce Appropriations," *1981 Congressional Quarterly Almanac* (Washington, D.C.: Congressional Quarterly, 1982), p. 368.

31. See "Senate Kills Abortion, School Prayer Riders," *1982 Congressional Quarterly Almanac* (Washington, D.C.: Congressional Quarterly, 1983), pp. 403–405.

32. See "School Prayer Amendments," *1983 Congressional Quarterly Almanac* (Washington, D.C.: Congressional Quarterly, 1984), pp. 301–302; "School Prayer Issue Flares in Many Guises," *1984 Congressional Quarterly Almanac* (Washington, D.C.: Congressional Quarterly, 1985), pp. 245–247.

33. See "Senate Rejects Bill to Permit School Prayer," *1985 Congressional Quarterly Almanac* (Washington, D.C.: Congressional Quarterly, 1986), pp. 234–235.

34. See Willmoore Kendall, with George W. Carey, "The 'Intensity' Problem and Democratic Theory," *American Political Science Review* 62 (March 1968):5–24.

35. Cited in Beaney and Beiser, "Prayer and Politics," p. 480.

36. Cited in ibid., p. 481.

37. Cited in *National Party Conventions, 1831–1980* (Washington, D.C.: Congressional Quarterly, 1983), p. 105.

38. Quoted in *New York Times*, October 29, 1964, p. 1.

39. *National Party Conventions, 1831–1980*, p. 118.

40. Ibid., p. 126.

41. Quoted in "Supreme Court Jurisdiction," p. 397.

42. "Town Hall Meeting, Independence, Missouri," September 2, 1980, *Public Papers of the Presidents of the United States* (Washington, D.C.: U.S. Government Printing Office, 1982), p. 958.

43. "Remarks to Out of Town Editors," October 17, 1981, in ibid., p. 958.

44. "Message to the Congress Transmitting a Proposed Constitutional Amendment on Prayer in Schools," May 17, 1982, *Public Papers of the Presidents of the United States* (Washington, D.C.: U.S. Government Printing Office, 1983), p. 647.

45. "Remarks at Kansas State University," September 2, 1982, in ibid., p. 1122.

46. See text of the State of the Union Address in *New York Times*, January 28, 1987, p. 6.

47. *Marsh v. Chambers*, 103 U.S. 3330 (1983), involved the Nebraska legislature retaining a single individual as chaplain; *Lynch v. Donnelly*, 104 S.Ct. 1355 (1984), involved a nativity scene in Pawtucket, Rhode Island; *Grand Rapids School District*

v. Ball, 105 S.Ct. 3216 (1985), involved enrichment/remedial programs that utilized parochial schools and parochial school teachers.

48. See "Family Feud: Reagan Conservatives Assail Solicitor General for His Independence," *Wall Street Journal*, September 6, 1984, p. 1.

49. U.S. Senate, *Hearings Before the Subcommittee on the Constitution of the Committee on the Judiciary on S.J. Res. 73 . . . and S.J. Res. 212*, 98th Cong., 1st sess., April 29, May 2, and June 27, 1983, pp. 16–26 and 346–355. Quote is on p. 17.

50. Ibid., pp. 96–99. Quote is on p. 98.

51. Donald E. Boles, *The Bible, Religion, and the Public Schools* (Ames: Iowa State University Press, 1965), pp. 48–56.

52. Cited in Dale Doak, "The Bible-Prayer Cases: Do Court Decisions Give Minority Rule?" *Phi Delta Kappan* (October 1963):23.

53. They were Colorado, Connecticut, Maryland, Michigan, Minnesota, Missouri, New Hampshire, New Mexico, North Carolina, Oregon, Rhode Island, South Carolina, Texas, Utah, Vermont, Virginia, West Virginia, Wyoming, and New York.

54. Doak, "The Bible-Prayer Cases," p. 23.

55. Cited in Beaney and Beiser, "Prayer and Politics," p. 481.

56. Ibid., p. 486.

57. Ibid., p. 487.

58. Ibid.

59. Cited in ibid., p. 490.

60. Cited in Donald R. Reich, "The Impact of Judicial Decision Making: The School Prayer Cases," in David H. Everson, ed., *The Supreme Court as Policy-Maker: Three Studies on the Impact of Judicial Decisions* (Carbondale: Southern Illinois University, Public Affairs Research Bureau, 1972), pp. 47, 50, 52.

61. Cited in Beaney and Beiser, "Prayer and Politics," p. 486.

62. Cited in Reich, "The Impact of Judicial Decision Making," p. 47.

63. H. Frank Way, Jr., "Survey Research on Judicial Decisions: The Prayer and Bible Reading Cases," *Western Political Quarterly* (June 1968):189–205.

64. Ellis Katz, "Patterns of Compliance with the *Schempp* Decision," *Journal of Public Law* 14 (1965):396–408.

65. Ibid., p. 407.

66. Robert H. Birkby, "The Supreme Court and the Bible Belt: Tennessee Reaction to the 'Schempp' Decision," *Midwest Journal of Political Science* (August 1966):304–319.

67. Roald Y. Mykkeltvedt, "The Response of Georgia's Public School Systems to the School Prayer Decisions: 'Whipping a Dead Horse,'" *Georgia State Bar Journal* (May 1973):425–441.

68. Ibid., p. 439.

69. Michael W. La Morte and Fred N. Dorminy, "Compliance with the *Schempp* Decision: A Decade Later," *Journal of Law and Education* (July 1974):399–407.

70. Kenneth Paul Nuger, "Teacher Compliance with *Wallace v. Jaffree* in Mobile County Schools" (Paper delivered at the annual meeting of the Midwest Political Science Association, Chicago, Illinois, April 9–11, 1987).

71. Reich, "The Impact of Judicial Decision Making," p. 66. Also see pp. 53–70 on California.

72. William K. Muir, Jr., *Law and Attitude Change* (Chicago: University of Chicago Press, 1973).

73. Richard M. Johnson, *The Dynamics of Compliance: Supreme Court Decision-Making from a New Perspective* (Evanston, Ill.: Northwestern University Press, 1967).

74. Kenneth M. Dolbeare and Phillip E. Hammond, *The School Prayer Decisions: From Court Policy to Local Practice* (Chicago: University of Chicago Press, 1971).

75. Ibid., p. 7.

Chapter 2

1. Joseph L. Galloway, with Jeannye Thornton, "Crackdown on Pornography—A No-Win Battle," *U.S. News and World Report*, June 4, 1984, p. 84. It is estimated that direct mail-order sales of pornography has increased from a "500 million-dollar business a few years ago to about 3 billion now" (p. 85).

2. Joseph W. Bishop, Jr., "The Warren Court Is Not Likely to Be Overruled," *New York Times Magazine*, September 7, 1969, p. 99.

3. These twenty states are Arizona, Colorado, Delaware, Florida, Hawaii, Kentucky, Louisiana, Massachusetts, Michigan, Montana, Mississippi, New York, New Jersey, Oklahoma, Pennsylvania, Rhode Island, Texas, Utah, West Virginia, and Wisconsin. See Daniel S. Moretti, *Obscenity and Pornography: The Law Under the First Amendment* (New York: Oceana, 1984), Appendix E, p. 127.

4. *American Booksellers Association, Inc. et al. v. William H. Hudnut III, Mayor of Indianapolis, et al.*, no. IP 84-791C (November 19, 1984).

5. For example, one bill defined obscenity as "an explicit representation, or detailed written or verbal description of an act of sexual intercourse, including genital-genital, anal-genital, or oral-genital intercourse, whether between human beings or between a human being and an animal, or of flagellation, torture, or other violence indicating a sado-masochistic sexual relationship." See S. 1400, 93rd Cong., 1st sess., section 1851(b)(2) (1973).

6. "Resolution Declaring that the Senate Reject the Findings and Recommendations of the Commission on Obscenity and Pornography," *Congressional Record* 116, 91st Cong., 2nd sess., December 17, 1970, p. 42318.

7. *Congressional Record*, 92nd Cong., 1st sess., January 25, 1971, p. 460.

8. "Obscenity Bill Pocket Veto," *Congressional Quarterly Weekly Report* (October 26, 1962):2061.

9. Donald Bruce Johnson, comp., *National Party Platforms*, vol. 2 (Urbana: University of Illinois Press, 1978), p. 683.

10. "Special Message to Congress on Forthcoming Legislative Proposals Concerning Domestic Programs," April 14, 1969, *Public Papers of the Presidents of the United States* (Washington, D.C.: U.S. Government Printing Office, 1971), p. 284. Nixon's comments in late 1968 are found in "General Government," *Congressional Quarterly Weekly Report* (December 27, 1968):3320.

11. "Text of President's Message on Obscenity," *Congressional Quarterly Weekly Report* (May 9, 1969):702.

12. "Statement About the Report of the Commission on Obscenity and Pornography," October 24, 1970, *Public Papers of the Presidents of the United States* (Washington, D.C.: U.S. Government Printing Office, 1971), p. 940.

13. "Special Message to the Congress Resubmitting Legislative Proposals," January 26, 1971, *Public Papers of the Presidents of the United States* (Washington, D.C.: U.S. Government Printing Office, 1972), p. 65.

14. Johnson, *National Party Platforms*, vol. 2, p. 904.

15. Ibid., p. 947.

16. Ibid., p. 972.

17. Donald Bruce Johnson, *National Party Platforms of 1980* (Urbana: University of Illinois Press, 1982), p. 5.

18. *Congressional Quarterly Almanac, 1984*, vol. 40 (Washington, D.C.: Congressional Quarterly, 1985), p. 51B.

19. "Child Protection Act of 1984: Remarks on Signing H.R. 3635 Into Law," May 21, 1984, *Weekly Compilation of Presidential Documents* 20, no. 4 (Washington, D.C.: Office of Federal Register, 1984), p. 743.

20. See PL 90-100, 90th Cong. The membership of the commission included William B. Lockhart, law professor, University of Minnesota Law School; Frederick H. Wagman, past president, American Library Association; Edward E. Elson, president, Atlanta News Agency; Thomas D. Gill, chief judge, Juvenile Court for the State of Connecticut; Edward D. Greenwood, psychiatrist, Menninger Foundation; Morton A. Hill, S.J., president, Morality in Media; G. William Jones, assistant professor of broadcast, Southern Methodist University; Kenneth B. Keating, former U.S. senator, who was replaced by Charles H. Keating, Jr., founder of Citizens for Decent Literature; Joseph T. Klapper, director, Office of Social Research, CBS; Otto N. Larsen, sociologist, University of Washington; Irving Lehrman, rabbi, Temple Emanu-El, Miami Beach, Fla.; Freeman Lewis, president, Washington Square Press; Winfrey C. Link, reverend, administrator of McKendree Manor Methodist retirement home, Hermitage, Tenn.; Morris A. Lipton, professor of psychiatry, University of North Carolina; Thomas C. Lynch, attorney general of California; Barbara Scott, deputy attorney, Motion Picture Association of America; Cathryn A. Spelts, South Dakota School of Mines and Technology; Marvin E. Wolfgang, sociologist, University of Pennsylvania.

21. *The Report of the Commission on Obscenity and Pornography* (New York: Bantam Books–New York Times Books, 1970), pp. 53–75.

22. Reported in Ray C. Rist, *The Pornography Controversy* (New Brunswick, N.J.: Transaction Books, 1975), p. 257.

23. Spiro Agnew, "Prepared Remarks," Salt Lake City, Utah, September 30, 1970.

24. Its membership included Henry Hudson, chairman, U.S. attorney for the eastern district of Virginia; Judith V. Becker, associate professor of clinical psychology, Columbia University; Diana D. Cusack, former vice-mayor of Scottsdale, Arizona; Park E. Dietz, professor of law, behavioral medicine, and psychiatry, University of Virginia; James C. Dobson, president, "Focus on Family," a syndicated radio program; Edward J. Garcia, federal judge, U.S. Court for Eastern District of California; Ellen Levine, editor, *Woman's Day*; Tex Lezar, counselor to former attorney general William French Smith; Rev. Bruce Ritter, president, Covenant House (a child care crisis center); Frederick Schauer, professor of law, University of Michigan; Deanne Tilton, president, California Consortium of Child Abuse Councils.

25. Attorney General's Commission on Pornography, *Final Report*, vol. 1 (Washington, D.C.: U.S. Government Printing Office, 1986), p. 229.

26. Robert Pear, "Panel Calls on Citizens to Wage National Assault on Pornography," *New York Times*, July 10, 1986, p. 10.

27. Philip Shenon, "Pornography Panel Barred from Publicizing Retailers," *New York Times*, July 4, 1986, p. 10. The original letter had its effect. Approximately five thousand five hundred 7-Eleven stores, two thousand Revco Drugstores, eight hundred Peoples Drugstores, the Dart Drug Corporation, Gray Drug Stores of Cleveland, Ohio, and Stop-N-Go Drug Stores withdrew adult magazines from their shelves. See Matthew L. Wald, "'Adult' Magazines Lose Sales as 8,000 Stores Forbid Them," *New York Times*, June 16, 1986, p. 11.

28. Attorney General's Commission on Pornography, *Final Report*, vol. 1, p. 326.

29. Ibid., p. 199.

30. Philip Shenon, "Obscenity Report Nears Completion," *New York Times*, May 3, 1986, p. 13.

31. Barbara Gamarekian, "Report Draws Strong Praise and Criticism," *New York Times*, July 10, 1986, p. 10.

32. Hallam and Falwell quoted in ibid.

33. Quoted materials found in ibid.

34. 29 FCC 2d 334 (1971).

35. In the Matter of Amendment of Part 76 of the Commission's Rules and Regulations Concerning the Cable Television Channel Capacity and Access Channel Requirements of Section 76.251. 87 FCC 2d 42 (1981).

36. In the Matter of Application for Review Filed by Decency in Broadcasting, Inc. of a Denial of Its Complaint Against Rahall Broadcasting of Indiana, Licensee of Station WFBQ (FM), Indianapolis, Indiana. 94 FCC 2d 1162-1163 (1983).

37. In re: Applications of Dena Pictures, Incorporated, Alexander Broadcasting Company, a Joint Venture d/b/a Kaye-Smith Enterprises; for Renewal of License of Station; Vincent L. Hoffart d/b/a, Hoffart Broadcasting, Seattle, Washington. 98 FCC 2d 671-672 (1984).

38. Postal Inspection Service, *Law Enforcement Reports* (Washington, D.C.: U.S. Postal Service, Summer 1983), p. 6.

39. Howard A. Davidson, "Sexual Exploitation of Children," *F.B.I. Law Enforcement Bulletin* (February 1984):28.

40. See 18 USC Sec. 552.

41. See 18 USC Sec. 1462, 1465; 19 USC Sec. 1305; and 18 USC Sec. 1699.

42. James C. N. Paul and Murray L. Schwartz, *Federal Censorship: Obscenity in the Mail* (Glencoe, Ill.: Free Press, 1961), pp. 90–91. It was found that during 1946–1956, rarely did any importer protest seizure by U.S. Customs. Ibid., p. 90.

43. Postal Inspection Service, *Law Enforcement Report* (Washington, D.C.: U.S. Postal Service, Winter 1984/1985), p. 4.

44. GAO Report, *Sexual Exploitation of Children—A Problem of Unknown Magnitude*, Report to Chairman, Subcommittee on Select Education, House Committee on Education and Labor, April 20, 1982, General Accounting Report, B-207117, p. 50.

45. Postal Inspection Service, *Law Enforcement Report* (Washington, D.C.: U.S. Postal Service, Spring 1984), p. 14.

46. Postal Inspection Service, *Law Enforcement Report* (Washington, D.C.: U.S. Postal Service, Winter 1983/1984), p. 7.

47. Postal Inspection Service, *Law Enforcement Report* (Washington, D.C.: U.S. Postal Service, Summer 1984), p. 6.

48. Postal Inspection Service, *Law Enforcement Report* (Washington, D.C.: U.S. Postal Service, Fall 1984), p. 9.

49. GAO Report, *Sexual Exploitation of Children*, p. 50.

50. U.S. Postal Service, Postal Inspection Service, *Law Enforcement Report 1977* (Washington, D.C.: U.S. Government Printing Office, 1978), p. 6; Edmund F. McGarrell and Timothy J. Flanagan, eds., *Sourcebook of Criminal Justice Statistics—1984* (Washington, D.C.: U.S. Government Printing Office, 1985), pp. 595 and 592.

51. GAO Report, *Sexual Exploitation of Children*, p. 7.

52. Harrell R. Rodgers, Jr., "Censorship Campaigns in Eighteen Cities: An Impact Analysis," *American Politics Quarterly* 2 (October 1974), especially pp. 375, 380–381, and 389.

53. Seth S. King, "Foes of Pornography Winning a Few Skirmishes, but Not the Major Battles," *New York Times*, C. ed., November 28, 1975, p. 52.

54. Ibid.

55. This definition of pornography was later expanded in the Model Anti-pornography Law to include "the graphic sexually explicit subordination of women through pictures and/or words that also includes one or more of the following: (i) women are presented dehumanized as sexual objects, things, or commodities; or (ii) women are presented as sexual objects who enjoy pain or humiliation; or (iii) women are presented as sexual objects who experience sexual pleasure in being raped; or (iv) women are presented as sexual objects tied up or cut up or mutilated or bruised or physically hurt; or (v) women are presented in postures or positions of sexual submission, servility, or display; or (vi) women's body parts—including but not limited to vaginas, breasts, or buttocks—are exhibited such that women are reduced to those parts; or (vii) women are presented as whores by nature; or (viii) women are presented being penetrated by objects or animals; or (ix) woman are presented in scenarios of degradation, injury, torture, shown as filthy or inferior, bleeding, bruised, or hurt in a context that makes these conditions sexual." See "Model Antipornography Law," *Ms.* (April 1985):46.

56. "2 Cable Porno Bans Defeated in Utah, Calif.," *Variety,* November 14, 1984, pp. 1, 98.

57. See footnote 3. Other state antipornography regulations are listed in Moretti, *Obscenity and Pornography,* pp. 127–129. Laws on sexual exploitation of children are discussed by Clifford L. Linedecker, *Children in Chains* (New York: Everest House, 1981), pp. 304–318.

58. Douglas H. Wallace, "Obscenity and Contemporary Community Standards: A Survey," *Journal of Social Issues* 29 (November 3, 1973):66.

59. Coke Brown, Joan Anderson, Linda Burggraf, and Neal Thompson, "Community Standards, Conservatism, and Judgments of Pornography," *Journal of Sex Research* 14 (May 1978):94.

60. Stuart Taylor, Jr., "High Court Backs Use of Zoning to Regulate Showing of Sex Films," *New York Times,* February 26, 1986, p. 1.

61. "Public Concerned About Porn, but Divided over Court Decision," *Gallup Opinion Index,* no. 142 (May 1977):5–6.

62. "Opinion Roundup: A Pornography Report," *Public Opinion* (September/October 1986):31.

63. "A *Newsweek* Poll: Mixed Feelings on Pornography," *Newsweek,* March 18, 1985, p. 60. These results were confirmed by a 1982 National Opinion Research Center General Social Survey, which found that 57 percent of the public thought that exposure to sexually explicit movies, books, and magazines would lead to "a breakdown of social morals." "Opinion Roundup," p. 32. A Gallup Poll showed 73–76 percent favored banning sexual violence in magazines, theaters, and video cassettes. *The Gallup Report,* no. 251 (August 1986):4–6.

64. Herbert McClosky and Alida Brill, *Dimensions of Tolerance* (New York: Russell Sage Foundation, 1983), p. 61. To the statement "novels that describe explicit sex acts have no place in a high school library and should be banned," 48 percent of the public, 35 percent of the community leaders, and 20 percent of the legal elites agreed; 53 percent of the public, 35 percent of the community leaders, and 20 percent of the legal elites agreed that "pornographic films can easily lead unbalanced people to commit violent sex crimes." Only 38 percent of the public but 43 percent of the community leaders and 56 percent of the legal elites agreed to this statement: "When it comes to pornographic films about sex, people should be allowed to see anything they want to, no matter how 'filthy' it is."

65. "Opinion Roundup," p. 31.

66. *Time*/Yankelovich Clancy Shulman, July 7–9, 1986, in "Opinion Roundup," p. 31.

67. Derived from raw data in James A. Davis and Tom W. Smith, *General Social Surveys, 1972–1982: Cumulative Codebook* (Chicago: National Opinion Research Center, July 1982).

68. Both the 1970 pornography commission report and a 1985 Canadian survey found that adolescents were more often exposed to pornography than adults. Attorney General's Commission on Pornography, *Final Report*, vol. 1, pp. 916 and 921.

69. "Opinion Roundup," p. 33.

70. *The Gallup Poll (Public Opinion 1976–1977)*, vol. 2 (Wilmington, Dela.: Scholarly Resources, 1978), p. 1029.

71. "Opinion Roundup," p. 33.

72. Marc B. Glassman, "Community Standards of Patent Offensiveness: Public Opinion Data and Obscenity Law," *Public Opinion Quarterly* 42 (Summer 1978):168.

73. Barry Sussman, "With Pornography, It All Depends on Who's Doing the Looking," *Washington Post National Weekly Edition*, March 24, 1986, p. 37.

74. *The Gallup Poll (Public Opinion 1976–1977)*, vol. 2, p. 1029.

75. McClosky and Brill, *Dimensions of Tolerance*, p. 210.

76. "Opinion Roundup," p. 32.

Chapter 3

1. For example, see Ramsey Clark, *Crime in America* (New York: Simon and Schuster, 1970).

2. See Edward C. Banfield, *The Unheavenly City Revisited* (Boston: Little, Brown, 1974).

3. Saleem A. Shah and Loren H. Roth, "Biological and Psychophysiological Factors in Criminality," in Daniel Glaser, ed., *Handbook of Criminology* (Chicago: Rand McNally, 1974), pp. 101–173.

4. President's Commission on Law Enforcement and the Administration of Justice, *The Challenge of Crime in a Free Society* (Washington, D.C.: U.S. Government Printing Office, 1967), pp. 147–157.

5. Clark, *Crime in America*, p. 38.

6. U.S. Department of Justice, *Report to the Nation on Crime and Justice* (Washington, D.C.: U.S. Government Printing Office, October 1983), p. 5.

7. See George Thomas Kuran, *The Book of World Rankings* (New York: Facts on File, 1979), pp. 337–345.

8. U.S. Dept. of Justice, *Report to the Nation on Crime and Justice*, p. 7.

9. President's Commission, *Challenge of Crime in a Free Society*, p. 4.

10. Ibid., pp. 50–51.

11. James Q. Wilson, *Thinking About Crime* (New York: Basic Books, 1975), p. 25.

12. Stephanie Riger, "On Women," in Dan A. Lewis, ed., *Reactions to Crime* (Beverly Hills, Calif.: Sage, 1981), pp. 49–52.

13. *The Gallup Report*, nos. 232-233 (January-February 1985):3.

14. Ibid.

15. John Galloway, *Criminal Justice and the Burger Court* (New York: Facts on File, 1978), p. 43.

16. Ibid., p. 12.

17. Wilson, *Thinking About Crime*, p. xii.

18. Interview with Attorney General Edwin Meese in "Reagan Seeks Judges with Traditional Approach," *U.S. News and World Report*, October 14, 1985, p. 67.

19. Stuart A. Scheingold, *The Politics of Law and Order* (New York: Longman, 1984), p. 151.

20. Ibid.

21. Ibid., p. 154.

22. Ibid., p. 155.

23. Roland K. L. Collins, "Reliance on State Constitutions: Some Random Thoughts," in Bradley D. McGraw, ed., *Developments in State Constitutional Law* (St. Paul, Minn.: West, 1985), p. 17.

24. Ibid., p. 2.

25. See, for example, Charles H. Sheldon, "Judicial Review and the Supreme Court of Washington, 1890–1986" (Unpublished manuscript); Donald E. Wilkes, Jr., "State Constitutionalism After Warren: Avoiding the Potomac's Ebb and Flow," in McGraw, ed., *Developments in State Constitutional Law*.

26. Collins, "Reliance on State Constitutions," p. 17.

27. Wilkes, "State Constitutionalism After Warren," p. 167.

28. Both cases are discussed in Sheldon, "Judicial Review and the Supreme Court of Washington," p. 22.

29. Galloway, *Criminal Justice and the Burger Court*, p. 6.

30. C. Herman Pritchett, *The American Constitution*, 3rd ed. (New York: McGraw-Hill, 1977), p. 481.

31. Ibid.

32. Ibid.

33. Michael Engel, *State and Local Politics* (New York: St. Martin's Press, 1985), p. 154.

34. Francis T. Cullen, Timothy S. Bynum, Kim Montgomery Garrett, and Jack R. Greene, "Legislator Ideology and Criminal Justice Policy: Implications from Illinois," in Erika S. Fairchild and Vincent J. Webb, eds., *The Politics of Crime and Criminal Justice* (Beverly Hills, Calif.: Sage, 1985), p. 69.

35. Herbert Jacob, *The Frustration of Policy: Responses to Crime by American Cities* (Boston: Little, Brown, 1984), p. 1.

36. Ann Heinz, Herbert Jacob, and Robert L. Lineberry, eds., *Crime in City Politics* (New York: Longman, 1983), p. 282.

37. Scheingold, *The Politics of Law and Order*, p. 139.

38. Ibid., p. 140.

39. Jacob, *The Frustration of Policy*, p. 5.

40. This categorization is from Charles A. Johnson and Bradley C. Canon, *Judicial Policies: Implementation and Impact* (Washington, D.C.: Congressional Quarterly, 1984), p. 164.

41. This tripartite division of labor is taken from Scheingold, *The Politics of Law and Order*, pp. 228–229.

42. Ibid., p. 180.

43. Martin A. Levin, *Urban Politics and the Criminal Courts* (Chicago: University of Chicago Press, 1977), pp. 5–6.

44. Research on local police departments is reported in Neal Milner, *The Court and Local Law Enforcement* (Beverly Hills, Calif.: Sage, 1971); Stephen Wasby, *Small Town Police and the Supreme Court: Hearing the Word* (Lexington, Mass.: Lexington Books, 1976).

45. Johnson and Canon, *Judicial Policies*, p. 168.

46. Robert R. Mayer, *Social Science and Institutional Change* (New Brunswick, N.J.: Transaction Books, 1982), p. 104.

47. L. Harmon Zeigler and G. Wayne Peak, *Interest Groups in American Society*, 2nd ed. (Englewood Cliffs, N.J.: Prentice-Hall, 1972), p. 197.

48. Ruth Marcus, "House Would Widen Use of Ill-Gotten Evidence," *Washington Post*, September 17, 1986, p. A16.

49. Albert P. Melone, "Criminal Code Reform and the Interest Group Politics of the American Bar Association," in Fairchild and Webb, *The Politics of Crime and Criminal Justice*, p. 38.

50. Aaron Epstein, "Burger Court Has Eased Limits on Search and Seizure," *Detroit Free Press*, June 8, 1986, p. 6B.

51. Carol S. Greenwald, *Group Power: Lobbying and Public Policy* (New York: Praeger, 1977), p. 289.

52. James D. Calder, "Presidents and Crime Control: Kennedy, Johnson and Nixon and the Influence of Ideology," *Presidential Studies Quarterly* 12 (Fall 1982):574–589.

53. Quoted in Scheingold, *The Politics of Law and Order*, p. 63. See Herbert L. Packer, *The Limits of the Criminal Sanction* (Stanford, Calif.: Stanford University Press, 1968), p. 153.

54. Scheingold, *The Politics of Law and Order*, p. 63.

55. Calder, "Presidents and Crime Control," p. 576.

56. Ibid., p. 577.

57. Ibid., p. 580.

58. Ibid., p. 581.

59. Richard M. Nixon, *Public Papers of the President of the United States* (Washington, D.C.: U.S. Government Printing Office, 1968), p. 728.

60. Ibid., p. 781.

61. Gerald R. Ford, *Public Papers of the President of the United States* (Washington, D.C.: U.S. Government Printing Office, 1975), p. 839.

62. Ibid., p. 840.

63. Ibid., p. 842.

64. Ibid., pp. 845–846.

65. Jimmy Carter, *Public Papers of the President of the United States* (Washington, D.C.: U.S. Government Printing Office, 1978), p. 839.

66. Ibid.

67. Statement by Stephen Trott, head of the Justice Department's Criminal Division; quoted in "Justice Under Reagan," *U.S. News and World Report*, October 14, 1985, p. 59.

68. Bertram Gross, "Reagan's Criminal 'Anti-crime' Fix," in Alan Gartner, Colin Geer, and Frank Riessman, eds., *What Reagan Is Doing to Us* (New York: Harper and Row, 1982), pp. 87–88.

69. Data supplied to the authors by the U.S. Bureau of Prisons, Administrative Office of the United States Courts, Washington, D.C., 1985.

70. Reagan, *Public Papers of the President*, pp. 401–402.

71. Joel Brinkely, "U.S. Panel Urges Testing Workers for Use of Drugs," *New York Times*, May 3, 1986, pp. 1, 3.

72. Joseph F. Sheley, *America's "Crime Problem": An Introduction to Criminology* (Belmont, Calif.: Wadsworth, 1985), p. 33.

73. Michael D. Reagan and John G. Sanzone, *The New Federalism*, 2nd ed. (New York: Oxford University Press, 1981), p. 130.

74. Ibid.

75. Scheingold, *The Politics of Law and Order*, p. 84.

76. Ibid, p. 85.

77. Twentieth Century Fund Task Force on the Law Enforcement Assistance Administration, *Law Enforcement: The Federal Role* (New York: McGraw-Hill, 1976), p. 40.

78. Malcolm M. Feeley and Austin D. Sarat, *The Policy Dilemma: Federal Crime Policy and the Law Enforcement Assistance Administration, 1968–1978* (Minneapolis: University of Minnesota Press, 1980), p. 40.

79. Ibid., p. 43.

80. Ibid., p. 41.

81. Ibid,. p. 44.

82. Ibid., p. 45.

83. Twentieth Century Fund, *Law Enforcement*, p. 4.

84. Feeley and Sarat, *The Policy Dilemma*, p. 50.

85. Twentieth Century Fund, *Law Enforcement*, pp. 28–29.

86. Ibid., p. 30.

87. Malcolm M. Feeley, *Court Reform on Trial: Why Simple Solutions Fail* (New York: Basic Books, 1983), p. 220.

88. Twentieth Century Fund, *Law Enforcement*, p. 31.

89. Feeley and Sarat, *The Policy Dilemma*, p. 58.

90. Ibid.

91. Quoted in Twentieth Century Fund, *Law Enforcement*, p. 32.

92. Ibid., p. 33.

93. "Meese Backs Reversal of Landmark Ruling," *The Spokesman Review* (January 22, 1987):A3.

Chapter 4

1. Robert J. Spitzer, *The Presidency and Public Policy: The Four Arenas of Presidential Power* (University: University of Alabama Press, 1983), pp. 172–173, fn. 5. I posit a refinement of Lowi's scheme by dividing each arena into "pure" and "mixed" types; see my "Promoting Policy Theory: Refining the Arenas of Power," *Policy Studies Journal* (June 1987):675–689.

2. Merrill Jensen, *The New Nation* (New York: Random House, 1962), p. 29.

3. Clinton Rossiter, *Seedtime of the Republic* (New York: Harcourt, Brace and World, 1953), p. 387.

4. Bernard Bailyn, *The Ideological Origins of the American Revolution* (Cambridge, Mass.: Belknap Press, 1967), p. 119.

5. Peter B. Feller and Karl L. Gotting, "The Second Amendment: A Second Look," *Northwestern University Law Review* 61 (March-April 1966):51.

6. John Levin, "The Right to Bear Arms: The Development of the American Experience," *Chicago Kent Law Review* 48 (Fall-Winter 1971):155.

7. Harold W. Chase and Craig R. Ducat, eds., *Corwin's The Constitution and What It Means Today* (Princeton, N.J.: Princeton University Press, 1973), p. 87.

8. Irving Brant, *The Bill of Rights: Its Origin and Meaning* (Indianapolis, Ind.: Bobbs-Merrill, 1965), pp. 486–487.

9. Legislative Reference Service, *The Second Amendment as a Limitation on Federal Firearms Legislation* (Washington, D.C.: Library of Congress, 1968), p. 6.

10. Ibid., pp. 6–7.

11. John K. Mahon, *The American Militia, Decade of Decisions, 1789–1800,* University of Florida Monographs, Social Science, no. 6 (Gainesville: University of Florida Press, 1960), pp. 20–21.

12. For examples, see Howard I. Bass, "Quilici v. Village of Morton Grove: Ammunition for a National Handgun Ban," *DePaul Law Review* 32 (Winter 1983):371–398; Lucilius A. Emery, "The Constitutional Right to Keep and Bear Arms," *Harvard Law Review* 28 (1914–1915):473–477; Eric S. Freibrun, "Banning Handguns: Quilici v. Village of Morton Grove and the Second Amendment," *Washington University Law Quarterly* 60 (Fall 1982):1087–1118; Ralph J. Rohner, "The Right to Bear Arms: A Phenomenon of Constitutional History," *Catholic University Law Review* 16 (September 1966):53–80; Roy G. Weatherup, "Standing Armies and Armed Citizens," *Hastings Constitutional Law Quarterly* 2 (1975):961–1001. For lower federal court rulings, see *American Law Reports, Federal* 37 (Rochester, N.Y.: The Lawyer's Co-Operative Publishing Company, 1978), pp. 706–707.

13. For examples, see David I. Caplan, "Restoring the Balance: The Second Amendment Revisited," *Fordham Urban Law Journal* 5 (Fall 1976):31–53; David T. Hardy and John Stompoly, "Of Arms and the Law," *Chicago Kent Law Review* 51 (Summer 1974):62–114.

14. John Crewdson, "Hard-line Opponent of Gun Laws Wins New Term at Helm," *New York Times*, May 4, 1981, p. B11.

15. Walter Isaacson, "Leading the Call to Arms," *Time*, April 20, 1981, p. 27.

16. Howard Kohn, "Inside the Gun Lobby," *Rolling Stone*, May 14, 1981, p.21.

17. Bill Keller, "Powerful Reputation Makes National Rifle Association a Top Gun in Washington," *Congressional Quarterly Weekly Report* (May 9, 1981):799.

18. Ibid., p. 800.

19. Ibid., p. 799.

20. "Firing Blanks," *Congressional Quarterly Weekly Report* (August 27, 1983):1232.

21. The NRA spent $1,037,175 for this purpose according to data supplied this author by the Federal Election Commission.

22. Ted Gest, "Battle over Gun Control Heats Up Across U.S.," *U.S. News and World Report*, May 31, 1982, p. 35.

23. Kohn, "Inside the Gun Lobby," p. 20.

24. "NRA, Liquor Industry Seek to Save BATF," *Congressional Quarterly Weekly Report* (April 3, 1982):730.

25. Kohn, "Inside the Gun Lobby," p. 20.

26. Julia Malone, "PAC-ing a Powerful Punch in November Elections," *Christian Science Monitor*, October 5, 1982, p. 12.

27. Michael Barone and Grant Ujifusa, *The Almanac of American Politics, 1984* (Washington, D.C.: National Journal, 1984), pp. 1341–1342.

28. *Common Cause News*, August 10, 1985.

29. Kohn, "Inside the Gun Lobby," p. 24.

30. *National Journal* (December 11, 1982):2148.

31. Malone, "PAC-ing a Powerful Punch in November Elections," p. 12.

32. For a survey of various gun groups, see Keller, "Powerful Reputation Makes National Rifle Association a Top Gun in Washington."

33. Isaacson, "Leading the Call to Arms," p. 27.

34. See, for example, Alan M. Gottlieb, *The Rights of Gun Owners* (Ottawa, Ill.: Green Hill Publishers, 1981).

35. "The Rhetoric of the NRA," *Vital Speeches of the Day* (October 1, 1983):758–761.

36. On June 3, 1982, the NRA ran a full page ad in the *New York Times* in the aftermath of the imposition of martial law in Poland. After noting that all firearms in Poland had been confiscated under the communist regime, the ad observed that

"so long as the Second Amendment is not infringed, what is happening in Poland can never happen in these United States."

37. U.S. Senate, Committee on the Judiciary, Subcommittee on the Constitution, *The Right to Keep and Bear Arms* (Washington, D.C.: U.S. Government Printing Office, 1982). The quoted materials to follow are found on page 14.

38. Robert Currin, "Is the NRA in Trouble?" *New York Times*, October 11, 1982.

39. Ibid., p. 24.

40. Tom Goldstein, "Straight Talk About Handguns," *Rolling Stone*, October 28, 1982, p. 23.

41. Walter Isaacson, "The Dual over Gun Control," *Time*, March 23, 1981, p. 33.

42. Gest, "Battle over Gun Control Heats Up Across U.S.," p. 35.

43. Richard Hofstadter, "America as a Gun Culture," *American Heritage* (October 1970):4.

44. "Whether It Sharply Reduces Crime or Not, Is a Federal Ban Worth Trying?" *New York Times*, April 5, 1981.

45. "Handgun Facts," Handgun Control, Inc., flyer.

46. See Library of Congress, *Gun Control Laws in Foreign Countries* (Washington, D.C.: Law Library, Library of Congress, 1981).

47. James D. Wright, Peter H. Rossi, and Kathleen Daly, *Under the Gun: Weapons, Crime, and Violence in America* (New York: Aldine, 1983), p. 221.

48. Ibid. Also see Hazel Erskine, "The Polls: Gun Control," *Public Opinion Quarterly* 36 (Fall 1972):455–469.

49. *The Gallup Report*, no. 215 (August 1983):3–4.

50. NORC, *General Social Surveys* (July 1982):87. The question was, "Would you favor or oppose a law which would require a person to obtain a police permit before he or she could buy a gun?"

51. Howard Schuman and Stanley Presser, "The Attitude-Action Connection and the Issue of Gun Control," in Philip J. Cook, ed., "Gun Control," *The Annals of the American Academy of Political and Social Science* (1981):40–47.

52. *The Gallup Report*, no. 215 (August 1983):3, and no. 237 (June 1985):17.

53. Wright, Rossi, and Daly, *Under the Gun*, p. 221.

54. *The Gallup Report*, no. 232-233 (January-February 1985):12–14.

55. *The Gallup Report*, no. 215 (August 1983):10, and no. 237 (June 1985):18.

56. Martin Rywell, *The Gun that Shaped American Destiny* (Harriman, Tenn.: Pioneer Press, 1957).

57. James Wycoff, *Famous Guns that Won the West* (New York: Arco, 1968), pp. 5–6. Also see Harold F. Williamson, *Winchester: The Gun that Won the West* (Washington, D.C.: Combat Forces Press, 1952).

58. Bob Nichols, "Should a Boy Have a Gun?" *Parents' Magazine* (October 1934):26, 77.

59. David Lester, *Gun Control: Issues and Answers* (Springfield, Ill.: Charles C. Thomas, 1984), pp. 98–99, 104. Also see David Lester, "Which States Have Stricter Handgun Control Statutes?" *Psychological Reports* 57 (August 1985):170.

60. "Kill the 'Cop-Killer' Bullets," *New York Times*, August 29, 1983.

61. "One Way to Stop the Teflon Bullet," *Newsday*, February 5, 1982.

62. See the NRA pamphlet, "The KTW Issue: A Media Made Hoax."

63. These cases are documented in the NCBH flyer, "Armor-Piercing Bullets Fact Sheet."

64. "Ban the Bad Bullets," *New York Times*, February 1, 1984.

65. Stephen Kleege, "Brookhaven Eyes Bullet Ban," *New York Times*, August 15, 1982, pp. 4–5.

66. "Bills on Bullets, 'Designer Drugs' Advance," *Congressional Quarterly Weekly Report* (December 28, 1985):2755.

67. Lee Kennett and James L. Anderson, *The Gun in America* (Westport, Conn.: Greenwood Press, 1975), pp. 197, 204, 211, 227, 238, 243.

68. Steven R. Weisman, "Reagan Tells of Initial Pain and Panic After Being Shot," *New York Times*, April 23, 1981.

69. All references to party platforms are drawn from copies supplied by the national committees.

70. Steven V. Roberts, "Rifle Group Viewed as Key to Gun Law," *New York Times*, April 5, 1981.

71. This pattern as predicted by Lowi's scheme is observed for the Omnibus Act in Spitzer, *The Presidency and Public Policy*, pp. 65–70.

72. "Gun Controls Extended to Long Guns, Ammunition," *Congressional Quarterly Almanac 1968* (Washington, D.C.: Congressional Quarterly, 1969), p. 552. The discussion to follow is based on pp. 555–556, 558, 560.

73. Ibid., p. 558.

74. Ibid., p. 560.

75. "Equalization Tax, Ammunition," *Congressional Quarterly Almanac 1969* (Washington, D.C.: Congressional Quarterly, 1970), pp. 334–336.

76. "Federal Gun Law," *Congressional Quarterly Almanac 1985* (Washington, D.C.: Congressional Quarterly, 1986), pp. 228–230.

77. Also see John Herbers, "Police Groups Reverse Stand and Back Controls on Pistols," *New York Times*, January 31, 1986; Richard Corrigan, "NRA, Using Members, Ads and Money, Hits Police Line in Lobbying Drive," *National Journal* (January 1, 1986):8–14; Howard Kurtz, "NRA Urging Repeal of Ban on Sale of New Machine Guns," *Washington Post*, August 28, 1986.

78. "NRA, Police Organizations in Tug of War on Gun Bills," *Congressional Quarterly Weekly Report* (March 1, 1986):502–504.

79. Ibid.; "House Committee Votes 35–0 for Controversial Gun Bill," *Congressional Quarterly Weekly Report* (March 15, 1986):598.

80. Linda Greenhouse, "House Passes Bill Easing Controls on Sale of Guns," *New York Times*, April 11, 1986.

81. "House Votes to Weaken U.S. Gun Control Law," *Congressional Quarterly Weekly Report* (April 12, 1986):783.

82. *U.S. Government Manual, 1983/84* (Washington, D.C.: U.S. Government Printing Office, 1983), pp. 437–438; *Federal Regulatory Directory, 1981–82* (Washington, D.C.: Congressional Quarterly Press, 1981), pp. 753–755.

83. "Gun Controls Extended to Long Guns, Ammunition," p. 552.

84. "U.S. Aides Find Gun Smuggling Is a Low Priority," *New York Times*, September 26, 1985.

85. Keller, "Powerful Reputation Makes National Rifle Association a Top Gun in Washington," p. 801.

86. Mary McGrory, "Pity the Poor, Suffering Gun Owners," *Ithaca Journal*, July 15, 1985.

87. "The Convertible Submachine Gun Boondoggle," *New York Times*, June 15, 1985.

88. Keller, "Powerful Reputation Makes National Rifle Association a Top Gun in Washington," p. 801.

89. "2 Regulatory Units Facing Budget Cuts," *New York Times*, February 14, 1981, p. 9; also see Phil Gailey, "White House Planning to Kill Firearms Enforcement Unit," *New York Times*, September 9, 1981, p. 1.

90. " . . . Any Gun You Want," *New York Times*, October 7, 1981, p. 26.

91. "Treasury, Postal Funds in Continuing Measure," *Congressional Quarterly Almanac 1982* (Washington, D.C.: Congressional Quarterly, 1983), p. 273.

92. Brant, *The Bill of Rights*, p. 486.

93. Robert A. Rutland, *The Birth of the Bill of Rights* (Chapel Hill: University of North Carolina Press, 1955), p. 229.

94. J. W. Peltason, *Corwin and Pelaton's Understanding the Constitution* (Hinsdale, Ill.: Dryden Press, 1976), p. 144.

95. National Commission on the Causes and Prevention of Violence, *Firearms and Violence in American Life* (Washington, D.C.: U.S. Government Printing Office, 1969), pp. 260–262. For a listing of the thirty-five state constitutions that make some mention of a right to bear arms, see Robert Dowlut, "The Right to Bear Arms: Does the Constitution or the Predilection of Judges Reign?" *Oklahoma Law Review* 36 (Winter 1983):102–105.

96. In *Robertson* the Court said that "the right of the people to keep and bear arms (article 2) is not infringed by laws prohibiting the carrying of concealed weapons."

97. Freiburn, "Banning Handguns," pp. 1102–1111; Bass, "Quilici v. Village of Morton Grove," p. 382.

98. Stuart Speiser, *Lawsuit* (New York: Horizon, 1980).

99. Donald E. Santarelli and Nicholas E. Calio, *Turning the Gun on Tort Law* (Washington, D.C.: Washington Legal Foundation, 1982); Richard Starnes, "The Handgun-Banners' Next Ploy," *Outdoor Life* (March 1983):54–57.

100. Elaine F. Weiss, "Guns in the Courts," *Atlantic* (May 1983):8–16. Also see "Pistol Liability Is Issue at Trial," *New York Times*, January 8, 1984.

101. Tom Stuckey, "Gun Foes Applaud Liability Ruling," *Cortland Standard*, October 4, 1985.

102. "Plastic Guns Defy Detectors, May Be on Market Soon Unless Ban Enacted," *Syracuse Post Standard*, April 9, 1986; "Ban on Plastic Guns Proposed by Lawmakers," *New York Times*, May 5, 1986.

Chapter 5

1. U.S. Commission on Civil Rights, "Affirmative Action in the 1980s: Dismantling the Process of Discrimination," (Washington, D.C.: U.S. Commission on Civil Rights, 1981), pp. 3–5.

2. See Morris Abram, "Affirmative Action: Fair Shakers and Social Engineers," *Harvard Law Review* 99 (1986):1312–1326.

3. They were Alaska, California, Colorado, Connecticut, Delaware, Hawaii, Idaho, Illinois, Indiana, Iowa, Kansas, Massachusetts, Michigan, Missouri, New Jersey, New Mexico, New York, Ohio, Oregon, Pennsylvania, Rhode Island, Vermont, Washington, and Wisconsin. Bureau of National Affairs, *State Fair Employment Laws and Their Administration* (Washington, D.C.: BNA, 1964), p. ii.

4. Congressional Quarterly, *Congress and the Nation*, vol. 1 (Washington, D.C.: Congressional Quarterly, 1964), p. 1634.

5. Ibid., p. 1629.

6. Ibid., p. 1610.

7. Ibid., p. 1635.

8. See, generally, Charles and Barbara Whalen, *The Longest Debate: A Legislative History of the 1964 Civil Rights Act* (New York: New American Library, 1985), especially Chapter 3.

9. Congressional Quarterly, *Congress and the Nation*, vol. 1, pp. 93a, 96a, and 1637.

10. See Gary Bryner, "Congress, Courts, and Agencies: Equal Employment and the Limits of Policy Implementation," *Political Science Quarterly* 96 (1981):411–430.

11. Congressional Quarterly, *Congress and the Nation*, vol. 2 (Washington, D.C.: Congressional Quarterly, 1969), p. 174.

12. Congressional Quarterly, *Congress and the Nation*, vol. 3 (Washington, D.C.: Congressional Quarterly, 1973), p. 6A.

13. Ibid., p. 500.

14. Ibid., p. 28a.

15. Ibid., p. 503.

16. Quoted in *Washington v. Davis*, 426 U.S. 229 (1976).

17. 29 C.F.R. section 1607, 1970.

18. 43 *Fed. Reg.* 38291, 1978. See cases cited in Joel William Friedman and George H. Strickler, Jr., *The Law of Employment Discrimination* (Mineola, N.Y.: Foundation Press, 1983), p. 96.

19. *Congressional Record* 110 (1964):8921.

20. Congressional Quarterly, *Congress and the Nation*, vol. 3, pp. 250–251.

21. But the Court shifted its position somewhat by finding that cases of employment discrimination brought under the Fifth Amendment required a stricter test of an intent to discrimination. See *Washington v. Davis*, 426 U.S. 229 (1976), a case brought by blacks who challenged the use of a written personnel test by a police department in selecting applicants for its officer training program; the Court upheld the use of the test even though it served to exclude a disproportionately high percentage of black applicants. This decision seems more in line with the school desegregation rulings in *Swann v. Charlotte-Mecklenburg*, 402 U.S. 1 (1971), and *Milliken v. Bradley* 411 U.S. 717 (1974), which emphasized the demonstration of discriminatory intent.

22. U.S. Senate, Committee on Labor and Human Resources, "Committee Analysis of Executive Order 12246," 97th Cong. (Washington, D.C.: U.S. Government Printing Office, 1982).

23. E.O. 9664, 3 C.F.R. 1943; E.O. 10210, 3 C.F.R. 1949; and E.O. 10308, 3 C.F.R. 1949.

24. E.O. 10479, 3 C.F.R. 1953; E.O. 10577, 3 C.F.R. 1954.

25. U.S. Senate, Committee on Labor and Human Resources, "Committee Analysis of Executive Order 12246," p. 9.

26. 3 C.F.R. 1963.

27. *Contractors Association of Eastern Pennsylvania v. Secretary of Labor*, 442 F. 2d 159, 3rd cir. (1971), cert. denied, 404 U.S. 854.

28. *New York Times*, December 21, 1969, p. 39.

29. Congressional Quarterly, *Congress and the Nation*, vol. 3, p. 498.

30. Ibid., pp. 498, 711.

31. Dom Donafede, "Blacks Await Performance of Promise," *National Journal* (November 30, 1974):1810.

32. See James W. Singer, "A Shake-up May Be in Store for Job Discrimination Efforts," *National Journal* (May 14, 1977):746–747; Bryner, "Congress, Courts, and Agencies," p. 417.

33. Michael J. Malbin, "Reagan's Platform: One He Can Run on in Wooing Democrats and Independents," *National Journal* (July 26, 1980):1221.

34. Dick Kirsten, "The Issue of Race," *National Journal* (January 23, 1982):164.

35. Timothy B. Clark, "Affirmative Action May Fall Victim to Reagan's Regulatory Reform Drive," *National Journal* (July 11, 1981):1248–1252.

36. Donna St. George, "Administration May Have to Shelve Its Relaxed Minority Hiring Rules," *National Journal* (October 22, 1986):2170–2173.

37. See Dan Fagin, "In Winning His Battle for Rights Commission, Did Reagan Lose the War?" *National Journal* (December 17, 1983):2622–2626.

38. Eric Press and Ann McDaniel, "A Right Turn on Race?" *Newsweek*, June 25, 1984, pp. 29–31.

39. George C. Eads, and Michael Fix, *Relief or Reform? Reagan's Regulatory Dilemma* (Washington, D.C.: Urban Institute, 1984).

40. Clark, "Affirmative Action May Fall Victim to Reagan's Regulatory Reform Drive," pp. 1248–1252.

41. St. George, "Administration May Have to Shelve Its Relaxed Minority Hiring Rules," pp. 2170–2173.

42. E.O. 11375, 32 *Fed. Reg.* 14303.

43. U.S. Senate, Committee on Labor and Human Resources, "Committee Analysis of Executive Order 12246," p. 12.

44. 33 *Fed. Reg.* 7804.

45. 41 C.F.R. sec. 60-2.10, 1970.

46. Ibid.

47. U.S. Senate, Committee on Labor and Human Resources, "Committee Analysis of Executive Order 12246," p. 17.

48. Ibid.

49. U.S. Civil Rights Commission, "Affirmative Action in the 1980s," p. 2.

50. Ibid., p. 17.

51. U.S. Senate, Committee on Labor and Human Resources, "Committee Analysis of Executive Order 12246," p. 16.

52. Congressional Quarterly, *Congress and the Nation*, vol. 2, p. 374.

53. Congressional Quarterly, *Federal Regulatory Directory*, 5th ed. (Washington, D.C.: Congressional Quarterly, 1986), pp. 149–150.

54. Kenneth B. Noble, "U.S. Labor Quits in Protest over Job Rights," *New York Times*, January 21, 1987, pp. 1, 9.

55. See Rochelle L. Stanfield, "The Black-Jewish Coalition—Shaken but Still Alive After Young Incident," *National Journal* (November 3, 1979):1849–1852.

56. Quoted in Fred Barbash and Kathy Sawyer, "A New Era of 'Race Neutrality' in Hiring?" *Washington Post National Weekly Edition*, June 25, 1984, p. 32.

57. Quoted in Herman Schwartz, "Affirmative Action," in Leslie Dunbar, ed., *Minority Report* (New York: Pantheon, 1984), p. 63.

58. Quoted in Carl Cohen, "The DeFunis Case, Race, and the Constitution," *Nation* (February 8, 1975):135–145.

59. Thomas Sowell, *The Economics and Politics of Race* (New York: Morrow, 1983).

60. See Randall Kennedy, "Persuasion and Distrust: A Comment on the Affirmative Action Debate," *Harvard Law Review* 99 (1986):1327–1346.

61. U.S. Civil Rights Commission, "Affirmative Action in the 1980s," p. 36.

62. *Statistical Abstract of the United States* (Washington, D.C.: U.S. Department of Commerce, Bureau of the Census, 1962), p. 382, and (1986), pp. 419–420.

63. Tom W. Smith and Paul B. Sheatsley, "American Attitudes Toward Race Relations," *Public Opinion* (October-November 1984):p. 15.

64. *The Gallup Report,* no. 224 (May 1984):29.

65. Seymour Martin Lipset and William Schneider, "The Bakke Case: How Would It Be Decided at the Bar of Public Opinion?" *Public Opinion* 1 (March-April 1978):41–42.

66. Anthony Neely, "Government Role in Rooting Out, Remedying Discrimination Is Shifting," *National Journal* (September 22, 1984):15.

67. Douglas Huron, "It's Fashionable to Denigrate Hiring Quotas—but It's Wrong," *Washington Post National Weekly Edition,* August 27, 1984, p. 23.

Chapter 6

1. See Raymond Tatalovich and Byron W. Daynes, *The Politics of Abortion: A Study of Community Conflict in Public Policymaking* (New York: Praeger, 1981).

2. Cyril C. Means, Jr., "The Phoenix of Abortional Freedom: Is a Penumbral or Ninth Amendment Right About to Arise from the Nineteenth-Century Legislative Ashes of a Fourteenth Century Common Law Liberty?" *New York Law Forum* 17 (1971):335–410.

3. This argument is made by Robert A. Destro, "Abortion and the Constitution: The Need for a Protective Amendment," *University of California Law Review* 63 (September 1975):1268.

4. James C. Mohr, *Abortion in America: The Origins and Evolution of National Policy, 1800–1900* (New York: Oxford University Press, 1978).

5. David W. Louisell and John T. Noonan, Jr., "Constitutional Balance," in John T. Noonan, Jr., ed., *The Morality of Abortion: Legal and Historical Perspectives* (Cambridge, Mass.: Harvard University Press, 1970), p. 225.

6. See Sherri Finkbine, "The Lesser of Two Evils," in Alan F. Guttmacher, ed., *The Case for Legalized Abortion Now* (Berkeley, Calif.: Diablo, 1967), pp. 15–25.

7. See Patricia G. Steinhoff and Milton Diamond, *Abortion Politics: The Hawaii Experience* (Honolulu: University Press of Hawaii, 1977).

8. See Lawrence Lader, *Abortion* (Indianapolis, Ind.: Bobbs-Merrill, 1966), and *Abortion II: Making the Revolution* (Boston: Beacon Press, 1973).

9. Roy Lucas, "Federal Constitutional Limitations on the Enforcement and Administration of State Abortion Statutes," *North Carolina Law Review* 46 (June 1968):753–754.

10. *People v. Belous,* 71 Cal. 2d 954, 458 P. 2d 194 (1969).

11. *United States v. Vuitch,* 305 F. Supp. 1032 (D.D.C. 1969).

12. Lader, *Abortion II,* p. i.

13. Cited in Lauren R. Sass, ed., *Abortion: Freedom of Choice and the Right to Life* (New York: Facts on File, 1978), p. 7.

14. Quoted in Eva R. Rubin, *Abortion, Politics, and the Courts* (Westport, Conn.: Greenwood Press, 1982), p. 88.

15. The seventeen cases decided during 1973–1986 were *Roe v. Wade, District Attorney of Dallas County,* 410 U.S. 113 (1973); *Doe v. Bolton,* 410 U.S. 179 (1973); *Bigelow v. Virginia,* 421 U.S. 809 (1975); *Connecticut v. Menillo,* 423 U.S. 9 (1975); *Planned Parenthood of Central Missouri v. Danforth,* 428 U.S. 52 (1976); *Beal v. Doe,* 432 U.S. 438 (1977); *Maher v. Roe,* 432 U.S. 464 (1977); *Poelker v. Doe,* 432 U.S. 519 (1977); *Colautti v. Franklin,* 439 U.S. 379 (1979); *Bellotti v. Baird,* 443 U.S. 622 (1979); *Harris v. McRae,* 448 U.S. 297 (1980); *Williams v. Zbaraz,* 448 U.S. 358 (1980); *H.L. v. Matheson,* 450 U.S. 398 (1981); *Akron v. Akron Center for Reproductive Health,*

Inc., 103 S.C. 2481 (1983); *Simopoulos v. Virginia,* no. 81-185 (slip)(1983); *Planned Parenthood Association of Kansas City, Missouri v. Ashcroft,* no. 81-1255 (slip)(1983); *Thornburgh v. American College of Obstetricians and Gynecologists,* 106 S.C. 2169 (1986).

16. The excluded case is *Connecticut v. Menillo,* 423 U.S. 9 (1975), a per curiam opinion upholding the conviction of a nonphysician who performed an abortion.

17. Eric M. Uslaner and Ronald E. Weber, "Public Support for Pro-Choice Abortion Policies in the Nation and States: Changes and Stability After the *Roe* and *Doe* Decisions," in Carl E. Schneider and Maris A. Vinovskis, eds., *The Law and Politics of Abortion* (Lexington, Mass.: Lexington Books, 1980), p. 214.

18. The question asked by Harris was, "In general, do you favor or oppose the U.S. Supreme Court decision making abortions up to three months of pregnancy legal?" See Harris Survey News Release (May 26, 1975), (April 18, 1977), (March 6, 1979). The Gallup question was, "The U.S. Supreme Court has ruled that a woman may go to a doctor to end pregnancy at any time during the first three months of pregnancy. Do you favor or oppose this ruling?" See *The Gallup Report,* nos. 244-245 (January-February 1986):17–18.

19. Judith Blake, "The Abortion Decisions: Judicial Review and Public Opinion," in Edward Manier, William Liu, and David Solomon, eds., *Abortion: New Directions for Policy Studies* (Notre Dame, Ind.: University of Notre Dame Press, 1977), p. 62.

20. Cited in Judith Blake, "The Supreme Court's Abortion Decisions and Public Opinion in the United States," *Population and Development Review* 3 (1977):59.

21. Cited in Peter Woll and Robert H. Binstock, *America's Political System,* 4th ed. (New York: Random House, 1984), p. 167.

22. Cited in *Congressional Record,* 98th Cong., 1st sess., June 27, 1983, p. S9154.

23. Cited in Edward Manier, "Abortion and Public Policy in the U.S.: A Dialectical Examination of Expert Opinion," in Manier, Liu, and Solomon, eds., *Abortion: New Directions for Policy Studies,* p. 15.

24. Cited in John Herbers, "Abortion Issue Threatens to Become Profoundly Divisive," *New York Times,* October 14, 1984, p. E3.

25. ACLU, "Abortion: A Fundamental Right Under Attack" (Pamphlet, n.d.).

26. Religious Coalition for Abortion Rights, "Sponsors and Members" (Pamphlet, 1978).

27. Religious Coalition for Abortion Rights, "Religious Freedom and the Abortion Controversy" (Pamphlet, 1978).

28. ACLU, "Abortion: A Fundamental Right Under Attack."

29. National Conference of Catholic Bishops, *Documentation on Abortion and the Right to Life II* (Washington, D.C.: National Conference of Catholic Bishops, n.d.), pp. 46–47, 55–56.

30. Frederick S. Jaffe, Barbara L. Lindheim, and Philip R. Lee, *Abortion Politics: Private Morality and Public Policy* (New York: McGraw-Hill, 1981), p. 79.

31. See Robert J. Spitzer, *The Right to Life Movement and Third Party Politics* (New York: Greenwood, 1987).

32. Quoted in Richard Phillips, "The Shooting War over 'Choice' or 'Life' Is Beginning Again," *Chicago Tribune,* April 20, 1980, section 12, pp. 13–14.

33. Text of debate found in *New York Times,* October 13, 1984, p. 10.

34. Text of debate found in *New York Times,* October 9, 1984, p. 15.

35. Quoted in Michael Coakley, "Archbishop Led Resurrection of Church-State Debate," *Chicago Tribune,* September 30, 1984, p. 6.

36. Quoted in Bruce Buursma, "Bernardin Vows Higher Profile on Local, U.S. Issues," *Chicago Tribune*, December 25, 1983, section 4, p. 1.

37. I commissioned The Roper Center at the University of Connecticut to analyze three questions asked on September 17–20, 1982, as reported in *The Gallup Report*, no. 206 (November 1982):8, 13, 19.

38. *The Gallup Report*, no. 191 (August 1981):46, 48, 50.

39. Peter Skerry, "The Class Conflict over Abortion," *Public Interest* (Summer 1978):70.

40. "Miscellaneous Issues," *Congressional Quarterly Weekly Report* (September 2, 1972):2222.

41. "Democratic Platform: 'A Contract with the People,'" *Congressional Quarterly Almanac 1976* (Washington, D.C.: Congressional Quarterly, 1977), p. 860.

42. "Text of 1976 Republican Platform," in ibid., pp. 907, 909.

43. Quoted in Carl Tucker, "Carter and Abortion," *Saturday Review*, September 17, 1977, p. 64.

44. Quoted in Laura B. Weiss, "1980 Presidential Campaign: Abortion Question Poses Constant Concern," *Congressional Quarterly Weekly Report* (March 15, 1980):734.

45. "1980 Republican Platform Text," *Congressional Quarterly Weekly Report* (July 19, 1980):2034.

46. "1980 Democratic Platform Text," *Congressional Quarterly Weekly Report* (August 16, 1980):2396.

47. "Text of 1984 Democratic Party Platform," *Congressional Quarterly Weekly Report* (July 21, 1984):1767.

48. "Text of 1984 Republican Party Platform," *Congressional Quarterly Weekly Report* (August 25, 1984):2110.

49. Lynn D. Wardle, *Restoring the Constitutional Balance: The Need for a Constitutional Amendment to Reverse Roe v. Wade, Hearings Before the Subcommittee on the Constitution of the Committee on the Judiciary, on S.J. Res. 3*, 98th Cong., 1st sess., February 28 and March 7, 1983, Appendix C, p. 70.

50. Maris A. Vinovskis, "The Politics of Abortion in the House of Representatives in 1976," *Michigan Law Review* 77 (1979):1790–1827.

51. Barbara Bardes and Raymond Tatalovich, "The House of Representatives and Abortion: Changing Patterns of Support Since the *Roe* Decision" (Paper delivered to the Southwest Social Science Association Convention, San Antonio, Texas, 1981).

52. Donald Granberg, "The United States Senate Votes to Uphold *Roe* versus *Wade*," *Population Research and Policy Review* 4 (1985):127.

53. "Hyde Amendment Reviewed: Supreme Court Considering Cases Challenging Congress' Curbs on Abortion Funding," *Congressional Quarterly Weekly Report* (April 19, 1980):1038.

54. Rachel Benson Gold, "Publicly Funded Abortions in FY 1980 and FY 1981," *Family Planning Perspectives* (July-August 1982):204.

55. Ibid.

56. Report by the Comptroller General of the United States, *Restrictions on Abortion and Lobbying Activities in Family Planning Programs Need Clarification* (GAO/ HRD-82-106), September 24, 1982 (Washington, D.C.: U.S. Government Printing Office, 1982).

57. Remarks by Congressman Lawrence J. Hogan, *Congressional Record*, 92nd Cong., 1st sess., June 21, 1973, pp. 20750–20752. Also see "Legal Services Program Transfer Stalled," *Congressional Quarterly Almanac 1973* (Washington, D.C.: Congressional Quarterly, 1974), pp. 581–585.

58. Remarks by Congressman David C. Treen, *Congressional Record,* 95th Cong., 2nd sess., September 6, 1978, pp. 28089–28091, 28096. Also see "Civil Rights Commission," *Congressional Quarterly Almanac 1978* (Washington, D.C.: Congressional Quarterly, 1979), pp. 789–790.

59. Stuart Taylor, Jr., "Foe of Abortion Is Confirmed as Solicitor General," *New York Times,* October 23, 1985, pp. 1, 14.

60. "Harassing Planned Parenthood," *New York Times,* July 31, 1982, p. 26L.

61. Richard J. Meislin, "U.S. Asserts Key to Curbing Births Is a Free Economy," *New York Times,* August 9, 1984, pp. A1, A8.

62. Ibid.

63. U.S. Senate, *Hearings Before the Subcommittee on Constitutional Amendments of the Committee on the Judiciary, on S.J. Res. 6, S.J. Res. 10, 11, S.J. Res. 91,* 94th Cong., 1st sess., 1976, Part IV, p. 250.

64. Alan Guttmacher Institute, *Abortions and the Poor: Private Morality, Public Responsibility* (New York: Alan Guttmacher Institute, 1979), p. 23.

65. Gold, "Publicly Funded Abortions in FY 1980 and FY 1981," p. 206.

66. National Abortion Rights Action League, *Legislative Update* (May 23, 1980).

67. Uslaner and Weber, "Public Support for Pro-Choice Abortion Policies in the Nation and States," pp. 214–219.

68. In 1972, these states were estimated to have a majority opinion favoring legalized abortion: Alaska, California, Colorado, Hawaii, Washington, Nevada, Oregon, Wyoming, Montana, Arizona, New Mexico, New York, Idaho, and New Jersey.

69. They are Alaska, Colorado, Hawaii, Washington, Oregon, New York, and Idaho.

70. They are Nevada, Idaho, and New Jersey.

Conclusion

1. Roger W. Cobb and Charles D. Elder, *Participation in American Politics: The Dynamics of Agenda-Building* (Baltimore, Md.: Johns Hopkins University Press, 1972), p. 183.

2. Mancur Olson, Jr., *The Logic of Collective Action: Public Goods and the Theory of Groups* (Cambridge, Mass.: Harvard University Press, 1965), pp. 160–161.

3. Neil J. Smelser, *Theory of Collective Behavior* (New York: Free Press, 1962), pp. 270 and 109.

4. See William Kornhauser, *The Politics of Mass Society* (Glencoe, Ill.: Free Press, 1959).

5. Richard Hofstadter, "The Pseudo-Conservative Revolt," in Daniel Bell, ed., *The New American Right* (New York: Criterion, 1955).

6. Max Weber, *Economy and Society* (New York: Bedminster, 1968), pp. 302–307, 901–940.

7. Joseph R. Gusfield, *Symbolic Crusade: Status Politics and the American Temperance Movement* (Urbana: University of Illinois Press, 1963).

8. Louis A. Zurcher, Jr., R. George Kirkpatrick, Robert G. Cushing, and Charles K. Bowman, "The Anti-Pornography Campaign: A Symbolic Crusade," *Social Problems* 19 (Fall 1971):236.

9. See Murray Edelman, *The Symbolic Uses of Politics* (Urbana: University of Illinois Press, 1964).

10. Ann L. Page and Donald A. Clelland, "The Kanawha County Textbook Controversy: A Study of the Politics of Life Style Concern," *Social Forces* 57 (September 1978):279.

11. Matthew C. Moen, "School Prayer and the Politics of Life-Style Concern," *Social Science Quarterly* 65 (December 1984):1070.

12. J. Wilbur Scott, "Status Politics and the Equal Rights Amendment: A Struggle over How Women Should Spend Their Days" (Paper delivered to the Southwestern Sociological Association Meeting, San Antonio, Texas, March 1982). He found that individuals who perceived a serious threat to the traditional women's roles as housewife and mother were most likely to oppose the ERA.

13. Eric Hoffer, *The True Believer* (New York: New American Library, 1958).

14. Cited in "A Congressman's Thoughts on the Pro-Life Movement," *Congressional Record*, 96th Cong., 2d sess., June 4, 1980, vol. 126, p. H4514 (daily edition).

15. See James Coleman, *Community Conflict* (Glencoe, Ill.: Free Press, 1957).

16. Smith, *The Comparative Policy Process*, p. 91 (see Note 7 in Introduction).

17. See Glendon Schubert, *Judicial Policy-Making* (Glenview, Ill.: Scott, Foresman and Company, 1965), Chapter 6.

18. Donald L. Horowitz, *The Courts and Social Policy* (Washington, D.C.: The Brookings Institution, 1977), p. 7.

19. Paul Brest, "The Fundamental Rights Controversy: The Essential Contradictions of Normative Constitutional Scholarship," *Yale Law Journal* 90 (1981):1063–1109.

20. John T. Noonan, Jr., "Raw Judicial Power," *National Review* (March 2, 1973):261.

21. See Raoul Berger, *Government by Judiciary: The Transformation of the Fourteenth Amendment* (Cambridge, Mass.: Harvard University Press, 1977).

22. Suppression of unpopular views does not end with the termination of armed hostilities. See Theodore J. Lowi, "Postwar Panic and the Chilling of Dissent," in his *The Politics of Disorder* (New York: Basic Books, 1971), pp. 102–119.

23. See Stuart Taylor, Jr., "Meese and His Candor," *New York Times*, August 3, 1985, p. 7; and "Administration Trolling for Constitutional Debate," *New York Times*, October 28, 1985, p. 10.

24. Walter F. Murphy, *Congress and the Court* (Chicago: University of Chicago Press, 1962), pp. 246–247.

25. See Linda Greenhouse, "Congress Approves Anti-Drug Bill as Senate Bars a Death Provision," *New York Times*, October 18, 1986, pp. 1, 9.

26. Donald R. Matthews and James W. Prothro, "Stateways Versus Folkways: Critical Factors in Southern Reaction to *Brown v. Board of Education*," in Gottfried Dietze, ed., *Essays on the American Constitution* (Englewood Cliffs, N.J.: Prentice-Hall, 1964), pp. 139–158.

27. Warren E. Miller and Donald E. Stokes, "Constituency Influence in Congress," *American Political Science Review* 57 (1963):45–56.

28. Aage R. Clausen, *How Congressmen Decide* (New York: St. Martin's Press, 1973).

29. Abraham H. Maslow, "A Theory of Human Motivation," *Psychological Review* 50 (July 1943):370–396.

30. See the discussion in Gusfield, *Symbolic Crusade*, p. 17.

31. See *The Gallup Report*, no. 219 (December 1983):5. Since 1935, the only social issue to be cited as the "most important problem" was race relations, which occurred in three years.

32. Richard E. Dawson, *Public Opinion and Contemporary Disarray* (New York: Harper and Row, 1973), pp. 7–8.

33. Seymour Martin Lipset, *Political Man: The Social Bases of Politics* (Garden City, N.Y.: Anchor Books, 1963), p. 92. Subsequent research has questioned his

hypothesis that education is the key explanatory variable. See Harry Holloway and John George, *Public Opinion: Coalitions, Elites, and Masses*, 2nd ed. (New York: St. Martin's Press, 1986), pp. 65–73.

34. John L. Sullivan, James Pierson, and George E. Marcus, *Political Tolerance and American Democracy* (Chicago: University of Chicago Press, 1982), p. 792.

35. *Report of the National Advisory Commission on Civil Disorders* (New York: Bantam Books, 1968).

36. Michael Corbett, *Political Tolerance in America: Freedom and Equality in Public Attitudes* (New York: Longman, 1982), p. 84

37. Samuel Stouffer, *Communism, Conformity and Civil Liberties* (New York: Doubleday, 1955).

38. See Clyde A. Nunn, Harry J. Crockett, Jr., and J. Allen Williams, Jr., *Tolerance for Nonconformity: A National Survey of Changing Commitment to Civil Liberties* (San Francisco: Jossey-Bass, 1978).

39. Jeremy Rabkin, "Office for Civil Rights," in James Q. Wilson, ed., *The Politics of Regulation* (New York: Basic Books, 1980), pp. 304–353.

40. See Harold Seidman, *Politics, Position, and Power*, 3rd ed. (New York: Oxford University Press, 1980), Chapter 6.

41. In *United States v. Darby*, 312 U.S. 100 (1941), the Supreme Court upheld the Fair Labor Standards Act of 1938, which prohibited the shipment in interstate commerce of goods produced by employees who were paid less than minimum wage or worked more than maximum hours as defined by that law.

42. For a historical overview, see Richard Hofstadter, *The Age of Reform* (Cambridge, Mass.: Harvard University Press, 1955).

43. Charles S. Bullock, III and Charles M. Lamb, *Implementation of Civil Rights Policy* (Monterey, Calif.: Brooks/Cole Publishing, 1984), p. 3.

ACRONYMS

AAP	affirmative action plan
ABA	American Bar Association
ACLU	American Civil Liberties Union
ALI	American Law Institute
ALL	American Life Lobby
BATF	Bureau of Alcohol, Tobacco, and Firearms
DWI	driving while under the influence
EEO	equal employment opportunity
EEOC	Equal Employment Opportunity Commission
FBI	Federal Bureau of Investigation
FCC	Federal Communications Commission
FEPC	Fair Employment Practices Committee
GAO	General Accounting Office
GOA	Gun Owners of America
HCFA	Health Care Financing Administration
ICC	Interstate Commerce Commission
ILA	Institute for Legislative Action
IRS	Internal Revenue Service
LEAA	Law Enforcement Assistance Administration
LSC	Legal Services Corporation
NAACP	National Association for the Advancement of Colored People
NARAL	National Association for the Repeal of Abortion Laws
	National Abortion Rights Action League
NCBH	National Coalition to Ban Handguns
NCPERL	National Coalition for Public Education and Religious Liberty
NORC	National Opinion Research Center
NOW	National Organization for Women
NRA	National Rifle Association
OEO	Office of Economic Opportunity
OFCC	Office of Federal Contracts Compliance
OFCCP	Office of Federal Contracts Compliance Programs

PAC   Political Action Committee

RCAR   Religious Coalition for Abortion Rights
RTL   Right-to-Life

SES   socioeconomic status
SPA   state planning agency
SRC   Survey Research Center

CASE INDEX

Abington School District v. Schempp, 5–6, 10, 12, 14, 16, 19–20, 28, 34–39

Adams v. Williams, 111, 138–139

Akron v. Akron Center for Reproductive Health, 183

Albemarle v. Moody, 155

American Booksellers Association v. Hudnut, 45–46

Argersinger v. Hamlin, 84

Beck v. McElrath, 21

Beal v. Doe, 183–184, 203

Bellotti v. Baird, 183

Benton v. Maryland, 84

Board of Trustees of Keene State College v. Sweeney, 152

Brown v. Board of Education of Topeka, xviii–xix, 214, 216, 220

Brown v. Texas, 83

Burstyn v. Wilson, 44

Butler v. Michigan, 42

City of Renton v. Playtime Theatres, 69

Coker v. Georgia, 84

Colautti v. Franklin, 183

Collins v. Chandler Unified School District, 20

Commercial Pictures Corp. v. Regents of the University of the State of New York, 44

Connecticut v. Menillo, 185

Cruikshank v. U.S., 118, 137

DeSpain v. Dekalb County Community School District, 20

Doe v. Bolton, 177, 181–182, 186, 215

Dred Scott v. Sandford, 118–119

Duffy v. Las Cruces Public Schools, 21

Eddings v. Oklahoma, 84

Edmund v. Florida, 84

Engel v. Vitale, 5–6, 10, 12, 14, 18–20, 25, 28, 31, 35, 39

Everson v. Board of Education, 13, 16–18, 23

Franks v. Bowman Transportation Co., 155

Fullilove v. Klutznick, 156

Furman v. Georgia, 87–89, 90

Furnco Construction Corp. v. Waters, 152

Gaines v. Anderson, 20–21

Gaston v. U.S., 154

General Electric v. Gilbert, 150–151

Gideon v. Wainwright, 84, 86, 99, 139

Gregg v. Georgia, 80, 84, 87–88

Griggs v. Duke Power, 152–154

Griswold v. Connecticut, 180–181, 215

Harrington v. California, 82

Harris v. McRae, 184, 204

International Association of Firefighters (Local 93) v. City of Cleveland, 156

International Brotherhood of Teamsters v. U.S., 154

Jacobellis v. Ohio, 41, 68

Jenkins v. Georgia, 68

Johnson v. Transportation Agency, 157

Karcher v. May, 39–40
Karen B. v. Treen, 20

Lemon v. Kurtzman, 22
Leon v. U.S., 82, 96
Lewis v. U.S., 118–119, 139

Maher v. Roe, 183–184, 203
Manual Enterprises v. Day, 42
Mapp v. Ohio, 82
McCleskey v. Kemp, 85
McDonnell Douglas Corp. v. Green, 152
Memphis Fire Department v. Stotts, 155
Miller v. California, 43–45, 56, 68
Miller v. Texas, 118, 137
Miller v. U.S., 118–119, 138–139
Minersville School District v. Gobitis, 13–14
Miranda v. Arizona, 83, 85, 94–95, 110
Morton Grove Case. See Quilici v. Village of Morton Grove
Murray v. Curlett, 5, 10, 12, 19, 38

New York v. Ferber, 45–46, 72
New York v. P. J. Video, 44

Oliver, In re, 82

Paradise v. U.S., 157
Paris Adult Theatre I. v. Slaton, 43
People v. Belous, 180–181
Planned Parenthood of Central Missouri v. Danforth, 182
Plessy v. Ferguson, 143–144
Poelker v. Doe, 184
Pope v. Illinois, 44, 68
Powell v. Alabama, 82
Presser v. Illinois, 118, 137

Quilici v. Village of Morton Grove, 124–125, 139–141

Regents of University of California v. Bakke, 156, 167
Regina v. Hicklin, 42, 45
Robertson v. Baldwin, 138
Roe v. Wade, 177–178, 180–182, 185–188, 190, 193, 198–200, 202–203, 206–209, 215, 217
Rogers v. Richmond, 83
Roth v. U.S., 42–43

Sheet Metal Worker's International Association (Local 28) v. EEOC, 156
Silverman v. U.S., 83
Southeastern Promotions, Ltd. v. Conrad, 44
Spano v. New York, 83
Stack v. Boyle, 84
Stanley v. Georgia, 43
State v. Ringer, 86
State v. Sheridan, 86
Stone v. Graham, 20

Texas Department of Community Affairs v. Burdine, 152
Thornburgh v. American College of Obstetricians and Gynecologists, 184–186, 206
Turner v. Fouche, 154

United Jewish Organization v. Carey, 156

Vuitch v. U.S., 181

Wallace v. Jaffree, 5, 10, 12, 14, 21–23, 34, 38–39
Weber v. U.S., 155
Weeks v. U.S., 86
West Virginia State Board of Education v. Barnette, 14
Wolf v. Colorado, 82
Wygant v. Jackson Board of Education, 155

Zorach v. Clauson, 34

GENERAL INDEX

Abortion, 1, 3, 210, and Chapter 6
Affirmative action, 1, 210, and
    Chapter 5
Agnew, Spiro, 51, 55
Alabama Civil Liberties Union, 11
American Association of School
    Administrators, 7
American Association of University
    Women, 179
American Bar Association, 92, 95–96
American Book Publishers Council,
    62, 64
American Booksellers Association, 56,
    62
American Citizens Concerned for Life
    (ACCL), 194
American Civil Liberties Union
    (ACLU), 7, 11, 57, 62–64, 72, 92–
    93, 96–97, 105, 145, 190–191
American Ethical Union, 11
American Federation of Labor/
    Congress of Industrial
    Organizations (AFL-CIO), 115,
    145, 149, 151, 159, 211
American Humanist Association, 11
American Indian Bar Association, 168
American Jewish Committee, 11
American Jewish Congress, 11, 63,
    93, 96–97
American Judicature Society, 93
American Legion, 64–65
American Library Association, 62–65
American Life Lobby (ALL), 194
American Lutheran church, 63–64
American Medical Association (AMA),
    194
American Nurses Association (ANA),
    194
American Parents Committee, 62–63

American Public Health Association,
    191–192
American Veterans Committee, 145
Americans for Democratic Action
    (ADA), 105, 145
Americans for Effective Enforcement.
    See Americans for Effective Law
    Enforcement
Americans for Effective Law
    Enforcement, 93, 96, 98
Americans United for Life, 191–193,
    206
Americans United for Separation of
    Church and State, 7
Anti-Defamation League of B'nai
    B'rith, 6, 11
Association for the Study of Abortion
    (New York), 179
Association of American Publishers,
    62–64
Association of Planned Parenthood
    Physicians, 191
Authors League of America, 62–64

Back to God Movement, 7
Bayh, Birch, 28–29
Bork, Robert, 209
Bureau of Alcohol, Tobacco and
    Firearms (BATF), 131–132, 134–
    136, 141, 221–222, 225
Bureaucracy, 2, 210
    and abortion, 203–207
    and affirmative action, 162–167
    and crime, 106–109
    and gun control, 134–136
    and pornography, 57–61
    and school prayer, 34–35
Bush, George, 127, 195
Business Roundtable, 161

California Committee on Therapeutic
    Abortion (Los Angeles), 179
Carter, Jimmy, 29, 32–33, 52, 95,
    101–102, 128, 160, 165, 197–198
Catholic War Veterans of U.S.A., 64
Catholics for Free Choice, 190
Center for Judicial Studies, 10, 12
Child pornography, 45–46, 50, 53,
    59–61
Christian Action Council, 193
Christian Broadcast Network, 12
Christian Crusade, 193
Christian Legal Society, 10
Christian Voice, 6, 30, 57
Church of Jesus Christ of Latter-day
    Saints. See Mormon church
Church of the Children of the Desert,
    61
Citizens Against Alcohol Related
    Traffic Accidents (CAARTA), 97
Citizens' Commission on Civil Rights,
    162
Citizens Committee for the Right to
    Keep and Bear Arms, 117, 131
Citizens for Decency Through Law,
    61–65
Citizens for Decent Literature. See
    Citizens for Decency Through
    Law
Citizens for Public Prayer, 7
Citizens for Public Reverence, 7
Citizens United for Life, 194
Civil Rights Acts
    1866, 143
    1964, xviii, 144, 146–149, 150–156,
    159, 167, 175, 202, 223
Commission on Law Enforcement and
    the Administration of Justice
    (1965), 104–105
Committee for the Preservation of
    Prayer and Bible Reading in
    Public Schools, 7
Committee for the Study of Handgun
    Misuse, 120
Committee on Constitutional
    Liberties, 63
Committee on Government Contract
    Compliance, 158
Comprehensive Crime Control Act of
    1983, 102
Congress, 2, 210

and abortion, 200–203
and affirmative action, 144–151
and crime, 103–106
and gun control, 128–134
and pornography, 46–49
and school prayer, 25–31
Constitutional Prayer Foundation, 7
Consumer groups, 92–95
Coolidge, Calvin, 126
"Cop-killer" bullets, 125–126
Council for Periodical Distributors
    Association, 62–63
Covenant House, 62–63
Crime, 1, 210, and Chapter 3
    and civil libertarian approach, 74,
    82, 84–86, 103, 109
    and law-and-order approach, 74,
    78–80, 82–86, 89, 109
Criminal process
    crime control model, 98
    due process model, 98

Danbury Baptists Association
    (Connecticut), 16
Death penalty, 79–81, 85, 87–91, 100
Direct Mail Advertising Association,
    64
Dirkson, Everett, 28–29, 32, 146
Doctors and Nurses for Life, 194
Drug Enforcement Administration, 96,
    103

Eisenhower, Dwight David, 127, 158,
    216
Environmental Protection Agency, 2
Episcopal church, 6
Equal Employment Advisory Council,
    161
Equal Employment Opportunity Act
    of 1972, 149–151
Equal Employment Opportunity
    Commission (EEOC), 144, 148–
    150, 153–154, 160–162, 164–166,
    221, 223–224
Equal Rights Amendment, 4, 199, 213
Eradication of Smut, 65
Establishment clause, 15–23
Exclusionary rule, 74, 82, 84, 102

Family Planning Services and
    Population Research Act (1970),
    204

Federal Bureau of Investigation (FBI), 58–59, 61, 96, 221
Federal Communications Commission (FCC), 58, 221
Federal Employment Practices Committee (FEPC), 157
Federalism, 2, 210
and abortion, 207–208
and affirmative action, 143–144
and crime, 86–92
and gun control, 124–126
and pornography, 66–69
and school prayer, 36–39
Federation of Women's Clubs, 65
Feminist Anti-Censorship Task Force (FACT), 65
Feminists for Life, 194
Ferraro, Geraldine, 195, 197, 199
Finkbine, Sherry, 179
Firearm Owners Protection Act (1986), 130–134
Ford, Gerald, 32–33, 52, 100–101, 160, 197
Foundation for Handgun Education, 120
Foundation on Violence in America, 120
Franklin, Benjamin, 33
Fraternal Order of Police, 92, 132
Free exercise clause, 16–19
Freedom Council, 10, 12

Goldwater, Barry, 24, 31, 49, 104
Greek Orthodox church, 6
Gun control, 1, 4, 210–211, and Chapter 4
Gun Control Act (1968), 120, 127–130, 134
Gun Owners of America, 117, 131
Gun Safety Institute, 120

Handgun Control, Inc., 119–121, 131
Hatch, Orrin, 27, 30–31, 118, 131, 202
Health Care Financing Administration (HCFA), 203, 221–222
Hellenic Bar Association of Illinois, 168
Helms, Jesse, 29–31, 202, 213
Hoover, Herbert, 31, 98
Humphrey, Hubert H., 24

Hyde amendment, 184, 190–191, 198–200, 202–204, 207, 209, 222

Interest groups, 2, 210
and abortion, 190–196
and affirmative action, 167–171
and crime, 92–98
and gun control, 113–122
and pornography, 61–66
and school prayer, 6–12
International Association of Chiefs of Police, 92, 102, 105, 125, 131
International Periodical Distributors Association, 62
International Planned Parenthood Federation, 206–207
Interstate Commerce Commission (ICC), 2

Japanese-American Citizens League (JACL), 145
Jefferson, Thomas, 16, 33, 112
Jehovah's Witnesses, 14
Johnson, Lyndon, 24–25, 32–33, 49–50, 99–100, 104–105, 127–129, 141, 146–147, 158–159
Judiciary, 2, 210
and abortion, 180–186
and affirmative action, 151–157
and crime, 81–86
and gun control, 136–141
and pornography, 42–46
and school prayer, 12–23

Kennedy, John F., 25, 31, 33, 49, 98–99, 105, 127, 145–146, 157–158, 216

Law Enforcement Assistance Administration (LEAA), 101, 104, 106–109, 221–222
Lawyers for Life, 192
Leadership Conference on Civil Rights, 145, 151
League of Women Voters, 93, 96
Legal Defense Fund for Unborn Children, 191–193
Legal Foundation of America, 10, 12
Legal Services Corporation (LSC), 102, 205, 222
Liberty Federation, 57

Liberty Foundation, 57
Lincoln, Abraham, 33
Lowi, Theodore J., 1–3, 111, 214,
    216–217, 224, and Foreword

Madison, James, 15–16
Maryland Interfaith Committee for
    School Prayer, 7
McGovern, George, 197
Medical Council on Handgun
    Violence, 120
Meese, Edwin, 53, 83, 102, 110, 132,
    206, 209, 217
Meese commission on pornography.
    See Presidential Commission on
    Obscenity and Pornography
Methodist TV, Radio, and Film
    Committee. See United Methodist
    church, TV, Radio, and Film
    Committee
Methodist Church Board of
    Temperance. See United
    Methodist church, Board of
    Temperance
Metropolitan Committee for Religious
    Liberty, 63
Militia Law of 1792, 113
Missouri Nurses for Life, 192
Mondale, Walter, 128, 195, 199
Moral Majority, 6, 10, 30, 193
Morality in Media, 62–65
Mormon church, 193
Mothers Against Drunk Drivers
    (MADD), 92, 97
Motion Picture Association of
    America, 62

National Abortion Rights Action
    League (NARAL), 180, 190–191,
    194
National Alliance Against Violence,
    120
National Alliance for Handgun
    Control Education, 120
National Association for Repeal of
    Abortion Laws. See National
    Abortion Rights Action League
    (NARAL)
National Association for Humane
    Abortion, 179
National Association for the
    Advancement of Colored People
    (NAACP), 93, 96–97, 121, 145,
    149, 160
National Association of Attorneys
    General, 92, 95, 105
National Association of College
    Stores, 62
National Association of Counties, 105
National Association of Evangelicals,
    6, 10, 64
National Association of Letter
    Carriers, 64
National Catholic Conference for
    Interracial Justice, 145
National Coalition Against Death
    Penalty, 97
National Coalition for Public
    Education and Religious Liberty
    (NCPERL), 7, 11
National Coalition to Ban Handguns
    (NCBH), 114, 120–122, 125, 135
National Committee for Human Life
    Amendment (NCHLA), 193
National Community Relations
    Advisory Council (Jewish). See
    National Jewish Community
    Relations Advisory Council
National Conference of Catholic
    Bishops, 193
National Council of Catholic Men, 64
National Council of the Churches of
    Christ, 6
National Council on Crime and
    Delinquency, 105
National Defense Act (1916), 113
National Education Association
    (NEA), 7
National Emergency Civil Liberties
    Committee, 192
National Firearms Act (1934), 128,
    130, 138
National Governors' Conference, 105
National Institute of Law Enforcement
    and Criminal Justice, 107–108
National Jewish Community Relations
    Advisory Council, 6, 11
National Lawyers Guild, 63
National League of Cities, 105
National Legal Aid and Defender
    Association, 92–93
National Medical Association, 168
National Organization for Women
    (NOW), 57, 151, 191–192, 198

National Organization of Black Law
  Enforcement Executives, 131–132
National Rifle Association (NRA), 111,
  113–122, 125–128, 130–136, 141,
  211–213, 219, 222
  and Firearms Civil Rights Legal
    Defense Fund, 117
  and the Institute for Legislative
    Action, 114–115
National Sheriffs' Association, 92,
  105, 131
National Troopers Association, 132
National Union of Police Officers, 92
National Urban League, 145
National Women's Christian
  Temperance Union, 64–65, 212
National Youth Prolife Coalition, 194
New York City Health and Hospitals
  Corporation, 204
New York State Catholic Welfare
  Committee, 62–63
Nixon, Richard M., 24, 32–33, 43, 48,
  50–52, 55, 57, 99–102, 104, 127,
  149, 159, 165, 197, 203, 205, 217

Obscenity. See Pornography
Office of Child Development, 100
Office of Criminal Justice, 98
Office of Economic Opportunity
  (OEO), 205
Office of Federal Contracts
  Compliance. See Office of Federal
  Contracts Compliance Programs
Office of Federal Contracts
  Compliance Programs (OFCCP),
  150, 153, 160–165, 167, 172, 221,
  223–224
Office of Management and Budget,
  108
Office of Technology Assessment, 141
Omnibus Crime Control and Safe
  Streets Act (1968), 104–107, 129,
  218, 221
Organized Crime Control Act (1970),
  103

Parents for Prayer, 7
Pastoral Plan for Pro-Life Activities,
  193
Patrolmen's Benevolent Association, 92
People for the American Way, 7, 209

Philadelphia Citizens Committee
  Against Pornography, 64
Philadelphia Plan, 149, 159, 163
Planned Parenthood Federation of
  America, 191–192, 194, 206
Planned Parenthood of New York
  City, 204
Playboy Enterprises, 56–57
Police Executive Research Forum, 132
Police Foundation, 132
Politics, types
  "direct-action," xviii
  mainstream, xiii–xvii
  "new," xii, xvi, xviii, xix–xx
  radical, xii, xiv–xvii, xx
  "single-issue," xviii
  "social movement," xviii
Pornography, 1, 3, 210, and Chapter
  2
Prayer Campaign Committee, 7
Presidency, 2, 210
  and abortion, 197–199
  and affirmative action, 157–162
  and crime, 98–103
  and gun control, 126–128
  and pornography, 49–57
  and school prayer, 31–34
Presidential Commission
  on Law Enforcement and
    Administration of Justice, 78, 99
  on Obscenity and Pornography, 48–
    49, 51, 53–57, 73
  on Organized Crime, 103
  on Population Growth, 197
Presidential Committee
  on Equal Employment Opportunity,
    146, 158
  on Government Contracts, 158
Pro-Choice Coalition, 190–191
Pro-Life Lobby, 191, 193–194
Project Prayer, 7
Public opinion, 2, 210, 218–220
  and abortion, 186–189
  and affirmative action, 171–175
  and crime, 77–81
  and gun control, 122–124
  and pornography, 69–72
  and school prayer, 23–25
Public policy, types
  competitive regulatory, 3
  constituent, xi, xv, xvii, 1

distributive, xi, xv, xvii
emotive symbolism, 3
patronage, xi
protective regulatory, 3
redistributive, xi, xv, xvii, 1, 211
regulative, xi, xv–xviii, 1, 74
social, xi, 3
social regulatory, xii, xix, 1, 111,
    210–211, 213–218, 220–221, 223–
    224
Public Works Employment Act (1977),
    151
Puerto Rican Legal Defense and
    Education Fund, 168

Reagan, Ronald W., 23, 30, 33–35,
    39, 53, 67, 102, 107, 120, 127,
    134–136, 140, 160–162, 165, 169,
    195, 197–200, 206–207, 209, 217,
    223
Religious Coalition for Abortion
    Rights (RCAR), 190–191
Right to Bear Arms, 111, 114, 117–
    118
Right-to-Life Committees, 192–194,
    198, 206, 211
Rockefeller, Nelson, 36
Roman Catholic church, 6, 193, 195–
    196
Roosevelt, Franklin D., 127–128, 157,
    216
Roosevelt, Theodore, 114, 126

Safe Streets Act. See Omnibus Crime
    Control and Safe Streets Act
    (1968)
St. Barnabas Medical Center (New
    Jersey), 64
School prayer, 1, 210–211, 219, 224,
    and Chapter 1
Society for Humane Abortion (San
    Francisco), 179
Society for Protection of Unborn
    Children, 194
Southern Baptist Convention, 6, 193

Southern Christian Leadership
    Conference, 145
State Patrol and Probation Officers'
    Association, 92
Stop ERA, 194
Story, Joseph, 16
Synagogue Council of America, 6, 11

Take Back the Night (TBTN), 65
Truman, Harry S, 157, 216

United Methodist church, 6, 120
    Board of Temperance, 64
    TV, Radio, and Film Committee, 63
    Women's Division of the Board of
        Global Ministries, 204
United Presbyterian church, 6
U.S. Catholic Conference, 191–192
U.S. Civil Rights Commission, 142,
    145, 161–163, 169, 205, 222
U.S. Coalition for Life, 194
U.S. Commission on Civil Rights. See
    U.S. Civil Rights Commission
U.S. Conference of Mayors, 105, 120
U.S. Customs, 58–61, 136, 221
U.S. Postal Service, 58–61, 64–65,
    221–222

Voting Rights Act (1965), 164

Wallace, George, 24, 36, 104
Washington, George, 112
Washington Legal Foundation, 93,
    96–97
Women Against Pornography (WAP),
    65
Women Against Violence Against
    Women (WAVAW), 65
Women Against Violence in
    Pornography, 65
Women's Christian Temperance
    Union. See National Women's
    Christian Temperance Union
Women Concerned for the Unborn
    Child, 194
Women's Democratic Club of
    Philadelphia, 65